A River
York: A
Camp?

Edited by Gareth Williams

The British Museum

This volume has been supported by

Historic England
York Archaeological Trust
The Viking Phenomenon

The Francis Coales Charitable Foundation are pleased to have been able to provide grant assistance towards the production of this publication

Publishers
The British Museum
Great Russell Street
London WC1B 3DG

Series editor
Sarah Faulks

A Riverine Site Near York: A Possible Viking Camp?
Edited by Gareth Williams

ISBN 978 086159224 1
ISSN 1747 3640

Front cover: items from 'A Riverine Site Near York' (ARSNY), including coins, weights, hack-silver and hack-gold, and three parts of a sword hilt. British Museum, selection from BM 2006,1203.1-111; 2008,4199.1-10; 2008,4200.1-26; 2010,8014.1-3

Printed and bound in the UK by 4edge Ltd, Hockley

Contents

Dedicated to the memory of Richard Andrew Hall 1949–2011

Acknowledgements

Mark Ainsley and Geoffrey Bambrook discovered the 'A Riverine Site Near York' (ARSNY) hoard and, by declaring it to the Portable Antiquities Scheme (PAS), set in train the archaeological investigations reported here. James Hare of Carter Jonas, land agent for the owners, was most helpful throughout, facilitating access and offering a variety of other assistance. The tenant farmers were equally gracious in permitting archaeological works to be inserted into their agricultural routines.

Simon Holmes, then based at the Yorkshire Museum as Finds Liaison Officer for the PAS, was the critical initial link between the finders and a number of individuals and institutions that subsequently became involved. At an early stage Dr Peter Addyman gave important advice and comment on the material and promoted its deeper study. At the PAS Dr Roger Bland and Dr Helen Geake were both involved in the early phases of the project. At the British Museum Leslie Webster provided advice and encouragement; Barry Ager and Gareth Williams provided comment on, respectively, the artefacts, and the coins and weights from the hoard, and on the related finds from the rest of the site.

Barry Ager and Gareth Williams are greatly indebted to Susan Youngs for her advice regarding the Celtic mount; at the British Museum grateful thanks are due to Susan La Niece for her analysis of the metal content of selected objects, to Alexandra Baldwin, Ana Tam, Ellen van Bork, Jamie Hood and Hayley Bullock for their later conservation work on the finds, to Stephen Crummy and Craig Williams for the illustrations, and to Lisa Voden-Decker, James Peters and Petra Rea for assistance with processing the finds for the Treasure report; also to Simon Holmes for arranging safe delivery of the hoard. Thanks are also due to Professor James Graham-Campbell for his help in identifying the finds, and for his more detailed discussion of the Irish harness mount, and to Jon Cotton for the reference to the ingot cache from Kingsway, London.

English Heritage (Yorkshire Region) (now Historic England), principally in the persons of Dr Keith Emerick, Inspector of Ancient Monuments, and Ian Panter (then Regional Science Advisor), have made supportive and helpful suggestions throughout. Stewart Ainsworth advised on the implementation of the topographic survey and landscape characterisation aspects of the project, and his observations were put into practice by Trevor Pearson, Abby Hunt and colleagues from the English Heritage Archaeological Investigation section based in York, working in conjunction with surveyors from Yorkshire Archaeological Trust (YAT). The project has also benefited from the involvement of other former and present English Heritage/Historic England staff, particularly Dr Chris Scull, Barney Sloane and Dr Pete Wilson.

There has also been keen interest and helpful comment from Neil Campling (formerly County Archaeologist) and Linda Smith (Rural Archaeologist) at the Heritage Unit, North Yorkshire County Council, while at the Yorkshire Museum both Mary Kershaw and Andrew Morrison were very supportive.

Keith Challis, now of the Department of Archaeology, University of York, was co-author of the original project design and contributed reports on the analysis of aerial photography, airborne laser altimetry (Lidar) and Airborne Thematic Mapper (ATM) data. Dr Andy J. Howard, then of the Institute of Archaeology and Antiquity, University of Birmingham, assessed the geoarchaeological potential of the site.

Initial geophysical prospection was undertaken by Louise Martin of the Archaeometry Branch, English Heritage Centre for Archaeology; subsequently coverage was extended by Ben Urmston of Geophysical Surveys of Bradford.

Excavations were directed, under difficult conditions, by Rhona Finlayson, who wrote a series of assessment reports and commentaries upon which parts of this synthesis are based. The excavation teams, which included professional staff from YAT and others recruited specifically for this project, laboured to good effect in extreme weather conditions.

Waterlogged timbers were sampled with the advice of Dr Allan Hall. Evaluation of biological remains was by John Carrott, Juliet Mant, Deborah Jaques and Stewart Gardner of Palaeoecology Research Services.

Derek Hamilton of English Heritage and Peter Marshall of Sheffield University are thanked for their help in selecting radiocarbon dating samples etc.

At YAT Dr Mark Whyman and Eliza Alqassar (now Buckinghamshire County Council) contributed to the background research on the site. Curation of artefacts was carried out principally by Rachel Cubitt and Christine McDonnell, and investigations of artefacts were carried out by staff in the Conservation Laboratory, including Julie Jones, Erica Paterson, Jim Spriggs, Ian Panter and Margrethe Felter. The human remains were assessed by Katie Tucker. Artefact research was undertaken by Nicky Rogers and pottery was assessed by Ailsa Mainman. Various electronic contributions were marshalled, coalesced and reformatted by Russell Marwood. Lesley Collett has drawn the objects and prepared the plans for publication.

Blaise Vyner provided invaluable advice on what could and could not be attributed to the prehistoric period, Terry Manby assisted with the identification of prehistoric pottery, and Peter Makey examined flints.

The interpretation of ARSNY presented here would not have been possible without detailed comparison with the sites of Torksey, Lincolnshire, and Woodstown, Co. Waterford. The late Dr Mark Blackburn was the first to recognise the location and significance of the Torksey site, and prior to his death there was a positive exchange of information about the two sites between Dr Blackburn, Richard Hall and Gareth Williams. This led to the development of a collaborative research project on Torksey by the Universities of York and Sheffield and the British Museum, subsequently carried on by the University of York alone. Gareth Williams would like to thank all the other members of the Torksey research team for sharing information on the project, and for permission to cite elements of their findings ahead of the main publication, especially Professor Julian D. Richards, Professor Dawn Hadley, Dr Samantha Stein, Hannah Brown, Dr Andrew Woods and Rachel Atherton. Ian Russell and Dr Stephen H Harrison provided valuable discussion of the Woodstown site prior to its final write-up, and Maurice Hurley, John Sheehan and James Eogan generously provided access to elements of the final report in advance of publication. Dr Cat Jarman has also kindly shared information on her ongoing work at Repton, while Professor Mark Horton was able to clarify details of the original excavations there. Gareth Williams would also like to thank Professor Martin Biddle for valuable discussion of both the published and unpublished data from Repton, and to all of the participants in the workshop on *Viking Winter Camps – organisation and movement* in Santiago de Compostela in September 2018, organised as part of *The Viking Phenomenon* research project, in conjunction with the Universities of Alicante and Santiago de Compostela.

YAT would like to extend special thanks to Frances Mee for pulling the report together after Richard Hall's death and to Gareth Williams for his invaluable help with the structure of the report and the interpretation of the site.

Thanks are also due to Dr Jane Kershaw, who contributed the chapter on single finds from Yorkshire, and also commented on the chapter on hoards and the concluding chapter. Interpretation of the multiple economies apparent at the ARSNY site has also benefited from discussions with Dr Kershaw and with Dr Andrew Woods. Comments from Professor James Graham-Campbell have been valuable since the site was first discovered, and thanks are also due for his willingness to contribute the appreciation of Richard Hall. The volume has also benefited from the input of the two peer reviewers, as well as from input in bringing this volume to publication from Dr JD Hill, Sarah Faulks, Edward Hulme and Rachel Tyson.

Final revisions and editing were undertaken by Gareth Williams while working on *The Viking Phenomenon* research project at the University of Uppsala, funded by the Swedish Research Council. This has permitted a more extended discussion of Viking winter camps than would otherwise be the case. Thanks are due to Professor Neil Price for agreeing that this work could fall within the project, and to Professor Price, Dr Charlotte Hedenstierna-Jonson, Dr John Ljungkvist and Dr Ben Raffield for useful discussions of winter camps and great armies more generally.

In addition to support from the British Museum, YAT and the *Viking Phenomenon* project, this publication has also received financial support from Historic England and the Francis Coales Charitable Foundation, for which the editor and publishers would like to express their gratitude.

Foreword

Gareth Williams

The site known as A Riverine Site Near York (ARSNY) came to archaeological notice in late 2003. Two metal detectorists, Mark Ainsley and Geoffrey Bambrook, had been detecting the site for some years, with the consent of the landowners and tenants, and had discovered a large number of single finds, predominantly of Anglo-Saxon and Viking date. The discovery in late 2003 of what appeared to be an associated group of coins, hack-silver and other related material led the finders to declare this discovery to the Portable Antiquities Scheme (hereafter PAS) as possible Treasure under the terms of the Treasure Act (1996). Resulting from this contact it became clear that the finders also had a large number of finds from the site in their possession, in addition to other finds already dispersed through sale.

The process by which the Treasure case developed into a research project is discussed in more detail below (see pp. 3–4); it suffices here to say that a collaborative project between York Archaeological Trust (hereafter YAT), English Heritage (EH) and the British Museum (BM) was developed under the leadership of the late Richard Hall, with financial support from both YAT and EH. This involved the archaeological investigation both of the immediate find-spot of the group of objects declared as possible Treasure, and the wider surrounding area from which other finds had been recovered, combined with the recording of a number of other objects from the site reported by the finders, some of which were also subsequently processed as Treasure. YAT (with input from EH and a number of external contributors) led on the investigation of the site and on the recording of the majority of the finds, while the BM led on the recording and interpretation of the coins, precious-metal objects and weights from the site. Investigations showed that the area from which the finds were recovered was surrounded by a large curving ditch, showing similarities to a pattern of D-shaped enclosure and shoreline generally regarded as characteristic of Viking settlements both in Scandinavia and elsewhere (see pp. 81, 88–9, 92), while the finds assemblage showed strong similarities to metal-detected finds recorded from the historically documented Viking camp at Torksey in Lincolnshire (Blackburn 2002; 2011; Hadley and Richards *et al.* 2016; see also below pp. 31–3, 41–5, 84–8). This combination prompted the interpretation of the site as a Viking camp of the late 9th century, an interpretation which is explored in detail below. At the time of the discoveries, there was considerable concern about possible illegal metal detecting on the site if the location was identified, and permission was only granted by the landowner for archaeological investigation if the anonymity of the site was guaranteed. The site was initially known by the fictitious name of Ainsbrook, comprising elements of the surnames of the two finders, and is referred to in some secondary literature by this name, but has been referred to here and in other recent publications as A Riverine Site Near York, or ARSNY for short, as this conveys some sense of the character of the site without revealing the exact location.

The plan was that Richard Hall should co-ordinate the publication of the site and the associated finds, but although he began this process he was prevented from completing this by his illness and untimely death. Following Richard's death, it was agreed that Frances Mee would be responsible for collating the various contributions into a single report, while I would provide an editorial overview of the whole report, and would also take over the responsibility for drafting the conclusions, in which the site is interpreted. This was based partly on Richard's notes, partly on my own, and partly on my recollection of discussions with Richard. A report was duly submitted by February 2012, to meet the deadlines stipulated as part of EH's funding support for the project, and I would like to thank Frances Mee and Ailsa Mainman, without whose efforts this deadline would not have been achieved.

The same report was submitted as a possible article to *Medieval Archaeology*. As anticipated, the response was that the report in its original form was too long for a journal article, but instead we were invited to consider turning it into a Society for Medieval Archaeology monograph instead, although it was noted that as it stood it was rather short for a monograph, so would need to be expanded, and this has resulted in the present volume. The report itself has been expanded in places, most notably in the contextual discussion and interpretation of the site. From very early on in the project it was clear that the finds, and other aspects of the site, showed strong similarities with those from the Viking site at Torksey, and also with the site at Woodstown near Waterford in Ireland, discovered in 2004. The initial ARSNY report drew comparisons with both sites, but the fact that interpretation of both Torksey and Woodstown has been ongoing throughout the intervening period means that it has been possible to explore that comparison, and the wider phenomenon of Viking camps in Britain and Ireland, rather more fully than was possible when writing the original report in 2011–12. The volume was also expanded by the addition of three further chapters to allow a fuller discussion of the implications of the site for the understanding of Viking currency and exchange, set in the wider context of hoards and single finds from the region, as well as from Viking York itself.

After the volume was expanded, the Society for Medieval Archaeology (SMA) imposed an additional requirement that the location of the site should be revealed. The anonymity of the site had not been an issue and was fully accepted in all of the discussions when we were invited to develop the volume as an SMA monograph, but subsequently the SMA Council changed their position on this. It would, of course, be preferable to include the exact location of the site here, since it would be valuable to the interpretation of the site to include discussion of place-names and of the wider landscape setting, and in other circumstances we would certainly have done so. However, this was impossible, given the commitments made to the landowner to keep the location of the site confidential. The volume has therefore been moved to its current publisher, and I am grateful to the British Museum for accepting it in their Research Publications series. I am, of course, aware that other archaeologists not involved in the project have chosen to disregard that confidentiality, but following further discussions with the landowner in which he confirmed his continued insistence on the anonymity of the site, both YAT and the BM feel ethically bound by the original agreement.

Attempts to resolve this issue have caused significant delays in the publication of ARSNY, which would otherwise have appeared some years ago. The intervening period has seen significant progress in the interpretation of the comparable site at Torksey in Lincolnshire. The site was initially investigated by the late Mark Blackburn of the Fitzwilliam Museum, Cambridge, in collaboration with a number of colleagues in the PAS, and it was possible to take full account when preparing this volume of Dr Blackburn's final work on the subject (Blackburn 2011). A further research project was developed on Torksey from 2011, with support from the British Academy, the Society of Antiquaries of London and the Robert Kiln Trust. This work was initially carried out in partnership by the Universities of York and Sheffield and the British Museum, subsequently by York and Sheffield without the British Museum, and a continuation project is now under way at the University of York. Information and interpretation from the ARSNY project was freely shared with the other members of the Torksey project team, and this report was essentially complete before the publication of the main report to date on the Torksey project (Hadley and Richards *et al.* 2016). That work is therefore cited only where it adds to the interpretation of ARSNY as it stood before the publication of that article, or where the discussion in the Torksey article supersedes either previous publications on Torksey (e.g. Hadley and Richards 2013) or unpublished personal communications from other members of the project team.

One of the most significant aspects of the ARSNY site, especially when considered with Viking Torksey, is that both ARSNY and Torksey appear to have their main focus of activity in the mid-870s, on the eve of large-scale Scandinavian settlement, thus bridging the gap between short-term raiding and permanent settlement. In this respect, both the scale of the two sites and the character of the finds recovered from them suggest a very different pattern from the interpretation of the Viking camp at Repton in Derbyshire by Martin Biddle and Birthe Kjølbye-Biddle (1992; 2001), which has hitherto provided the paradigm for the camps of the *micel here*, or 'great raiding army' of the 860s and 870s. Recent years have also seen new work in and around Repton by Cat Jarman both in the course of her doctoral research and subsequently, and I have benefited from a number of discussions with Dr Jarman, as well as from various lectures and conference presentations which she has given on the subject. However, since most of Dr Jarman's work is not yet published, while work on Professor Biddle's project is also still ongoing, discussion in this volume of Repton is largely restricted to published work.

Although place-names of Scandinavian origin indicate widespread rural settlement in England, few non-urban sites have yet been investigated in detail, and understanding of Anglo-Scandinavian settlement in England has been dominated by the towns, following the Coppergate excavations in York, although the so-called 'Five Boroughs', with the exception of Lincoln, have so far not produced comparable material. Similarly, understanding of Viking settlement in Ireland has been dominated by the major towns, especially Dublin and Waterford, and Woodstown provides important new evidence of the phase of pre-urban

Plate 1 Assemblage of items from ARSNY, including coins, weights, hack-silver and hack-gold, and three parts of a sword hilt. British Museum, selection from 2006,1203.1-111; 2008,4199.1-10; 2008,4200.1-26; 2010,8014.1-3

Viking settlements known as *longphuirt* ('ship camps' or 'ship fortresses'), which has been reinforced by the discovery of elements of the *longphort* phase in Dublin itself, and of the site of the *longphort* of Linn Duachaill, near Annagassan, Co. Louth (see pp. 89–90). A number of towns, or at least substantial pre-urban settlements, in the Viking homelands – most notably Hedeby and Ribe in Denmark, Kaupang in southern Norway, and Birka in Sweden – can be seen to predate the Viking settlement of England in the 870s, but the bulk of Scandinavian society was rural. The same is broadly true of Britain and Ireland prior to the Viking settlements, although both *wics* and (more debatably) large monastic sites provide a more extensive pattern of pre-urban or proto-urban settlement prior to the late 9th century than can be found in Scandinavia. Nevertheless, the transition to urbanisation during the period of Viking settlement has previously been difficult to trace archaeologically, but ARSNY and Torksey now offer important insights into how that transition took place. The role of the Viking camps of the 860s and 870s both as campaign forts and as an evolutionary stage on the road towards urbanisation is thus discussed in some detail.

The second area in which ARSNY – again with parallels in the finds from Torksey – offers particularly important insights is the field of exchange. Prior to the Viking conquest of Northumbria in 866–67, monetary exchange was based on copper-alloy coins known to modern scholars, though probably not to contemporaries, as stycas, whereas exchange in the Viking kingdom of Northumbria was characterised by what has been labelled a 'dual economy', comprising at different times a structured and well-regulated silver coinage minted at York, and the use of bullion, including intact ornaments, ingots, imported coin, and cut fragments of any of the above, known as hack-silver (Graham-Campbell 2001a). The Coppergate excavations revealed evidence of minting, as well as of the use of coins (Pirie *et al.* 1986), while weights and balances also point to a more limited use of bullion (Mainman and Rogers 2000, 2559–64), but interpretation of both the coinage and the character of the economy, or economies, in Viking Northumbria has traditionally been based primarily on a limited number of hoards from the Viking period. The growth of metal detecting since the 1970s, coupled with the systematic recording of single finds first of coins and since the late 1990s of other archaeological material, has added another dimension. Over the same period, the number of hoards from the Viking period has also increased dramatically.

ARSNY adds yet another dimension, providing as it does a large assemblage of objects relating to exchange from a single site, apparently largely concentrated into a very short period of time, but spanning the transition from the pre-Viking styca coinage to the characteristic Viking economy, although the site probably ceased to be occupied on any scale before the introduction of the silver coinage minted in

York from *c.* 895. The site assemblage contains what may plausibly be interpreted as a distinct hoard, plus other coins (both silver and copper alloy), silver bullion, gold bullion, a fragment of a balance and one of the largest groups of Viking weights found to date in Britain or Ireland (**Pl. 1**). These finds and their significance are discussed extensively in the main report, but it was felt that the evidence from ARSNY could usefully be contextualised by comparison with other recent finds from the region. Accordingly, three additional contributions have been included to complement the discussion of means of exchange in the ARSNY report. In the first, I survey the evidence provided by Viking hoards from Yorkshire, including the important Vale of York hoard (2007) and the recent hoards from 'Near Bedale' and 'Near York' (both 2012) together with a number of more established hoards. For the second, Dr Jane Kershaw has kindly provided a chapter on single finds from Yorkshire of Scandinavian/Anglo-Scandinavian character, relating to exchange, which forms part of her larger AHRC-funded postdoctoral research project into such material across England. In a final short chapter I bring the material from ARSNY together with the hoards, single finds and the previously published material from York itself to provide an overview of the key developments in the character of exchange in Yorkshire between the Viking settlement of the mid-870s and the end of the Anglo-Scandinavian kingdom of Northumbria in 954.

The scholarly papers in this volume are preceded by a short appreciation of Richard Hall's contributions to Viking archaeology by Professor James Graham-Campbell, and I would like to thank Professor Graham-Campbell on behalf of the other contributors for his willingness to provide this introduction to what has become, in effect, a small memorial to Richard and his work. Richard's interests in the Vikings went far beyond York, and indeed beyond Anglo-Scandinavian towns, but the extent to which towns have dominated our understanding of the archaeology of Viking settlement in England for a generation is in large part due to Richard's extraordinary contribution to the subject. Both his leadership and his many personal contributions have led to an exemplary body of publication, both for the specialist and the general reader, concerning the Coppergate excavations in particular, and Anglo-Scandinavian York more generally, culminating in the posthumous publication of the interpretation of Coppergate as a whole (Hall *et al.* 2014). He also produced definitive studies of the archaeological evidence for Viking settlement in the 'Five Boroughs' of Lincoln, Stamford, Nottingham, Derby and Leicester (Hall 1989; 2001), as well as a major survey of both Anglo-Saxon and Viking towns and urbanisation (Hall 2011). While his premature death meant that he was unable to see the publication of the ARSNY project through to completion, it is typical that he was so pivotally involved in the investigation of a site which offers so much for the interpretation of a key phase in the early development of Viking urban settlement in England.

Richard also appreciated the importance of integrating numismatics within the wider body of archaeological evidence, from his own early work on Viking coin finds in Ireland (Hall 1973–74) to collaborations with Elizabeth Pirie, Marion Archibald and other numismatists on the publication of the coins from the Coppergate excavations (Pirie *et al.* 1986), and with Mark Blackburn and others on the important interdisciplinary volume, *Aspects of Anglo-Scandinavian York* (Hall *et al.* 2004). It is to be hoped that he would therefore have enjoyed the wider discussions of currency and exchange that complement the ARSNY report within this volume. On a more personal note, I would also like to record my gratitude for the encouragement and support that Richard extended to me, as he did to so many others, from our first meeting when I was still a postgraduate student. It is in memory of that friendly and encouraging attitude, as well as in recognition of his enormous contribution to Viking studies, that this volume is dedicated to Richard Hall.

Chapter 1
Richard Hall and Viking Archaeology

James Graham-Campbell

In the 'Introduction' to the main paper in this volume Richard Hall describes, in modest manner, his role in the initial attempt to establish a context for a group of coins and metalwork that had been submitted to the PAS, in 2003, by metal detectorists who had been working for several years on an unidentified site that was first given the invented name of 'Ainsbrook', but is now known as 'A Riverine Site Near York' (ARSNY). Indeed, much gratitude is owed to Richard for his insistence that something needed to be done to investigate the find circumstances of this assemblage – and not least that such needed to be done most urgently given the then state of the site itself, even though it involved the commitment of YAT resources.

The situation at the time was confused. I well remember my amazement on making the calculation that if the find-place was indeed the location of a Viking boat grave, as was initially being suggested, then the apparent spread of clench nails/boat rivets implied the burial of a vessel the size of the Gokstad ship. If true, such would have been a most remarkable find of exceptional status (even by Scandinavian standards), being of a size far in excess of any documented boat grave from Scandinavian Scotland, the Isle of Man or Iceland. For a Viking archaeologist such a discovery did indeed demand immediate investigation – even more so than would normally be considered applicable to the apparent association of a Viking warrior grave with a Viking silver hoard, although silver hoards are themselves rare inclusions in Viking burials.

Anyway, as documented below, Richard was able not only to dispose of the 'boat grave' hypothesis, but also to call into question the suggestion that the assemblage derived from a Viking warrior burial at all. On the other hand, 'the large hole dug by the detectorists to extract the hoard' left nothing to assist him in the elucidation of the manner – let alone the occasion – of the deposition of this group of Anglo-Saxon/Viking-Age coins and metalwork, 'loosely referred to as a hoard', and the additional 'group of miscellaneous iron objects ... found while unearthing the hoard'.

Such was the frustrating start to the ARSNY project with which Richard then remained fully involved until his death, with the results published here serving in some part to honour Richard's extensive contributions to Viking archaeology.

Richard's research interests from his postgraduate years at Southampton University were focused on the origins and development of the towns of the Danelaw, beginning with Derby (Hall with Coppack 1972; Hall 1974a), as brought together in his classic paper 'The Five Boroughs of the Danelaw: a review of present knowledge' (1989). Richard was to return to this subject, with a focus on 'the East Midlands', for his paper to the Thirteenth Viking Congress, when held in Nottingham (Hall 2001; see also Hall 2011).

Richard joined the York Archaeological Trust in 1974, as Excavations Supervisor, and found himself directing the excavation of the row of waterlogged pre-Conquest tenements (16–22 Coppergate) that constituted the 'The Viking Dig' (cf. Hall 1984a; 2011). The spectacular nature of the archaeological evidence that was so painstakingly recovered, in terms of buildings, artefacts and palaeoenvironmental data, propelled Richard onto the international Viking scene. The findings were given initial prominence by the Anglo-Danish Project's exhibition, 'The Vikings in England and in their Danish Homeland' – first seen in Copenhagen and Aarhus in 1981, and then in the Yorkshire Museum, from April to October 1982 (with the opening ceremony performed by HRH the Prince of Wales). Indeed, the Project's chairman, Kenneth Pearson, explained in his 'Foreword' to the catalogue: 'As for the exhibition, half of it has been excavated from the Viking Coppergate site in York' (Roesdahl *et al.* 1981, 9).

It was likewise in 1981 that Richard joined the (Ninth) Viking Congress which met that year in the Isle of Man, establishing himself as a regular member who had become, by the time of the Sixteenth Viking Congress (Iceland, 2009), the English national representative for archaeology. In the meantime, he had delivered one of the key-note addresses (Hall 1994a) at the Twelfth Viking Congress (Sweden, 1993) and had served as a member of the organising committee of the Thirteenth (Nottingham, 1997), when he had personal responsibility for the highly successful post-Congress tour, based in York. Further international commitments connected with Viking archaeology involved active service as consultant to the Swedish State Archaeological Service, for the Birka excavations, and on the Kaupang Excavation Project Council, in Norway.

In an exemplary manner, Richard followed the completion of the Coppergate excavations with the publication of *The Viking Dig* (Hall 1984a; Hall *et al.* 2014) – a well-deserved success, indicative of his ability to combine his scholarship with appeal to a wide audience. Its successor was the *English Heritage Book of Viking York*, or *Viking Age York* (Hall 1994b; see also Hall 2004), but of course any editor of an atlas, encyclopaedia, handbook or exhibition catalogue, in need of a succinct summary concerning 'Viking York' turned to Richard who would not disappoint (e.g. Hall 2008). Along with ARSNY, Richard continued working on the definitive publication of Coppergate until his final illness, and this appeared posthumously as *Anglo-Scandinavian Occupation at 16–22 Coppergate: Defining a Townscape* (Hall *et al.* 2014).

Viking-Age towns are not for study in isolation and Richard was properly concerned with the wider context of Scandinavian settlement in England, including his survey of the archaeological evidence, as known in the 1990s, which he admirably summarised for a Danish conference on 'The Vikings in the West' (Hall 2000), following on from his 'key-note' address to the Twelfth Viking Congress in 1993 (as noted above).

It should not be forgotten, however, that Richard's academic involvement with Viking archaeology commenced during his undergraduate days at Queen's University, Belfast. There, under the guidance of Michael Dolley, he carried out the research for his 'Check-List of Viking-Age Coin Finds from Ireland' (Hall 1973–4). Richard's further publications of Viking-Age material from Ireland consisted of an important arm-ring hoard from Cushalogurt, Co. Mayo (Hall 1973), and the first modern accounts of two Viking graves in the immediate vicinity of the Scandinavian settlement at Dublin (Hall 1974b; 1978). It is no surprise therefore that he should have chosen to include Ireland in his Shire Archaeology publication, *Viking Age Archaeology in Britain and Ireland* (Hall 1990). The fact that this highly recommended 'booklet' was deemed worthy of a reprint 20 years on (2010) serves to highlight its invaluable nature as an introductory survey of its subject, written – with clarity – from personal knowledge of the material evidence.

Richard's ability to address a general audience, whether as author, lecturer or tour-guide, is further exemplified by his book *Exploring the World of the Vikings*, commissioned by Thames & Hudson (Hall 2007; paperback edition, 2013). In the words of one reviewer (Gazzoli 2012), this provides 'a comprehensive and accessible account of the entire Viking phenomenon … from a thoroughly up-to-date perspective', in a book that is not only 'well-written', but also 'engaging'. It has been translated into six foreign languages.

Brian Ayers wrote in his fine obituary of Richard, for the Society of Medieval Archaeology of which Richard had been president (2002–04), that he had had the good fortune to be 'a man in the right place at the right time' (Ayers 2012, 298). Indeed, 30 years ago it was said of Richard that 'he has made, through his Coppergate excavations, the single greatest contribution ever to the study of Anglo-Scandinavian urbanism' (Addyman and Black (eds), introducing Hall 1984b, 71). The outstanding nature of this contribution is such that it was recognised by a conference in Richard's memory in March 2014 organised jointly by the York Archaeological Trust and the University of York: 'The World of the Vikings – 40 Years of Viking Archaeology in York'. This has subsequently developed into an annual symposium in Viking studies bearing Richard's name and organised by the York Archaeological Trust.

Chapter 2
A Riverine Site Near York: A Possible Viking Camp?

Richard Hall and Gareth Williams with Barry Ager and Nicola Rogers, and with contributions from Stewart Ainsworth, Keith Challis, Gordon Cook, Rhona Finlayson, James Graham-Campbell, Derek Hamilton, Andy J. Howard, Richard Kelleher, Ailsa Mainman, Peter D. Marshall, Louise Martin, Catherine Mortimer, Ben Urmston and Penelope Walton Rogers

Introduction
Richard Hall

A Riverine Site Near York (ARSNY) came to archaeological notice when metal detectorists, operating with the landowners' and tenants' permission, unearthed a group of Anglo-Saxon and Viking-Age coins and metalwork in association, they believed, with traces of human bone. They declared the discovery to the PAS in late 2003, and this group of objects came to be loosely referred to as a hoard. A small number of iron clench nails within this group suggested to some that this assemblage could represent the remains of a Viking ship burial. The detectorists also handed over a second group of miscellaneous iron objects they had found while unearthing the 'hoard'.

Over a number of years the detectorists had already found in this immediate vicinity many hundreds of objects, most of which they dated to the early medieval period and, more specifically, to the 8th–9th/10th centuries. With the exception of some coins which had been shown to the late Elizabeth Pirie, this material had not been brought to archaeological attention. Some iron objects had been discarded at the field edge and were now retrieved; much had been dispersed by sale and could not now be studied, although the detectorists had some records, as well as some memories, of what had been found, and of approximately where.

Following expert advice from a range of individuals and institutions (see Acknowledgements), EH indicated its willingness to receive a project design for investigation and characterisation of the site, largely by means of non-invasive techniques. The aim, as initially conceived, was to examine and contextualise the hoard's find-spot, and to provide data that would assist in the understanding and management of the site.

While the project design was being considered, surface conditions around the hoard's find-spot degenerated because of erosion, caused by heavy rain and exacerbated by the agricultural regime. YAT, concerned that significant evidence might be lost, obtained permission to undertake limited excavations in March 2004, precisely targeted at the hoard's find-spot; YAT bore the cost of these excavations. They uncovered no sign of a boat, but did locate various archaeological features as well as the large hole dug by the detectorists to extract the hoard. Concurrently, EH undertook a geophysical survey of part of the area defined by the detectorists' find-spots. This added further interest by revealing, *inter alia*, part of a substantial curving ditch-like feature.

The project design initially agreed by EH included topographic survey, further geophysical survey, geoarchaeological survey, the analysis of aerial photographs, airborne laser altimetry (Lidar) and Airborne Thematic Mapper (ATM) data, and an assessment of other archaeological and historical data. Following the collection, analysis and interpretation of these data, another project design for further investigative work in the form of trial trenching was put to EH and, after some negotiation, agreed and implemented. No further archaeological investigation has been undertaken.

This report presents the artefacts unearthed by the metal detectorists up to February 2008, and summarises and interprets the archaeological information gathered throughout the project. All parties involved – the landowners, their tenants, those working the land, the detectorists and the archaeologists – recognised that the site was potentially vulnerable to trespass, damage and theft by treasure hunters operating illegally. The site's location has therefore remained confidential. This unavoidably restricts some aspects of the information which can be made public in this report, for example in discussing topographical and historical information.

'The site' available for examination during this project was defined on the basis of topography, land ownership and the area within which the detectorists had permission to operate. While the topographic survey incorporated the river's floodplain, geophysical survey was confined to an area of higher ground adjacent to the floodplain, within which finds had also been recovered.

The site and its non-invasive investigation

Geoarchaeological assessment of the site
Andy J. Howard

Geological background

Glacial deposits

The Vale of York is one of the largest of a number of glacially overdeepened lowland river basins in the UK. It extends for *c.* 100km from the Humber Estuary in the south to the River Tees in the north and for *c.* 40km from the Pennine foothills in the west to the Yorkshire Wolds/Hambleton Hills in the east.

During the last glacial maximum in the Dimlington Stadial (*c.* 26,000–13,000 years BP) of the Late Devensian, glacier ice fed from snow accumulation centres in the Lake District, Cheviots and further north entered the Vale of York and was augmented by ice flowing down Swaledale, Wensleydale, Nidderdale and Wharfedale from local Dales accumulation centres (Catt 1991). Glacial and meltwater processes within and beneath the icesheet led to the deposition of extensive deposits of till and fluvioglacial sands and gravels. Ice flowing down the east coast blocked the Humber Estuary, resulting in drainage impediment and the creation of proglacial Lake Humber. This lake rose initially to a short-lived high level of about 30m OD, with littoral sands and gravels deposited around the margins. Its level then dropped transiently to below minus 4m OD, possibly draining away entirely, before rising again to a more prolonged low level of approximately 7.5m OD. The sediments formed in Lake Humber, mainly during the later, low-level phase, consist largely of laminated clays with marginal sands. These deposits, together with upper sands of post-lacustrine fluvial origin, are for historical reasons known collectively as the 25-Foot Drift. A bone fragment found within the littoral sands and gravels near Brantingham yielded a radiocarbon age of nearly 22,000 years BP, and provides an estimated age for the high-level lacustrine phase and coeval ice surge (Gaunt 1981; Gaunt *et al.* 1992; Gaunt 1994). A minimum age for the deposition of the silts and clays of Lake Humber is provided by the radiocarbon date of approximately 11,000 years BP gained from the organic part of a soil developed on these sediments at West Moor, north-east of Doncaster (Gaunt 1994).

The site

The site is located on a prominent ridge flanking the east bank of the River Ouse, and this rolling countryside, approximately 20km behind the York moraine, is typical of a deglacial landscape where deposition beneath, within and upon the surface of the icesheet has been important. In addition to deposition during glaciation, landforms and sediments associated with the melting of the icesheet during climatic amelioration at the end of the Devensian, such as kettle holes, are also locally important and may contain important environmental records. Mapping by the British Geological Survey has classified the ridge as a mixture of sandy till covered by small patches of glacial sand and gravel, and excellent exposures of the sediment body are located in an abandoned pit. These exposures reveal approximately 10m of coarse, sub-bedded, rounded gravels. The gravels comprise local Triassic quartzite and sandstone, and Carboniferous chert and crinoidal limestone from the Yorkshire Dales. These deposits are typical of glacial outwash sediments and the planform of the ridge (a sinuous landform) suggests that it is part of a complex of eskers (englacial stream deposits), mapped in this part of the Vale of York.

Approximately 1m of fine to medium, structureless, pebbly sand was recorded overlying the coarse gravel deposits and this was probably deposited during a period of low meltwater flow, perhaps during the waning stages of glaciation. However, this pebbly sand is not of uniform thickness across the exposure, but in some places infills depressions up to 2m wide and 1m deep within the gravels. The depressions are probably relict glacial and periglacial features, possibly formed by a combination of freeze-thaw processes (cryoturbation) and the melting of blocks of ice within the sediment sequence (ground ice collapse depressions).

Implications for archaeology

Critically, from an archaeological perspective, it suggests that the thickness of subsoil is likely to be variable across the ridge but this variability would be difficult to map unless recorded as 'patterned ground' on aerial photographs (see Howard 1995). The varying thickness of subsoils preserved within these structures may well explain some of the vegetation and soil contrasts observed within the remote-sensed datasets (particularly the multispectral imagery).

No organic sediments were observed within either the gravels or the overlying pebbly sands, although this is not surprising since these sediments were deposited under full glacial (i.e. cold climate) conditions when vegetation would have been very sparse.

Aeolian deposits

With climatic amelioration from around 13,000 BP, the Vale of York icesheet retreated and melted leaving extensive tracts of fine-grained sand, silt and clay spread across the landscape. The return of cold climate conditions between 11,000 and 10,000 years BP (the Loch Lomond Stadial) led to the reworking of the finer-grained fluvioglacial sediments and the creation of extensive tracts of blown sand (usually referred to as coversands) across large areas of the Vale of York.

The site

Although no coversands are mapped in the immediate vicinity of the site, the hedgebanks around the survey area indicate considerable evidence for aeolian activity, with accumulations of wind-blown sands up to 1m thick. Whilst these wind-blown sediments were initially deposited during the Late glacial period (Matthews 1970; Gaunt *et al.* 1971), radiocarbon dating of organic material within sands at East Moor, near Sutton on the Forest, indicates sediment reworking, tentatively dated to episodes of Anglo-Saxon and/or medieval forest clearance (Matthews 1970). Radley and Simms (1967) documented more recent wind erosion of these fine-grained deposits to the north and east of York during the winter and spring of 1967. This recent episode of sand destabilisation was linked to a combination of unusually dry conditions, high temperatures and changing farming practices relating to the cultivation of sandy areas, which prior to enclosure had served as parish commons and moors.

Implications for archaeology

The reworking of coversand deposits during the Holocene may have resulted in both the erosion and burial of archaeology within this landscape. However, without radiometric dating control it is impossible to delimit these periods of increased aeolian activity. Whilst the spread of finds across the site appears quite even, there are notable blank areas and sharp limits to the distribution, especially on the eastern side of the scatter. Since a considerable build-up of wind-blown sediment can be observed along the hedge bank of the track along the eastern edge of the site, the potential for burial in this zone may well merit further investigation.

Alluvial deposits

At the beginning of the Holocene, or slightly earlier, the plug of glacial material blocking the Humber Estuary was breached. This allowed the newly establishing rivers of the region to incise their courses across the Vale of York, locally down to minus 20m OD, in response to continuing low sea levels. Through time, marine transgression associated with climatic amelioration resulted in sedimentation and infilling of these incised courses (Gaunt 1981; 1994; Long *et al.* 1998; Metcalfe *et al.* 2000; Kirby 2001). Upstream of tidal influence, the low-gradient river systems of the Vale have been characterised by low rates of lateral movement and relatively high rates of fine-grained (sand, silt, clay and peat) sedimentation (Macklin *et al.* 2000; Taylor *et al.* 2000). Deposition probably occurred in a series of multi-channelled, anastomosed systems with documentary and cartographic evidence indicating that many of these river patterns survived in the southern part of the Vale of York and Humberhead Levels until large-scale drainage and land reclamation in the early 17th century AD (Dinnin 1997).

The identification of episodes of river incision and sedimentation in the Yorkshire Ouse basin through radiocarbon dating of organic materials recovered from alluvial units has shown that variations in Holocene river activity, principally flood frequency and magnitude, can be correlated with periods of climate change and, particularly in the last 1,000 years, with human impact (Macklin *et al.* 2000). Since the Bronze Age, progressive deforestation associated with pastoral and arable farming has probably enhanced both run-off and the supply of fine-grained sediments to river valley floors. Since the 11th century AD and during the last 250 years, the base-metal mining industry of the Yorkshire Dales has been a major source of fine-grained sediments for rivers of the Ouse basin (Hudson-Edwards *et al.* 1999).

The site

The site is located on Pleistocene sediments and sits approximately 10m above the surrounding floodplain, marked by a sharp terrace edge slope. The Holocene floodplain situated below comprises a single flat terrace surface approximately 100m wide. Augering revealed approximately 1.3m of coal-rich, grey, gleyed sandy silty clay overlying coarse sands and gravels. A single (previously excavated) test pit in the central part of the floodplain confirmed this stratigraphy. These dark-coloured sandy sediments, rich in coal, are typical of mining-age material of the late medieval and predominantly post-medieval period (Hudson-Edwards *et al.* 1999), although detailed geochemical analysis would need to be undertaken in order to confirm this assumption.

The topography of the valley floor and presence of marsh vegetation along the interface between the valley floor and terrace slope suggested that a palaeochannel might be located in this area. However, coring through the area revealed a maximum of 1.2m of humic silty clay, typical of overbank alluviation; overlying sand and significant in-channel sediments were not recorded.

To the east of the site, a small, enclosed, alluvial basin is recorded by the British Geological Survey (BGS). Coring through this basin revealed approximately 0.5m of humic clay and well-preserved peat overlying coarse-grained sands and gravels. The basin was waterlogged, which suggests that organic sediments should be well preserved.

Implications for archaeology

The Holocene floodplain surface at ARSNY is probably of relatively recent origin and it is unlikely that *in situ* archaeology, contemporaneous with the material from the site, will be located on the floodplain surface. Although reworked archaeology may be included in the floodplain sediments, any *in situ* archaeology is likely to be buried within the floodplain (but may already have been reworked or removed by fluvial processes). The small, waterlogged alluvial basin identified through BGS mapping has the potential to preserve and provide proxy records of land use and climate.

Floodplain hydrology

The contemporary channel of the River Ouse is relatively straight and entrenched approximately 5m below the floodplain surface, though during high discharge events the Holocene floodplain is fully inundated. In this reach, the river is stable since the channel bank is well vegetated with grass and willow and there is even some evidence of active sediment deposition. In the central area of the floodplain, two springs were recorded where water and sediment issued onto the ground surface building small mounds of sediment. These springs appear to be part of a complex groundwater system in this part of the valley floor, with additional springheads located on the slope below the terrace edge.

Implications for archaeology

The stability of the river channel in this reach of the valley floor suggests that even if the site extended onto the Holocene floodplain, the area is unlikely to be significantly affected by fluvial erosion in the medium-term future unless management regimes in the valley floor corridor change. The presence of springheads on the floodplain suggests that the hydrology of the valley floor is complex, but that the potential for organic preservation is likely to be high.

Valley side sediments

The terrace slope separating the site from the Holocene valley floor is steep (approximately 50 degrees) and covered by a mixture of scrub vegetation and wet grassland. The foot of the slope is characterised by at least two very low angle prograding alluvial fans, indicating the movement of sediment from further upslope, importantly, from the area of the site. Bare patches of fan indicate that erosion is an ongoing process and sedimentary structures within the fan sediments (dune and ripple structures) indicate quite high water flow velocities. Coring through the most active of these fan deposits indicates at least 1m of coarse sand has been deposited at the valley floor edge.

Coring further up the terrace slope above the fan deposits revealed an interesting sequence of waterlogged sediments, which appear to be perched above the contemporary floodplain; colluvial sediments are also present. This sequence recorded through augering of the central part of the floodplain was replicated at the northern end of the study area. The presence of waterlogged sediment above the valley floor is unusual, but is probably explained by the presence of spring-lines issuing from the valley side.

Implications for archaeology

The presence of fresh alluvial fan deposits indicates active erosion of the terrace surface on which the site is situated. This erosion has significant implications for the preservation of *in situ* archaeology, some of which may well have already been reworked into the alluvial fan deposits. Any future investigations of this site should include test pitting of the valley floor fans, and the associated colluvial sediments, which may also mask or incorporate reworked archaeology. Erosion has most probably been exacerbated by land use regimes in the recent past and evidence of poaching and gullying has been observed around animal feeding areas; once these foci of degradation become established, erosion can soon be exacerbated if appropriate mitigation strategies are not put in place.

Summary conclusions

- The site is situated on a glacial landform above the Holocene valley floor of the River Ouse. Natural geological processes have resulted in an uneven distribution of the upper pebbly sands across the landscape and this may explain some of the vegetation and soil contrasts observed within the remote-sensed datasets.
- Wind-blown sands of unknown age have been identified around the site and these may have both eroded and buried archaeology.
- The Holocene floodplain surface at ARSNY is probably of relatively recent origin and it is unlikely that *in situ* archaeology, contemporaneous with the material from the site will be located on the floodplain surface. Although reworked archaeology may be included in the floodplain sediments, any *in situ* archaeology is likely to be buried within the floodplain.
- The small, waterlogged alluvial basin identified through BGS mapping has the potential to preserve and provide proxy records of land use and climate.
- The stability of the river channel in this reach of the valley floor suggests that even if the site extended onto the Holocene floodplain, the area is unlikely to be significantly affected by fluvial erosion in the medium-term future unless management regimes in the valley floor corridor change.
- The presence of springheads upon the floodplain suggests that the hydrology of the valley floor is complex, but that the potential for organic preservation is likely to be high.
- The presence of fresh alluvial fan deposits indicates active erosion of the terrace surface on which the site is situated. This erosion has significant implications for the preservation of *in situ* archaeology.
- Associated colluvial sediments may also mask or incorporate reworked archaeology.

Topographic survey at ARSNY
English Heritage Archaeological Investigation section, York

Introduction

Between 29 November and 6 December 2004, members of the English Heritage Archaeological Investigation section based in York worked with a team from YAT to compile a topographic survey of an area of land in North Yorkshire. Specific details concerning the location have been omitted from this report due to concerns over access to the site and issues with metal detecting.

The survey covered an area of 31ha (76 acres), bounded to the west by the top of the slope down to the river and to the east along a 'green lane' which provides access to the site. The survey area is divided into seven fields. Individual fields are either defined by hedges or by post and wire fences. The southernmost field, Field 1, has small copses at the north-west and south-west corners whilst the rest of the area had been ploughed prior to the start of the survey. A track, used by pig farmers, at the eastern edge of the field was surveyed but was ploughed out shortly afterwards. The middle two fields (Fields 2 and 3) were used for rearing pigs immediately before the start of survey work. This had left a pattern of temporary trackways but it was not possible to record these fully as the two fields were ploughed over during the course of the fieldwork, removing all surface traces of that previous land use. Field 4 had been ploughed in the recent past but was fallow at the time of the survey apart from the north-east quarter, which had been used for rearing pigs prior to the start of the fieldwork. This area was ploughed during the course of the survey. At the south-east corner of Field 4, a post-and-wire fence divides a triangular-shaped plot from the rest of the field. This plot is rough ground and contains a small, square fenced area. Fields 5 and 6 were under pasture and encompass the north-west and west sides of the high ground respectively and lower ground beyond it. An area of rough, boggy ground on the edge of the high ground within Field 6 had been fenced off (Field 7).

The survey was undertaken to a specification previously agreed between EH and YAT to produce a short, written analytical summary of any earthworks and an AutoCad map of the site showing topographic features; erosion features; a contour model of the area with contours at 0.5m intervals; the location of the permanently marked survey points positioned around the site during the course of the survey; the position of the geophysical survey grid established by GSB Prospection; and significant earthwork features.

Survey methodology

The field survey was carried out using Trimble 4800 and 4700 dual frequency Global Positioning Satellite (GPS) systems related to a base station on site. The base station had previously been established using the GPS equipment and related to the National Grid (OSGB36) through a transformation programme which calculated its position relative to three Ordnance Survey active GPS stations at Carlisle, Glasgow and Newcastle. Ten permanent and intervisible stations were established on the site to allow future work with conventional survey equipment. The positions of the stations are marked by 1m-long metal ground anchors and their positions are indicated on the English Heritage survey plan. Additional survey details were provided in areas with poor satellite visibility using a Trimble 5600 series Total Station theodolite, and the plan position fixed by reference to the permanently marked survey stations. The 2D plot of the site was produced from the GPS data using Key Terra-Firma and AutoCad software. Sufficient 3D GPS points were surveyed to generate contours on the survey plot at 0.5m intervals.

The survey was undertaken by Trevor Pearson and Abby Hunt (EH) and Rhona Finlayson and Michael Andrews (YAT). The report was edited by Stewart Ainsworth (EH).

Natural topography

High ground, formed from glacial sands and gravels, on the south and east of the survey area falls away steeply on the west to the floodplain of the river and to the floor of a tributary valley to the north. The north-facing slope incorporates two distinct terraces which are probably relict river terraces formed by glacial meltwater. To the west there are two quite deeply incised hollows reaching from the edge of the floodplain to the crest of the escarpment. They are natural erosion features but it is possible that the sides of the southern hollow have been artificially steepened (see below).

Landscape history

The boundaries between Fields 1 and 2, Fields 2 and 3, and Fields 3 and 4 have slightly curving alignments which probably perpetuate the reversed 's' pattern of medieval open-field ploughing with oxen. The field pattern does not extend below the escarpment, suggesting the medieval open-field did not continue across the low ground on the north and west of the survey area.

The map sequence from the first edition 1:10,560 Ordnance Survey map published in 1855–6 to that published in 1952–3 does not reveal any significant landscape change during the past 150 years. The maps show the same basic field pattern as today, though cross-divisions in Fields 1 and 2 and subdivisions within Field 6 have disappeared in the last 50 years.

Survey results

Erosion gullies

Before the survey commenced, there were a number of erosion gullies visible in Field 2 which had been created by surface run-off down the escarpment. However, there was no opportunity to map all of these before they were filled in and the field ploughed over. As a result, only Gully 1 was surveyed in its entirety. This started as a slight, narrow channel about 7m from, and running parallel to, the southern boundary, but became deeper to the west as it went further down slope and joined with Gully 2 from the north. Gully 2 consisted of a narrow, 30m-long channel contained in a much wider, shallow-sided linear depression that continued on northwards beyond the end of the gully. The wider depression was probably the combined result of water erosion and the use of the feature for access by pig farmers.

There were a further four narrow gullies 50m to the west of Gully 2 running roughly parallel from east to west down the slope. There was no opportunity to survey these completely and it is possible there were other gullies in this area which were ploughed out before the start of the survey.

Earthworks

The ploughed fields (Fields 1–4) were devoid of any significant earthwork traces, apart from in Field 1 where a slight curving depression towards the west side of the field (Earthwork 1) is most likely to be a continuation of the southernmost of the two natural hollows cutting the escarpment. However, it is possible that it indicates the line of a partially infilled ditch.

Earthwork 2 in Field 5 is a roughly oval mound, around 22m in length and 17m wide, situated on the crest of the slope at the north-west angle of the escarpment. The mound is around 0.4m high on the west and north but is less prominent on the south and east. The mound has no obvious interpretation but is probably agricultural in origin.

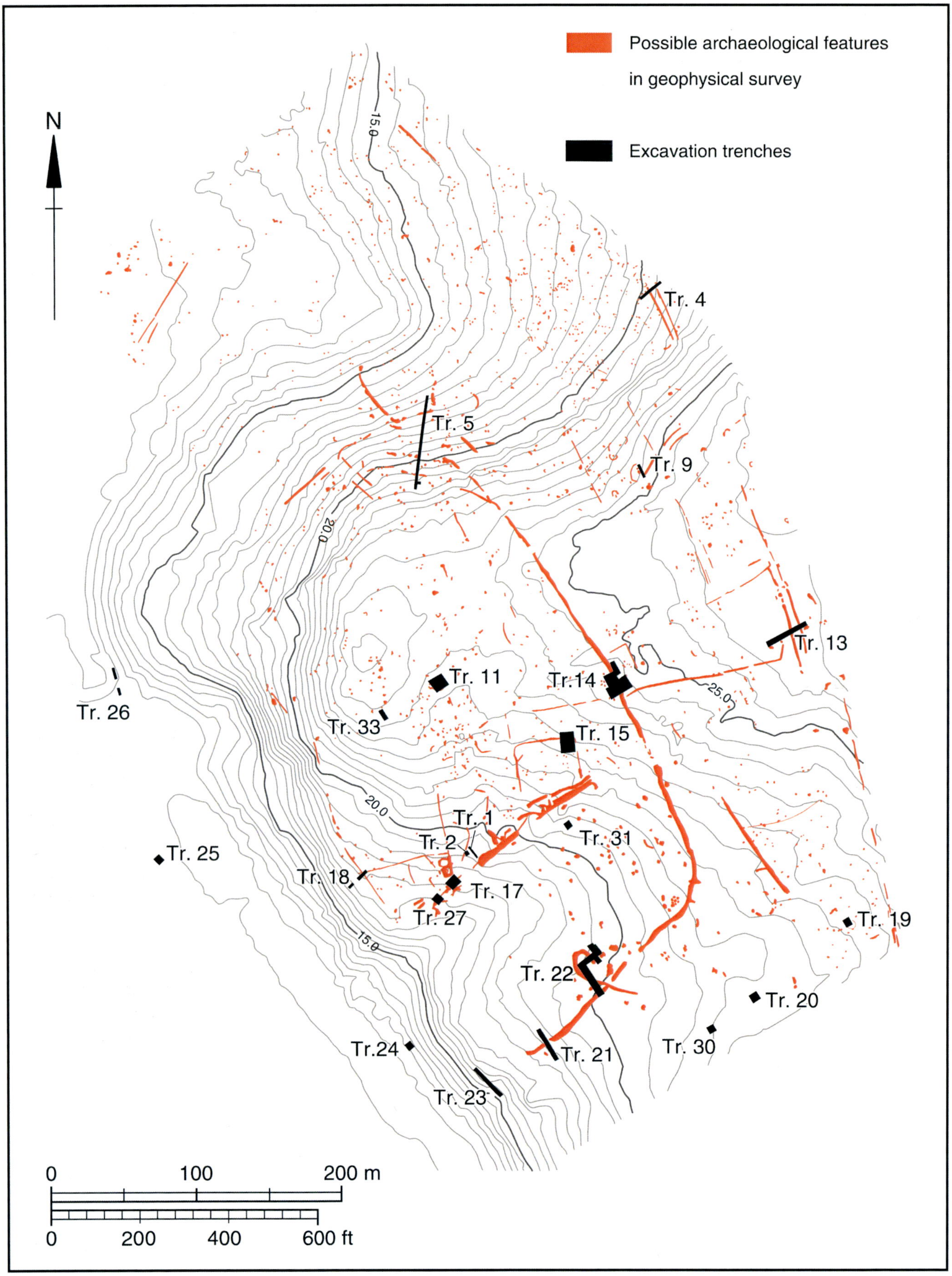

Figure 1 Location of excavation trenches and features revealed by geophysical survey. © York Archaeological Trust

Towards the south of the same field at the bottom of the slope, Earthwork 3 is a prominent, flat-topped bank which starts on the slope of the escarpment on the east and extends across the low ground to the west outside the limits of the survey area, to end at the top of the river bank. The bank is a quite long-lived feature of the landscape as it is depicted on the first edition 1:10,560 Ordnance Survey map published in 1855–6. There are slight traces of a ditch on the north side of the bank, which presumably provided material for construction. The bank is quite low on the slope but increases in height to 0.5m at the foot of the escarpment, though it is cut by several erosion hollows, probably caused by livestock. The tributary stream on the west and north sides of Field 5 passes beneath the earthwork in a culvert. This suggests that the bank was not constructed to act as a dam to retain the flow of this watercourse. This interpretation is supported by two other observations. Firstly, to the east, the feature rises over 2m in height up the slope which is further than would have been necessary to impound the flow of the stream. Secondly, for the bank to have functioned as a dam it would have needed to turn to the north for a considerable distance in order to prevent water from escaping into the river and there is no evidence for this. The siting of the bank seems significant as it acts as a barrier across a narrow strip of land between the river and the tributary valley to the north. This suggests that it was constructed as a flood bank dividing poorly drained land to the south from improved pasture to the north.

Earthwork 4 is a short length of very slight bank on the slope in Field 5, immediately to the east of Earthwork 3 and on a slightly more southerly alignment, parallel with the southern edge of the field. There is no actual contact between the two earthworks that might indicate a relative chronology, though it appears on plan that Earthwork 4 could be cutting across the line of Earthwork 3 and may therefore be later. At one point, the bank bulges out slightly to the south and could indicate the start of a second bank at right angles heading towards the existing field edge. If this interpretation is correct, then it might be evidence that the bank formed part of an animal pen or small enclosure along the edge of the field.

Earthwork 5 is in the south-west corner of Field 5. It consists of a wide bank with a shallow ditch part way down the middle. The bank aligns with a manhole 5m to the east in Field 6 and is presumably connected with an underground drain.

Earthwork 6 in Field 6 is a narrow bank that carries on the line of the fence on the south side of Field 7. The bank presumably indicates that this enclosed area was larger at sometime although there is no plan evidence of this on the Ordnance Survey mapping consulted.

Earthwork 7 is a broad, south-facing scarp on the west side of Earthwork 6. This could be a continuation of the north side of the hollow on the escarpment further to the east or possibly the remnant of a trackway heading towards the foot of the escarpment from the edge of the river.

In addition to these definite earthworks, the sides of the southernmost of the two natural hollows on the escarpment in Field 6 appear to have been artificially steepened, perhaps to incorporate the hollow in a land boundary or defensive ditch extending eastwards in Field 1.

Lidar and airborne multispectral imaging
Dr Keith Challis (Department of Archaeology, University of York)

Aerial photographs from the National Monuments Record collection were researched, but were found not to be informative. Environment Agency Lidar data from two survey flights were used for analysis and visualisation of terrain across the study area. They also provide evidence for some of the earthworks and erosion features which were identified in the topographic survey. Lidar intensity data assisted in delineating an ill-defined area of homogeneous soil/subsoil character, which was also evident in multispectral Daedalus Airborne Thematic Mapper data, supplied by NERC (Natural Environment Research Council), which may relate to a variation in the drift geology, soil or subsoil, and which coincides with the majority of metal-detected finds. It is conceivable that this area of homogeneous soil/subsoil may have played some role in influencing the disposition and extent of past activity across the site; equally, subsoil variations may have affected archaeological survival or the ability of detectorists to identify buried artefacts.

Geophysical survey
Richard Hall

An initial 4.4ha geophysical survey was carried out by the EH Centre for Archaeology, under the supervision of Louise Martin; its results prompted an extension of geophysical coverage, undertaken by Ben Urmston of GSB Prospection Ltd. These surveys revealed a complex multi-period landscape (**Fig. 1**). Linear and curvilinear ditch-like anomalies have an overall plan form that can be interpreted as enclosures, field systems and trackways. Additionally, there are abundant coherent groups of pit-type anomalies that may represent foci of settlement or activity. There is also some evidence for possible industrial activity, albeit confused by modern and historic agriculture; and there is evidence for ridge and furrow agriculture (see **Fig. 40**).

This overall pattern shows some consistency of alignment, but these features do not align with a large, apparently D-shaped or sub-rectangular enclosure ditch, also observed in the topographic survey. Despite its high visibility in places, there are uncertainties about its course at its northern return westwards, and indeed there may be more than one phase of ditch at this point. Geophysics did not identify a barrier along the fourth side of the enclosure (to the west); this does not necessarily rule out the original existence of such a feature, which may be undetectable due to the presence of a field boundary, or may have been eroded away.

Among the discrete positive responses, mainly recorded within the ditched area, some are very strong and at least five appear along the line of the ditch itself. These may well be (thermoremanent) hearths, an interpretation which would correlate with the evidence for metalworking seen among the artefacts (see pp. 48, 82–3). The remainder of the anomalies may be pits, or more deeply buried/less well-fired hearths.

Plate 2 Coins from the hoard: pennies of Alfred of Wessex and Burgred of Mercia, and fragmentary dirham, showing obverses (rows 1–3) and reverses (rows 4–6), Top row within each group (l–r) sfs147, 146, 150, 148. Middle row (l–r) sfs151, 149, 153, 154. Bottom row (l–r) sfs152, 155. British Museum, 2008, 4199.1-10

The early medieval material reported here must be seen in the context of earlier use of the site, the details of which may be found in the YAT Archive and which will be published elsewhere in due course. In summary, the excavation revealed evidence for prehistoric activity hereabouts, with Mesolithic, Later Neolithic/Early Bronze Age and Beaker phases all represented by lithics. There was ceramic evidence for AOC ('all-over corded') Beaker activity, mostly associated with an annular ditch outside the main enclosure which is interpreted as the remains of an isolated barrow. Iron Age/Romano-British activity was represented by pottery in both traditions, by small numbers of Roman coins, metalwork and ceramic building materials, and by geophysical and/or excavated evidence for enclosures and trackways.

The hoard: A closely associated group of Viking-period and late Saxon finds

Barry Ager and Gareth Williams

This group of 121 finds, including items of precious metal, was retrieved by metal detectorists from a small, closely confined area, and forms a distinct and separate assemblage in relation to other artefacts from the ARSNY site. The find-spot was later investigated archaeologically (see **Fig. 27**), but no further information directly relevant to the hoard and its circumstances of deposition was recovered (see pp. 1, 65–6). This group was given the treasure reference 2004T13. The absence of clear contextual information means that this group cannot be definitely identified either as grave goods or as a deliberately deposited hoard, and it is possible that some of the items included are only with this group by chance. However, given the finders' account of the material being found in a concentrated area, and given that the coins, bullion, balance fragment and weights make a plausible group, it seems likely that the core material should be considered as a group which is genuinely distinct from the site assemblage as a whole, even if it is not possible to draw firm conclusions as to the circumstances of its deposition. Following a coroner's inquest, at which the precious-metal finds were declared Treasure and the non-precious-metal finds Treasure by association, the hoard was acquired by the British Museum in 2006 (registration numbers of non-coin items: BM 2006, 1203.1–111; registration numbers of coins BM 2008, 4199.1–10). For consistency, all objects from the site, including BM acquisitions, are referred to by the small finds (sf) numbers drawn up by YAT. An apparent discrepancy in overall numbers is accounted for by the British Museum having separately registered a number of items (e.g. hack-silver, ingot droplets) which YAT had numbered collectively.

The coins (Pl. 2)

Gareth Williams

Of the ten coins, nine are of late 9th-century date. Seven were in the name of Burgred, king of Mercia (852–74), and two in the name of Alfred, king of Wessex (871–99). All nine are of the so-called Lunettes type, issued jointly as part of a monetary and political alliance between the two kings (Pagan 1974; Keynes 1998; Williams 2008a; Lyons and Mackay 2008). This type circulated freely in both kingdoms, and therefore across most of England south of the Humber (apart from East Anglia), although the pre-Viking Northumbrian coinage system was almost completely separate from that south of the Humber (see below, pp. 36–7, 42–3, 104–6). Three examples of the Lunettes type in the name of Burgred have been found in York but are interpreted as having been brought there by Vikings, rather than relating to pre-Viking trade (Blackburn 2004, 344, 347).

The tenth coin is a fragment of an Islamic silver dirham of the Umayyad dynasty (AH 41–132/AD 661–750), of the reformed coinage (AH 79–132/AD 690–749). Fragmentary Islamic coins are typical within Viking hoards of the late 9th and early 10th centuries from Britain (Lowick 1976; Brooks and Graham-Campbell 2000; Graham-Campbell 2001b; Naismith 2005; Williams 2007; 2009; 2011a), as well as from productive sites linked with Viking activity, e.g. Torksey (Blackburn 2002, 92–3; 2011, 229–30). A total of 60 dirhams, including 12 from Yorkshire, have been recorded as single finds from England (Naismith 2005; Kershaw, this volume, pp. 117–19), and most, if not necessarily all of these can also be linked with Viking activity. Dirhams, whether from hoards, sites or single finds, are often in fragmentary condition and should be regarded as hack-silver rather than as coins *per se*.

The coins are as follows:

- Sf146. Silver penny of Alfred of Wessex (871–99), Lunettes sub-type B (N626), moneyer Cuthwulf. Cracked.
  Obv. +ΛELBRED/REX
  Rev. CVÐVLF/.MON./.ETΛ:.
  Weight: 1.31g; Die axis: 90°

- Sf147. Silver penny of Alfred of Wessex (871–99), Lunettes sub-type A (N625), moneyer probably Heremod. Fragmentary, having apparently been bent and snapped. Small quantities of green accretion on both sides.
  Obv. +ΛELBRE____X
  Rev. __[R]EMO/[D]MO:./__Λ.
  Weight: 0.76g; Die axis: 270°

- Sf148. Silver penny of Burgred of Mercia (852–74), Lunettes sub-type A (N423), moneyer Cynehelm.
  Obv. BVRGREDREXM
  Rev. CYNEHL/.:MON:./.:ETΛ:.
  Weight: 1.25g; Die axis: 90°

- Sf149. Silver penny of Burgred of Mercia (852–74), Lunettes sub-type A (N423), moneyer Eadulf.
  Obv. BVRGREDREM
  Rev. EΛDVLF/.:MON./.:ETΛ:.
  Weight: 1.24g; Die axis: 270°

- Sf150. Silver penny of Burgred of Mercia (852–74), Lunettes sub-type A (N423), moneyer Cenred.
  Obv. BVRGREDREXI
  Rev. CEHRED/MON./.ETΛ:.
  Weight: 1.34g; Die axis: 90°

- Sf151. Silver penny of Burgred of Mercia (852–74), Lunettes sub-type A (N423), moneyer Dudwine.
  Obv. BVRGREDREXM
  Rev. DVDPINE/MON/ETΛ:.
  Weight: 1.33g; Die axis: 90°

Sf152. Silver penny of Burgred of Mercia (852–74), Lunettes sub-type E ii (N427) variant, moneyer Tata. Pierced centrally, small quantities of green accretion on both sides.
Obv. +BVRGRED RE
Rev. TATA /MOH/ETA
Weight: 1.27g; Die axis: 180°

- Sf153. Silver penny of Burgred of Mercia (852–74), Lunettes sub-type E ii (N427) variant, moneyer Bernheah. Pierced centrally, small quantities of green accretion on both sides.
Obv. BVRGRED REX
Rev. BER_EA/HMON/ETA
Weight: 1.27g; Die axis: 180°

- Sf154. Silver penny of Burgred of Mercia (852–74), Lunettes sub-type E ii (N427) variant, moneyer Beagstan. Pierced centrally, edge badly chipped in three places, quantities of green accretion on both sides.
Obv. _VRGRED RE
Rev. BEA_ZTA/MON/ETA
Weight: 1.27g; Die axis: 0°

- Sf155. Islamic silver dirham of the Umayyad dynasty (AH 41–132/AD 661–750), of the reformed coinage (AH 79–132/ AD 690–749), mint uncertain, date of issue uncertain (AH__2). Only a small fragment of the coin survives.
Weight: 0.55g

The Lunettes coinage was issued between 871 and 874, and the presence of examples of the rare sub-class E (N427) suggests a *terminus post quem* for the coin assemblage of 873–74, very close to the end of the circulation period of this coinage type, *c.* 875 (Williams 2008a). It is of variable silver quality, and declined to a very low level before its replacement by the Cross-and-Lozenge type, in good silver, issued jointly by Alfred and Burgred's successor Ceolwulf II of Mercia (874–*c.* 879) (Blackburn and Keynes 1998; Blackburn 2003; Williams and Naylor 2016). The improvement in quality makes it likely that the Lunettes coins would have ceased to circulate fairly quickly in Mercia and Wessex, and the presence of Lunettes coins has been taken to imply a fairly precise dating of sites south of the Humber; Lunettes finds at Torksey and Repton have plausibly been linked with the over-wintering of the *micel here* in 872–3 and 873–4 respectively (Biddle *et al.* 1986a; Biddle *et al.* 1986b; Blackburn 2002, 91; 2011, 225).

However, since the coins currently under consideration were found outside the area of controlled coinage circulation south of the Humber, it is not possible to date the hoard so securely with complete confidence. Nevertheless, a number of factors do point to a deposition date in the mid-870s. Firstly, in the absence of any of the coins of Viking Northumbria or East Anglia issued in large quantities from the late 890s (Blackburn 2004; 2005; 2006; Williams 2011a, 42–9; 2014a), it is probably reasonable to assume a deposition date prior to *c.* 895. The hoard also lacks any of the anonymous imitative Viking issues derived from Alfred's coinage produced from *c.* 880 onwards, although the volume of this coinage is less certain than that of the later types, so the significance of their absence cannot easily be assessed, especially given the small size of the hoard. Nevertheless, their absence points to deposition before the 880s. A further refinement to the dating may possibly be made on the basis of the absence of test marks from the coins. Anglo-Saxon coins found in Viking contexts often show signs of having been tested for bullion content, by bending, nicking the edges, pecking the faces, or even biting (Archibald 1990; 2011). Testing by bending and edge-nicking is recorded in England from the early 870s, but pecking is first recorded *c.* 890, and this date frame appears to be confirmed by hoards from other areas of the Viking world (Archibald 1990; 2011; Blackburn 2001; Graham-Campbell 2001a; Moesgaard 2011). Given the gap in hoard evidence between the 870s and the 890s, together with the relative paucity of single finds from this period, it is not possible to indicate exactly when the practice of pecking was introduced, but Marion Archibald (2011) argues convincingly that the most likely context for the introduction of pecking was the transition to good silver coinage with the introduction of the Cross-and-Lozenge type in the mid-870s, as the only time in which good and bad silver coins routinely circulated together, thereby necessitating testing for quality, although the recent discovery of the Watlington hoard of *c.* 879–80, which on preliminary examination shows no sign of pecking (Williams and Naylor 2016) indicates that this practice was not yet universal in Viking exchange systems in England by that time. One of the coins (sf147) has been bent, and appears to have snapped as a result, but it is not immediately apparent whether this is the result of Viking-Age testing, or subsequent accidental damage. Another coin (sf149) has a possible edge nick, although this is more probably just a crack. More significantly, none of the coins show any evidence of pecking, and following Archibald's argument this would suggest that they may well have been deposited no later than the 870s, although it would be rash to build too much on negative evidence. Thirdly, coins of the Lunettes phase did not appear in Viking hoards of the 890s and later, suggesting that they were withdrawn from circulation in Northumbria as well as elsewhere, probably because of widespread rejection of their poor silver quality rather than because of any formal control (Williams 2009; 2011a, 42), although the current rarity of Viking hoards which can be firmly dated between the mid-870s and *c.* 890 means that we cannot state definitively that this withdrawal took place immediately after the introduction of the Cross-and-Lozenge type. It is notable, however, that the one substantial documented hoard of the Cross-and-Lozenge phase, found near Watlington in Oxfordshire in 2015, excludes Lunettes coins but includes significant numbers of coins of the Cross-and-Lozenge phase along with gold and silver bullion and imported Frankish coins (Williams and Naylor 2016). A second hoard found around the same time in Herefordshire, but without secure provenance, and not yet fully recorded, also includes coins of the Cross-and-Lozenge phase but none of the Lunettes phase.

Finally, the hoard needs to be seen in the context of the overall coin assemblage from elsewhere on the site. Apart from a few late strays which appear to post-date the main phase of occupation on the site, the assemblage terminates in a single example of a Lunettes type of Burgred (sf267) and

another of the following Cross-and-Lozenge type of Ceolwulf II (874–*c.* 879) (sf1385), suggesting that the coin supply to the main period of activity on the site ended in the mid-870s (see further below, p. 36). It therefore seems safe to say that the hoard was deposited between *c.* 874 and *c.* 895, while circumstantial evidence suggests very strongly that it was buried at the very beginning of that period.

Three of the Anglo-Saxon coins (sfs152–4) have been pierced centrally, although it is uncertain whether this was for use as mounts on weights, characteristic of Viking weights of the late 9th and early 10th centuries, especially from England and Ireland (Williams 1999; see also below, p. 22), or as pendants or dress ornaments, or for some other purpose. No trace of lead could be found on the surface of the pierced coins, indicating that even if it was intended to mount them on weights, this had not occurred prior to deposition. One of these coins (sf154) is also badly chipped. As noted above, another Anglo-Saxon coin (sf147) is only fragmentary, although it is unclear whether this reflects more recent damage. The Islamic coin is also fragmentary. This again suggests secondary usage of the coins as silver bullion rather than use in a controlled monetary system, and it is likely that the entire coin assemblage should be considered simply as bullion, especially when taken with the presence of weights and hack-silver (see below). Given the small size and weight of the pieces of hack-silver, the coins and hack-silver are probably best considered together in monetary (rather than typological) terms as a single mixed hoard of low-value items of silver bullion, rather than as two distinct groups. This fits a broader pattern of monetary use in the areas of Viking settlement in northern England in the late 9th century (Graham-Campbell 2001a; Williams 2007; see also Kershaw, this volume, pp. 116–27; Williams, this volume, pp. 36–45, Chapter 5). Given the evidence for metalworking on the site (see below, pp. 9, 33, 48, 82–3), the possibility that the coins and bullion were intended as raw material for metalworking cannot be completely excluded. However, both groups of weights are of types more typically associated with bullion exchange than metalworking (see below, pp. 20–31) and Kershaw (this volume, pp. 121–2) notes the presence of similar weight types at Cottam B, which currently lacks any evidence for metalworking. Furthermore, if the hoard is seen as associated with a grave, then there are direct parallels for the presence of weights and balances in wealthy Viking graves in the British Isles and elsewhere, whether these are seen as relating to trade or the distribution of plunder/tribute (Crawford 1987, 126; Owen and Dalland 1999, 118–21). The coins and hack-silver can therefore perhaps most plausibly be interpreted as the contents of a purse.

Artefacts

Barry Ager

Surface metal analyses conducted at the British Museum indicated the approximate precious-metal contents noted for each object below.

Gold

Sf142: gilded and gold circular stud with blue glass cabochon setting on top; diameter 10mm (**Fig. 2**). Double-tiered with twisted beaded wire round the lower tier and a plain collet for the setting above; gold content of the lower edge of the setting, 51% approx. Two rivets fix the stud to a corroded fragment of a copper-alloy sheet backing plate. The stud is late Saxon, 8th or possibly early 9th century in date, and may be from a piece of jewellery such as a pin, or possibly from a bronze vessel. It is comparable, for example, with the riveted central bosses of the heads of the 8th-century silver-gilt Witham pins, which were originally set with glass in collets enclosed by two plain wires on either side of a twisted wire (Wilson 1964, 132–4, no. 19, pl. 18); or, more closely, with the circular, silver-gilt setting of a red glass cabochon forming the head of a probably 8th-century silver pin from Low Santon, North Lincolnshire, on which the setting is enclosed by a plain collet and a collar of three twisted wires (Evans 2004, no. 119, fig. 119). Also, 28 studs with (blue glass) cabochon settings were spaced around the interior and base of the lost silver hanging bowl from the River Witham, of the mid- to late 8th, or possibly early 9th century (Graham-Campbell 2004a, 358–71, figs 1–2 and 6). The studs of the bowl appear from the surviving illustrations to have had plain collets above a collar of two twisted wires above a milled ring. A further comparison may be made with the Anglian blue glass and silver stud of *c.* 800 from 16–22 Coppergate, York (Tweddle *et al.* 1999, 258, no. 83, fig. 80) with a plain collet enclosed by two rings of twisted wire and filigree with two small prongs on the back for attachment (as on the ARSNY stud), that is in turn comparable with bosses on the lining of the 8th-century, repoussé-decorated, silver-gilt bowl from Ormside churchyard that may have been made in York (Hall 1984, 33–4, fig. 29; Roesdahl *et al.* (eds), 1981, illusts on p.41; Wilson 1984, 64, pls 56–7 and 159).

Silver

The silver component of the hoard comprises one silver ingot, four ingot droplets (only two of which contain more than 10% silver) and six pieces of hack-silver (sf144:1–11), and ten coins (sfs146–55) (see above, pp. 11–12).

i) The ingot (sf144:1) consists of a short bar with rounded ends and lateral projections; it has been cast in a simple open mould and then hammered fairly smooth on top and bottom; length 27mm; weight 6.96g; 94% silver. The initial form of the silver ingot before working is typical of the Viking/Anglo-Scandinavian period in England. Its weight falls within the lower range of its type. Similar examples occur in the well-known Viking silver hoards from Cuerdale, Lancashire (deposited *c.* 905–10; Graham-Campbell 2011, 73–86), and Chester (deposited around 965; Webster 1953; Graham-Campbell 2011, 11–13, 157–8, no. 11, fig. 1.12), as well as in Scandinavia and the Netherlands. Ingots, whole and fragmentary, are also included in the main site assemblage (see pp. 33–5), and in the assemblage from Torksey (Blackburn 2011, 223–4, 226, 233–6). Several recent single finds of Viking-period ingots have been reported from across a wide geographical area, mostly but not exclusively from areas of Viking settlement, e.g. from Temple Normanton, Derbyshire (DCMS 2000, 49), Eccleston, Cheshire, and Sandhurst, Gloucestershire (DCMS 2003, 46–8), Hindringham, Norfolk (DCMS 2004, 50–1) and Roxby cum Risby, North Lincolnshire (DCMS

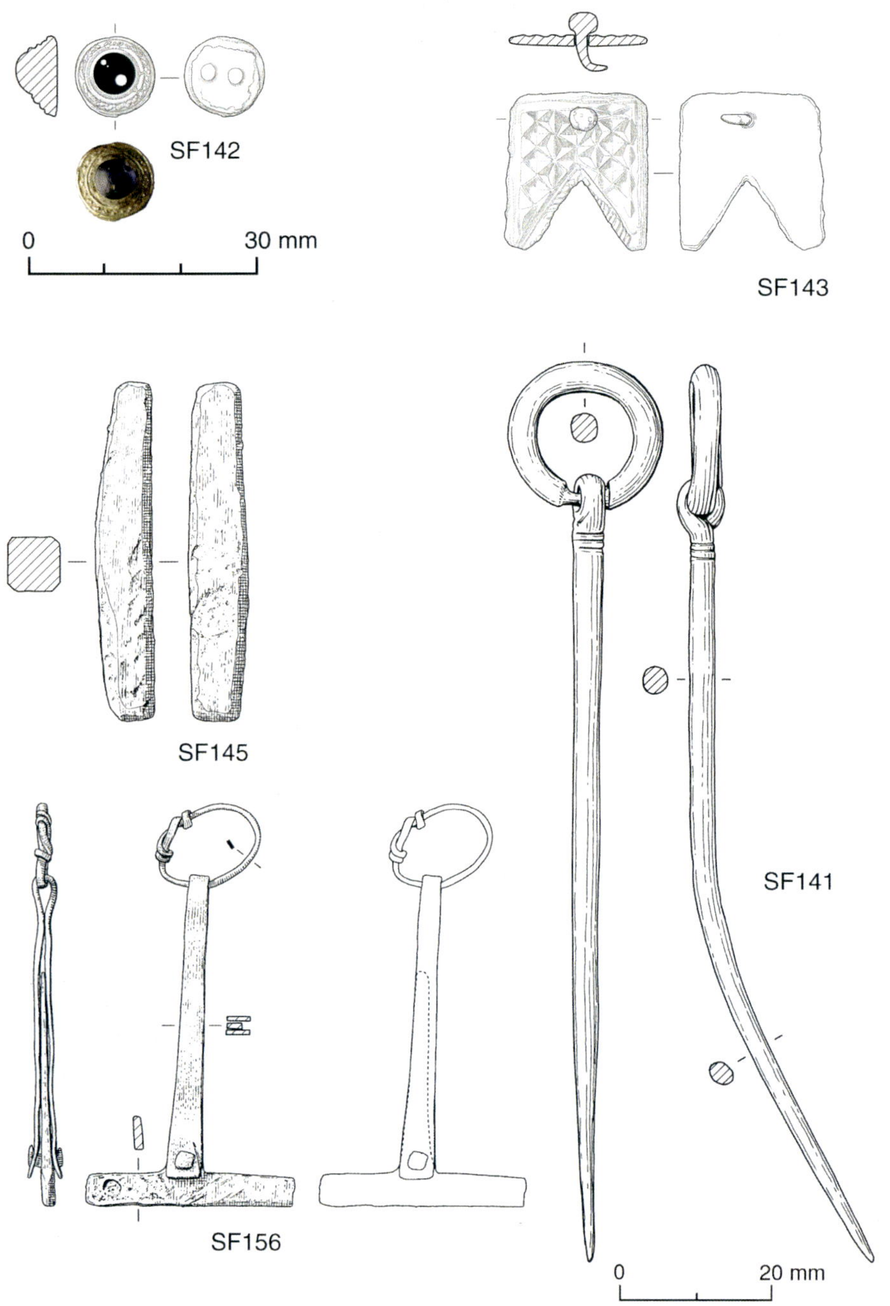

Figure 2 Objects from the hoard: copper-alloy ringed pin (sf141); gilded and gold circular stud with blue glass cabochon setting (sf142); gilded, cast copper-alloy mount (sf143); copper-alloy ingot (sf145); part of a copper-alloy folding balance (sf156). British Museum

2009, 109; further, more recent examples are recorded on the database of the PAS). Twelve single finds of silver ingots of typical Viking-Age form from Yorkshire (four complete and eight cut fragments) are discussed in more detail below by Jane Kershaw (see pp. 114–16). Such ingots could have been used as bullion in payments or trade transactions, as well as a source of metal for jewellery-making. While not all such ingots are diagnostically Anglo-Scandinavian, this example is typical of ingots from Viking hoards, as noted above.

ii) The four larger pieces of hack-silver comprise: sf144:2, a roughly cast and hammered fragment, length 24mm, weight 6.0g, 96% silver; sf144:3, a curved fragment of a square-sectioned bar, length 18mm, weight 7.67g, 98% silver; sf144:4, one end cut from an ingot, width 15mm, weight 4.84g, 96% silver; and sf144:5, a section of strip, length 11mm, weight 2.06g, 98% silver.

There are also two very small fragments of silver, sfs144:7–8: widths *c.* 5mm, weight 0.36g and 0.37g, 97% and 99% silver respectively. The two silver droplets, sfs144:9–10, are roughly plano-convex, diameters 8mm and 5mm, weight 1.37g and 0.85g, 98% and 97% silver respectively. The other two droplets, sfs144:6 and 11, are of leaded bronze and lead-tin alloy respectively, diameter 6mm each, weight 0.55g and 0.76g. An associated copper-alloy ingot is described below (sf145). Again, there are parallels to the hack-silver in the main site assemblage (see pp. 33–6), and the hack-silver pieces can also be compared with those from many Viking-period hoards. A number of comparable finds are recorded from the productive site at Torksey (Blackburn 2011, 223–4, 226, 233–6), while single finds of hack-silver from Yorkshire are discussed by Kershaw below (see pp. 116–17).

The total weight of the silver items above is 30.48g.

Copper alloy

i) Hammered, copper-alloy ingot of tapering square section with chamfered edges (sf145), length 41mm, weight 11.48g (**Fig. 2**). It was closely associated with the silver items above according to the metal detectorists who found it. Copper-alloy ingots are unusual finds in early medieval Britain, e.g. a Viking-Age example from Saham Toney, Norfolk (Gurney 2001, 704), while two of rectangular section and of similar size to the ARSNY find are recorded from middle Saxon London and long bar ingots from Kingsway on the edge of *Lundenwic* are also held by the Museum of London (Malcolm and Bowsher 2003, 274, 276; Bayley *et al.* 2014).

ii) Gilded, cast copper-alloy mount (sf143), flat, rectangular with a V-shaped cut-out in one of the short sides and a ball-headed rivet opposite, length 21mm, width 19mm (**Fig. 2**). The front is decorated with a ribbed border and a lattice of chip-carved rosettes, etc. It may be broadly compared with an 8th-century, Irish-style, chip-carved rectangular plaque from the site of a Viking-period beach market at Meols, Cheshire (Griffiths *et al.* 2007, 63, pls 9, 316, and V, 316). Susan Youngs suggests, more appositely, that the ARSNY mount may be half a framing plate for a lozenge-shaped setting of, presumably, glass or amber, such as those that appear with a symbolic significance on the stem and base of the Derrynaflan chalice of the early 9th century, and are imitated in the borders of the Book of Kells and Irish sculpture of the late 8th–9th century. The complete plate would have formed part of a rectangular, composite border panel from something potentially ostentatious, e.g. a shrine or book-cover, and the rivet may be from re-use after the original had been dismantled (S. Youngs, pers. comm.; Henry 1974, 24–5, 29, 55; Youngs 1989, no. 124). The lozenge featured on brooches in the first half of the 9th century, possibly as a Christian symbol (Richardson 1984, 32; Youngs 1989, nos 77–8, 80–1 and 84). Decorative, gilded, Irish-style jewellery and fittings, mainly of the 8th to early 9th century, were often re-used by the Vikings in both Britain and Scandinavia in the 9th century (Wamers 1985; Sheehan 2013; Pitts 2014, 9). It is of further significance that a number of northern English place-names in the Domesday survey incorporate Gaelic personal names, whether of Irish or Scottish derivation (Edmonds 2009), since both this mount and a ringed pin (below) may have been obtained by their Viking owner as the result of loot or trade, but they may also partly reflect a Gaelic-Scandinavian background.

iii) Copper-alloy ringed pin (sf141) with long shank bent roughly halfway along and a plain ring of circular section hinged by a narrow rod through a closed loop at the top of the shank (length 120mm overall, diameter of ring 20mm) (**Fig. 2**). There are three close grooves incised round the top of the shank below the loop. The pin is an example of Fanning's plain-ringed, loop-headed type of dress or shroud fastener, adopted from the Irish in the 9th century by the Scandinavians in the British Isles and northern Europe (Fanning 1990; Fanning 1994, 15–23). The plain-ringed, loop-headed form is typical of the late 9th–early 10th centuries especially, although it originated in pre-Viking Ireland. In Britain, ringed pins of various types occur mainly in Anglo-Scandinavian urban centres, as at York, reflecting Hiberno-Norse contacts, although a number of single finds have also been recorded from graves and nineteen complete or partial examples from Meols alone, while two silver examples form part of the Skaill Hoard, Orkney, deposited *c.* 960–80 (Graham-Campbell 1995, 36, nos 24:51 and 110, pl. 46; Griffiths *et al.* 2007, 67–9, pls 10–11 and V, nos 370–88).

iv) Copper-alloy part of a folding balance of Steuer's Type 6 (sf156) consisting of the central section of the beam with pointer, the hanging arm hinged to the base of the pointer by a copper-alloy rivet, and a knotted wire ring passing through the looped top of the arm (height excluding ring 43mm, remaining width of beam 27mm) (**Fig. 2**). One end of the beam section is pierced by a rivet hole with traces of an iron rivet for hinging a missing long arm, whilst the other end is broken to a similar length. The resulting T-shape suggests that the balance may have been re-used as a Thor's hammer pendant when no longer usable for weighing (**Pl. 3**) (for the pendants, see Graham-Campbell 2011, 125–6). Complete examples of folding balances are well known from Scandinavian Viking-period contexts (Graham-Campbell 1980, 88, no. 306, pl. 306; Armbruster 2002; Steuer 2007a).

Copper-alloy weights **(Pl. 3)**
Gareth Williams

v) Four cubo-octahedral weights (**Fig. 3**): sf157:1 in the form of a cube with faceted corners, the six square faces each punched with six dots and framed by grooves (weight 3.60g, width 9mm); sf157:2, same form, each square face punched with four annulets (weight 2.89g, width 8mm); sf157:3, same form, each square face punched with three annulets (weight 1.97g, width 7mm); sf157:4, same form, each square face punched with two dots (weight 1.47g, width 6mm). The form is typical of the Viking period and other English finds are recorded, e.g. from Torksey, Lincolnshire (Blackburn 2011, 236–9; Geake 2010; see also PAS website for more recent finds). Several other examples were included in the general finds assemblage from the ARSNY site, and these are discussed more fully below (pp. 20–3). With reference to the hoard, however, it is worth noting that this weight type was apparently introduced in Scandinavia *c.* 860–70 (Pedersen 2007, 132), although such weights continued to be used into the 10th century.

Lead weights **(Pl. 3)**
Gareth Williams

Four cylindrical weights (**Fig. 3**): sf158:1, stub of a rivet on top, probably originally for fixing a piece of decorative metalwork (weight 7.41g, diameter 13mm); sf158:2, pierced by a dome-headed iron rivet (weight 6.57g, diameter 15mm); sf158:3, plano-convex with seven or eight round marks on the flat face and stub of a rivet(?) on the edge (weight 5.64g, diameter 13mm); sf158:4, with slightly raised rim and central dot on both faces (weight 1.79g, diameter 8mm).

The lead weights are typical of the Viking/Anglo-Scandinavian period in the British Isles and Scandinavia (e.g. Graham-Campbell 1980, 88–9, nos 306–8, pls 306–8; Williams et al. 2014, 59, nos 50–2). Like the cubo-octahedral weights from the hoard, the lead weights are consistent with the general pattern of the weights assemblage from the site. Lead weights marked with dots or incisions are common in

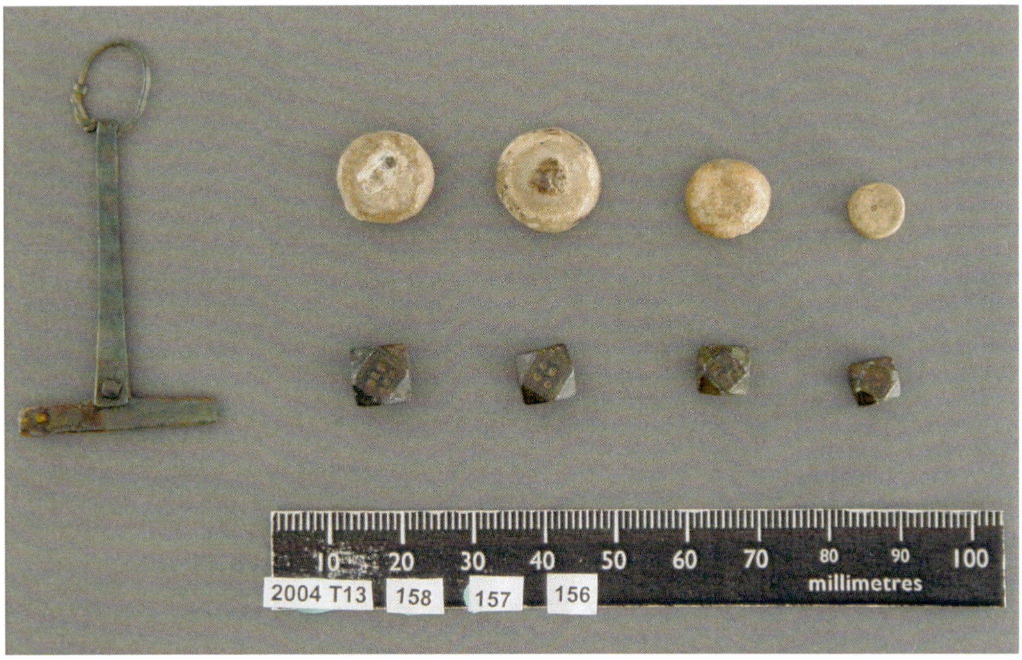

Plate 3 Balance fragment and weights from the hoard (sfs156, 157:1–4, 158:1–4). British Museum, 2006,1203.16, 104-111

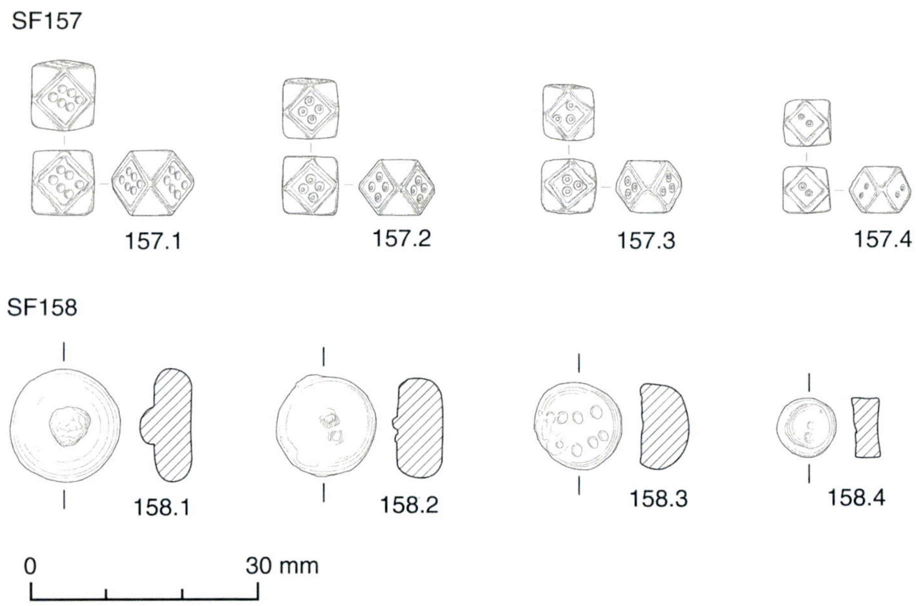

Figure 3 Objects from the hoard: four cubo-octahedral weights (sfs157.1–157.4) and four cylindrical weights (sfs158.1–158.4). British Museum

Scandinavia, and are known from both 9th- and 10th-century contexts (Pedersen 2007, 148–55). Lead weights with decorative insets or caps are more typical of Insular Viking finds, although they are also known in small numbers from Scandinavia (ibid., 131; Baastrup 2013). Weights of this type cannot be dated precisely, but again there are arguments for dating their introduction to the 860s and 870s, although they continued to be used over a longer period (see below, p. 22).

Ironwork

Barry Ager

i) Three pieces from the hilt of a sword (sf133), comprising the pommel, part of the tang of rectangular section (partly missing at the lower end) and a downward-curved, lentoid lower guard with pointed ends (**Fig. 4**). The pommel is of trilobate, sub-triangular form with a curved-up base and a lobe projecting on either side of the apex; solid iron with no evidence of inlays (width 55mm, height 42mm). The guard has a slot for the tang and a groove for the shoulders of the blade (length 85mm, width 25mm). The trilobate pommel and curved guard are typical of swords of Petersen's Type L, mainly of the mid- to late 9th century, although extending into the beginning of the 10th century (Petersen 1919, 112–16). The pointed ends of the guard suggest a late date in the series, which generally has rounded ends, and tending towards Evison's derivative 'Wallingford Bridge' type (Evison 1967, 163). The pommel and lower guard from a sword, or swords, of this type were found residually in medieval contexts at Fishergate, York (Rogers 1993, 1431–3, fig. 702, nos 5262–3, which notes further examples of the type from British sites, including a pommel from 10th-century levels at Coppergate, York). The decoration of the silver mounts surviving on a number of these swords, however, particularly those in the Trewhiddle style, confirms that they are late Saxon in origin, not Viking, although they occur in Viking graves in both Scandinavia and Britain (Evison 1967, 161; *pace* Peirce 2002, 74–6). An iron pommel of the type, mounted with gold plaques, was

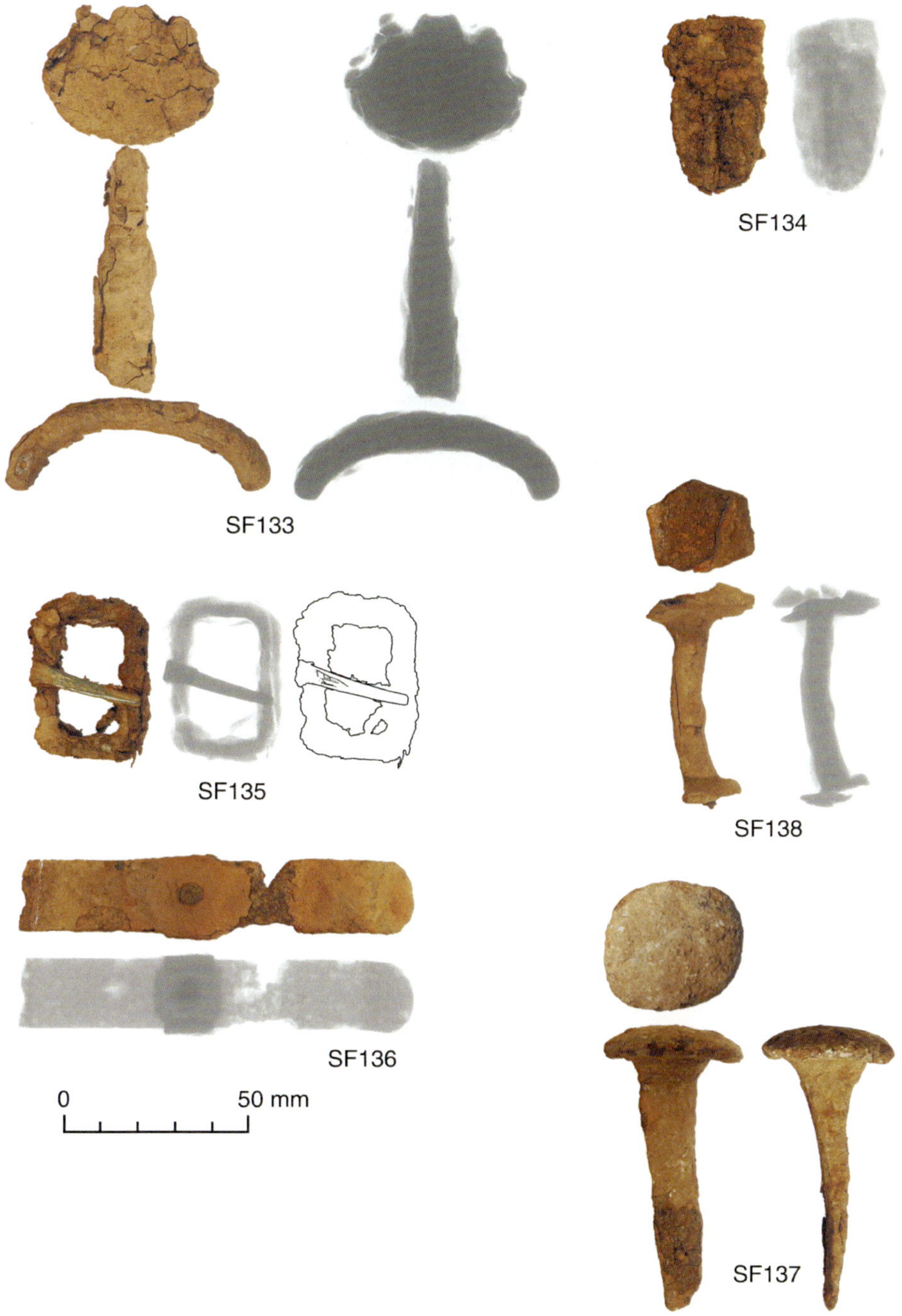

Figure 4 Objects from the hoard: three pieces from the hilt of a sword (sf133); tongue-shaped strap-end (sf134); buckle (sf135); binding strip (sf136); nail with domed square head (sf137); clench rivet and rove (sf138). British Museum

discovered recently in a Viking-Age hoard from Bedale, North Yorkshire (PAS Find-ID YORYM-CEE620 (no. 1); see also below, pp. 111–12).

ii) Four pieces of a sword (sf132), comprising the pommel, the upper end of the blade with the tang, the pointed lower end and a short section from the centre (**Fig. 5**). The solid iron pommel is of trilobate, sub-triangular form with a curved-up base; the top of one of the slight lobes on either side of the apex has broken off (width 63mm, height 30mm). The blade is very corroded, but shows evidence of the pattern-welding technique in a herringbone pattern of three twisted strips along the middle (Lang and Ager 1989, pattern B1); (length of upper end and tang 232mm, width 45mm surviving, length of central section 70mm, length of lower end, 300mm approx; i.e. total surviving length 602mm). The lower end is bent around its mid-point and slightly again above the tip, which is possibly damage resulting from agricultural activity rather than a sign of 'ritual killing'. The pommel is a very simple version of Petersen's late Anglo-Saxon L-type, without any visible evidence for plating or inlay. The sword is of the same mid- to late 9th-century date as the sword hilt (sf133) above. It was found with a whetstone (see 'Stone' below).

iii) Tongue-shaped strap-end with square-section midrib on front and damaged split end, of Thomas Class E, Type 3 (sf134) (**Fig. 4**); two rivets towards the top edge, a corner section of which is missing on one side (length 46mm, width 25mm); no visible evidence for plating; possibly associated with buckle (sf135). This form is found in Anglo-Scandinavian areas and is related to Continental and late Saxon tongue-shaped types of the late 9th and 10th centuries (Thomas 2004, fig. 4, 28).

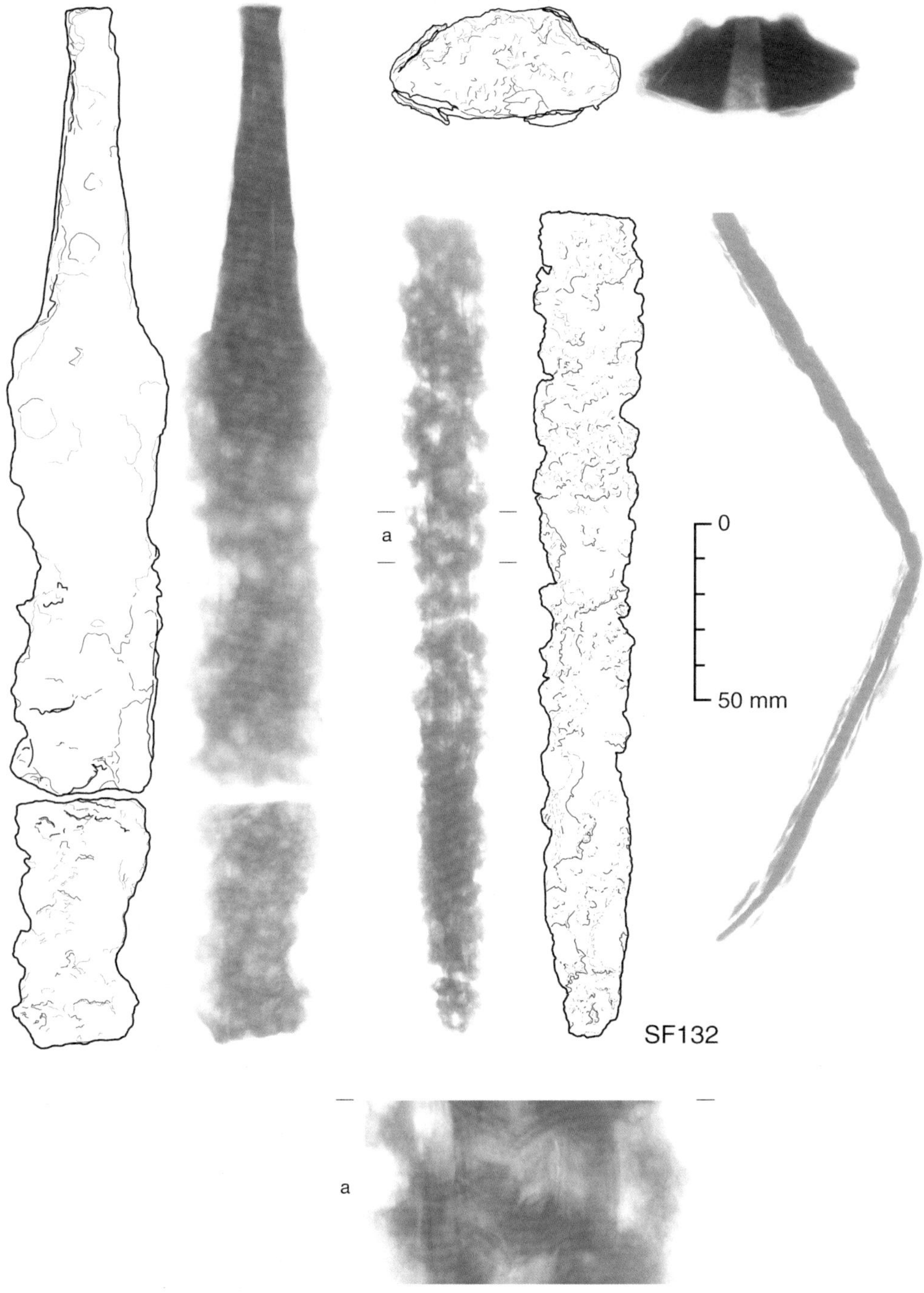

Figure 5 Objects from the hoard: four pieces of a sword (sf132). British Museum

iv) Rectangular buckle-loop with rounded corners and copper-alloy tongue with a series of approximately parallel, roughly incised lines towards the hinge end (sf135), length 42mm, width 30mm (**Fig. 4**); no visible evidence for plating; possibly associated with strap-end (sf134) above. Buckles of this type without belt plates were generally used on the girth-straps of horse-harnesses (Müller-Wille 1973, 32, fig. 7, 3).

v) Binding strip rounded at one end (bent) and broken at the other (sf136) (**Fig. 4**); a square iron collar is riveted round the central section; probably modern (length 105mm).

vi) Large nail with domed square head and wide, flattened, tapering shank (sf137), length 75mm (**Fig. 4**).

vii) Clench rivet with a damaged, square rove and round head, part of which is missing (sf138), length 60mm (**Fig. 4**). This type of rivet was used by both late Saxon and Viking-period carpenters to fasten overlapping planks for a variety of purposes, e.g. for roofs, boats, doors and the bodies of carts. Both of the latter were occasionally re-used as coffins, as at the ringfort of Fyrkat, Denmark (Roesdahl 1977, 14, 131–2, figs 109, 172; Rogers 1993, 1410–12, fig. 689, nos 5115 and 5130; Thomas 2008, 375–6, fig. 27, 7–8).

viii) Domed square head of large nail or rove of clench rivet with stub of shank surviving (sf139), width 25mm.

ix) Rectangular head of nail or rove of clench rivet with stub of shank surviving (sf140), length 28mm.

Stone

Whetstone (sf159), grey-brown, rectangular and slightly tapered at one end, the edges and corners slightly chipped (length 110mm; width 18mm); found with sword (sf132) above. For recent literature on early medieval whetstones, including examples from York, see references in: Rogers 1993, 1313–16; Wamers 1998, 45–6; Steuer 2007b.

Conclusions
Barry Ager and Gareth Williams

Without any archaeological evidence for the circumstances in which this group of objects were committed to the ground in close proximity, it is on the basis of the artefacts themselves that suggestions may be made. The coins and silver make a clear grouping, although with parallels in the general finds assemblage, and can reasonably be considered to be a single hoard. While weights would not normally be hoarded together with precious metal, there are parallels in the Talnotrie hoard, Kirkcudbrightshire, deposited at a similar date (see below, p. 37), and in hoards from other parts of the Viking world, e.g. one of the hoards from Gnezdovo in Russia (Williams *et al.* 2014, 264), while a balance fragment was also discovered with a hoard of Northumbrian stycas from Bamburgh, Northumberland, dated to the mid-860s (DCMS 2006, 184). The other finds are less obviously associated, and the interpretation of the deposit depends to some extent on whether or not they are all considered to be a single associated group.

The hoard could have been deposited as a discrete group of precious and non-precious-metal items, representing perhaps a merchant's stock in trade. Alternatively, the deposit could represent an interment, in which the swords, whetstone, and balance and weights were disposed around the body in typical Scandinavian fashion, and with the costume items (ringed pin, strap-end, buckle, and possibly the re-used Celtic mount, which had been attached by a rivet to something, perhaps a belt), presumably on the body. The silver objects/hack-silver and coins could possibly have been kept together in a purse, which may also have held the gold and blue glass stud, since it appears to have been removed from a vessel or piece of jewellery rather than to have been part of the dead man's costume. It seems unlikely that the stud was just a stray piece in the (putative) grave, although the presence of a purse containing such an assortment of precious metal rather than just coins would be unparalleled in Viking graves from the British Isles.

The finders reported seeing traces of bones, which they took to be human, when digging out the artefacts. No bones were discovered during the archaeological investigation of the burial site, but organic survival was poor over much of the entire site, and relatively little bone was recovered during excavations.

The hoard can be dated with certainty to *c.* 874–95 on the basis of the dates of the minting of the coins, and there is strong evidence for believing that it was buried at the very beginning of this period. The typological dating of the main associated objects which do not show secondary usage is consistent both with the broader and narrower datings.

The objects were found in a confined area, and the combination of material is certainly plausible as a single assemblage, with the exception of a few medieval and more modern items which simply happen to have been found in the same place. At the same time, given the clear evidence for dispersal of finds across the site as a result of ploughing and other activity the possibility cannot be excluded that other non-associated objects from the same cultural context may have been found in close proximity to the main deposit by chance, along with the later medieval and post-medieval items. The continued association of all the finds listed above with the hoard should thus be considered to reflect the find circumstances rather than a definitive interpretation of a single deposition.

Trade and exchange at ARSNY

Introduction
Gareth Williams

In addition to the coins, weighing equipment and silver bullion in the hoard, items apparently relating to trade and exchange comprise one of the largest groups of objects recorded from the site. These include a fragment of an equal-armed folding balance, up to 283 weights, 2 pieces of hack-gold, 70 pieces of silver and 106 coins from the key period of activity in the late 9th century, as well as smaller numbers of later coins which apparently represent casual loss over several centuries rather than concentrated exchange activity on site. The exact number of objects relating to trade and exchange is debatable since, while some of the objects can be clearly identified as weights, there is some ambiguity as to whether all of the putative weights really are weights rather than gaming pieces or counters, while some of the gold and silver objects may relate to metalworking and production rather than to exchange within a bullion economy (see below). Nevertheless, the mixture of weighing equipment, bullion and coins has parallels with those from a number of Viking-Age urban or pre-urban sites in Scandinavia and the Baltic, as well as with other sites in Britain and Ireland. To date, this is the largest such assemblage from Britain, with the exception of the Viking winter camp at Torksey in Lincolnshire (Blackburn 2011), and is a substantial body of material even by Scandinavian standards. Other large assemblages of related material have recently been recorded from Ireland at the Woodstown 6 site, near Waterford (Sheehan 2014; 2015; Wallace 2013, 308–9; 2014) and from an assemblage dispersed along the course of the River Blackwater in Co. Armagh and Co. Tyrone, including *inter alia* silver, lead and copper-alloy ingots, hack-silver, both plain lead weights and lead weights with decorative insets derived from Insular metalwork, a single pan from a pan-balance (with parallels at Kilmainham/Islandbridge on the outskirts of Dublin, and York), and waste products relating to metalworking (Bourke 2010, 22–7, 30, 35–7, 46, 71–5 ; Wallace 2013, 311–12).

***Folding balance* (Fig. 6)**
Nicola Rogers

A fragmentary folding balance made of copper alloy (sf1159) comprises the pointer and beam up to the hinged ends of both arms. The folding form of balance appears to date from *c.* 800 onwards (Kruse 1992, 72), and examples have been recovered from late Anglo-Saxon, Anglo-Scandinavian and medieval deposits. Typologically, these balances are difficult to date more precisely, particularly when incomplete (*ibid.*).

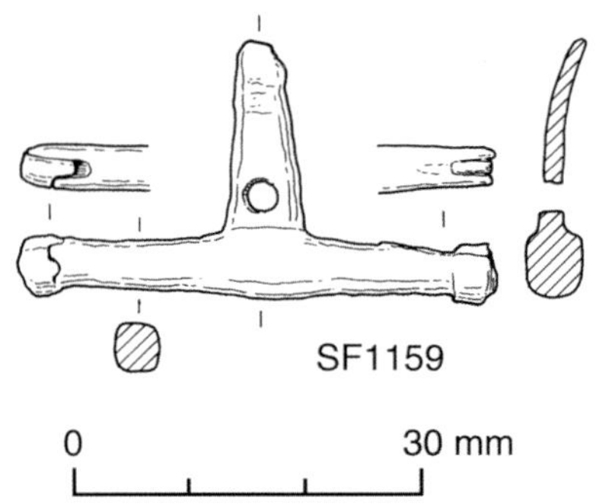

Figure 6 Part of a copper-alloy folding balance (sf1159). © York Archaeological Trust

Fragments of four folding balances were found in Anglo-Scandinavian levels at Coppergate, York (Mainman and Rogers 2000, 2559–61), while another has been recovered from an early 15th-century context at the Bedern foundry, also in York (Ottaway and Rogers 2002, 2952). Sf1159 may possibly date therefore from some time between the 9th and 15th centuries. A folding balance was also found in the ARSNY hoard (sf156, **Fig. 2** and **Pl. 3**, see above p. 15).

Weights
Gareth Williams

Classification of weights

The weights from ARSNY take a wide variety of forms, unlike the more homogeneous assemblages from some Scandinavian sites. This probably reflects the fact that, as discussed below, the main period of activity on the site coincided with the adoption of new weight types in the Scandinavian homelands, while other types with more parallels in Britain and Ireland than in Scandinavia can best be seen as an independent development as a result of the Viking raiding and settlement there in the third quarter of the 9th century. Other weights are of more generic type with parallels in both Britain and Scandinavia dating back to the pre-Viking period. Accordingly, while it is not possible in most cases to assign a very precise place (or even culture) of origin for the weights, a single classification system based on form is proposed here (**Table 1**). Not all of the weight types in the classification system are represented in the ARSNY assemblage, or at any single Viking-Age site. However, with the growing body of evidence available for study in this field, a single system of classification should make for more convenient comparison in future.

Viking-Age weights fall into two main categories. The first contains two types, typically made of copper alloy, or of copper-alloy shells with iron or lead cores, produced to more or less regulated weight standards, and usually with a design reinforcing their 'formal' status. These are the oblate-spheroid (type A), sometimes referred to in the literature as truncated or flattened spheres, and the cubo-octahedral (type B), also referred to in the literature as polyhedral and, in metal-detecting circles, as 'dice-weights'. Both types are recognised as reflecting monetary contact with the Islamic world, as they imitate the design and, more debatably, the weight standards (see below), of Islamic copper-alloy weights. While this type of weight originated in the Islamic world, examples have been found in large numbers in a variety of sites from Viking-Age Scandinavia, and there is some evidence for their production both at Birka and on Gotland (Sperber 1996; 2004; Steuer 1987; 1997; Gustin 2004; Pedersen 2008, 121, 132–40). A date of *c.* AD 870–80 for the introduction of both types in Scandinavia was proposed by Heiko Steuer (1987, 460; 1997, 12), but the re-excavation of both Birka and Kaupang has led to a redating of the introduction of the cubo-octahedral weights to *c.* AD 860–70 (Gustin 2004; Pedersen 2008, 132). Until recently, both types were seen as predominantly confined to Scandinavia, but a growing number of cubo-octahedral weights have been recorded in England, both on major sites and as stray finds. The largest group of these from one site comes from the proposed Viking camp at Torksey, and a preliminary publication of these, together with other strays known at that time, was published by Mark Blackburn in 2002. Both the Torksey corpus and the wider corpus of single finds have expanded significantly since then, with the 28 recorded finds of this type from the ARSNY site (sfs157:1–4, 163, 825, 1428–49) representing the largest group from the British Isles after Torksey (**Pl. 4**). More recent lists of Torksey material appear in Brown (2006) and Blackburn (2011), and work is currently under way to record additional material and to provide a unified catalogue of all the finds from the Torksey site (see below pp. 84–6; for finds elsewhere see also Geake 2010; Kershaw 2017; and the PAS website for more recent finds). A single example of the cubo-octahedral type has also been recorded from the important site of Woodstown, near Waterford in Ireland, together with a larger but unmarked object of the same shape in silver, which has also been interpreted as a weight (e.g. Valante 2008, 42–3). However, this interpretation of the object has recently been questioned by Patrick Wallace in his study of the Woodstown weights (see below, pp. 40–1).

No certain example of the iron/copper-alloy oblate-spheroid type has been recovered from ARSNY, although a single heavily corroded iron object from the excavation (sf815) may possibly be the core of a weight of this type. It is possible that the rarity or absence of this type at ARSNY may reflect its slightly later date, as only three are recorded from Torksey compared with at least 57 cubo-octahedral weights, whereas the more long-lasting sites of Kaupang and Birka suggest a more typical ratio of one oblate-spheroid to two cubo-octahedrals (Blackburn 2011, 239). However, given the relatively small size of these objects, and the fact that detectorists initially dismissed iron objects from both Torksey and ARSNY as later intrusions, it is possible that weights of this type are under-represented in the finds record from both sites.

Weights of both oblate-spheroid and cubo-octahedral form are also recorded in lead, bridging the gap with the second main group of Viking weights. These lead weights take a wide variety of forms, with less overall regularity of standards. In particular times and places, greater regulation does appear to have applied, as at Dublin in the 10th century, where Wallace (1987, 212) has proposed a standard of 26.6g. Across the Viking world a range of standards has been suggested, with varying degrees of tolerance (see below), but the extent to which firm original weights can be

Main classification	Sub-classification	Decoration
A. Oblate-spheroid	1.Copper alloy/iron 2. Copper alloy 3. Lead	a. Sub-Islamic b. Abstract c. Undecorated
B. Cubo-octahedral	1.Copper alloy/iron 2. Copper alloy 3. Lead	Main classification by number of pellets in square faces; additional decoration may include individual pellets on triangular faces, borders of lines or pellets on square and/or triangular faces
C. Biconical	1.Copper alloy/iron 2. Copper alloy 3. Lead	a. Undecorated b. Inset c. Capped d. Enamelled e. Punch-marked
D. Cylindrical/discoid	1. Flat 2. Straight side 3. Concave side 4. Convex side	a. Undecorated b. Inset c. Capped d. Enamelled e. Punch-marked
E. Oval	1. Flat 2. High, vertical side 3. High, sloping side	a. Undecorated b. Inset c. Capped d. Enamelled e. Punch-marked
F. Domed	1. High side 2. No side, flat bottom 3. No side, domed bottom	a. Undecorated b. Inset c. Capped d. Enamelled e. Punch-marked
G. Conical	1. Truncated cone 2. Full cone, flat bottom 3. Full cone, rounded bottom	a. Undecorated b. Inset c. Capped d. Enamelled e. Punch-marked
H. Pyramid	1. Truncated pyramid, flat bottom 2. Truncated pyramid, rounded bottom 3. Full pyramid, flat bottom 4. Full pyramid, rounded bottom	
I. Rectangular prism	1. Flat 2. High, vertical side 3. Cubic 4. High, sloping side	a. Undecorated b. Inset c. Capped d. Enamelled e. Punch-marked
J. Rectangular prism with concave edges	1. Flat 2. High, vertical side 3. Cubic 4. High, sloping side	a. Undecorated b. Inset c. Capped d. Enamelled e. Punch-marked
K. Re-used decorative object, filled with lead		
L. Miscellaneous lead		

Table 1 Classification of Viking/Anglo-Scandinavian weight types

attributed to all of the surviving examples is debatable. Many show cracking or chipping, and only a small variation in weight would fundamentally skew some of the calculations based on particularly precise units, while even on perfectly preserved objects it is difficult to distinguish between deviation around an agreed standard, multiple standards or a complete lack of precise standards (Kruse 1988, 294; 1993, 195; Williams 2004, 84). Furthermore, with so many variations in shape and size, it is not absolutely certain that all of the lead objects classified as weights are in fact weights rather than, for example, gaming pieces.

Undecorated lead weights are difficult to date precisely on typological grounds, but seem to have been in use at least from the early Viking Age, and certainly from well before the introduction of the Islamic-influenced copper-alloy weights discussed above. The creation of lead versions of the cubo-octahedral and oblate-spheroid forms suggests an assimilation of the new style of weights into the wider pool of lead weights, reflecting the variety of weight standards, as well as the flexibility of form seen in lead weights. So much variety of form may at first seem surprising, with eight main shapes (types C–J), and several sub-types. However, such variety may well have served a functional purpose, as it acted as an aid to visual recognition. Whether or not one postulates the use of regular standards, it seems clear at the least that there were multiple standards in use, and it must have been necessary for the parties to any transaction to ensure that any measurement was carried out in accordance with an acceptable standard, if only a personal one. Having immediately recognisable sets of weights would prevent deliberate switching or accidental confusion which might occur between similar-looking weights of slightly different standards.

Plate 4 Selection of the cubo-octahedral weights from ARSNY (sfs1428–49). Selection from British Museum, 2008,4200.1-26

This need for recognition probably explains two further categories of weights. Although the majority of the lead weights described above are plain and undecorated, the majority of the forms are susceptible to decoration. Within Scandinavia, the most common form of decoration on weights was by punch-marking, either with pellets or annulets, or a combination of the two. This form of decoration is well documented, for example, from the Kaupang weights assemblage, and there has been some speculation that the markings may in some cases relate to regular standards, although this certainly does not appear to be invariably the case (Pedersen 2008, 150–5). With the exception of type F (domed) and some type G (conical) weights, the various forms of lead weight could also be ornamented with additional material. This normally takes the form of fragments of metalwork, usually Insular, more rarely of Scandinavian origin, and frequently undiagnostic. The fragments are in some cases set into the top of the weight, pushed into the soft lead, or placed into a shaped recess. In other cases, the fragments are mounted onto the weights as caps, sometimes secured with pins. Rather more rarely, a similar effect is achieved by enamelling directly onto the surface of the weight (including one example with a face design from Woodstown, and another (BM 2000, 0101.2) with a geometric design, found in East Yorkshire). While some of these are highly decorated, the fact that some of the insets are mere blobs or roughly shaped undiagnostic fragments suggests that decoration alone is not the main purpose of including the insets.

These 'decorated' weights are also known from Scandinavia, but are comparatively rare there. Two examples with coin-insets are known from a single Norwegian grave (Skaare 1976, 44–5, 144; see also below), while a handful of examples with fragments of Insular metalwork are known from Denmark (Baastrup 2013). By contrast, the type is known from a number of Viking sites around Britain and Ireland, again including both Torksey and Woodstown, as well as the Blackwater assemblage, the site at Llanbedrgoch on Anglesey and the burial from Kiloran Bay on Colonsay (Kruse 1992; Graham-Campbell and Batey 1998, 119–20; Redknap 2009; Bourke 2010, 26, 72–5; Ó Floinn, with Bourke, 2014, 181–91), and from a growing number of single finds (Williams 1999; Redknap 2009; Kershaw, this volume, pp. 120–1).

A final related category (type K) also includes re-used metalwork, but with the fragments either hollow or filled in with lead. Unn Pedersen (2008, 127) has noted the difficulty of attributing these as weights without a clear archaeological context, but the interpretation of at least some of the Irish examples as weights seems very plausible. Zoomorphic weights of this type are recorded from Norway (Pedersen 2008, 175–7), Kiloran Bay and Dublin, although not from the Woodstown assemblage (Williams *et al.* 2014, 24, 265; Wallace 2014, 226; Ó Floinn, with Bourke, 2014, 187), while two examples of decorative projections from Viking oval brooches, packed with lead, have also been recorded, from Bute and Orkney respectively (J. Barrett and B. Crawford, pers. comm.).

The distribution of the type K weights suggests origins in Ireland and Scotland. The various types of lead weights with added decoration are comparatively rare in Scotland, but the presence of several such weights in the assemblages from ARSNY, Torksey, Llanbedrgoch, Woodstown and the River Blackwater, together with a wider spread of single finds, coupled with the re-use of both Insular metalwork and Anglo-Saxon coins, suggests that this type originated in England and/or Ireland. The type is rare enough in Denmark that they are referred to as 'Irish weights' (Baastrup 2013). Since in many cases the metalwork re-used may be considerably older than the weight itself, it rarely provides very useful direct evidence for dating the production of the weight, and dating of use therefore derives from archaeological context. However, one sub-group can be more precisely dated, as the decorative additions take the form not of fragments of metalwork, but of re-used coins. Again, this group seems to be rare in Scandinavia, although two examples are recorded from a grave at Fjære in Aust-Agder, Norway (Skaare 1976, 44–5, 144), but rather more common in England. The total number of known examples has expanded significantly since the publication of a corpus of possible and certain examples (Williams 1999), with examples from ARSNY (sf1566–7), Torksey and Blackwater, as well as stray detector finds (Kershaw this volume, p. 121; see also the PAS database for more recent examples outside Yorkshire). The dating of the coin-weights suggests that their production was concentrated in the first decade or so after the arrival of the *micel here* in England in 865. A substantial majority of these weights use Northumbrian copper-alloy stycas of various dates, widely used and produced until the conquest of Northumbria in 866–7. Four examples (two from Kingston in Dorset, one said to be from near Malton in North Yorkshire, one from the Blackwater assemblage) use pennies of the Lunettes coinage issued by Æthelred I (865–71) and Alfred (871–99) of Wessex (Archibald 1998; Williams 1999, 19–21; Bourke 2010, 74–5). This type was apparently rapidly demonetised after the re-introduction of a good silver coinage *c.* 874–75 by Alfred of Wessex and Ceolwulf II of Mercia (874–*c.* 879) (Blackburn and Keynes 1998; Blackburn 2003; see also discussion of the hoard from the ARSNY site above on pp. 11–12). Only one example (Williams 1999, no. 22) uses later coins, with two separate halves of pennies, both of a Circumscription Cross type and probably dating from the early 10th century. It seems likely that the coin-weights were therefore predominantly produced in the late 860s and early 870s, and the other weights using fragments of metalwork may well be of similar date, which would fit well with the presence of such weights at Torksey in particular, and also at Llanbedrgoch and Kaupang. However, the fact that the fashion for coin-weights largely disappeared with the re-introduction of good silver coins in the mid-870s may simply indicate that good silver was considered too valuable to waste in weights of this sort, and weights with other forms of inset (typically copper alloy, with or without traces of gilding) may well have continued to be produced over a longer period. Kershaw (2013, 100, 148; this volume, p. 121) notes the re-use in a decorated lead weight from Kilnwick, East Yorkshire, of a fragment from a Scandinavian oval brooch of Petersen's Type 51 E, dating from the late 9th or early 10th century, which may indicate that this particular weight was made somewhat after the core period of the 860s and 870s suggested above.

With all of the decorated weights, there is a question of why the decoration was applied. In some cases, a purely 'decorative' function is plausible. A number of weights use complete faces, or self-contained decorative motifs cut from larger items, probably mostly book mounts, reliquaries and the like. Such weights are often attractive, and symmetrically shaped, so it is clear that some attention has been given to appearance. One such 'face' mount is recorded from ARSNY (sf1577), with other weights with face-shaped caps recorded as single finds from near Tadcaster, North Yorkshire (PAS Find-ID SWYOR-EF9E81), Ixworth, Suffolk and near Furness, Cumbria (Youngs 1989, nos 135–6), and Øster Vandet, near Thisted in Denmark (Baastrup 2013, 13), as well as an enamelled mask as decoration on one of the lead weights from Woodstown (Wallace 2014, 247–8, WWT 100). However, as noted above, in other cases the decoration is little more than a blob or scrap of contrasting metal, and it is hard to imagine that this was done for aesthetic purposes. Some of those involving Northumbrian stycas are also less than entirely attractive. It is possible that some of the designs may have been adopted to give a symbolic status to the weights, and the possibility that the use of coins as decoration was intended to reflect the 'official' status of the weights has previously been suggested (Archibald 1998; Williams 1999; Pedersen 2008, 168–9). Maria Panum Baastrup (2013) has suggested that such finds in Denmark may, like other finds of imported objects, have acted as signifiers of the overseas connections, and therefore the wealth and status, of the owners. However, this would not explain the re-use of Insular metalwork in such weights in Britain and Ireland, where they are relatively common, compared with only six recorded weights of this type in Denmark. This suggests that if the decorated weights did have such social connotations in Scandinavia, any status derived from their 'exotic' character was secondary to their original function within the Insular Viking milieu.

An alternative explanation is simply, as indicated above, that the users of weights needed to be able to recognise their own weight sets instantly, to avoid confusion or fraud in exchange transactions, and that coins, decorative metalwork, and mere scraps all served to personalise weights sufficiently to avoid confusion. In one example from ARSNY (sf1570), a small cubo-octahedral weight (or the surface from one) has been re-used for the same purpose. In this respect, it is interesting that even the more regulated cubo-octahedral weights have elements of customisation. The variation in borders and in the decoration (or not) of the triangular faces allowed individual sets to be distinguished, and one example from ARSNY (sf1430) appears to have been deliberately personalised by incising a rough cross or X into one of the triangular faces. It therefore seems appropriate that the coin-weights should be considered together with the other decorated weights rather than as a distinct group (as opposed to the separate group of Anglo-Saxon coin-weights impressed with official coin-dies also discussed in Williams 1999), and that the decoration, like the variation in form, should be seen as a means for distinguishing individual weights more easily. As such, the presence of 'decoration', and how it was applied, functions as a third level of classification for the weights as a whole.

A summary list of probable weights from the site (excluding those from the hoard discussed above), arranged according to this classification, is presented in **Table 2**.

Function of weights

Most if not all of the weights considered here were intended for use with equal-armed pan-balances, well known both as grave finds and as site finds from around the Viking world, including the two fragmentary examples from ARSNY (sfs156, 1159; **Figs 2, 6**). Such balances functioned with a high degree of accuracy, although experimentation suggests that the precise degree of accuracy varies from type to type, with sensitivity also varying in proportion to the total mass weighed, sensitivity diminishing as the total mass increases (Pedersen 2008, 138–40). This means that the vast majority of the weights here, typically small and light, were well

Sf number	Class	Weight	Dimensions in mm Diameter (d), length (l), width (w), height (h)	Description/features
815	A1?	12.87g	17–18(d)	Roughly spherical iron object, rusted and heavily worn. Possible core from oblate-spheroid weight
1420	A3c	7.48g	14(d) x 8.5(h)	Smoothed edges, plain, chipped
1421	A3c	11.68g	15(d) x 9(h)	Plain
1422	A3c	8.14g	18(d) x 8(h)	Plain, slightly chipped
1423	A3c	25.01g	22(d) x 10(h)	Plain, irregular shape
1424	A3c	12.51g	17(d) x 8(h)	Plain
1425	A3c	2.53g	10(d) x 5(h)	Plain
1426	A3c	2.91g	11(d) x 5.5(h)	Irregular shape, chipped
1427	A3c	7.76g	14(d) x 9(h)	Slightly chipped, rounded top, concave base
163	B2	1.42g	6.5(w)	2 pellets per side, border of straight lines on square faces, single pellet on triangular faces
1428	B2	4.05g	9(w)	6 pellets per side, border of pellets on square faces, single pellet on triangular faces
1429	B2	3.78g	9(w)	6 pellets per side, border of pellets on square faces, border of straight lines on triangular faces
1430	B2	3.74g	9(w)	6 pellets per side, border of straight lines on square faces, triangular faces blank except for one incised with a rough cross
1431	B2	3.72g	9(w)	6 pellets per side, border of straight lines on square faces, border of straight lines on triangular faces
1432	B2	3.42g	8.5(w)	6 pellets per side, heavily worn and corroded
1433	B2	3.26g	8(w)	6 pellets per side, border of pellets on square faces, triangular faces blank, worn and corroded
1434	B2	3.13g	9(w)	6 pellets per side, border of straight lines on square faces, triangular faces blank
1435	B2	2.45g	7.5(w)	4 pellets per side, border of notched lines on square faces, single pellet on triangular faces
1436	B2	2.40g	8(w)	4 pellets per side, border of pellets on square faces, single pellet on triangular faces
1437	B2	2.16g	7.5(w)	4 pellets per side, very worn and corroded, slightly chipped
1438	B2	2.43g	8(w)	4 pellets per side, worn, slightly chipped edges
1439	B2	2.17g	8(w)	4 pellets per side, very worn and corroded, chipped edges
1440	B2	2.09g	7.5(w)	4 pellets per side, border of straight lines on square faces, triangular faces blank
1441	B2	2.37g	7.5(w)	0 pellets per side, badly chipped, unfinished?
1442	B2	1.99g	7(w)	3 pellets per side, very worn
1443	B2	1.92g	6.5	3 pellets per side, border of pellets on square faces, triangular faces blank
1444	B2	1.92g	7.5(w)	3 pellets per side, border of straight lines on square faces, triangular faces blank
1445	B2	1.91g	7.5	3 pellets per side, pellets on square faces, triangular faces blank
1446	B2	1.81g	8(w)	3? pellets per side, very worn, rounded edges, triangular faces blank
1447	B2	1.51g	7(w)	2 pellets per side, very worn, rounded edges
1448	B2	1.27g	6(w)	2 pellets, border of notched lines on square faces, single pellet on triangular faces
1449	B2	0.58g	5(w)	0 pellets, all faces blank
825	B3	1.25g	6.5(w)	2 pellets per side, straight lines on square faces, triangular faces blank, worn
258	D1a	1.29g	11(d) x 2(h)	
311	D1a	1.79g	11(d) x 3(h)	
1450	D1a	11.78g	15(d)	
1451	D1a	9.21g	19.5(l) x 18(w) x 5(w)	
1452	D1a	6.90g	15.5(d) x 5(h)	Slightly chipped
1453	D1a	4.53g	16(d) x 4(h)	Slightly irregular shape, chipped around edge
1454	D1a	4.12g	15(d) x 4(h)	Irregular shape, worn, slightly chipped

Table 2 Weights from ARSNY

Sf number	Class	Weight	Dimensions in mm Diameter (d), length (l), width (w), height (h)	Description/features
1455	D1a	3.75g	11(d)	
1456	D1a	3.59g	10(d)	Rounded edges, slightly chipped
1457	D1a	2.74g	11(d)	Slightly angular, between cylinder and circle
1458	D1a	1.47g	10(d) x 3(h)	
1459	D1a	1.31g	10.5(d) x 3.5(h)	Slightly chipped edge
1494	D1a	11.97g	24(d) x 4(h)	Rough cross lightly incised on one face
1495	D1a	7.56g	23(d) x 4(h)	Small oval hole through centre, irregularly shaped punch-marks on each face. Possibly not a pan weight, but a weight for some other purpose
1543	D1a	70.58g	35(d) x 9(h)	Rounded edges
1545	D1a	2.11g	10.5(d) x 2(h)	
1552	D1a	1.22g	10(d) x 2(h)	Rough surfaces, slightly chipped
1558	D1a	6.39g	23(d) x 2(h)	Uneven surfaces
1564	D1a	7.42g	24(d) x 2(h)	Bent, uneven surfaces
1576	D1b	–	35(d)	Blob of ?copper in centre, chipped edges
1460	D2a	27.50g	22(d) x 10(h)	Chipped face and edges
1461	D2a	22.29g	16(d) x 13.5(h)	Chipped on side
1462	D2a	15.67g	17(d)	Slightly irregular shape, uneven surfaces
1463	D2a	14.72g	16(d) x 11(h)	2 straighter sides, notched down one
1464	D2a	10.24g	20(d) x 5(h)	Slightly chipped
1465	D2a	7.20g	14(d) x 7.5(h)	Slightly concave, slightly chipped
1466	D2a	6.95g	14(d) x 7(h)	Most of surface worn/chipped
1467	D2a	6.80g	13(d) x 7.5(h)	Slightly rounded edges, slightly chipped on edge
1468	D2a	3.14g	10.5(d) x 5(h)	
1469	D2a	3.12g	9(d) x 7(h)	
1470	D2a	1.61g	9(d) x 5(h)	Irregular shape, chipped side
1484	D2a	3.42g	12(d) x 5(h)	Concave faces, chipped edges
1489	D2a	4.04g	10(d) x 8(h)	
1491	D2a	3.48g	11(d) x 6(h)	Chipped edge, very slightly domed
1498	D2a	3.80g	12(d) x 5(h)	Slightly chipped, worn edges
1500	D2a	3.28g	12(d) x 4(h)	Slightly chipped edges
1501	D2a	7.26g	17(d) x 5 (h)	Pitted surfaces, slightly concave on one face, chipped
1503	D2a	3.42g	10(d) x 6.5(h)	Slightly concave top and bottom
1511	D2a	14.63g	18(d) x 8(h)	Slightly concave on top and bottom
1528	D2a	11.99g	17(d) x 7(h)	Chipped
1530	D2a	15.18g	20(d) x 7(h)	Slightly chipped
1537	D2a	7.36g	13.5(d) x 7(h)	Concave on one face, indented on other
1563	D2a	11.38g	13(d) x 13(h)	Concave surfaces
1571	D2c	–	25(d)	Flat lead cap on top of main weight, overlapping sides. Small inset in centre, may be top of pin holding cap in place
1485	D2e	1.50g	10(d) x 4(h)	2 pellets on one face, chipped
1551	D3a	8.31g	11.5(d) x 9.5(h)	
1556	D3a	7.34g	12(d) x 11(h)	Chipped
780	D4a	0.84g	6(d) x 3(h)	
1471	D4a	24.40g	19.5(d) x 12(h)	Hole in each face, but not pierced all the way through
1472	D4a	22.58g	21(d)	Concave, top and bottom
1473	D4a	18.26g	17(d) x 9(h)	

Table 2 (continued) Weights from ARSNY

Sf number	Class	Weight	Dimensions in mm Diameter (d), length (l), width (w), height (h)	Description/features
1474	D4a	15.85g	16(d) x 12(h)	Large hole in one face, chipped
1475	D4a	12.50g	11(d)	Slightly chipped
1476	D4a	7.25g	12(d) x 9(h)	Slight chips on side and edge
1477	D4a	7.22g	14.5(d) x 7.5(h)	Irregular shape, uneven surface
1478	D4a	6.72g	12.5(d) x 9(h)	Very irregular shape, chipped
1479	D4a	6.51g	15(d) x 6(h)	Concave top and bottom, worn edges
1480	D4a	3.57g	11(d) x 6(h)	Chipped
1481	D4a	2.47g	10.5(d) x 5(h)	Chipped
1482	D4a	2.23g	10(d) x 6 (h)	Concave on one surface, rounded edges, slightly chipped
1483	D4a	5.43g	12(d) x 6(h)	Rounded edges, indentations on each face, one spear-shaped
1486	D4a	2.13g	11(d) x 4(h)	Concave and slightly chipped on one face
1487	D4a	2.44g	12(d) x 4.5(h)	Rounded edges, chipped
1488	D4a	11.40g	18(d) x 6(h)	Rough edges and faces, chipped
1490	D4a	3.31g	14(d) x 4(h)	Indented on one face, chipped edge on other face
1492	D4a	1.37g	11(d) x 3.5(h)	Chipped edges
1493	D4a	7.11g	12(d) x 9(h)	One face entirely chipped off, some marks in exposed surface. Decorative cap/inset removed?
1496	D4a	7.38g	11.5(d) x 9.5(h)	Slightly chipped on edge
1497	D4a	2.51g	10(d) x 5(h)	Slightly rounded edge, slightly chipped
1499	D4a	1.46g	10(d) x 4(h)	Chipped edges
1502	D4a	11.40g	14(d) x 12(h)	One lipped surface with bright metal face. Probably had styca inset, lost relatively recently. Base uneven slope, probably broken in antiquity
1504	D4a	7.19g	14(d) x 8(h)	Chunk missing from one side, edges chipped
1505	D4a	12.79g	14(d) x 12(h)	Uneven surfaces, rounded edges
1506	D4a	2.58g	12(d) x 4(h)	Slightly concave on top and bottom, rounded edges, slightly chipped
1507	D4a	6.89g	14.5(d) x 6(h)	Badly chipped surface and edges
1508	D4a	2.25g	12(d) x 4(h)	Slightly chipped
1510	D4a	3.45g	12(d) x 6(h)	Concave on top and bottom
1527	D4a	25.64g	22(d) x 8(h)	One face slightly concave, and edge slightly chipped, edges rounded
1529	D4a	86.04g	28(d) x 15(h)	One face concave, with deep scratch, the other very uneven. Edges slightly rounded, slightly chipped
1531	D4a	7.34g	14(d) x 7(h)	Slightly chipped
1532	D4a	11.72g	15(d) x 8(h)	Slightly concave on one face, rounded edges
1533	D4a	22.74g	20(d) x 9(h)	Concave on both faces, slightly chipped
1534	D4a	6.91g	14.5(d) x 6(h)	Slightly chipped
1535	D4a	6.64g	14(d) x 5(h)	Uneven shape, slightly chipped
1536	D4a	22.87g	21(d) x 10(h)	Very slightly domed
1538	D4a	5.10g	16(d) x 4.5(h)	Irregular shape, chipped and worn
1539	D4a	6.97g	15(d) x 5.5(h)	Slightly chipped
1541	D4a	7.07g	13(d) x 7(h)	Slightly concave on one face, slightly chipped
1542	D4a	23.43g	17(d) x 16(h)	Rounded faces, chipped
1546	D4a	1.74g	9(d) x 3(h)	Chipped
1548	D4a	1.58g	8.5(d) x 3(h)	Badly chipped
1549	D4a	1.44g	9(d) x 5(h)	Slightly chipped
1553	D4a	1.94g	8.5(d) x 5(h)	Irregular shape, slightly chipped
1554	D4a	1.68g	9(d) x 5.5(h)	Irregular shape
1555	D4a	3.22g	13(d) x 5(h)	Irregular shape
1557	D4a	2.04g	12(d) x 10(h)	
1559	D4a	4.09g	11(d) x 8(h)	

Table 2 (continued) Weights from ARSNY

Sf number	Class	Weight	Dimensions in mm Diameter (d), length (l), width (w), height (h)	Description/features
1560	D4a	3.31g	13(d) x 3(h)	Slightly chipped
1561	D4a	2.90g	11(d) x 4.5(h)	Slightly chipped
1562	D4a	1.27g	11(d) x 2(h)	Rough, uneven surface
1565	D4a	2.96g	12(d) x 4(h)	Plain
1566	D4b	37.97g	19(d) x 18(h)	Styca of moneyer Eardwulf inset. Underside also recessed as if to hold inset, and slightly hollow
1567	D4b	8.38g	16.5(d) x 8(h)	Styca, possibly of Aethelred II, inset, rounded edges, slightly chipped
1568	D4b	–	36(d)	Chip-carved gilt fragment inset, rounded edges. Chipped on one edge
1569	D4b	–	18(d)	Chip-carved inset, rounded edges, chipped on underside
1570	D4b	22.71g	20(d) x 12.5(h)	Face of 2-dot cubo-octahedral weight inset on top, blob of ?copper alloy inset on bottom. Rounded edges, chipped
1572	D4b	–	15(d)	Small gold/gilt pellet in centre of top, rounded edges
1573	D4b	–	24(d)	Irregular shape, rounded edges, blob of copper alloy
1509	D4e	2.79g	10(d) x 6(h)	4 notches on face forming cross pattern, chipped
1561	D4e	0.84g	12(d) x 1(h)	Faded impressions on both faces
1574	D4e	–	19(d)	6 pellets in 2 lines of 3, rounded edges, slightly chipped
1575	D4e	–	19(d)	Indented surface, with 6 pellets, either as punch-marks or possibly as the result of an inset pressed in and subsequently lost
1550	E1a	2.15g	13.5(d) x 2(h)	Worn, one edged straight, chipped
1540	E2a	12.91g	18(d) x 9(h)	Slightly uneven shape
1547	E2a	4.97g	13(d) x 9(h)	Irregular shape, chipped
1578	E3b	–	24(l) x 16(w)	Chip-carved gilt inset
1577	E3c	–	20(l) x 17.5(w)	Gilt copper face, probably cut from Irish shrine or book mount, set as cap
1544	F1a	13.24g	11(d) x 19(h)	Very high in relation to diameter, lines carved into the side
1602	F1a	8.94g	17(d) x 16(h)	Slightly pointed dome, hollow, badly chipped around base, possibly gaming piece rather than weight
1606	F1a	3.82g	11(d) x 7(h)	Hole in top, tiny hole in base
1648	F1a	10.85g	14(d) x 14(h)	Slightly chipped
1608	F1b	–	20(d)	Blob of copper alloy
1609	F1e	–	15(d)	Circle of 6 pellets on dome
1579	F2a	15.14g	20(d) x 8(h)	Smoothed edges
1580	F2a	1.7g	9(d) x 6(h)	Uneven curve
1581	F2a	4.13g	14(d) x 7(h)	Uneven (chipped?) top
1582	F2a	1.98g	10(d) x 6(h)	Uneven shape
1583	F2a	4.33g	14(d)	
1584	F2a	6.10g	16(d)	Chipped on bottom edges
1585	F2a	12.39g	16(d)	
1586	F2a	23.16g	19(d)	Rough surfaces
1587	F2a	7.68g	17(d)	Top chipped off
1588	F2a	21.41g	20(d)	Flattened surface on top
1603	F2a	2.94g	10(d) x 8(h)	2 elevated ridges
1604	F2a	3.80g	12(d) x 10(h)	Plain
1605	F2a	6.31g	17(d) x 8(h)	Uneven sides, badly chipped
1607	F2b	–	27.5(d)	Copper pellet inset
1600	F3a	157.64g	38(d)	Unusually large, shallower dome to underside
1601	G1a	16.37g	21(d) x 16(h)	Hollow, slightly chipped, crack on side near top, possibly gaming piece rather than weight
1610	G1a	18.92g	19(d) x 14(h)	Rounded edges
1611	G1a	10.72g	15.5 (d) x 11(h)	Slightly chipped at base
1612	G1a	11.60g	15(d)	
1613	G1a	23.72g	19(d) x 18(h)	Slightly uneven on one side

Table 2 (continued) Weights from ARSNY

Sf number	Class	Weight	Dimensions in mm Diameter (d), length (l), width (w), height (h)	Description/features
1614	G1a	4.38g	11(d) x 11(h)	Chip at edge of base
1615	G1a	1.78g	11(d)	Notch in middle of top
1616	G1a	15.85g	16(d)	Chipped around base, slightly concave base
1618	G1a	13.69g	16(d) x 11(h)	Slightly chipped, concave base
1619	G1a	28.55g	15(d) x 18(h)	Very steep sides
1620	G1a	24.60g	18(d) x 13(h)	Slightly chipped on base
1622	G1a	11.07g	15(d) x 10(h)	Irregular shape, sloping top, rounded edges
1623	G1a	23.60g	17(d) x 14(h)	Slightly chipped
1624	G1a	7.60g	12(d) x 10(h)	Sloping top, uneven sides, slightly chipped base
1626	G1a	15.39g	19(d) x 16(h)	Large chip at base
1627	G1a	9.15g	14.5(d) x 11(h)	Chipped base and side
1628	G1a	7.69g	14(d) x 10(h)	Chipped base
1633	G1a	13.22g	16.5(d)	Hole in bottom
1634	G1a	3.65g	11(d)	Slightly concave base
1636	G1a	14.59g	15(d) x 15(h)	Chipped, rounded surfaces
1641	G1a	21.93g	17(d) x 16(h)	3 lumps at top, probably gaming piece rather than weight
1645	G1a	13.05g	15(d) x 15(d)	Slightly concave top, 2 markings on base: one round and one crescent-shaped, but possibly accidental rather than deliberately shaped
1647	G1a	23.72	16(d) x 20(h)	Possible markings on base, one round and one crescent-shaped, slightly chipped edges to base
1625	G1b	11.11g	15(d) x 12(h)	Chip-carved gilt fragment inset in top
1629	G2a	2.37g	9(d) x 12(h)	Slightly concave base
1630	G2a	10.53g	15(d) x 14.5(h)	Uneven base, slightly chipped
1631	G2a	15.94g	17(d)	
1632	G2a	8.59g	15(d)	Slightly chipped base
1638	G2a	6.43g	12(d) x 20(h)	Bulging 'head' at top of cone. Probably gaming piece rather than weight, some decoration on head
1639	G2a	11.88g	17(d) x 15(h)	Leaning to one side, chips or marks on vertical face
1640	G2a	9.93g	16(d) x 20(h)	Leaning to one side, rounded top, flared towards base, possible gaming piece
1642	G2a	19.91g	17(d) x 24(h)	Large hole in base, small hole on one side, heavily faded marking at top, perhaps eyes and a mouth, possible gaming piece
1643	G2a	14.34g	15(d) x 18(h)	Rounded top, leaning to one side, flared towards base, possible gaming piece
1644	G2a	3.30g	8(d) x 13(h)	Rounded top, high sides in relation to diameter, slightly flared towards bottom, possible gaming piece
1646	G2a	23.84g	19(d) x 15(h)	Small hole in base, rounded top
1649	G2a	1.70g	10(d) x 8(h)	Rounded top, flared towards bottom, possible gaming piece, slightly chipped
1635	G3a	113.61g	35(d)	Slightly domed underside
1621	H1	5.27g	12(d) x 10(h)	2 concave sides, 2 straight
1637	H1	19.86g	15(d) x 22.5(h)	Straight edges, leaning, possible gaming piece
1650	H1	23.30g	18(l) x 16.5(w) x 12.5(h)	Flat top, slightly chipped on one edge
1651	H2	23.09g	18(l) x 16(w) x 17(h)	Leaning, flattened top, slightly rounded bottom, slightly chipped
1675	I1a	2.42g	12(l) x 11(w) x 3.5(h)	Slightly chipped corner
1690	I1a	1.69g	8(l) x 7(w) x 2(h)	Imperfect shape, one corner rounded
1653	I2a	12.42g	15.5(l) x 15(w) x 7(h)	Rounded edges, rough surface on one face
1654	I2a	12.71g	17(l) x 15.5(w) x 8(h)	Chipped edge, one corner missing
1655	I2a	2.03g	9(l) x 8(w) x 6(h)	Chipped corner and edges
1658	I2a	3.45g	12(l) x 11(w) x 5(h)	Hole in one face, one side rounded
1659	I2a	7.12g	14(l) x 13(w) x 6(h)	One corner chipped, scratches on one face
1660	I2a	1.59g	7.5(l) x 7.5(w) x 5(h)	One side rounded

Table 2 (continued) Weights from ARSNY

Sf number	Class	Weight	Dimensions in mm Diameter (d), length (l), width (w), height (h)	Description/features
1661	I2a	2.31g	11(1) x 8(w) x 5.5(h)	Chipped corners
1662	I2a	1.43g	8(l) x 8(l) x 5(h)	Slightly chipped
1665	I2a	3.82g	12.5(l) x 10(w) x 5.5(h)	One side concave
1666	I2a	2.69g	9.5(l) x 9(w) x 6(h)	Slightly domed top
1668	I2a	7.10g	12.5(l) x 12.5(w) x 7.5(h)	Chipped edges and corners, slightly concave faces
1669	I2a	2.56g	11(l) x 8(w) x 6(h)	Chipped side
1670	I2a	4.15g	11(l) x 11(w) x 6(h)	Slight lip on one edge, chipped on one corner
1672	I2a	5.05g	10(l) x 9(w) x 7(h)	Slightly chipped
1673	I2a	3.39g	11.5(l) x 10.5(w) x 4.5(h)	
1676	I2a	10.94g	15(l)	Chipped sides and corner
1677	I2a	2.21g	9(l)	
1678	I2a	21.56g	17(l)	Large indentation in one face
1679	I2a	5.26g	13(l) x 13(w) x 5.5(h)	Very rounded edges and corners
1681	I2a	4.69g	10(l) x 9(w) x 7(h)	One side diagonal, slightly rounded corners
1684	I2a	21.73g	18(l) x 16(w) x 9.5(h)	
1685	I2a	5.94g	15(l) x 4.5(h)	Slightly rounded edges and corners
1686	I2a	28.60g	17.5(l) x 16(w) x 12(h)	Slightly chipped on faces
1691	I2a	10.73g	16(l) x 12.5(w) x 8(h)	Plain, rounded edges
1692	I2a	15.80g	18(l) x 16.5(w) x 8(h)	Rounded, uneven faces, one face slightly concave
1694	I2a	3.81g	10(l) x 6(h)	One side diagonal
1695	I2a	10.98g	10(l) x 14.5(h)	Slightly rhomboid, one concave face
1698	I2a	2.56g	10(l) x 9(w) x 4(h)	One side concave
1699	I2b	–	17.5(l) x 16(w)	Chip-carved fragment inset in one face
1702	I2b	–	24.5(l) x 24(w)	Copper blob inset in one face
1701	I2e	–	16(l) x 15(w)	5 pellets stamped in square border
1703	I2e	–	14(l) x 14 (w)	2 pellets in centre of one face
1656	I3a	2.18g	8(l) x 7(w) x 7(h)	
1667	I3a	2.61g	8(l) x 7(w) x 8(h)	Chipped side
1674	I3a	2.53g	8(l) x 8(w) x 6(h)	Chipped corners
1680	I3a	1.48g	7(l) x 6(w) x 5(h)	Rounded corners
1687	I3a	1.90g	8(l) x 7(w) x 5.5(w)	Slightly worn edges
1693	I3a	4.75g	11(l) x 9(w) x 9(h)	One side diagonal, slightly chipped
1652	J1a	11.09g	19(l) x 19(w) x 5(h)	
1696	J1a	4.15g	13.5(l) x 11(w) x 3(h)	
1700	J1b	–	21(l) x 17.5(w)	Chip-carved fragment inset in one face
1657	J2a	2.90g	12.5(l) x 12.5(w) x 4(h)	One corner lost in antiquity
1664	J2a	2.65g	10(l) x 9.5(w) x 6(h)	3 chipped corners
1671	J2a	10.69g	17(l) x 16(w) x 7(h)	Slightly concave edges, corners chipped
1682	J2a	11.07g	13(l) x 13(w) x 9(h)	Slightly concave sides and surfaces
1683	J2a	11.04g	19(l) x 5(h)	
1688	J2a	9.98g	15(l) x 12(w) x 6(h)	2 convex and 2 concave sides, concave faces
1689	J2a	6.06g	12(l) x 9(w) x 7.5(h)	
1697	J2a	3.00g	10(l) x 4(h)	
1705	L	45.22g	22 x 20(d)	Near spherical, with 2 small holes in either side. Possibly not a weight

Table 2 (continued) Weights from ARSNY

suited for use in such fine balances, with combinations of different weights providing a range of permutations. Few of the weights are as heavy as the postulated Viking ounces in the range *c.* 24–26.6g, while the smallest weight from the assemblage (sf1449), at 0.58g, was sufficient to tip the balance around 1mm on a payload in the order of 1 ounce. Only two weights, by far the largest at 157.64g (sf1600) and 113.61g (sf1635), would be rather heavy to be used in this type of balance. However, although steelyards (which operate with a single large weight attached to the iron bar) are known in the Viking Age (Pedersen 2008, 125), there is no sign that these weights were designed for suspension, and Pedersen (2008, 139) notes that there are recorded instances of sets of weights and balances from graves in which the heavier weights were far heavier than the ideal maximum weight of the balance; it may be that a greater variation was simply tolerated in large transactions, or that larger pan-balances existed than have yet been discovered.

The Islamic-style weights of regulated standards have generally been interpreted as being intended for the weighing of precious metals for use in exchange, with the possible refinement that the smaller cubo-octahedral weights represented equivalent values in gold to the values of silver represented by the corresponding oblate-spheroid weights (Steuer 1987, 467; Pedersen 2008, 155). Given the somewhat limited evidence for the use of gold in bullion transactions, and the vast numbers of cubo-octahedral weights found in Scandinavia, this particular interpretation may be overly precise and it seems more likely that the markings on weights of both types were intended to represent the relative place of an individual weight within a set rather than a correspondence between different types of weight, or even a very precise correspondence between weights of the same type and 'denomination' (see below). Nevertheless, the basic premise that such weights were intended for use as measuring bullion in transactions seems likely.

The same is true for any of the types of decorated weights mentioned above. Weights and balances have been found in a large number of Viking graves in Scandinavia, as well as in a few examples from the British Isles. Such graves have often been interpreted as 'traders' graves', but recent scholarship has tended to stress the wide variety of types of transaction (social and legal as well as purely commercial) for which exchange of bullion might be appropriate (Samson 1991; Gaimster 1991; 2007; Kruse 2007; Pedersen 2007, 159–61; Sindbæk 2011, 42–8). The decorated weights from Kiloran Bay on Colonsay are associated with a grave of some status, which also includes a sword, and the same is true of the punch-marked weights from Scar on Sanday (Owen and Dalland 1999, 118–21). Barbara Crawford (1987, 126) has noted that scales and weights would also be necessary in the division of spoils or tribute by a chieftain or military leader.

The plain lead weights, being less distinctive, were perhaps less well suited to use in transactions, although variation in size and shape may have been of some assistance in distinguishing between individual weights in a set. However, many of the sites with significant assemblages of weights appear to have been centres for production as well as of exchange, and, in some cases, plain weights have been found in what have been interpreted as workshop areas, giving rise to the suggestion that such weights may have been used for measuring quantities for metalworking (Pedersen 2007, 166–8). This could be of value in measuring appropriate quantities for moulding, especially if the items being moulded were intended to be weight-adjusted, as with some types of arm-ring. They could also have been useful for adjusting the relative quantities of different components when creating alloys. In this context it is important to note the evidence, in the form of part-finished objects and waste products, of metalworking on the site (see pp. 48, 82–4), as well as at Torksey and Woodstown (see pp. 85, 87), which also have large weight assemblages.

However, the presence of significant quantities of plain lead weights in areas associated with metalworking may simply indicate that weights were among the categories of objects being produced in these areas. Moulds for various types of object have been discovered at a number of sites, including moulds for the more complicated cubo-octahedral and oblate-spheroid weights at Birka (Pedersen 2007, 121). I am not aware of moulds for plain lead weights having been identified, and certainly none has been recorded from the ARSNY site, but such moulds must have existed, and the more visually interesting lead weights decorated with punch-marks, added metalwork or enamelling must also have begun as undecorated lead casts. The plain casts could thus in many cases represent unfinished rather than completed objects. A detailed comparison to establish whether multiple weights may have originated in the same cast could be revealing in this respect, but has not been carried out in this instance.

It is also possible that many items have been wrongly identified as weights, and that they have some other function entirely, or that measurement of weight formed only part of their function. There are three possibilities. The first is that some of the plain pieces may be gaming pieces rather than weights. A board game like *hneftafl* has mostly pieces of one type, with a single king piece differentiated. Thus clusters of lead pieces of more or less uniform size, shape and weight could represent gaming pieces, with different forms corresponding to different sets.

A second possibility is that they were used as a form of reckoning counter, like late medieval lead tokens, late medieval and early modern copper-alloy jettons, or modern gambling chips. Given the diversity of form which precious metal took in the Viking economy, with complete coins of different types, and both ingots and hack-silver of hugely varying sizes, reckoning counters might well have been useful for calculating the size of payments in silver, whether for the purpose of gambling or for commercial transactions, with the detailed weighing of silver only taking place after the basic sum had already been calculated. Again, pieces of roughly uniform size and weight would make sense for such a function, with the added possibility that such pieces could double as both reckoning counters and weights.

A final possibility would take this a step further, with base-metal weights actually forming a currency level below that of silver bullion. Such an explanation has no place in established explanations of silver economy, but the recent revival of interest in 'commodity money' (see below) raises interesting possibilities. If lead was seen as a commodity, which for metalworking purposes it presumably was, then transferring it in measured amounts would have enabled it to function more flexibly in exchange in societies which were not yet completely monetised; this certainly applies to the whole of the Viking world in the 9th century. Again, such an explanation would be consistent with the concentration of lead weights at various sites which were centres both for production and exchange.

Weight standards

Much has been written on weight standards in the Viking Age, and recent detailed discussion is provided by Pedersen (2007, 140–4) and Kilger (2007). A number of different 'ounces' have long been proposed for the Viking Age, all clustering in the area around 25g. A.W. Brøgger (1921, 95) proposed both a light ounce (øre) of 24.59g, subdivided into three *ertogs* of 8.19g, replacing a heavier 'old Norwegian' ounce of 26.5g, which he saw as subdivided into seven, but which his contemporary Asgaut Steinnes (1927) preferred to divide into 20 nominal penny-weights of *c.* 1.33g, although the almost complete absence of pennies of any description from early Viking-Age Norway makes this an unlikely basis for a weight system in this period; a division into seven is also less than obvious. More recent interpretations of the ounce have been clustered in the same areas, with a unit of 26.6g proposed for the Dublin weights, including recent finds of 9th-century date as well as the 10th-century standardised weights on which this figure was originally based (Wallace 1987, 206–7; 2013, 313–15). The 'old Norwegian' and Dublin ounces also correspond very closely with two weights of 26.65g each recovered from the boat burial at Scar on Sanday (Owen and Dalland 1999, 118–26). A very slightly lighter target unit of 26.15 ± 0.9g is proposed by John Sheehan (1998, 178–9; 2009, 67; 2014, 202) for weight-adjusted arm-rings from Ireland, with around two-thirds of the broad-band arm-rings studied by Sheehan corresponding to multiples of this target. The fact that the remaining third do not correspond to this target value may indicate that those functioned purely as ornaments rather than as deliberately weight-adjusted rings with a dual function in display and currency, in contrast to those of standardised weight. This may also reflect the fact that not all Hiberno-Scandinavian arm-rings were necessarily produced in the same place, with possible evidence of the production of such rings from both Torksey and Llanbedrgoch (see below, pp. 36, 40). With a difference of only around 0.5g from Wallace's Dublin ounce, and allowing for deviation around both targets, this can probably be safely seen as a variation on the same basic standard.

A somewhat lighter target of 22–23g is proposed by Pat Wallace (2013, 313–15; 2014, 228–32) for the Woodstown weights. Here the difference is sufficiently different from the Dublin standard of 26.6g that this should probably be considered a distinct standard, and Wallace suggests that this is in part a chronological difference, reflecting the fact that the Woodstown assemblage is on the whole earlier than that from Dublin. The Woodstown weight-standard also seems less tightly controlled than that of Dublin, which would be consistent both with the clearer evidence for centralised authority in 10th-century Dublin, and with the interpretation of 'personalised' weights in the late 9th century suggested above (see p. 21). Reflecting this variation, some of the Woodstown weights come closer to a unit of 24g.

A unit of *c.* 24 ± 0.8g was proposed by Richard Warner (1976) for the plain weight-adjusted arm-rings characteristic of Viking Scotland in the 10th century, and known as 'ring-money', although on Warner's own figures there is often considerable variation apparent around the nominal target weight. A figure of *c.* 24g has also been proposed for the oblate-spheroid weights in Sweden, although Sperber (1996, 110) suggests that there may have been two separate standards for this type of weight, at 24g and 25.4g. The latter weight is six times the size of Sperber's proposed unit of the *mitqāl* (4.233g), an Islamic weight based around the gold dinar, which he also proposes as the basis for the cubo-octahedral weights, although with two contrasting sub-systems which he labels the Islamic market system and the Islamic-Swedish system, with the former representing a weight standard derived directly from the Islamic world, and the latter a local variant.

Sperber's calculations give two smaller units of 0.71g and 0.8g, which are taken as the underlying units for the different sizes of cubo-octahedral weight in his two systems. Since these figures were drawn primarily from two different assemblages, they may reflect genuinely different standards, but could equally indicate slightly different calibration at different sites around the same basic standard. Mark Blackburn (2002, 96–8), in his examination of cubo-octahedral weights from Torksey and other English finds, argued that these could be seen as reflecting both Sperber's 0.8g standard and a lighter unit of 0.65g, typically with the smaller weights with fewer dots following the 0.8g standard and the larger weights the 0.65g standard, rather than a single standard weight per dot applying across whole sets, as Sperber had suggested. However, some individual examples differ appreciably from the target weights associated with these units, and Blackburn noted that the sample was too small to make a very strong case for such precise standards. He also noted the possibility that the markings may have served simply to identify weights of different sizes within a set, rather than specific multiples of a common standard. Blackburn (2011, 237–8) recently revisited this subject in the light of the expanded corpus of weights now recorded from Torksey, and came to similar conclusions, although he broadened the range of the higher weight standard to 0.75–0.8g.

The 24 single finds of cubo-octahedral weights from ARSNY (sfs163, 825, 1428–49), plus the four from the hoard (sf157:1–4), make a significant addition to the 28 originally considered by Blackburn, and the weight distribution of both groups is mapped in **Table 3**, together with a further nineteen weights from Torksey recorded by Hannah Brown (2006, table 1), although not all of the weights are sufficiently well preserved to be used for the analysis of weight standards. Comparison indicates that the mean value of the ARSNY weights is in most cases lower than for the English assemblage generally, but by such a small margin that it is unlikely to be significant. The weights with three, four and

Value (number of dots/ annulets)	Weight of examples (g)*	Mean weight†	Mean weight per dot	Target weight at 0.65g per dot	Target weight at 0.71g per dot	Target weight at 0.8g per dot
6	4.22, 4.1, **4.05**, *3.87*, *[3.8]*, *3.78*, **3.78**, **3.74**, **3.72**, *3.7*, 3.69, **3.6**, *3.55*, *[3.5]*, **[3.42]**, **[3.26]**, 3.41, [3.4], *3.22*, **[3.13]**	3.75 (3.78)	0.63 (0.63)	3.9	4.26	4.8
4	**2.89**, 2.69, 2.68, *2.61*, *2.6*, *2.6*, 2.6, *2.59*, *2.53*, **2.45**, **[2.43]**, **2.40**, **[2.37‡]**, *2.24*, **[2.17]**, **[2.16]**, **2.09**, *2.06*	2.5 (2.46)	0.63 (0.61)	2.6	2.84	3.2
3	*[2.33]*, *2.31*, *2.13*, *2.09*, 2.0, **1.99**, **[1.97]**, *1.94*, **1.92**, **1.92**, **1.91**, 1.83, *[1.82]*, **[1.81‡]**, *[1.7]*, *1.67*, *[1.66]*	1.97 (1.94)	0.66 (0.65)	1.95	2.13	2.4
2	*1.63*, 1.6, *1.53*, **[1.51]**, *1.51*, 1.5, *1.5*, **1.47**, *1.44*, **1.42**, ***[1.32]***, *1.29*, **1.27**, **[1.25]**, *[1.16]*, *[1.01]*	1.47 (1.39)	0.74 (0.69)	1.3	1.42	1.6
1	0.93, *0.86*, *0.73*	0.84	0.84	0.65	0.71	0.8
0	**0.58**	0.58	0.58	–	–	–

Table 3 Analysis of the weight standards of cubo-octahedral weights from ARSNY, Torksey and other English sites

*Weights in **bold** come from ARSNY, those in ***italics*** from Torksey, those in normal type from elsewhere or unprovenanced. Data from Torksey and elsewhere are taken from Blackburn 2002, table 1, and Brown 2006, table 1. More recent finds from Torksey and elsewhere have not been included. Weights given in square brackets indicate that the example is too worn, corroded or otherwise damaged to reflect accurately the original weight, and these have been excluded from the calculations of mean weight.

†The first figure in this and the adjacent column is drawn from all of the examples in suitable condition. The bracketed figures are drawn from ARSNY material alone.

‡These weights have no visible value markings and have been assigned to particular values on the basis of their size.

six dots each provide mean values of 0.66, 0.63 and 0.63g respectively, bracketing Blackburn's suggested 0.65g unit, and close enough to suggest a common standard. However, the two-dot weights provide a mean value of 0.74g, between Sperber's two units, and the one-dot weights a mean of 0.84g, above even Sperber's higher unit of 0.8g, although the sample here is particularly small. However, the unity of the three-, four- and six-dot weights may also be exaggerated, as the mean figures for each size incorporate examples which differ significantly not just from the mean but from the main cluster for each size. While the mean for the three-dot weights falls into the main cluster of values for weights of this size, the mean for the four-dot weights falls below the main cluster, and that for the six-dot weights above, suggesting a lower target value per dot for the six-dot weights, and a slightly greater difference between the target values for the two weights than the mean for each size would suggest. Furthermore, the ARSNY assemblage contains one example (sf1449) with no dots at all, and a target weight of only 0.58g. The small size suggests that the absence of decoration is deliberate (unlike larger weights which also lack markings and may be unfinished, e.g. sf1441), signifying the smallest weight in a set, but this undecorated weight comes rather closer to a single unit in the 0.6–0.65g range than the one-dot weights of 0.86g and 0.93g recorded by Blackburn.

Altogether, there is considerable variation in weight between different examples of the same 'denomination', and between different target weights per dot for those different denominations. On the available evidence, this does not suggest that any of the suggested target weights can be accepted as standard with any confidence. Deviation from any given target tends to be considerably greater than the variation between different proposed targets, and this suggests both a fairly broad weight standard and that the markings were intended more to denote relative positions within individual sets than absolute and widely accepted weight standards. However, as the corpus of such weights from England continues to grow, it is likely that this can be revisited with rather more statistical validity in the foreseeable future. A study by Helen Geake (2010) on an overlapping corpus of cubo-octahedral weights recorded through the PAS follows a different (and in my opinion less statistically meaningful) method, making it difficult to compare her results usefully with either Blackburn's or my own, although the raw data is a valuable resource. I have not attempted to incorporate the additional weights discussed by Geake into my own calculations, as she does not provide sufficient discussion of the condition of individual weights for me to calculate whether or not any should be excluded as too damaged to provide statistically useful data, an approach followed by both Blackburn and myself in our respective analyses of the cubo-octahedral weights.

Also ultimately derived from the Islamic world is the weight standard of the so-called 'Permian rings' at *c.* 100g, giving a sub-unit of *c.* 25g (Hårdh 1996, 58–65; 2007a), while Susan Kruse (1988, 294) suggests a broader unit of 25–26g on the basis of Viking silver ingots from England and Wales. The metrological precision of some of these distinctions is dubious, and it is uncertain how far distinctions in different times and places genuinely reflect different weight standards imposed by local authorities; how far they represent local variation in the calibration of a standard weight imposed by an invisible 'market'; and how far they represent the over-precise constructions of modern scholars. This becomes even more of a problem with smaller units, since there does seem to be a concentration in assemblages at many sites of weights around one-third of an ounce (the *ertog*) and one-sixth of an ounce (the half-*ertog*, now labelled the þveiti by Christoph Kilger (2007, 316)). The þveiti stands at *c.* 4g in Kilger's calculations, but could range up to *c.* 4.4g based on other hypothetical ounces, a range which also encompasses Sperber's *mitqāl* of 4.233g. A concentration of weights around the 4.00–4.25g unit, and of multiples of this unit, is recorded from a variety of sites, and the fact that odd-numbered multiples of this unit appear not infrequently as weights suggests that this, rather than the larger ounce or the *ertog*, may be the key unit (Pedersen 2007, 145). Multiples of the *ertog* and the þveiti are also observable in silver bullion (Kruse 1988, 294; Williams 2004, 83).

However, with units so close together, the standard deviations required to fit objects to any of the proposed systems are often higher than the variations between different systems, so that an individual weight could be seen as broadly consistent with a number of slightly different systems. This problem is exacerbated by the fact that it is frequently unclear just how far chipping, wear and corrosion may have altered any individual weight. Except on sites where there is a sufficient body of evidence to provide a clear local trend, and where tighter local controls may have applied, it seems safer to postulate a broader unit of 4.0–4.4g for the þveiti, and 24.0–26.6g for the ounce (Kruse 1988, 294; 1993, 195; Williams 2004, 84). Sheehan (2011, 403) has also proposed a broad unit of *c.* 25–26g for the Viking-Age bullion economy in general, while accepting some of the tighter standards discussed above for specific groups of material. The ARSNY assemblage supports these broad units, but does not reliably suggest a tighter standard, although it is notable that a number of pieces are chipped and worn, and, with such small differences between nominal standards, this may affect the quality of the data here and elsewhere. A detailed analysis of the weight distribution of the lead weights is therefore not provided here, although all the individual weights are recorded in **Table 2**, together with factors such as chipping which might affect those weights. This may usefully be revisited in the future in comparison with other material, as the corpus of Viking weights from England continues to expand.

Gold and silver
Barry Ager and Gareth Williams

In addition to the hack-silver from the hoard and other Treasure items treated separately (see above, pp. 13–14), the assemblage from the site contains two pieces of hack-gold and 70 pieces of silver (see **Table 4**). These were processed as Treasure under the terms of the Treasure Act (1996). Although these pieces were found separately and distributed across the site, and each therefore potentially represented a case of treasure, they were dealt with as a single case, with the reference 2007 T186 (DCMS 2009, 106). The silver items can be summarised as follows:

- Hack-silver: 36
- Broken fragment: 3
- Ingot: 1
- Pin/pinhead: 3
- Medieval buckle tongue: 1
- Droplet from metalworking: 17
- Other metalworking waste: 9

With the exception of the medieval buckle tongue, all of the gold and silver objects are either identifiably Viking or Anglo-Saxon, or non-diagnostic but consistent with the predominantly Viking-Age assemblage. The objects basically fit into two main groups, with the hack-silver and ingot falling into a category of object normally associated with a quasi-monetary economy based on silver bullion, while the droplets and melted fragments appear to represent casual waste from metalworking. The broken fragments and the pin(head)s could be regarded either as bullion or as raw material for metalworking. The stubs of base-metal shanks in the pinheads (nos 70–1) perhaps indicate that the latter is more likely in their case. Given the wider evidence for metalworking on the site (see pp. 48, 82–4), the possibility that some or all of the hack-silver may have been intended for re-use in metalworking rather than any monetary function cannot be ruled out, and there is a similar dilemma concerning the interpretation of stray finds of hack-silver from other sites which apparently combined both production and exchange (Hårdh 2008). Equally, the small silver droplets formed as by-products of metalworking could have been used to make fine adjustments to the weight of larger sums of bullion, and such droplets and other types of casting waste are occasionally found in hoards (Graham-Campbell 2011, 193; Sheehan 2014, 196, 206–7). Some of the weights used, and the proposed weight units on which they were supposedly based (see pp. 31–3), are tiny, and, if such fine adjustment was expected for the weights, it must also have been expected for the silver. This is also reflected in the small size and weight of the smallest pieces of hack-silver. One of the notable features of the use of silver in the Viking Age is its flexibility, since it could function in both coin-based and bullion economies, as well as in a more 'social' economy based on display; the ease with which items could be melted down meant those which might appear at first sight to represent one form of economy might equally well provide material for another (Graham-Campbell 2001b; Williams 2007; 2011a).

Hack-gold is comparatively unusual, as it is not normally found in hoards, and it is rare even as a site find. Nevertheless, fragments of hack-gold are also known from the assemblage from Torksey and examples of both gold ingots and hack-gold are known as single finds (Blackburn 2007a, 75–6; 2011, 233–5; see also Kershaw, this volume, pp. 116–17). A single piece of hack-gold is also recorded in the Watlington hoard (Williams and Naylor 2016, 11–12). The usual absence of hack-gold from Viking-Age bullion hoards may well indicate a difference in function as well as value, and it is interesting that the huge gold neck-ring from Tissø in Denmark (Jørgensen and Vang Petersen 1998, 300–2), which is composed of twisted gold rods comparable to the hack-gold fragments from both ARSNY and Torksey, and which had been partly disassembled, apparently with the intention of recycling, was found in an area of the site associated with metalworking (L. Jørgensen, pers. comm.). It is not unreasonable to assume that the hack-gold from ARSNY may also have been similarly intended for re-use in metalworking. However, this is not the only possibility, and both Blackburn (2007a, 75–6) and Kershaw (this volume, pp. 123–4; 2019) point to the growing evidence for the use of gold as well as silver bullion in the Viking Age, while the presence

Sf number	Treasure reference number	Description	Largest dimension	Weight
1225	1	Viking hack-gold fragment of round-sectioned rod	13mm	2.49g
1226	2	Viking hack-gold fragment of square-sectioned rod	7mm	0.86g
1227	3	Viking hack-silver fragment of roughly hexagonal rod	8mm	0.70g
1228	5	Viking hack-silver fragment	7mm	1.20g
1229	7	Viking hack-silver fragment of oval section, from an ingot	12mm	2.61g
1230	8	Viking hack-silver fragment of an ingot	9mm	0.92g
1231	9	Viking hack-silver fragment	9mm	0.50g
1232 and 1233	13 and 36	Viking hack-silver sheet fragments (x2), joining together and lightly incised with rough circles on the inner side. They possibly derive from a convex ornamental disc of a type found in Viking hoards in southern Sweden, e.g. from Assartorp and Östra Herrestad (Hårdh 1976, pls 33, 9 and 52: I, 8)	14mm (sf1232) and 13mm (sf1233)	0.50g (sf1232) and 0.50g (sf1233)
1234	14	Viking hack-silver fragment, flat, ornamented with punched annulets and wavy line on one side and with test marks on the plain side, cut from the edge of a band-shaped arm-ring	11mm	0.63g
1235	16	Viking hack-silver fragment, cut from round droplet/ingot	10mm	1.18g
1236	17	Viking hack-silver fragment, half-oval in section, cut from an ingot	7mm	1.62g
1237	20	Viking hack-silver fragment	6mm	0.51g
1238	21	Viking hack-silver fragment cut from the end of an ingot	6mm	0.89g
1239	26	Viking hack-silver fragment of rectangular-section rod	8mm	0.27g
1240	27	Viking hack-silver fragment, apparently from crude ingot	21mm	7.18g
1241	28	Viking hack-silver fragment, apparently from crude ingot, with test marks. Surface metal analysis conducted at the BM indicated an approximate silver content of 66%, the remainder being copper with small amounts of lead and gold	18mm	11.18g
1242	30	Viking hack-silver fragment, cut from a lozenge-sectioned arm-ring, with test marks	22mm	7.95g
1243	31	Viking hack-silver fragment, cut from a lozenge-sectioned arm-ring, with test marks	24mm	3.05g
1244	34	Viking hack-silver fragment, cut from a hammered ingot of roughly trapezoidal section	7mm	1.51g
1245	37	Viking hack-silver fragment	9mm	1.60g
1246	40	Viking hack-silver fragment, cut from an ingot	11mm	2.76g
1247	42	Viking hack-silver fragment, cut from an ingot	16mm	9.13g
1248	45	Viking hack-silver fragment, cut from the terminal of a punch-marked, penannular, band-shaped arm-ring	11mm	1.46g
1249	46	Viking hack-silver fragment, from rectangular-sectioned rod/arm-ring, with hammered angles and test marks	15mm	4.77g
1250	47	Viking hack-silver fragment, cut from a lozenge-sectioned rod, slightly curved	11mm	1.94g
1251	49	Viking hack-silver fragment, probably cut from an ingot	8mm	1.11g
1252	50	Viking hack-silver fragment, cut from the terminal of a penannular, band-shaped arm-ring, decorated on one side with interlocking punched triangles	11mm	1.24g
1253	51	Viking hack-silver fragment, cut from the end of an ingot	5mm	0.74g
1254	52	Viking hack-silver fragment	7mm	0.99g
1255	54	Viking hack-silver fragment, cut from the end of an oval-sectioned ingot	9mm	2.78g
1256	55	Viking hack-silver fragment, curved and cut from an oval-sectioned ingot, with test marks	18mm	9.15g
1257	56	Viking hack-silver fragment	5mm	0.27g
1258	57	Viking hack-silver fragment, cut from an oval-sectioned ingot	9mm	1.03g
1259	58	Viking hack-silver fragment, cut from a lozenge-sectioned ring	5mm	0.65g
1260	60	Viking hack-silver fragment, cut from a transversely punch-marked, band-shaped arm-ring	12mm	1.20g
1261	61	Viking hack-silver fragment of cylindrical rod, possibly cut from the shank of a pin	13mm	0.86g
1262	39	Viking silver fragment (probably broken rather than hack-silver), from the end of a hammered, rectangular-sectioned ingot	12mm	1.30g
1263	44	Broken silver fragment, from jewellery/ornament of uncertain date; dumb-bell shaped with pierced ends	12mm	0.74g

Table 4 Gold and silver single finds from ARSNY (Treasure case 2007 T186)

Sf number	Treasure reference number	Description	Largest dimension	Weight
1264	59	Viking silver fragment	6mm	0.44g
1265	66	Silver fragment with incised geometric ornament, broken from a spherical object of possibly late Anglo-Saxon date	12mm	0.78g
1266	72	Corroded fragment of a small, late Saxon finger-ring with a circular bezel engraved with a back-turned animal with a dotted body in 9th-century Trewhiddle style enclosed by a rim punched with minute triangles; only part of the hoop survives. Surface metal analysis conducted at the BM indicated an approximate silver content for the ring of 94–98%, the remainder being copper with small amounts of lead and gold	14mm	0.4g
1267	25	Viking silver ingot, oval-shaped, with test marks	20mm	6.74g
1268	32	Anglo-Saxon silver ball-headed pin with collar; shaft broken. This compares with 9th-century bronze examples from Whitby monastery in the BM	24mm	2.36g
1269	70	Silver pinhead, with stub of bronze shank. Although not a recognisably Viking type of object it seems probable that it is contemporary with the other finds	8mm	1.32g
1270	71	Silver pinhead, broken, with stub of iron shank (see previous comment)	11mm	2.37g
1271	18	Medieval silver tongue from a buckle, or pin of a brooch, tip missing (cf. Egan and Pritchard 1991, fig. 329)	2mm	1.20g
1272	4	Viking(?) silver droplet of metalworking debris	4.5mm	0.18g
1273	10	Viking silver droplet	8mm	1.56g
1274	11	Viking silver droplet	12mm	1.29g
1275	12	Viking silver droplet	6mm	0.55g
1276	15	Viking silver droplet/ingot	10mm	1.45g
1277	22	Viking silver droplet	9mm	1.03g
1278	23	Viking silver droplet/ovoid ingot	14mm	3.80g
1279	29	Viking silver droplet	5mm	0.56g
1280	38	Viking silver droplet	7mm	0.60g
1281	41	Viking silver droplet	4mm	0.24g
1282	48	Viking silver droplet	6mm	0.67g
1283	53	Viking silver droplet	5mm	0.41g
1284	64	Viking flattened silver droplet/ovoid ingot	8mm	0.85g
1285	67	Silver droplet or pinhead. Although not a recognisably Viking type of object it seems probable that it is contemporary with the other finds	8mm	1.65g
1286	68	Silver droplet or pinhead (see previous comment)	9mm	2.05g
1287	69	Silver droplet or pinhead (see previous comment)	8mm	1.73
1288	6	Viking(?) melted silver fragment	7mm	0.76g
1289	19	Viking(?) fragment of melted silver	20mm	3.96g
1290	24	Viking fragment of melted silver	12mm	0.59g
1291	33	Viking fragment of melted silver	12mm	2.54g
1292	35	Viking fragment of melted silver	10mm	1.01g
1293	43	Viking fragment of melted silver	18mm	2.93g
1294	63	Viking fragment of melted silver	10mm	0.32g
1295	65	Viking silver waste from metalworking	6mm	0.33g
1296	62	Silver fragment in the shape of a cluster of granules (metalworking waste?), of uncertain date	10mm	1.61g

Table 4 (continued) Gold and silver single finds from ARSNY (Treasure case 2007 T186)

of hack-gold in the Watlington hoard also points to use as bullion. The fact that Torksey, ARSNY and Watlington all apparently date to the mid–late 870s and all contain hack-gold fragments of comparable size may indicate a particular tendency to the use of small-scale gold bullion within the *micel here* of 865–79 (see p. 104) and perhaps the settlement period that followed. The same flexibility between coinage, bullion and complete ornaments would apply to both gold and silver, although gold always seems to have been considerably rarer than silver (Williams 2011b, 338), and it is interesting that a trial-piece for an imitative gold solidus of Louis the Pious was amongst the finds at Torksey, together with another for a base-silver Lunettes penny (Blackburn 2002, 93–4; 2011, 225, 228), indicating that coin-striking might also be among the activities associated with sites of this type. However, the same site also included what appears to be trial-pieces for testing punches typical of punch-marked Hiberno-Scandinavian arm-rings and other decorated silver of Scandinavian character (Blackburn 2011, 242), and a comparable trial-piece was also found at Llanbedrgoch, Anglesey (Redknap 2000, 84; 2009, 37–8), a site with a number of similarities to ARSNY. Given the other evidence for metalworking on the ARSNY site (see pp. 48, 82–4), the re-use of both hack-silver and hack-gold in the manufacture of ornaments must remain a strong possibility.

The majority of the gold and silver objects are thus to some extent ambiguous in function, whatever their form. Their likely purpose is discussed further below (pp. 43–4), together with the coins and weights.

The coins
Richard Kelleher and Gareth Williams

The assemblage of coins recorded from the site includes 20 Roman coins (not discussed here), 90 Northumbrian copper-alloy stycas of the 9th century (including three from the excavation: sfs272, 381, 770), a debased silver Lunettes-type penny of Burgred of Mercia from the excavation (sf267), a silver penny of the Cross-and-Lozenge type of Ceolwulf of Mercia, two pennies of the Pyramids type of Edward the Confessor, fourteen fragmentary dirhams, five late medieval coins, nine post-medieval coins, three jettons (reckoning counters) and a battered silver disc which may also be a coin (**Table 5**). A large number of other stycas had previously been discovered on the site, and are said to have been recorded by the late Elizabeth Pirie, but a thorough examination of her archive (at that time in the National Museums of Scotland) revealed no records which could positively be identified with the site. The stycas contain a mixture of issues, terminating in coins of Osberht (*c.* 848–67) and several blundered issues, normally also dated to Osberht's reign. Late styca hoards and assemblages typically contain earlier issues, so all of the stycas represented here are largely what one might expect to find in the final stages of circulation prior to the Viking conquest of 866–7. While some of the stycas are too poorly preserved to be legible, the majority date from the 840s or later, with surprisingly few from the reign of Eanred (*c.* 810–40/1). The stycas thus seem to have been deposited over a comparatively short period of a few years rather than indicating continuous occupation of the site throughout the 9th century. As discussed in more detail below (pp. 42, 79–80, 130–1), stycas have typically been seen as indicative of pre-Viking activity, but an increasing number of stycas found in Viking contexts, including an assemblage from Torksey (Blackburn 2011, 225), suggests that they may have continued to be used for some years after the Viking conquest, and even raises the possibility that some of the blundered derivative issues may be Viking imitations.

The Lunettes penny is contemporary with those in the hoard and the single coin of the Cross-and-Lozenge type dates from the mid- to late 870s, while the dirham fragments, although not precisely datable, are also consistent with the first phase of settlement in the 870s, and with the weights assemblage. Like the weights, the combination of Northumbrian stycas, Lunettes pennies and dirham fragments directly parallels the assemblage from the Viking winter camp at Torksey (Blackburn 2011). Beyond this settlement phase there are no coins from the Anglo-Scandinavian period, while the absence of any significant concentration in the later coins suggests that there was never a major focus of commercial activity on the site beyond the early settlement phase, although the site was clearly utilised, whether intermittently or continuously, over a period of several centuries.

The coins, weights and bullion: discussion and interpretation
Gareth Williams

The hoard and site assemblage from ARSNY currently represents by far the most significant single body of material relating to Viking precious-metal economies from northern England dating from the settlement period of *c.* AD 875–900. However, it is possible that part of the even larger assemblage from Torksey may also be associated with this period, despite the fact that it can be clearly linked with the occupation of Torksey in 872–3, shortly before the beginning of permanent settlement is recorded, and also before the partial collapse of the Mercian kingdom in 874 (Blackburn 2002; 2011). Current interpretation of the Torksey assemblage is inclined to see the Viking occupation of that site (as distinct from the site of the later Anglo-Saxon *burh* slightly to the south) as relating almost exclusively to the winter camp of 872–3 (Hadley and Richards *et al.* 2016, 28–33), although the possibility of more prolonged occupation cannot be ruled out. Dating of both the hoard and the single finds suggests that it was likely that activity at ARSNY began in the immediate aftermath of the Viking settlement of Northumbria from 875 onwards, and thus at an important moment in the political history of the region. Comparison with other material suggests that it was an equally important moment from an economic perspective.

Comparison with other hoards of the late 9th century

Comparison between hoards and site finds/stray finds is not straightforward, since it has been argued that while site finds and stray finds generally represent casual loss, and thus a random sample of monetary items which were in circulation at the time of loss, hoards generally represent monetary items withdrawn from circulation and are thus possibly less representative of circulation as a whole (Blackburn 2003). This is not always necessarily the case, since it is sometimes unclear whether smaller hoards were deliberately deposited, rather than representing the casual loss of a single small purse, but the principle of applying caution is certainly a good one. It is also important to note that while Viking hoards may contain any combination of jewellery, ingots, hack-silver and coins, they rarely include weights or balances, and thus exclude a significant group of evidence which is better represented both in site assemblages and grave finds as well as, increasingly, single finds (for the last, see Kershaw, this volume, pp. 119–23). However, it is interesting that at ARSNY, the hoard (if all the objects attributed to it genuinely belong together) appears to correspond very closely with the wider assemblage, containing as it does a mixture of weights, coins, and highly fragmented silver bullion, and a brief comparison with hoards as well as sites is instructive. The following section considers how the ARSNY material compares with other hoards deposited in England during the same general period. A more detailed overview of the chronological development of Viking and Anglo-Scandinavian hoards in the region over a longer period is provided elsewhere (Williams, this volume, Chapter 3).

The hoard is the latest in a group which can be identified with the documented activity of the *micel here*, in the decade of activity 865–75. Nicholas Brooks and James Graham-Campbell (2000) have noted a broad correspondence between coin-dated hoards within this period, and the sites at which the Viking *micel here* is recorded as raiding and/or over-wintering, and this trend is reinforced by the discovery of two further hoards from Bamburgh dating from this broad period. For the first hoard, found in two distinct parcels by metal detectorists near Bamburgh, see Pirie 2004; DCMS 2006, 184. The second, found during excavations at Bamburgh Castle in 2009, could only be partially identified when initially examined, as some of the coins were too corroded for clear identification, but appeared on the available evidence to be somewhat earlier than the ARSNY hoard. That hoard has now been conserved, but has not yet been re-examined in detail. In most cases, these hoards are drawn from local currency (copper-alloy stycas north of the Humber, base-silver Lunettes pennies to the south) and therefore cannot be firmly identified as Viking rather than Anglo-Saxon deposits, although the group includes Lunettes pennies comparable to those from ARSNY from Viking graves at Repton *c.* 873–4 (Biddle *et al.* 1986a; Biddle *et al.* 1986b), while the Croydon hoard of *c.* 871–2 is more characteristically Viking, containing as it does ingots and hack-silver as well as both locally issued and imported coins (Brooks and Graham-Campbell 2000). However, Croydon does not show the extreme fragmentation of silver visible at ARSNY, nor the characteristic pecking of later hoards.

The year 2015 saw the discovery of two hoards dating from *c.* 879–80. The Watlington hoard contained a little over 200 silver pennies (extensive fragmentation in the ground means that the exact total is uncertain) of the Cross-and-Lozenge phase (874–*c.* 879), issued both by Alfred of Wessex and Ceolwulf II of Mercia, as well as by Archbishop Æthelred of Canterbury. The hoard terminates in a single coin of the Two-Line type of Alfred, introduced *c.* 879–80. In addition to the coins, the hoard contains intact arm-rings, ingots, hack-silver and a single piece of hack-gold. Work on the hoard is ongoing at the time of writing, but initial examination reveals no sign of test marks (Williams and Naylor 2016). A further hoard of almost exactly the same date, also found in south-western Mercia, was found earlier in 2015, but only partially reported. At the time of writing it is the subject of an ongoing police investigation, so it is not possible to discuss the contents in detail, but it also appears to contain predominantly coins of the Cross-and-Lozenge phase, terminating in a single coin of the subsequent phase, and with some non-numismatic material. Again, initial examination of the objects recovered does not indicate testing, but it appears unlikely that all of the hoard has been recovered, in which case it is likely that the coins recovered may represent the more attractive coins selected for sale.

There is then a significant gap in the hoard record before the deposition of hoards from Stamford (Brooks and Graham-Campbell 2000; Blackburn 2005) and Ashdon, Essex (Blackburn 1989), followed by a substantial group of silver hoards from northern England and around the Irish Sea from the early 10th century (Graham-Campbell 2001a; Williams 2009; 2011b). These hoards represent a distinctly different phase in the economy of Viking England, with widespread pecking, the presence of both Anglo-Saxon and Anglo-Viking coinage in good silver, the presence of bullion in varying degrees of fragmentation, and the complete exclusion of the coin types circulating in both northern and southern England prior to the Viking settlement. A hoard from St-Pierre-sur-Dives in Normandy (Cardon *et al.* 2008) reflects the same general trends, but the gap between the mid-870s and the 890s is partly filled by the later of two hoards from Westerklief in the Netherlands (Bestemann 2004; 2009). The earlier hoard (*c.* 850) contains intact jewellery, coins and substantial items of bullion, but the later hoard of *c.* 880 shows the same fragmentation of silver bullion visible at ARSNY. A small hoard from Ablaincourt (dép. Somme) of Frankish coins deposited in the 880s or very early 890s also shows evidence of pecking (Moesgaard 2013).

Viking hoards from Scotland typically reflect the silver economy of the 10th and 11th centuries (Graham-Campbell 1995), but it is relevant to consider the status of a small hoard from Talnotrie in Kirkcudbrightshire, deposited in the early to mid-870s. The Viking status of this hoard has been regarded as ambiguous, since it is atypical of Viking hoards generally, containing a mixture of Insular gold and metalwork, together with a lead weight capped with a copper-alloy disc of Insular chip-carved workmanship, and thirteen coins, comprising four Burgred Lunettes pennies, six stycas, one fragmentary denier of Louis the Pious, and two dirham fragments (Maxwell 1912–13; Webster and Backhouse 1991, 273–4; Graham-Campbell 1995, 3–4; Brooks and Graham-Campbell 2000, 89–90). Brooks and Graham-Campbell suggest a possible association with Halfdan's raiding in Northumbria in 874–5, and the similarity of both the date and the character of the hoard to the ARSNY assemblage suggests very strongly that it represents the same stage of economic development. While not a hoard as such, the combination of stycas, weights and a balance from the grave at Kiloran Bay, dated only to 'towards the end of the [9th] century or even 900' (Graham-Campbell and Batey 1998, 118–22), seems to fit the same pattern.

Sf number	Description	Weight
Northumbrian stycas		
1298	Eanred (*c.* 810–40/1), moneyer Eardwulf	0.60g
1299	Eanred, moneyer uncertain, fragmentary	0.60g
1300	Eanred, moneyer uncertain	1.02g
1301	Aethelred II (840/41–44, 844–48/850), moneyer Alchere	0.82g
1302	Aethelred II, moneyer Brother	0.85g
1303	Aethelred II, moneyer Coenred or Eanred	0.71g
1304	Aethelred II, moneyer Eanred	0.99g
1305	Aethelred II, moneyer Eardwulf	0.97g
1306	Aethelred II, moneyer Eardwulf; obverse very worn	1.02g
1307	Aethelred II, moneyer Eardwulf	0.84g
1308	Aethelred II, moneyer Eardwulf	0.78g
1309	Aethelred II, moneyer Eardwulf	0.64g
1310	Aethelred II, moneyer Eardwulf	1.06g
1311	Aethelred II, moneyer Eardwulf	0.54g
1312	Aethelred II, moneyer Eardwulf	0.86g
770	Aethelred II, moneyer Eardwulf	1.11g
1313	Aethelred II?, moneyer Eardwulf; obverse illegible, glassy patina	0.58g
1314	Aethelred II?, moneyer Eardwulf; obverse illegible, glassy patina	0.95g
1315	Aethelred II, moneyer Ethelweard?; reverse corroded	0.61g
1316	Aethelred II, moneyer Fordred, fragment	0.53g
1317	Aethelred II, moneyer Monne; badly chipped	0.64g
1318	Aethelred II, moneyer Monne	0.94g
1319	Aethelred II, moneyer Wulfred?	0.87g
1320	Aethelred II, 'Edilred' reverse	0.91g
1321	Aethelred II, moneyer uncertain	1.07g
1322	Aethelred II, moneyer uncertain	0.84g
1323	Aethelred II, moneyer uncertain	0.59g
1324	Aethelred II, moneyer uncertain	0.63g
1325	Aethelred II, moneyer uncertain	0.70g
1326	Aethelred II, moneyer uncertain	0.73g
1327	Redwulf (844), moneyer Coenred	0.95g
1328	Osberht (848–67), moneyer Monne	0.98g
1329	Osberht, moneyer uncertain	0.63g
1330	Osberht, moneyer uncertain	0.44g
1331	Osberht, moneyer uncertain; corroded	0.93g
1332	Osberht retrograde, moneyer uncertain	0.77g
1333	Osberht, moneyer uncertain; heavily worn	1.04g
1334	Osberht, moneyer Monne	1.00g
1335	Archbishop Wigmund (837–54?), moneyer Hunlaf	0.85g
1336	Archbishop Wigmund, moneyer Coenred	1.06g
1337	Archbishop Wigmund?, moneyer illegible	0.39g
381	Archbishop Wulfhere (854–900), moneyer Wulfred	0.87g
1338	EAN___/illegible	0.68g
1339	Blundered, derived Aethelred II/moneyer Eanred	0.50g
1340	Blundered, derived Aethelred II/moneyer Eardwulf	0.57g
1341	Blundered, derived Aethelred II; reverse illegible; corroded	0.82g
1342	Blundered, derived Osberht; reverse illegible	0.69g
1343	Blundered, derived Archbishop Wigmund	0.55g

Table 5 Single finds of medieval and post-medieval coins from ARSNY

Sf number	Description	Weight
1344	Blundered, derived moneyer Eardwulf	0.54g
1345	Blundered, derived moneyer Eardwulf	0.61g
1346	Blundered	0.65g
1347	Blundered	0.52g
1348	Blundered; corroded	0.73g
1349	Blundered	0.76g
1350	Blundered	0.97g
1351	Blundered	0.57g
1352	Blundered	0.44g
1353	Blundered	0.66g
1354	Blundered	0.62g
1355	Blundered	0.88g
1356	Blundered	0.56g
1357	Blundered	0.80g
1358	Blundered	0.83g
1359	Blundered	1.04g
1360	Blundered	0.48g
1361	Blundered	0.75g
1362	Blundered/illegible; corroded	1.07g
1363	Blundered/illegible; reverse corroded	0.80g
1364	Blundered/illegible	0.62g
1365	Blundered/illegible; corroded	0.67g
272	Illegible; corroded	0.94g
1366–84	Illegible (x19); in many cases corroded	0.79g, 1.10g, 0.85g, 0.67g, 0.79g, 0.62g, 0.74g, 0.59g, 0.55g, 0.68g, 0.72g, 0.31g, 0.47g, 0.63g, 0.40g, 0.51g, 0.60g, 0.52g, 1.12g
Anglo-Saxon silver pennies		
267	Burgred of Mercia (852–74), silver penny (two pieces), type A, moneyer Dudwine	0.935g
1385	Ceolwulf II of Mercia (874–*c.* 879), Cross-and-Lozenge type, moneyer Liafwald; four fragments, incomplete	0.70g
1386	Edward the Confessor (1042–66), Pyramids type, moneyer Dutholf of York	1.15g
1387	Edward the Confessor, Pyramids type, mint and moneyer uncertain; small fragment only	0.25g
Dirhams		
1388–1401	Dirham fragments (x14). All were too fragmentary to be assigned to individual rulers, mints, or years of minting, with the exception of sf1401, which was minted at Balkh	0.21g, 0.25g, 0.20g, 0.49g, 0.37g, 0.91g, 0.39g, 0.31g, 0.55g, 0.59g, 0.18g, 0.33g, 0.22g, 0.69g
Later medieval		
1402	Cut halfpenny of Henry II, Short Cross type 1c, moneyer Pieres of London	0.72g
1403	Cut halfpenny of Richard I, Short Cross type 4a, moneyer Turkil of York	0.36g
1404	Penny of Alexander III 1st coinage, type VIII?, moneyer Andrew of Roxburgh; in 4 pieces	1.21g
1405	Penny of Edward I, class 2, London	0.95g
1406	Penny of Edward I or II, London	0.72g
Post-medieval		
1407	Silver penny of Elizabeth I, martlet mint mark	0.84g
1408	Silver half groat of James I, 2nd coinage	0.77g
1409	Fragment of silver shilling of James I, rose mint mark	0.79g
1410	Scottish silver 20 pence of Charles I, 2nd coinage	0.26g

Table 5 (continued) Single finds of medieval and post-medieval coins from ARSNY

Sf number	Description	Weight
1411–13	Twopences (turners) (x3) of Charles II, 1663	2.21g, 1.42g, 1.43g
1414	Farthing of George II (Ireland), young head (1736–55), clipped	
1415	Copper halfpenny of George III (1760–1820), heavily worn and scratched; metal detected from spoil	
Jettons		
1416	Nuremberg Rose/Orb type of Hans Krauwinckel	0.81g
1417	Nuremberg Rose/Orb type, uncertain variety	1.35g
1418	Token imitating French coins of Louis XIV	0.62g
Uncertain		
1419	Battered silver disc, may be a coin	1.71g

Table 5 (continued) Single finds of medieval and post-medieval coins from ARSNY

Comparison with sites in Scandinavia

An increasing number of sites in Scandinavia have comparable assemblages of coins, weights and hack-silver from the late 9th century. Coin assemblages are typically dominated by the dirhams (often fragmentary), of which a small number are recorded from ARSNY, while coins from western Europe are surprisingly scarce, given the volume of recorded raiding and tribute-taking in western annals in the late 9th century. Not surprisingly, Northumbrian stycas are extremely rare in Scandinavia, although less so than previously recognised (Bogucki 2009; see also below, p. 44). Hack-silver seems to develop for currency purposes from the 860s (Hårdh 2008), in response to the influx of dirhams, rather than to western coinage, with increased fragmentation over time probably reflecting an increased monetary use. Weights are recorded in large numbers, and include the sub-Islamic cubo-octahedral (from *c.* 860) and oblate-spheroid (from *c.* 870) copper-alloy weights, together with punch-marked and plain lead weights (see pp. 20–3). As noted above, lead weights capped or inset with Insular metalwork are considerably less well known in Scandinavia than in Britain and Ireland, and appear to represent the exportation of an Insular Viking tradition to Scandinavia.

The sites containing such monetary and/or bullion assemblages include a number of urban or proto-urban sites, of which the most important published sites are Kaupang (Skre 2007a; 2007b; 2011a), Birka (Ambrosiani 2004; 2008) and Hedeby (Wiechmann 1996; Hilberg 2011), although a new site of comparable significance has recently been discovered at Heimdalsjordet, close to the famous Gokstad burial mound in Vestfold, Norway (Bill and Løchsen Rødsrud 2017). These sites typically combine production and exchange on a large scale. However, a similar combination of function can also be found at a number of pre-urban sites from the Viking Age and earlier, which show evidence of production and exchange combined with non-urban functions. These have variously been identified as manorial centres, cult centres or more vaguely as 'central places'. Among the most important for comparison with ARSNY are Tissø (Jørgensen 2003), Uppåkra (Hårdh 2000; 2008) and Sorte Muld (Adamsen *et al.* 2009), representing a spread across southern Scandinavia, and demonstrating the same general economic trends as the urban sites in the same area already mentioned, although it is important to recognise the significance of local and regional variation in silver economies in Scandinavia in this period (Hårdh 1996; Williams 2011b, 338–40).

Comparison with sites in Britain and Ireland

In Britain and Ireland, three sites bear close comparison. Llanbedrgoch on Anglesey has produced coins, weights and bullion, although on a smaller scale (Redknap 2004, 156–68; 2009; Besly 2006, 704, 715). It is less clear that this site saw extensive production as well as exchange, although a lead trial-piece for decorative punches suggests the manufacture of Hiberno-Scandinavian punch-marked arm-rings (see above, p. 36), but the finds assemblage certainly points to the existence of an exchange system in the Irish Sea based around a mixture of coins and bullion in the late 9th century, and both Llanbedrgoch and other stray finds reflect the use of Insular decorated weights. The absence to date of any cubo-octahedral weights from the site may indicate that the main period of economic activity in the late 9th century is slightly earlier than that of ARSNY, but this absence may not be significant, given the smaller corpus of finds, and unlike ARSNY there is unequivocal evidence for continued activity on the site in the 10th century.

A rather more significant comparison may be drawn with Woodstown, near Waterford. This is interpreted as a *longphort* site of the 9th century (for further discussion of Woodstown and of this category of site in general, see below, pp. 86–90), although some of the finds point to continued occupation (or re-occupation) in the 10th or even 11th centuries (O'Brien *et al.* 2005; McNamara 2005; Russell *et al.* 2007; Valante 2008, 42–3; Harrison 2013; Russell and Hurley, with Eogan, 2014). Like ARSNY, the site has only been partially investigated, but has revealed a large assemblage, pointing towards both production and exchange, and containing over 200 weights, and 42 pieces of non-numismatic silver. These include two complete ingots; 24 hack-silver ingot fragments; six hack-silver fragments of arm-rings, six pieces of casting waste; two fragments of hack-silver from a sheet and a rod respectively; a brooch fragment, which may or may not be hack-silver; and an object, apparently made of silver, which looks like a version of one of the cubo-octahedral weights known from ARSNY and elsewhere (Sheehan 2014, 205; 2015). This piece was initially identified as a weight (e.g. Sheehan 2008, 291–2), but this is rejected by Wallace (2013, 308; 2014, 226) in his study of the Woodstown weights, although he does not explain his reasoning. A cubo-octahedral weight in silver would be unique, although Sheehan (2014, 206) notes that the metal content of the object has not been tested, and that the silver appearance may be misleading. However, two examples of what appear to be silver conical pan weights were found close to the suggested *longphort* site of Fairyhill, Co. Sligo, and it is tempting to see these as parallels to the Woodstown weight (Kelly and O'Donovan 1998, 14; Sheehan 2014, 206; Williams 2015, 110–11), and to see all three in the context of a dual role for weights in which the weights themselves might serve as a form of currency (Steuer 2009, 297–8; Williams 2015, 113; see also below, p. 44). Furthermore, the object weighs 2.51g, and while this does not obviously fit into the weight standard proposed by Wallace for the Woodstown weights assemblage as a whole (see above, p. 31), it is consistent with the target weight for four-dot cubo-octahedral weights from Birka proposed by Ola Kyhlberg (1980, 261) and with the mean weight of cubo-octahedral weights from England in general and ARSNY in particular (see above, pp. 31–2). There is only one other cubo-octahedral weight from Woodstown: a large piece in lead (WWT14), which falls outside the main group, although it is paralleled by a find from East Yorkshire, now in the BM (BM 2000, 0201.7), so it is unsurprising that the silver weight piece should fall outside the typical weight standards of an unrelated group of weights. It is also unsurprising that there should be fundamentally different categories of weight at the same site, given the diverse composition of Viking raiding forces in the 9th century (see below, pp. 92–3). The remainder of the weights are lead pan weights, including both undecorated and decorated varieties, of several different types (for a full catalogue, see Wallace 2014, 233–55).

Coins are less well represented than weights and bullion, although two dirham fragments are recorded (Rispling 2014). In part this reflects a fundamental difference between England and Ireland, in that Ireland did not have a coin-based economy prior to the Viking settlements of the 9th century, and hoard evidence only suggests widespread importation of coin from England in the 10th century. Evidence of a predominantly bullion economy at Woodstown is thus consistent with the broader picture of Viking Ireland in the 9th century (Sheehan 2014; 2015). At the same time, metallurgical analysis suggests that imported dirhams provided an important source of raw materials for the manufacture of Hiberno-Scandinavian jewellery (Kruse and Tate 1995), while historical sources and archaeological finds make it clear that some of the Viking forces in Ireland in the mid–late 9th century also raided in the coin-using societies of Anglo-Saxon England and Francia (McLeod 2014, 112–71), so some coin is likely to have entered Ireland at this time, even if it was then largely recycled. The site shows evidence of metalworking, including the testing and possibly reworking of silver (Sheehan 2014, 206–7; 2015; Young 2014a; 2014b) so this may partially explain the absence of coin. At the same time, the almost complete absence of coins suggests that the main period of activity on the site was slightly earlier than that of ARSNY. This impression is reinforced by the presence in such a large assemblage of only one sub-Islamic cubo-octahedral weight and another larger weight of the same shape, since the use of these weights in Viking trade became widespread in the course of the 860s (see pp. 20–1, **Pl. 4**), and they are well represented at both Torksey and ARSNY although activity at Woodstown must continue at least into the 860s for even one cubo-octahedral weight to be present.

Closer still, both chronologically and geographically, is the massive assemblage from Torksey, in Lincolnshire, identified with the winter camp of the *micel here* in 872–3. The site is primarily known through metal-detected finds recorded over a period of many years. Unfortunately much information has been lost, but ongoing recording of finds from the site, especially by Rachel Atherton and Kevin Leahy of the PAS, and by Mark Blackburn of the Fitzwilliam Museum, has led to a substantial body of material from the site being recorded on the PAS database. Preliminary publication of the site by Blackburn (2002; 2007c; 2011) indicates strong similarities with ARSNY, although a full study of the site and its assemblage is needed. A preliminary study of the site has been carried out as a collaborative project led by the Universities of York and Sheffield and the BM (Hadley and Richards 2013, and see below pp. 84–6), and this has included geophysical and topographical surveys, fieldwalking, a limited amount of trial excavation and systematic recording of both existing and new metal-detected finds (for further details of the Torksey research project, see https://www.york.ac.uk/archaeology/research/current-projects/torksey).

Coins from the site include Lunettes-type Anglo-Saxon pennies, stycas and dirhams, as well as some Carolingian coins, together with a range of gold and silver bullion and weights, including both cubo-octahedral weights and lead weights decorated with Insular metalwork or coins, as well as plain lead weights. The assemblage is larger in all of these areas than that from ARSNY, although without the waste products from cupellation recorded from ARSNY (see p. 48). The main run of coins probably terminates just before ARSNY's, reflecting the historically documented activity in 872–3, although precise dating within the Lunettes coinage is problematic, and it is also difficult to be certain exactly how long the dirham fragments may have circulated before deposition. Given the continued importance of Torksey as one of the main towns in Lincolnshire in the 10th and 11th centuries, some continuity of activity on the site, rather than a one-off occupation in 872–3, can certainly not be ruled out, but the site of the late Anglo-Saxon *burh* was at a separate location slightly to the south of the Viking site, and it is possible that all of the Viking/Anglo-Scandinavian finds represent a very condensed period of activity consistent with the winter camp of 872–3. However, the datable association with the *micel here* provides useful corroboration for the introduction of both highly fragmented hack-silver and cubo-octahedral weights by the early to mid-870s, which has direct relevance for the interpretation of the ARSNY finds.

On leaving Torksey, the *micel here* moved to Repton in Derbyshire, site of a major monastery with close associations with the Mercian royal house, and established a winter camp there in 873–4. The site has been investigated by Martin Biddle and Birthe Kjølbye-Biddle (1992; 2001), and included a mass grave, which yielded five pennies of the

Lunettes type, consistent with a deposition date in the early 870s (Biddle *et al.* 1986b). There were also several individual burials associated with Viking activity on the site, and one of these also contained five pennies of the same period, as well as a gold finger-ring (Biddle *et al.* 1986a; Biddle and Kjølbye-Biddle 2001, 65). A handful of other Anglo-Saxon and Frankish coins from the site are all either too early or too late to be associated with the *micel here* (Grierson *et al.* 1986; Biddle *et al.* 1986a). The site as a whole has not yielded a substantial assemblage of coins, weighing equipment and bullion comparable with those found at ARSNY and Torksey, although a few larger objects including an axe and two swords had earlier been recovered from the site, and three copper-alloy pins of comparable date were found during the Biddle excavations, one in the defensive ditch (for further discussion of the defences see p. 89), and two in later contexts (Biddle and Kjølbye-Biddle 2001, 58–9). However, the comparative rarity of small finds at Repton almost certainly reflects the different circumstances of the recovery of material from the sites rather than a different character of occupation. The Torksey and ARSNY assemblages have largely been recovered through metal detecting in open agricultural sites whereas fieldwork at Repton did not involve metal detectors and was constrained by the modern use of the site by the churchyard (which will also have led to some disturbance of the archaeology in some of the excavated areas) and Repton School. It should also be noted that comparison with the size of Torksey, ARSNY and Woodstown suggests that only a small proportion of the Repton camp was investigated, rather than the whole camp as interpreted by the excavators (see below, p. 89 for more detailed discussion). It is therefore unsurprising that much less material relating to exchange has been recovered from Repton, but that such as there is appears consistent with finds from ARSNY and Torksey.

The finds from these 9th-century sites contrast notably with the two important urban settlements of Dublin and York. In the latter case, the evidence for exchange reflects a more coin-based economy, including evidence of local coin production, in the form of dies and trial-pieces, as well as circulation in the form of a number of single finds (Pirie *et al.* 1986). This is because the excavated layers largely post-date the introduction of locally minted Anglo-Scandinavian coinage from the 890s onwards, which seems thereafter to have dominated exchange within the city itself, if not necessarily in the hinterland (Blackburn 2005; 2006; Williams 2009; 2011b; this volume, Chapter 5). The Coppergate excavations yielded only two weights of the oblate-spheroid type (type A according to the classification above) (Mainman and Rogers 2000, 2564) and no silver bullion. There are no weights or silver bullion from the recent Hungate excavations, although there is an ingot mould (Sf10175) from a possibly 10th-century pit backfill (Context 5205) (Nicky Rogers, pers. comm.). However, ingots were not exclusively used for bullion (see pp. 14–15), and this may relate to metalworking rather than to bullion exchange. The three hoards from the city itself deposited during the period of Viking rule (Coney Street, late 860s–870s; Walmgate, *c.* 915 and Coppergate, early 940s) contain only coins, as does one parcel of a hoard discovered 'Near York' in 2012, but another parcel found within a few metres of the other contained four ingot fragments, as did hoards from Bossall/Flaxton, Goldsborough, Bedale and the 'Vale of York', while a hoard from Selby (Graham-Campbell 2008) contained only intact arm-rings of Hiberno-Scandinavian character (see Williams, this volume, Chapter 3, for more detailed comparative discussion of the Yorkshire hoards).

Dublin also seems to have had a tightly controlled coin-based economy following the introduction of local minting in the mid–late 990s (Blackburn 2008), but prior to this there is clear evidence for a bullion economy in the form of a substantial corpus of at least 180 weights from Dublin (Wallace 1987; 2013), which pre-dates the minting of coinage in Dublin in the 990s. However, the interaction of coinage and bullion in Ireland in the 10th century is complicated (Sheehan 2007; Blackburn 2007b; Bornholdt Collins 2010), and the Dublin weights of the 10th century seem to reflect both more standardised design and a much more tightly controlled weight standard in the 10th century than appears visible in the 9th-century sites (Wallace 1987; 2013). As new excavations uncover more of the earlier layers of Viking Dublin (e.g. Simpson 2005; 2010), it will be interesting to see whether finds more comparable to ARSNY, Torksey and Woodstown emerge. Another site at Annagassan, Co. Louth, may prove interesting in this respect. So far only preliminary excavations have taken place, but as at ARSNY and Torksey more extensive geophysical surveys suggest more extensive occupation (Kelly 2015, 77–84). The Annagassan site has been identified as the historically documented *longphort* (see below, p. 89) of Linn Duachaill. In terms of items of monetary significance, initial investigations have so far revealed only two pieces of hack-silver (Kelly 2015, 83; Williams 2015, 95–6), but it is important to recognise that the finds from ARSNY and Torksey have largely been recovered through metal detecting, which was not used in the investigation of the Annagassan site.

Bullion and monetary economies

The period *c.* 870–95 saw major changes in monetary economy, both to the north and the south of the Humber. To the north, the received wisdom is that the copper-alloy styca coinage characteristic of pre-Viking Northumbria ceased to be produced around the beginning of this period, probably immediately after the deaths of the rival Northumbrian rulers Osberht and Ælle in 867, although the blundered anonymous coinage found in late Northumbrian hoards, and at ARSNY, cannot be precisely dated. It is therefore possible that production continued into the late 860s or even possibly the early 870s, although there is currently no clear indication that this was the case, and further detailed work comparing the late blundered issues is required to resolve this question one way or the other. South of the Humber, the base-silver Lunettes coinage of Alfred and Burgred was replaced by a pure silver coinage under Alfred and Ceolwulf II, *c.* 874–75, with a further reform undertaken by Alfred following the disappearance of Ceolwulf II from the historical record, *c.* 879–80 (Archibald 1991, 286; Blackburn and Keynes 1998; Blackburn 2003, 205–14). Alfred's London monogram type was produced at the time of this reform, celebrating the extension of West Saxon authority over London, and a Two-Line type was also introduced, which lasted for the remainder of Alfred's reign. Coins in the names of Æthelred and Oswald were issued in East Anglia from *c.* 870, and a short-lived coinage in the name of Athelstan II (Guthrum) from *c.* 880, and substantive 'national' coinages were introduced by Viking rulers in both Northumbria and East Anglia from *c.* 895 (Blackburn 2005; 2006). Viking coins imitating the designs and inscriptions of Alfred's coinage probably preceded these 'national' coinages, and although these are normally attributed to the midlands, filling in the gap between East Anglia and Northumbria, it is just as likely that some of these imitations were also produced to the north of the Humber (Williams 2011a, 48–9). However, since all of the types which were commonly imitated post-date Alfred's second reform, there is no reason to suppose that any imitative coinage was available in Northumbria prior to 880, unless the blundered stycas already mentioned fall into this category. The coin stock potentially available in Northumbria in the mid-870s thus consisted of stycas and pre-reform Southumbrian Lunettes which had not yet disappeared from circulation, together with the first reformed coinage of Alfred and Ceolwulf II, and imported Islamic dirhams and Carolingian deniers. All but the last of these are represented at ARSNY.

This coincides with a period in which hack-silver was becoming a standard means of exchange in Scandinavia, reflecting an increasingly widespread bullion economy. Bullion met many of the requirements of a monetary economy in that it could be used for the core functions of means of exchange, measurement of value and storage of wealth, lacking only the guarantee of value of a more fully monetised economy. Despite this, and despite the lack of standard-sized monetary units of silver, the value of silver could effectively be regulated by the market through a combination of quantity, measured by weight, and quality, measured by various forms of testing, including the standard 'pecking' apparently introduced around this time (see above). This meant that weights of silver could be used as a unit of account, whether or not the silver was physically present. Furthermore, the bullion economy was if anything more flexible than the coin economies of the time for physical payments, since between them hack-silver and ingots provided a much wider range of effective 'denominations' than coinage almost completely restricted to the penny in England, the denier on the Continent, and the dirham in the Islamic world and Scandinavia.

This bullion economy can now be clearly observed in three separate coin-dated contexts from the early to mid-870s in England, in the Croydon hoard (871–2), the Torksey assemblage (872–3) and the hoard and assemblage from ARSNY (*terminus post quem* 874–5). The greater fragmentation in the latter two cases may represent a chronological development, but more probably reflects the selection criteria of the person who deposited the Croydon hoard, as hack-silver from this period also typically shows less fragmentation in hoards than in site finds (Hårdh 2008). Further evidence for the same economy, perhaps slightly earlier, may be found in the assemblage from Woodstown and in the hoard and assemblage from Llanbedrgoch, as well as from the assemblage from the River Blackwater. The presence of Islamic coins and also of sub-Islamic weights common in Scandinavia suggests that the driving force for this economic model came from southern Scandinavia. At the same time, the presence in Scandinavian contexts of the decorated lead weights more characteristic of Viking Britain and Ireland, together with the spread of pecking (apparently introduced by Vikings in England between *c.* 875 and *c.* 890), indicates that economic influences travelled in two directions.

Other uses for bullion: social economies and commodity money

The monetary value of silver was not based on silver as a purely neutral medium of exchange. Silver and gold were valued for their use in a non-monetary economy which went back far beyond the Viking Age. Within this broad 'status' economy, precious metal was used for the visual display of wealth, in the form of jewellery, decorative weapon fittings, etc., and the transfer of wealth in the form of precious metal was central to a number of different categories of 'social' exchange, including tribute payments, gift exchange and the rewarding of followers with visible symbols both of the wealth of the lord or chieftain making the gift and of the ongoing relationship between lord and follower. Ring-giving, and the giving of ornate swords, are recurrent symbols of lordship, but rings also had a role in judicial fines and religious ritual (Samson 1991; Gaimster 1991; 2007; Graham-Campbell 2001b; Kruse 2007; Sindbæk 2011; Williams 2007; 2011b). A much-quoted passage in the travel account of Ibn Fadlan makes it clear that the same transaction between Arab and Rus traders could be seen as monetary purchase from the Arab perspective, and a form of barter or exchange in which silver dirhams were seen as a conveniently pre-measured commodity for the production of high-status jewellery from the Rus perspective. Weight-adjusted jewellery effectively bridged this gap, and the standardised weights of Permian rings reinforce Ibn Fadlan's account of neck-rings being produced from set numbers of dirhams, even if the numbers in his account seem exaggerated (Gaimster 1991, 117; Hårdh 2007a; Graham-Campbell 2007, 215–16; Williams 2007, 182; 2011b, 353).

This role of silver as commodity draws attention to a further category of economy, which is the so-called commodity economy. It seems likely that only a small proportion of exchanges, especially in the early Viking Age, were carried out with the involvement either of coin or of any other form of precious metal. This does not mean that all exchanges were based around barter, which relies on both parties to a transaction wanting what the other has to offer, and may require renegotiation of the relative value of different commodities on every occasion in response to supply and demand. Instead, different commodities could function as 'commodity money', fulfilling the various monetary functions described above, but with values clearly founded in their utility. Clearly some commodities had greater potential for the long-term storage of wealth (iron, grain or textiles over fish, for example) but anything which could be traded on, rather than being used/consumed by the parties to an exchange, had the potential to be commodity money, as long as it could be measured in regular units. These were self-defining in some cases (livestock, hides, etc.), but measured units of capacity or weight meant that a wide variety of commodities could in fact function as commodity money (Skre 2011b; Gullbekk 2011a; Gullbekk 2011b; Williams 2011b, 352; Critch *et al.* 2019; Hayeur Smith 2019).

Against this background, silver or even gold bullion was effectively just another form of commodity money, as long as there was a demand for precious metal. The fact that those sites (as opposed to hoards) which feature finds of coins, hack-silver and weights often also show evidence of metalworking reflects this. Speculation as to whether hack-silver should be seen as a means of exchange or raw material for production to a great extent creates a false dichotomy, as it could be both at the same time, as could a coin, or even an intact piece of jewellery. Furthermore, silver droplets and other products of casting appear not only in site assemblages such as ARSNY, Torksey and Woodstown, but also in hoards, in which they clearly functioned as very small items of bullion alongside cast ingots and hack-silver (Graham-Campbell 2011, 193; Sheehan 2014, 196, 206–7). Although some hoards, such as Talnotrie, can be interpreted as metalworking hoards, the presence of casting waste in the Cuerdale hoard suggests that the boundaries between silver production and silver bullion are more blurred than has sometimes been recognised. This is particularly apparent in a crucible melt from Kaupang in Norway, comprised of dirham fragments and other hack-silver, sufficiently melted in the crucible for the objects to have fused, but not so far melted that the original items are no longer discernible (Blackburn 2007c, 32–4). One may reasonably assume that this is a failed piece of preparation for metalworking, yet the result is a perfectly functional item of bullion.

This approach to silver bullion has implications for other metals in this period. Gabor Thomas (pers. comm.) has suggested that the economic function of iron hoards in the Viking Age would benefit from further study. The presence of undiagnostic pieces of iron at ARSNY and other sites may also in some cases represent the presence not only of complete objects now corroded beyond recognition, but also of ingots or broken items awaiting re-use. Of more interest for ARSNY, however, the interplay of currency and commodity should also influence how we consider both stycas and undecorated lead weights. A focus on silver economies has meant that numismatic commentators, including the present writer, have tended to assume that stycas would be of little or no interest to the Vikings. However, if we consider the stycas firstly against the background that widespread familiarity both with silver coin and hack-silver now appears to have been only a comparatively recent development in Scandinavian society by the 860s and 870s, and secondly the importance of copper as a raw material for bronze and other copper-alloy ornaments, fittings and utensils, then stycas would certainly have had a value as a commodity, while their broadly standardised weight meant that they could perfectly well have functioned as a form of commodity money. As noted above, stycas are recorded not only from Torksey and ARSNY, but from the Talnotrie hoard and the Kiloran Bay burial, as well as from several examples, provenanced and unprovenanced, as insets for decorated lead weights. Stycas are also recorded in small numbers, both as coins and as weight-insets in Viking contexts in Scandinavia and the Baltic (Skaare 1976, 44–5, 144; Williams 1999, 23–4; 2011b, 354; Bogucki 2009). Furthermore, the parcel of stycas found at Bamburgh in 2004, terminating in coins of Osberht, together with the anonymous blundered issues, was found along with the central section of a folding balance (DCMS 2006, 184), indicating very clearly that at the point of deposition they were measured by weight rather than face value. While there is no clear indication whether they were deposited by an Anglo-Saxon or a Viking, either is possible for such a late deposition, while there is nothing to indicate an association between coins and balances across the wider history of Northumbrian stycas. One may also note the presence of a copper-alloy ingot in association with the ARSNY hoard (see p. 15), and of copper-alloy ingots at Torksey (Blackburn 2011, 235–6) and in the River Blackwater assemblage (Bourke 2010, 46). This also falls into a wider pattern of circulation of copper-alloy ingots in Viking-Age Scandinavia, and especially of brass ingots (e.g. Warnke 1992–93; Sindbæk 2003), brass also being the most common alloy of which stycas are made.

Similarly, lead also contributed to bronze-making, in addition to items produced purely in lead, such as a lead 'Valkyrie' figure from the site (see below, pp. 58–9), and the decorated weights. While it is not necessary to interpret the undecorated weights as anything more than simple weights, it is possible that they may, as measured units of a useful commodity, have had an additional function as a form of low-value commodity money. Lead ingots are also known in Viking contexts. It may, of course, be argued that iron, copper alloy and lead at ARSNY and similar sites need not have any function in exchange, and that their purpose relates purely and simply to production, and a number of base-metal items from ARSNY are interpreted straightforwardly as production waste (see below, p. 48). However, it is in their value as materials for metalworking that the potential value of these materials as bullion/commodity money depends. The possibility that copper alloy and other base metals may have functioned as bullion must therefore be considered (Williams 2011b, 354; 2015, 113–14; Blackburn 2011, 236), although a fuller investigation of the possibility is needed before this can be accepted as more than a hypothesis.

If non-precious metals may have had a role as low-value bullion, worked Insular items of copper alloy may also have featured in the social exchanges discussed above. As recently noted by John Sheehan, although Insular metalwork in gilt copper alloy may have had 'little intrinsic or bullion worth, this may have been compensated for by its great artistic value. It was generally of a much higher quality than most contemporary Scandinavian ornament-types and this is what may well have made it of value in the Norse gift-exchange system, as well as its exotic nature.' There are over 500 such fragments from Norway, predominantly in female graves, and often featuring cut-up mounts and other ecclesiastical items recycled into brooches and other ornaments (Sheehan 2013, 818–19). Similar items are also found in Denmark, but on a much smaller scale, with the main focus for such material being south-western Norway (Wamers 1998).

ARSNY has produced numerous fragments of Insular jewellery and mounts, although as it is far from certain that these relate to exchange they have been listed by category in the following section rather than here. Many of these could easily have been lost in the process of recycling into the sort of ornaments found in Norway. Most notable amongst these is a splendid Irish harness mount, with parallels in Scotland and Norway as well as in Ireland itself, and James Graham-Campbell (see p. 64) suggests that this piece is particularly likely to have been lost at an intermediate stage between its original function as a harness mount and a new role as a brooch. Fragments of Insular and Carolingian metalwork are also a feature of the Torksey assemblage (Blackburn 2011, 230–3), and there is also a substantial group of cast and gilt copper-alloy mounts and other objects from Woodstown (Ó Floinn, with Bourke, 2014), while similar copper-alloy objects, and particularly mount fragments, make up a large proportion of the River Blackwater assemblage (Bourke 2010, 27–31, 37–71). The presence of these fragments in all four assemblages indicates that such fragmentation of Insular objects was common in Viking sites in Britain and Ireland in the late 9th and early 10th centuries. The fact that all of these assemblages also feature lead weights with decorative insets made of fragments of Insular metalwork (see above, p. 22) suggests that at least some of the individual fragments may also have been intended for this purpose. However, given that there is also evidence for metalworking in all four assemblages, and given the clear evidence for a taste for recycled Insular metalwork in jewellery in Scandinavia, it is likely that production of such jewellery was a feature of these sites, and that the acquisition of such 'objects of desire' for their value within a social rather than a bullion economy was one of the motivations for Viking raids on Britain and Ireland in this period (Sheehan 2013, 817–21).

Conclusion

Some of the interpretations above are necessarily speculative, but the recent burst of research activity on related issues in Scandinavia in this period, combined with the unprecedented nature and scale in Britain of the material now available from ARSNY and Torksey, means that it is possible to consider fundamental reinterpretations of the nature of exchange in the first wave of Viking settlement in England. A more flexible interpretation of the nature of exchange, based primarily on the ARSNY assemblage, appears to make sense of what had previously seemed to be a series of anomalies, including the presence of a balance in the Bamburgh hoard, and the presence of complete stycas in the Talnotrie hoard and the Kiloran Bay burial. The recent discovery of comparable assemblages at Llanbedrgoch, Torksey, Woodstown and the River Blackwater also suggests that ARSNY is not an isolated case.

The Woodstown report (Russell and Hurley, with Eogan, 2014) appeared as this one was in the final stages of preparation, while listing and interpretation of the finds from Torksey by Andrew Woods is ongoing. Once all of the data relating to all three sites are more readily available (and, in the case of Torksey, more complete), it should be possible to test the interpretations suggested here through more detailed comparisons. The steadily increasing corpus of single finds of related material from around the north of England studied by Dr Jane Kershaw provides a further point for future comparison.

What is clear in the meantime, however, is that activity at the ARSNY site had its focus at a key moment in the Viking settlement of Northumbria. Whether or not it was part of the primary settlement of 875, it cannot be much later, and it certainly stands at a point between the destruction of monetary status quo of pre-Viking Northumbria, and the period in the 890s when Viking rulers of Northumbria including Guthfrith, Siefredus and Cnut sought to enter the mainstream of European kingship, as well as monetary practice, by issuing Christian regal coinage. This is a period in which the economy of the later Viking Age was taking shape, but in contrast to the decade immediately prior to permanent settlement, the period *c.* 875–95 is poorly served by hoards, especially within the kingdom of Northumbria (see Williams, this volume, Chapter 3), while the excavated contexts from Anglo-Scandinavian York represent a later phase of monetary activity. ARSNY thus currently provides a unique source of information on the nature of exchange in northern England around the time that the Viking invaders switched from migratory warfare (see pp. 129–31) to permanent settlement. At the same time, as discussed above, the dating of the site coincides with a period of two-way influences between Viking Britain and Scandinavia on the character of metal-based exchange. This means that while Northumbria itself may have reverted to mainstream Anglo-Saxon monetary practice within a couple of generations, the phase of monetary interaction and experimentation represented by ARSNY and comparable sites had a more lasting influence on the wider Viking world, and ARSNY is thus of international rather than purely local or even national significance for our understanding of the development of exchange systems in the Viking world.

Other Insular and Anglo-Scandinavian artefacts
Nicola Rogers

Context of finds

The artefacts described and discussed here are from a number of discrete groups of material found at different times: most by the detectorists, some in YAT's excavations. Their varying origins can be tracked through reference to their small find numbers, which were allocated in batches. Sfs78–131 are the so-called 'hedgerow finds': metal-detected items, principally of iron, which had been discarded at the field edge before archaeologists became involved. Artefacts from YAT's excavation of the first two trenches, in 2004, include sfs160–240. Five objects brought in by the detectorists in the summer of 2004 are numbered sfs241–46. Artefacts from YAT's 2005 excavations comprise sfs250–910. Further finds from the detectorists include sfs911–1223; these were examined in February 2008, and represent the latest set of artefact discoveries to be included here.

Early Anglo-Saxon material (Fig. 7)

All of this material was metal detected. It included fragments of two possible great square-headed brooches (sfs1144 and 1106) and of two cruciform brooches (sfs1075 and 1109), all identified by Dr Cath Mortimer; a copper-alloy pinhead (sf1110) identified by Penelope Walton Rogers; and a copper-alloy wrist or sleeve clasp (sf1149). In addition to these personal items, a lead-alloy plug, sf1132, possibly from an early Anglo-Saxon cremation urn, was found during metal detecting.

Great square-headed brooches

Sf1144 is probably part of a catch-piece from a great square-headed brooch; the obverse depicts the mask of a human face, a feature characteristic of Hines Group IV great square-headed brooches (Hines 1997, 48–58). Of the five brooches Hines includes in this group, three have masks forming side and terminal lobes on the foot plate (*ibid.*, 50); Hines suggests that these masks are characteristically Scandinavian (*ibid.*, 57). The Group IV brooches in Hines' study were recovered from Lincolnshire, Leicestershire and Suffolk.

A perforated and decorated disc (sf1106) which has one edge bent is possibly a roundel from a great square-headed brooch. Decorative roundels or discs were applied to brooches belonging to several of Hines' groups, including Groups II, XVI and XVII (Hines 1997, 13–138). Hines notes finds of brooches of Group XVII from Yorkshire at Thornborough Pasture near Catterick and also from Flixborough (Evans and Loveluck 2009, 3–4).

Great square-headed brooches as a type originated in Scandinavia in the 5th century, but derivatives of the form had appeared in Kent and the Saxon and Anglian zone of England by the early 6th century and were a form worn by women (*ibid.*, 1).

Cruciform brooches
Catherine Mortimer

Fragments of two cruciform brooches were identified. Only a small portion of sf1075 remains, from the area at the base of the bow to the top part of the animal head. The poor surface condition means that it is difficult to see some of the details. The catch at the back was broken and mended, using an additional copper-alloy plate and rivets, now also broken. Traces of gilding are visible, particularly within the deeply recessed areas of the floral motif and parts of the lappet.

The extant lappet indicates that this must be either a Mortimer Type D or Type Z brooch. The floral motif between the lappets is unusual amongst cruciform brooches, but there is a close parallel from Norton (Cleveland), grave 22 (Sherlock and Welch 1992, fig. 8), although on sf1075 the petals are arranged diagonally, rather than perpendicularly as on the Norton example. The Norton example is a well-developed Type Z4 brooch which means it has elements typical of cruciform brooches but with a head plate more closely resembling that of square-headed brooches. The lappets on sf1075 are poorly preserved and, on this basis, it seems equally possible that they may have been of the highly developed zoomorphic form seen on Type Z brooches or the rather simpler form seen on many Type D brooches. However, the presence of gilding means it is more likely that this is a Type Z brooch, and that the lappets may, with a little imagination, be compared to the 'creeping animal' style of lappet seen on many Type Z brooches. This is normally seen as a late form (6th century), which the association with a Frankish belt set from Norton, grave 22, would tend to confirm.

Part of the head plate and most of the bow are preserved on sf1109. The bow has multiple lines running top to bottom, with a round boss on the top of the medial ridge. Unusually, on each side towards the edge of the bow, one of the lines runs uninterrupted into the flat area of the head plate, ending in a curl abutting another round boss. Above the head plate boss, there is a small piece of curved ornament which shows signs of wear. This could result from heavy use, but the curved ornament is very low down on the head plate compared with most brooches and the head plate would have had a very truncated appearance. Both the bosses are quite simple designs, one with a central ring-and-dot punch-mark, one with a large central dot surrounded by smaller dots. Further punch-marking on the bow ridges seems to be intended to produce segmentation of the ridges (thus resembling beading on wire), although this was not done with any precision. The pin is not extant but would have pivoted between the two pin lugs. There appears to be a small hole in the casting towards the edge of the head plate. The zoomorphic ornament shows poor symmetry.

This fragment could be either a zoomorphic cruciform brooch (Type Z) or a square-headed brooch. Amongst these brooch types, heavily ridged bows and zoomorphic detail within the wings of the head plate are common but there are no examples that closely resemble sf1109. The form of the head plate, particularly the arrangement of the panelling, seems slightly more likely to be related to cruciform brooches, including an example from Sleaford (Lincolnshire), grave 50 (Thomas 1887, pl. XXIII, fig. 1). Heavy ridging can be seen in several Type Z cruciform brooches including Empingham II (Rutland), grave 73 (Timby 1996, fig. 126), although it is much more neatly executed than on sf1109. A Hines Group XXII square-headed brooch from Driffield (East Yorkshire) is a rare example of bow ridges running into the head plate area although there are no other points of comparison (Hines 1997, pl. 82a). On the basis of the style of ornament, this brooch is likely to be 6th century.

Wrist clasp

One of a pair of copper-alloy wrist or sleeve clasps, sf1149 is an almost complete plate, having a wavy rear edge, a decorated bar, and fastening hooks on the other edge. These clasps originated in Scandinavia where they were worn by both sexes (Walton Rogers 2007a, 123), but in the Anglian region of Britain, in which they became a standard garment fastener, they were used almost exclusively by women on the ends of the sleeves of their inner dresses (*ibid.*, 123, 154). They were in use from the end of the 5th century to perhaps the third quarter of the 6th century (*ibid.*, 177, 184). This example seems to be a Hines Type B20 (Hines 1984, 92–3), believed to date to the 6th century. Although typically found in cemeteries, wrist clasps were easily lost and occur in non-

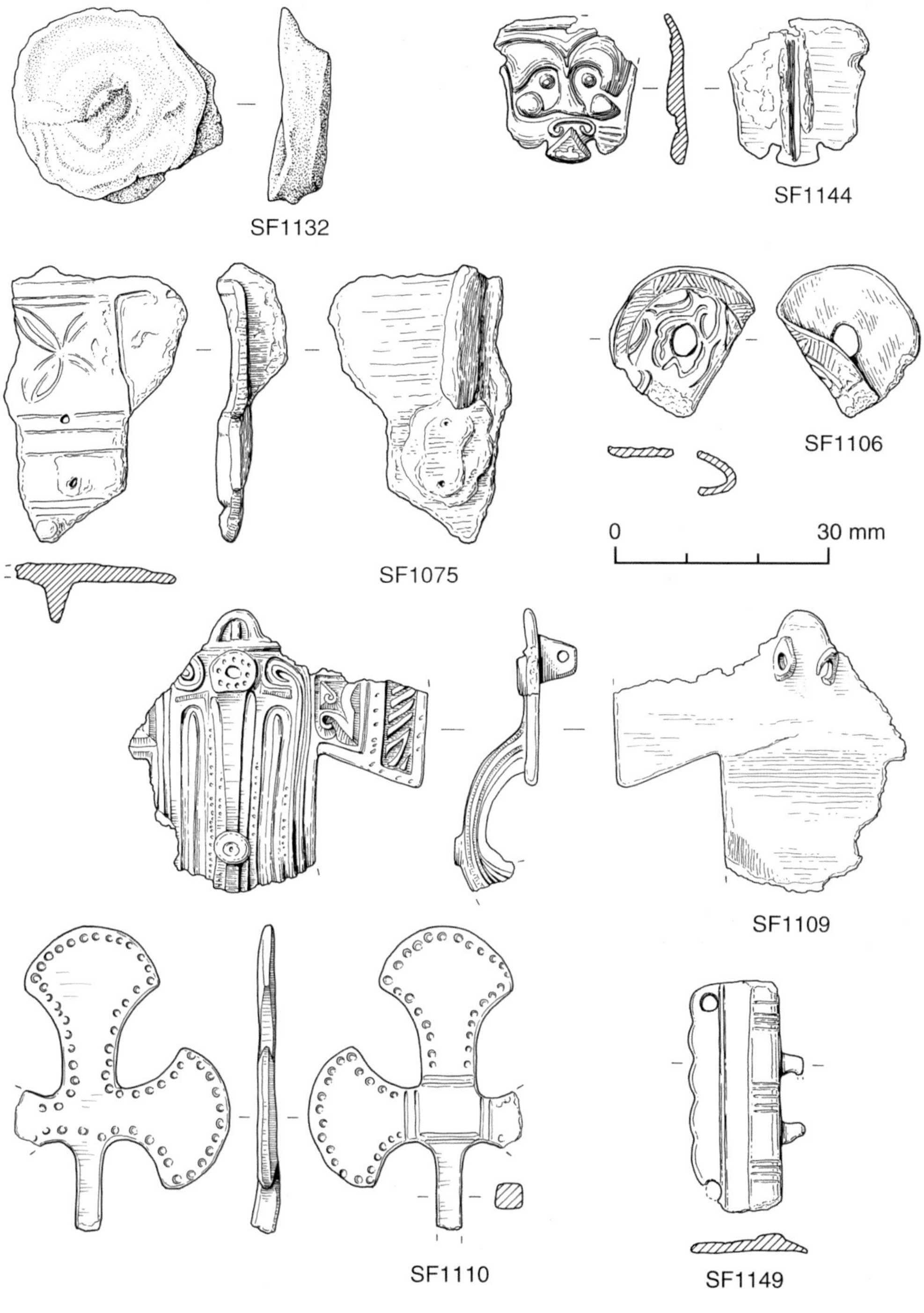

Figure 7 Early Anglo-Saxon material: fragments of two possible great square-headed brooches (sfs1144 and 1106) and of two cruciform brooches (sfs1075 and 1109); a copper-alloy pinhead (sf1110); a copper-alloy wrist or sleeve clasp (sf1149); a lead-alloy plug, possibly from a cremation urn (sf1132). © York Archaeological Trust

burial contexts; for example, five were recovered at the site of a farmstead at Orton Hall, near Peterborough (Howe and Mackreth 1996, 103–4).

Copper-alloy pin
Penelope Walton Rogers

Sf1110, a trefoil-shaped object with stamped decoration on front and back, almost certainly represents the head of an Anglian woman's garment pin. Trefoil-headed pins were originally grouped by Ross with cross-headed pins of the later 6th to mid-7th century (Ross 1991, I, 241), but it can be argued that this type more naturally belongs with trefoil-headed brooches of the later 5th to early 6th century (Penn and Brugmann 2007, 24–5, 58, 69–70), and with other types of pin with a flat head and a shaped outline. There is an example of a pin with a similar profile, and with stamped decoration on front and back, from the cemetery at West Heslerton, North Yorkshire, grave 8, where it was found with brooches dated to the period from the late 5th to the third quarter of the 6th century (Haughton and Powlesland 1999, I, 103 and II, 7). The flat plane and crescentic terminal is also reminiscent of a gilt pin from the cemetery at Sleaford, Lincolnshire, grave 95, found with metalwork of similar date (Thomas 1887, 394, pl. XXIV). The Sleaford and West

	Number of small finds	Weight in grams
Copper-alloy waste	5	16
Ironworking slag	12	4818
Lead object/waste	31	372
Slag (not identifiable)	14	593
Stone	3	538
Vitrified furnace lining	4	158
White-metal sheet	1	2
Total	**70**	**6497**

Table 6 Metalworking waste

Heslerton pins are 150mm and 172mm long respectively, which confirms a date before the AD 560–80 watershed when pins shortened dramatically (Walton Rogers 2007a, 126). These long pins were exclusive to women and were probably used to fasten a shawl or head-veil (*ibid.*, 159–61).

Cremation urn plug

A lead-alloy plug sf1132 might derive from a 5th- to 6th-century cremation urn. At the Anglo-Saxon cemetery at Cleatham, Lincolnshire, it was recorded that 1–2% of cremation urns had been deliberately perforated and plugged with molten lead (Leahy 2007a, 82).

Craftworking and manufacture

Metalworking
Catherine Mortimer

Litharge

Ten samples of litharge cake, found by the detectorists, weigh 1380g. 'Litharge' means lead oxide, but litharge cakes are produced in the cupellation process, when refining debased silver. The silver alloy is melted with lead and then heated in an oxidising atmosphere in a small flat hearth or container together with something absorbent, like crushed bone. The copper and other non-precious metals oxidise and are then combined with the lead compounds. The silver does not oxidise and remains as a silvery droplet or button on the surface, which can then be picked off. This leaves behind a flat-based, dense 'cake', sometimes with a noticeable dished central area where the silver had been.

These litharge cakes indicate that a small container, about 80 or 90mm in diameter, was used to contain the process. In one case, sf1044, there seems to be a trace of ceramic or unreacted lining attached to the underside. Unusually, some traces of silver are visible to the naked eye; these would normally have been scrupulously removed and remelted. The litharge is mainly grey in colour, but some items are greenish, suggesting higher levels of copper compounds.

Metalworking waste

About 6.5kg of metalworking and other waste was examined, identified and weighed (**Table 6**).

Five of the ironworking slag samples are part or whole smithing hearth bottoms, plano-convex lumps which are formed at the base of working smithing hearths, before being raked out. One of these, the unstratified sf223, is particularly large (2160g, maximum width 190mm) and is unlikely to have travelled far. Other ironworking slag is classified either as smithing slag lumps (broken-up smithing hearth bottoms) or just ironworking slag. No hammerscale was detected amongst the debris within sample bags, but specks of ferrous material on the large stone 'anvil' sf327 may relate to ironworking.

A further 593g of slag was not identifiable as being from a specific high-temperature process, although some of it may have been from non-ferrous metalworking, as it is pale in colour (sfs847 and 861). Of the four samples of vitrified furnace lining, one item (sf279) has copper-alloy deposits within it, but the others could have come from any of a number of high-temperature processes.

Five pieces of copper-alloy waste are probably casting waste. The 31 samples of lead waste or lead objects were typically very small, and most are probably spillages from casting, although it is impossible to tell whether some might be from lead-rich objects being heated, accidentally or otherwise. Some lead-rich items are more distinctive; sf303 seems to be a discarded casting of an object with a hollow interior, and sf828 is part of a small lead ingot. Other items have post-casting evidence. Sf778 is an irregular sheet, roughly curled up; sf826 is a thick strip with knife marks; and there is a spillage with possible toolmarks (part of sf779).

Also examined were three stone items and a white-metal sheet fragment. One of the stone samples (sf210) has vitrified 'glazing' on it, which shows contact with high temperatures, but it is not known what process this reflects.

Most of the different material types were scattered without distinct concentrations in particular trenches. For example, Trench 11 samples include copper-alloy, lead and ironworking waste, together with possible silver waste (sf266). However, large numbers of lead-waste small finds were found in backfills in Trench 14 and nearly all the fired clay (probably not related to metalworking) was found in Trench 22, amongst dumping contexts which also included burnt cobbles. There is no structural evidence for where the metalworking took place.

Several different types of metalworking took place on or around the site, in locations as yet undiscovered. Iron smithing took place in the vicinity, with the very large smithing hearth bottom suggesting a relatively large hearth. Copper-alloy casting and silver working seem to have been of lesser importance than lead working, which used casting and cold-working techniques.

Textile production
Penelope Walton Rogers

Fibre preparation

A possible textile processing spike of early medieval or medieval date (sf338) could derive from a wool-comb or a flax heckle (Walton Rogers 1997, 1727).

Spinning

A total of 28 eight spindle whorls, all of lead alloy, were recovered, all but one (sf287) by metal detecting (**Table 7**). A further 27 lead-alloy objects are probably weights rather than whorls, as they seem too crudely formed to perform as whorls. Eight of the spindle whorls are of biconical form which dates them to the 15th century or later; these are not discussed further.

Spindle whorls of truncated conical and hemispherical forms conform to Walton Rogers Type A (Walton Rogers 1997, 1736–7). This form arrived in Britain during the course of the 6th century and remained in use in Yorkshire, Lincolnshire and East Anglia until the 10th century (Walton Rogers 2014).

Walton Rogers Type B whorls include discoidal or annular forms, which were found in late 10th- to early 12th-century deposits at Coppergate (Walton Rogers 1997, 1737), but were also known in the Iron Age and Roman periods (Walton Rogers 2007a, 24–5). One of the discoidal whorls from the site (sf985) could be Roman, as these tended to have small perforations with a diameter of 4–6mm (*ibid.*, 23–4); sf985 has a perforation of 4.5mm.

Perforations of 4–6mm are typically Roman, 6–9mm are early and middle Anglo-Saxon, and 9–11mm are late Anglo-Saxon (Walton Rogers 2007a, 23–4); on this basis, the whorls of types A and B are represented equally in both the early–middle Saxon and late Saxon periods (**Table 8**).

The weights of the whorls reflect the types of yarns being produced, the lighter weights being used for finer quality yarns (**Table 9**). Fifty percent of the whorls fall into a weight range of 15–35g; at Brandon (Suffolk) 16 out of 19 whorls fell into this range (Walton Rogers 2014). Both of these sites were probably producing yarns of different quality for use in a variety of fabric-types. In contrast, at Flixborough, most of the whorls weighed between 10g and 20g (Walton Rogers 2009, 283); this is taken to indicate an emphasis on finer quality yarns, such as top-quality wool and linen textiles (Walton Rogers 2007b, 107).

Truncated conical/ hemispherical	Annular/discoidal	Biconical
14	6	8

Table 7 Forms of the spindle whorls

4–5.9mm	6–8.9mm	9–10.9mm	11mm+
2	8	8	2

Table 8 Diameters of the perforations of the spindle whorls

0–14.99g	15–34.99g	35–49.99g	50g+
3	10	6	1

Table 9 Weights of the spindle whorls

Woodworking **(Fig. 8)**

Nicola Rogers

An almost complete iron axe head (sf130) was metal detected. The T-shaped head, with a blade length of 126mm, would have been suitable for shaving the faces of planks, beams and boards (Morris 2000, 2108). It is a form of axe head used from the 8th century (*ibid.*) into the medieval period, and is one of the types of axe most commonly shown in medieval illustrations of carpentry (Goodall 1980, 23). Other woodworking tools include spoon bits (sfs305 and 762), one definitely of early medieval date, and a punch (sf389).

Leatherworking

Of two possible leatherworking awls (sfs766 and 814), one can be assigned stylistically to the early medieval period.

Multi-purpose tool

A stone hone assignable stylistically to the early medieval period was also found (sf285).

Household equipment

Nicola Rogers

Rotary quern

Part of a lower stone of a sandstone rotary quern, sf259 was excavated from a possible dump of industrial waste (**Fig. 9**). Rotary querns were widely used in the Anglo-Saxon and Anglo-Scandinavian periods (Ottaway and Rogers 2002, 2799), but declined in use following their prohibition in the 12th century (Biddle and Smith 1990, 882).

Structural ironwork

Structural ironwork found on the site comprises looped staples (sfs251 and 282) (**Fig. 9**), iron rivets (sfs379 and 817), and clench bolts and/or roves (sfs383, 384, 386 and 760). All, except for three of the bolts, came from early medieval features.

Keys

Two iron keys were recovered during the excavations, both from early medieval contexts. Sf260 is a small key for a fixed lock, probably from a casket (**Fig. 9**). It is fairly crudely made, the bow being formed simply from a flattened rounded end with a perforation. The rectangular bit is at right angles to the stem, the end of which projects beyond the bit. There is non-ferrous plating on the bow and stem. This form of key is known in the Roman period and a similar though much larger key of that period has been found in London (Manning 1985, 94, no. O58). Sf280 is a barrel padlock key with a looped upper end with suspension ring through it, and a two-pronged bit at right angles to the stem. This is similar to an Anglo-Scandinavian key found at Coppergate (Ottaway 1992, 676, no. 3663).

Box mounts **(Fig. 10)**

Possible box mounts of copper alloy with gilding were recovered during excavation of an early medieval pit (sfs276–7, 290). The fragments have been cut out of sheet, forming a continuous openwork band which, when studied *in situ*, appeared to form a corner, suggesting attachment to two sides of a rectangular vessel such as a box or chest. Strips form the top and bottom borders of the band, enclosing a pattern of triangles with pierced discs attached, linked together at the apexes of the triangles. At one end of the band there are rivet holes. The mounts may best be compared with those attached to a wooden bucket found during drainage works at Clonard, Co. Meath, Ireland (Youngs 1989, 121, no. 119). The Clonard bucket is one of eight that have been recovered previously from sites in

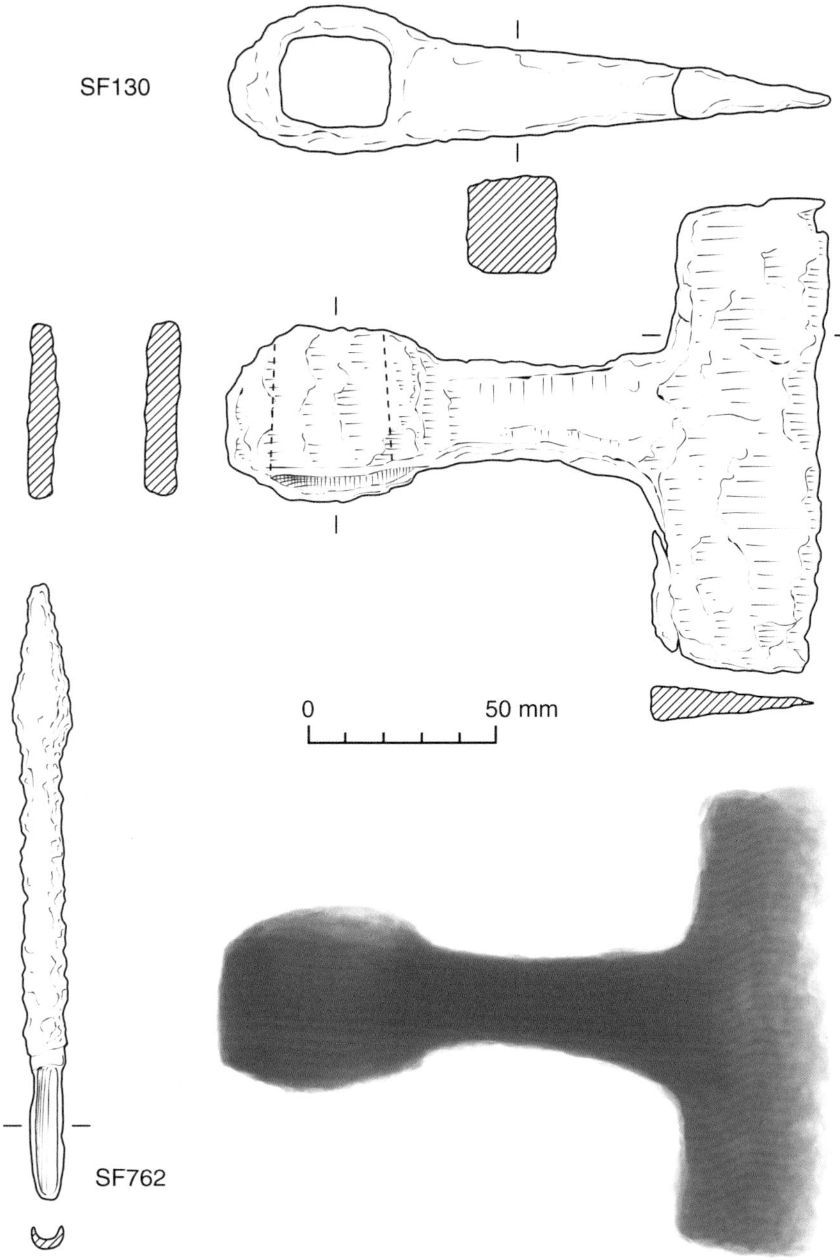

Figure 8 Woodworking tools: iron axe head (sf130) and spoon bit (sf762). © York Archaeological Trust

Ireland, all with engraved or openwork mounts, and dated to the 9th century (*ibid.*).

Drop handles

Two iron drop handles were found during the excavations, both in early medieval contexts. One (sf269), which has been made of a twisted strip, closely resembles handles found at Coppergate in Anglo-Scandinavian (Ottaway 1992, 646, nos 3502–5) and 11th- to 13th-century deposits (Ottaway and Rogers 2002, 2808, nos 11919–20). Sf278 is incomplete.

Dress accessories and personal items

Belt fittings

Strap-ends **(Figs 11–14)**

In addition to a fragment of handle or strap-end, made of iron, found by the detectorists when digging out the hoard (sf68), a total of 41 early medieval strap-ends were recovered at the site: of these one (sf900) was found during excavation, the others by detectorists. Apart from sf927, which is made of lead alloy, all are of copper alloy.

Anglo-Saxon and Viking-Age strap-ends have been divided into seven classes, A–G (Thomas 2003; 2004). The largest group here comprises sixteen which fall into Thomas Class A (Thomas 2003, 2–4). While the split attachment-end appears common to all strap-ends from this period, Class A strap-ends are characterised by the typical use of two or more rivets at the split end, the trilobate palmette motif below the rivets, convex-sided plates bearing decoration, and stylised animal head terminal (**Figs 11–12**).

The central fields of the upper plates of sfs918 and 939 both feature well-defined creatures, typical of Trewhiddle-style decoration (Wilson 1964, 21–35), which Thomas sub-groups into Class A, Type 1, the largest of the sub-groups of this Class (Thomas 2003, 2).

On sf918, interlace develops from the beast, and the decoration has been inlaid with a lead/silver metal. Features of

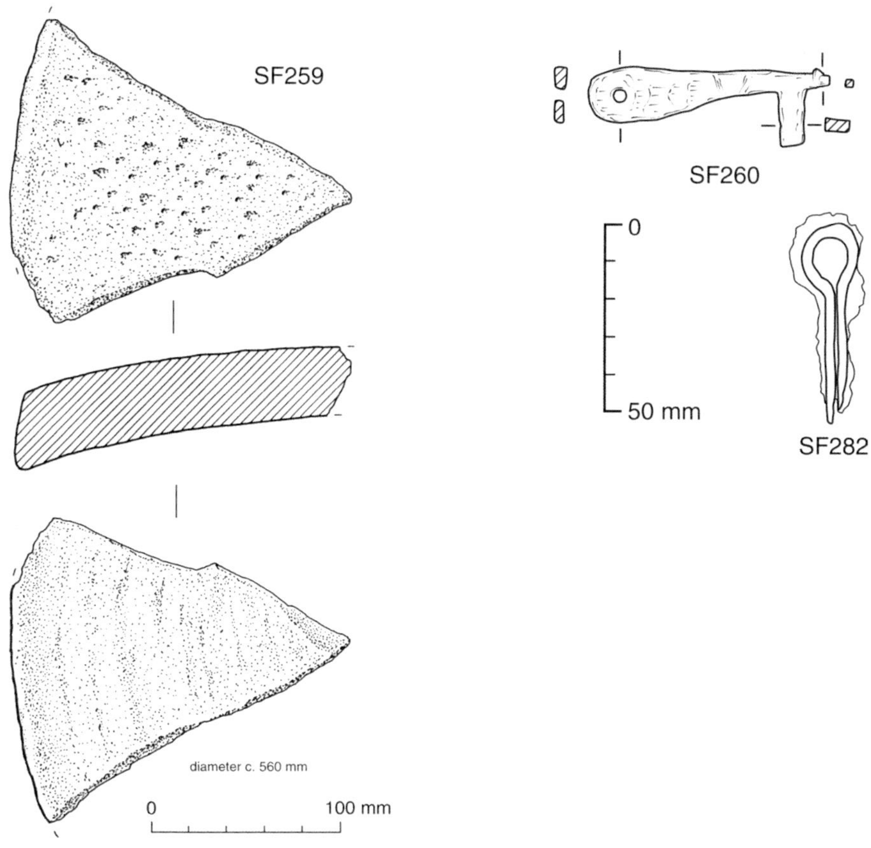

Figure 9 Household equipment: part of a lower stone of a sandstone rotary quern (sf259); looped staple (sf282); iron key (sf260). © York Archaeological Trust

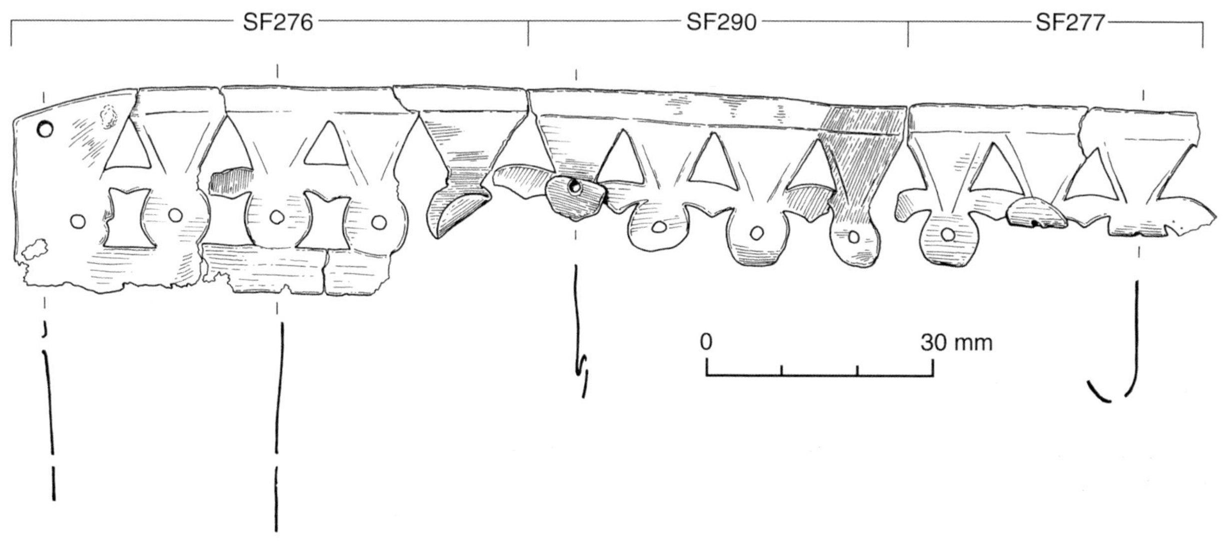

Figure 10 Possible box mounts of copper alloy with gilding (sfs276–7 and 290). © York Archaeological Trust

the zoomorphic terminal such as the comma-shaped ears and bulging eyes, and the palmette with interlaced tendrils, are paralleled on a strap-end from Coldingham Priory, Berwickshire (Wilson 1964, 32–3, fig. 3), and the strap-ends in the Poppleton (York) hoard, and appear geographically restricted to counties north of the Humber (Thomas 2006, 159–60).

Although slightly damaged and subsequently repaired, sf939 has the classic, crouching Trewhiddle-style animal with angled hip and splayed toes, and speckling on the body, as well as a beaded border.

Opposed serpent-like beasts occur on two strap-ends. On sf917, the thickest parts of their bodies curve round, almost touching the palmette below the rivets of the split end; their heads with mouths open, possibly swallowing the tips of their tails, look towards the zoomorphic terminal. The heads of the more slender snake-like creatures on sf946, however, look to the upper corners of the central field, which appears tightly sandwiched between a large but squat zoomorphic terminal and a compressed palmette. Similarly interlaced beasts – quadrupeds rather than serpents – can be seen on a strap-end from the multi-period site at Middle Harling, Norfolk (Margeson 1995a, 60, fig. 41, no. 68). The decoration on sf934 is unclear, but may feature another interlaced serpent-like body.

The decoration in the main fields of three strap-ends has been divided up into panels, and all have beaded borders.

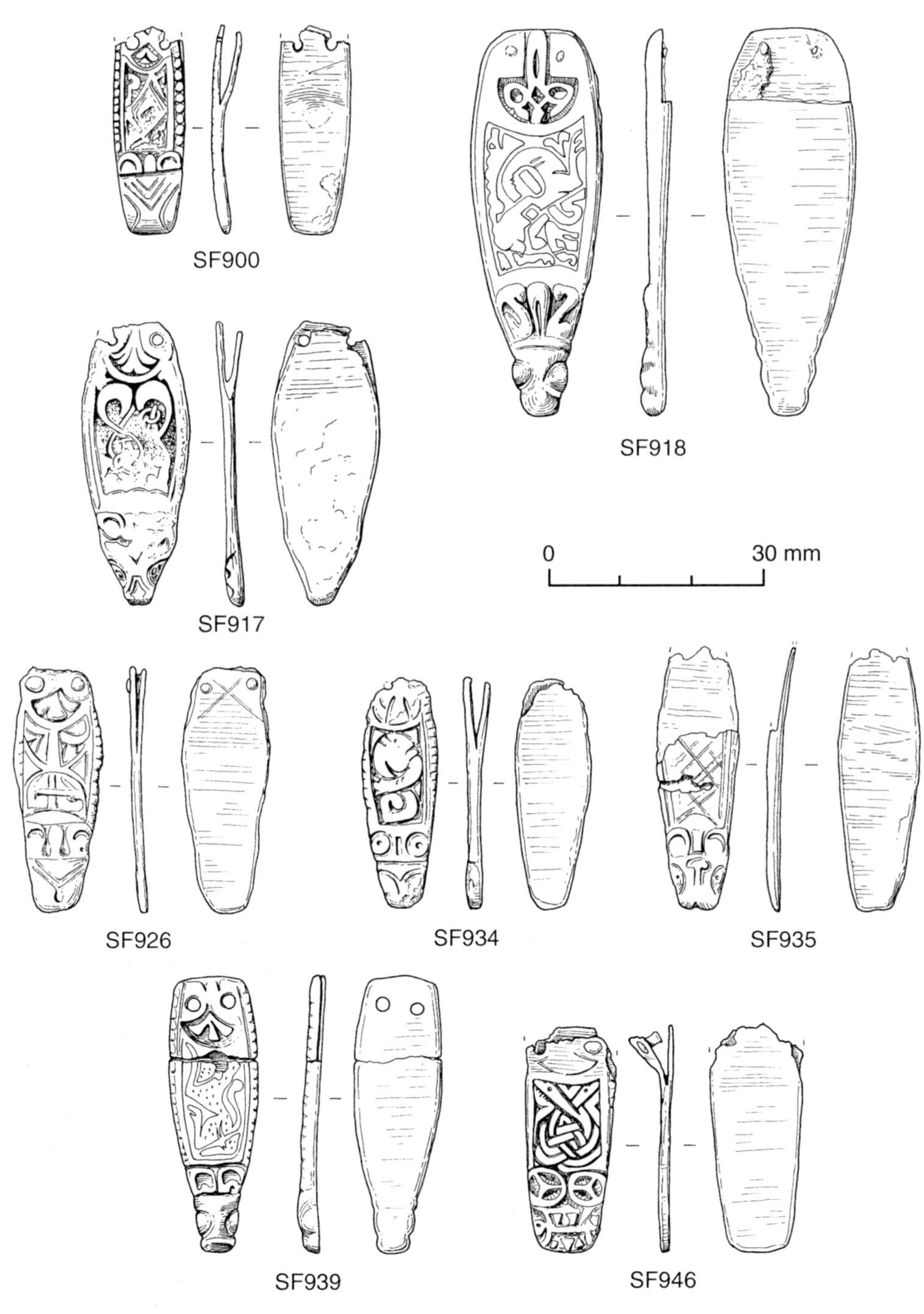

Figure 11 Thomas Class A strap-ends (sfs900, 917, 918, 926, 934, 935, 939 and 946). © York Archaeological Trust

The central field of sf926 is divided into three or four panels, some of which contain possible interlace; although incomplete, it is clear that sf947 also had decoration divided into panels. Both are very similar to two strap-ends found at Cottam in the East Riding of Yorkshire (Haldenby 1990, 56, nos 4.4, 4.5), although this trait of division into panels is thought to be more typical of strap-ends from south-east England (Thomas 2003, 2). Another example, sf900, bears traces of silver inlay. A possible strap-end fragment sf1076, which has no original edges, also appears to bear panels of interlace decoration.

Thomas Class A, Type 2, comprises strap-ends decorated with a diverse range of patterns, curvilinear and geometric (Thomas 2003, 2). Sf935 falls into this group: although part of the upper plate has broken away, sufficient survives to indicate that a cross-hatched pattern with possible gilding originally filled the central field. Similar decoration was noted on two strap-ends from Fishergate, York, one deriving from an 8th-century ditch or pit (Rogers 1993, 1350–1, nos 5317, 5321), and another from Brandon, Suffolk, where it was suggested that an origin in the 8th century may be as likely as one in the 9th (Riddler, with Evison and Rogers, 2014).

Other strap-ends fall into Class A, but are too worn for decoration to be interpreted (sfs930, 932, 933, 937), or too fragmentary to be identified further to type (sfs936, 938, 942).

Five strap-ends fall into Thomas Class B (**Fig. 12**), which differs primarily from Class A in having straight or slightly tapering sides, and a tendency to be narrower. Both sfs929 and 941 are decorated with interlace, unfortunately rather

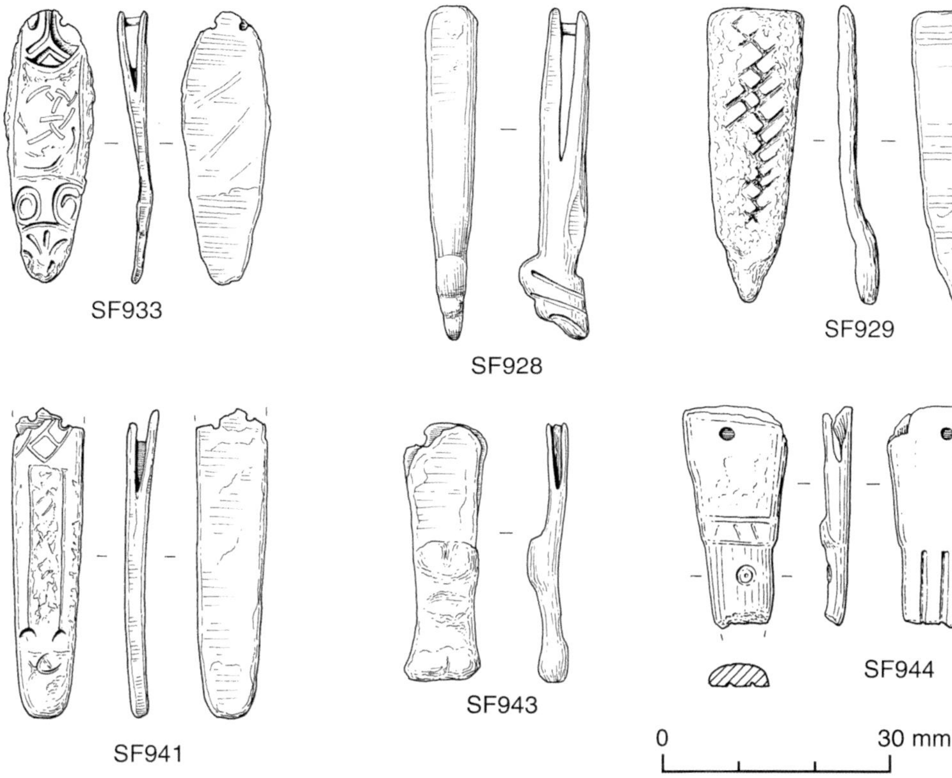

Figure 12 Thomas Class A (sf933) and Class B (sfs928, 929, 941, 943 and 944) strap-ends. © York Archaeological Trust

worn on both examples; that on sf929 appears to cover the entire area of the upper face that survives, and is similar to strap-ends from Fishergate, York (Rogers 1993, 1350–2, no. 5319), and Aggersborg, Jutland, Denmark (Graham-Campbell 1980, 52, no. 187). On sf941 the interlace fills a central field. These strap-ends seem to resemble those in Thomas Class B, Type 5, a form which Thomas suggests is typically found within the Danelaw (Thomas 2003, 5). Sf944 has a broad wedge-shaped split end with a single rivet, a collar, and a narrow incomplete body decorated with ring-and-dot; being fragmentary, it is less easy to categorise but seems most similar to others of this class. Sf943 seems largely complete, although the original surface of the upper end of the upper plate may have been lost. The sides of the strap-end are slightly concave, and the large animal head terminal stands proud of the upper plate. With its broad snout and faint transverse ridges, the head appears most similar to that on a strap-end thought to be from Staxton, North Yorkshire (Tweddle 1992, 1149, fig. 575b). The use of relief animal heads is typical of the Class B, Type 4, form (Thomas 2003, 5–6), examples of which have been found at Fishergate, York (Rogers 1993, 1351, no. 5320), and Cottam, East Riding of Yorkshire (Haldenby 1990, 56, no. 4.7; 1992, 28–30, no. 3.1).

Type 6 within Thomas Class B differs in having the animal head terminal displayed side on (Thomas 2003, 6), and sf928 takes this form. On these strap-ends, the terminal seems to provide the main decorative feature: on sf928, the profile of the head has a rounded ear, a brow above the eye and an extended snout with rounded end. Thomas notes that this form of animal head is diagnostic of the Ringerike and Urnes styles, and of 11th-century date (*ibid.*).

The second largest class of strap-end as identified by Thomas is his Class E, broadly defined as tongue-shaped, which he divides further into five types (Thomas 2004, 1–4). The second largest group found here, with fourteen examples, equates to Thomas Class E, Type 3, characterised by a median rib (**Fig. 13**). Some are decorated: sf919 has V-shaped notches running the length of the rib and around the edge, while sf924 has a double rib, and the whole of the upper plate is decorated with ring-and-dot motifs. The fragmentary sf949 has ring-and-dot running down the rib, and horizontal lines filling the fields to either side.

Of particular interest amongst this group is sf920, which is clearly an unfinished E3 strap-end: the tip is incomplete, and casting flash remains along one edge, indicating that this example was discarded due to poor casting. Sf1151 also appears to be an unfinished E3 strap-end. A lead-alloy Type E3 strap-end sf927 may be a pattern or model for casting such strap-ends in copper alloy (Leahy 2003, 143).

Thomas attributes these Class E strap-ends to an Anglo-Scandinavian metalworking tradition developing during the latter 9th and 10th centuries (Thomas 2000, 242). He notes that examples have been found in the Irish Sea region, at Peel Castle on the Isle of Man, and Cathedral Green, Carlisle (*ibid.*, 249), while at least nine others have been recovered within the Danelaw, mostly by metal detectorists (*ibid.*, fig. 23), including one from Cottam (Haldenby 1992, 31, fig. 3, no. 9). Outside Britain, two Class E strap-ends are known from Scandinavia, and another from Domburg, the Netherlands (Thomas 2000, 249).

Sf931 has suffered significant corrosion, but appears to be of Thomas Class F, defined as typically having a split end, zoomorphic terminal and double-sided decoration incorporating a roundel and interlace (Thomas 2004, 4). It has a single rivet through the split end, with a possible collar beneath, and straight sides with a perforated roundel at the

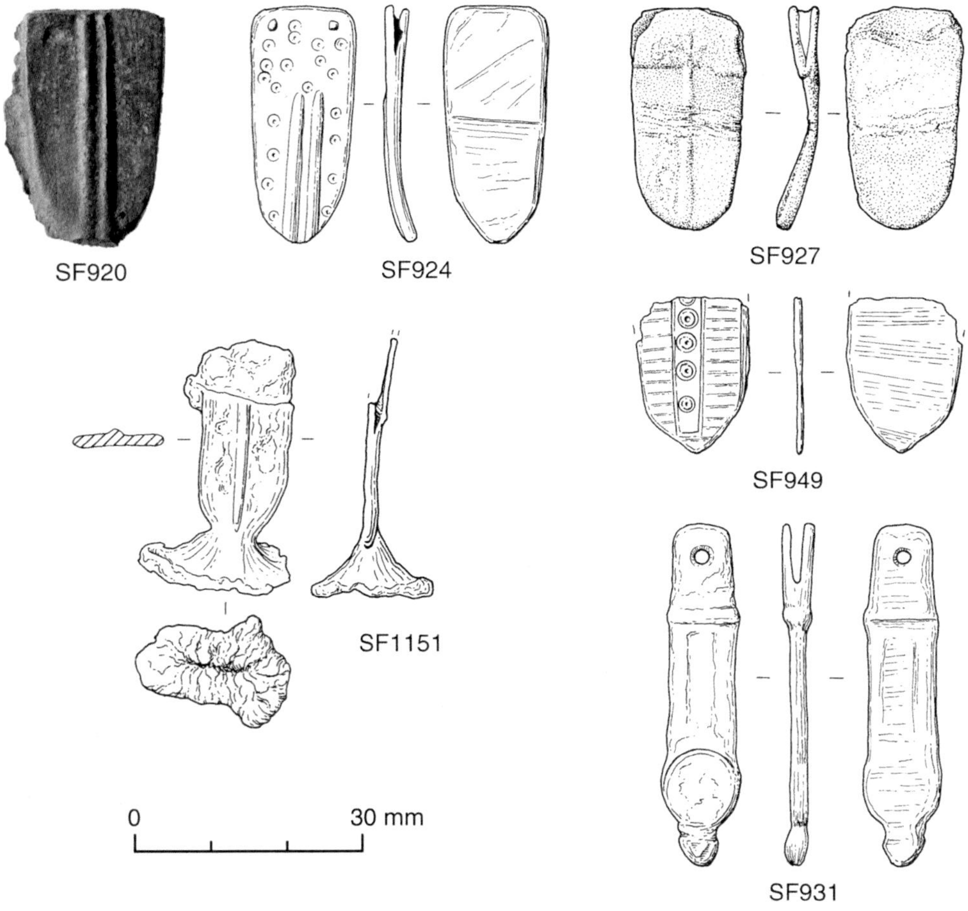

Figure 13 Thomas Class E (sfs920, 924, 927, 949 and 1151) and Class F (sf931) strap-ends. © York Archaeological Trust

lower end (visible on x-ray), with a rounded but featureless terminal at the tip. There are traces of decoration on both faces but this is impossible to identify, and any zoomorphic features on the terminal have also been lost. Thomas notes that this form is likely to originate from 9th-century Ireland, being subsequently adopted within the Irish Sea region by Scandinavian settlers, and possibly produced in 10th-century Dublin (Thomas 2000, 246). Examples have also been found within the Danelaw, however, as at Ashby-de-la-Launde, Lincolnshire; some of these seem sufficiently similar to strap-ends from Ireland and the Irish Sea region to indicate that they were manufactured in that area, a category into which sf931 may also fit. Thomas suggests copies were also made within the Danelaw itself, but that these tend to lack perforations through the roundels (*ibid.*, 249).

A number of unusual strap-ends appear to have few parallels (**Fig. 14**). Three may have been formed from other pieces of metalwork that have been cut down. Sf945 is rectangular, with a small split at the upper end, the upper part of which has broken off. It has raised mouldings with decorative notches at both ends, and two transverse grooves across the centre. The incomplete and sub-rectangular sf948 also has traces of a transverse groove; above this, part of the upper plate has broken away, and the lower plate has at least three rivet holes. Also sub-rectangular, but with a single central rivet at the split end, sf950 has four ring-and-dot motifs, one of which has been bisected by a deeply cut groove which possibly marks where a replacement split end had been created. This appears to be a strap-end which has been reworked and re-used.

Buckle plates (Fig. 15)

Two buckle plates (sfs925 and 952) are decorated with designs which are so similar to those found on known 9th-century strap-ends that they must surely have been made as companion pieces, forming matching sets, although the companion strap-ends themselves were not found. This has been identified as a fashion which is rarely seen in Anglo-Saxon contexts, but was widespread in Carolingian areas and the Viking homelands in the 9th and 10th centuries (Thomas 2000, 249). Sf925 has a split end with a square terminal which is decorated with a roundel of two concentric circles filled with grooving, one rivet going through the circles, a second being central within the circles. Below the terminal the plates expand towards the hinged end. The grooved decoration continues along the edges, the field between being filled with interlace, and terminates in two circles with central perforations, with triangular notches at the circumferences. The loops of the hinge are also grooved. This buckle plate with its interlace and roundels must have been designed to partner a Thomas Class F strap-end (see sf931 above). This buckle plate is very similar to examples found at Meols (Griffiths 2007, 62, pl. 8, no. 309) and Eynsham Abbey, Oxfordshire (Thomas 2001, 46, fig. 4.7c).

Made of pure silver but incomplete, sf952 is missing the buckle end of the upper plate. The other end of the upper plate is notched, with two rivets, and the panel below depicts a Trewhiddle-style backward-looking beast possibly with its own tail in its mouth.

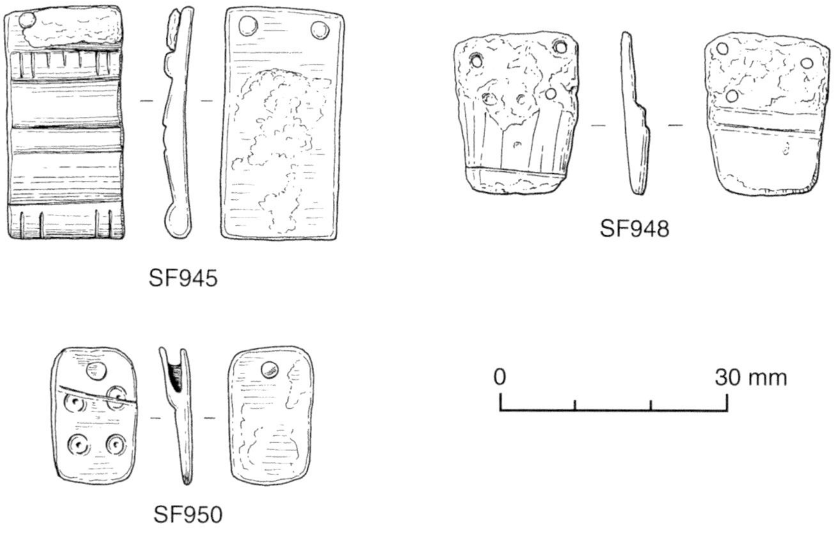

Figure 14 Unusual strap-ends with few parallels: sfs945, 948 and 950. © York Archaeological Trust

Strap guides **(Fig. 15)**

Nine strap guides – also known as belt slides – were recovered, sfs1153 (1), 1154 (1), 1155 (1), 1156 (3), 1157 (2), 1158 (1), including two which appear part made or unfinished. All are of copper alloy apart from sf1155, which is made of lead alloy. All the strap guides take the same basic form, being a sub-discoidal, oval or lozenge-shaped plate, with a central rib, and a projection to each side which is bent down and inwards forming an opening for attachment to a belt. Both unfinished examples are misformed, one with half of its lozenge-shaped plate missing (sf1158), the other with the rib placed off-centre (part of sf1156); both also have casting flashes still attached. The lead-alloy strap guide sf1155 may have been a pattern piece. It seems likely that these fittings were made alongside the Class E strap-ends, also decorated with a central rib and also possibly manufactured on the site.

Similar iron guides, including probable part-made examples, were recovered at Coppergate, York, all from mid-9th- to late 10th-century deposits (Ottaway 1992, 688–90, nos 3778–80, 3785–7). Another, of slightly different form, was found there in association with a spur, and was thought possibly to have been manufactured on the site in the Anglo-Scandinavian period (*ibid.*, 690, 698–704, figs 304, 306, no. 3832). Other possible functions include use on waist belts, or for fastening leggings or footwear (Goodall and Paterson 2000, 128). It has been suggested that these belt fittings are specifically Scandinavian, either being found in such contexts, or, if recovered without a context, decorated with motifs attributable to Viking influence (*ibid.*, 128–9);

Figure 15 Buckle plates (sfs925 and 952) and strap guides (sfs1153 and 1154). © York Archaeological Trust

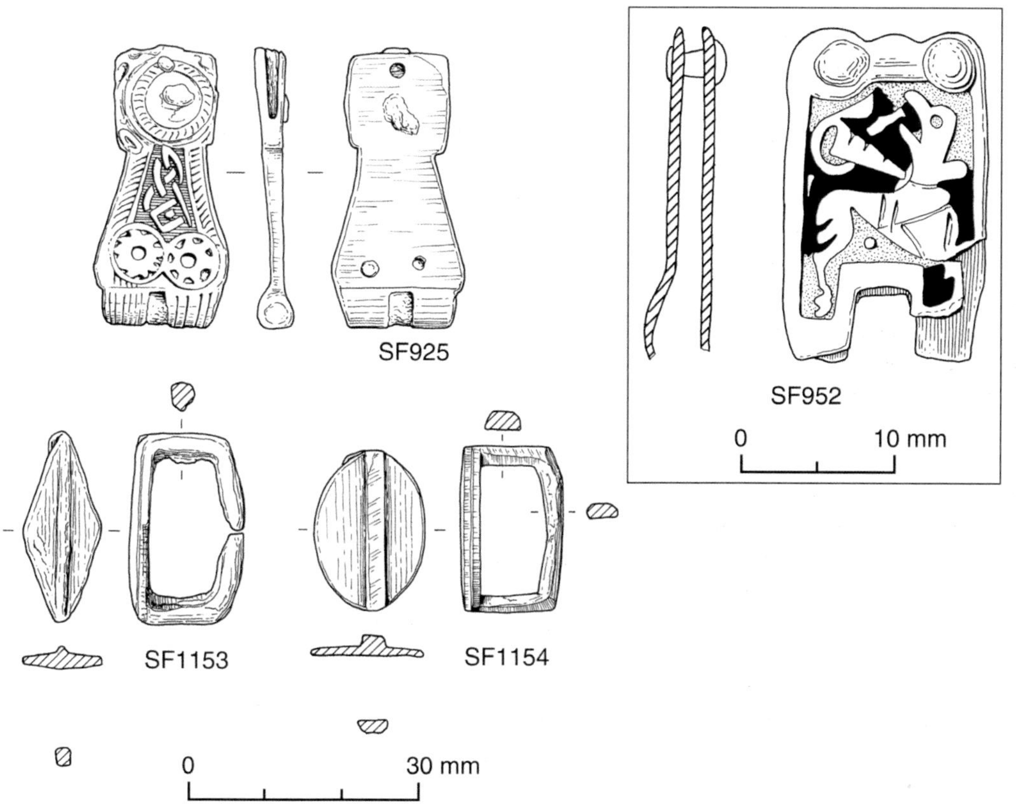

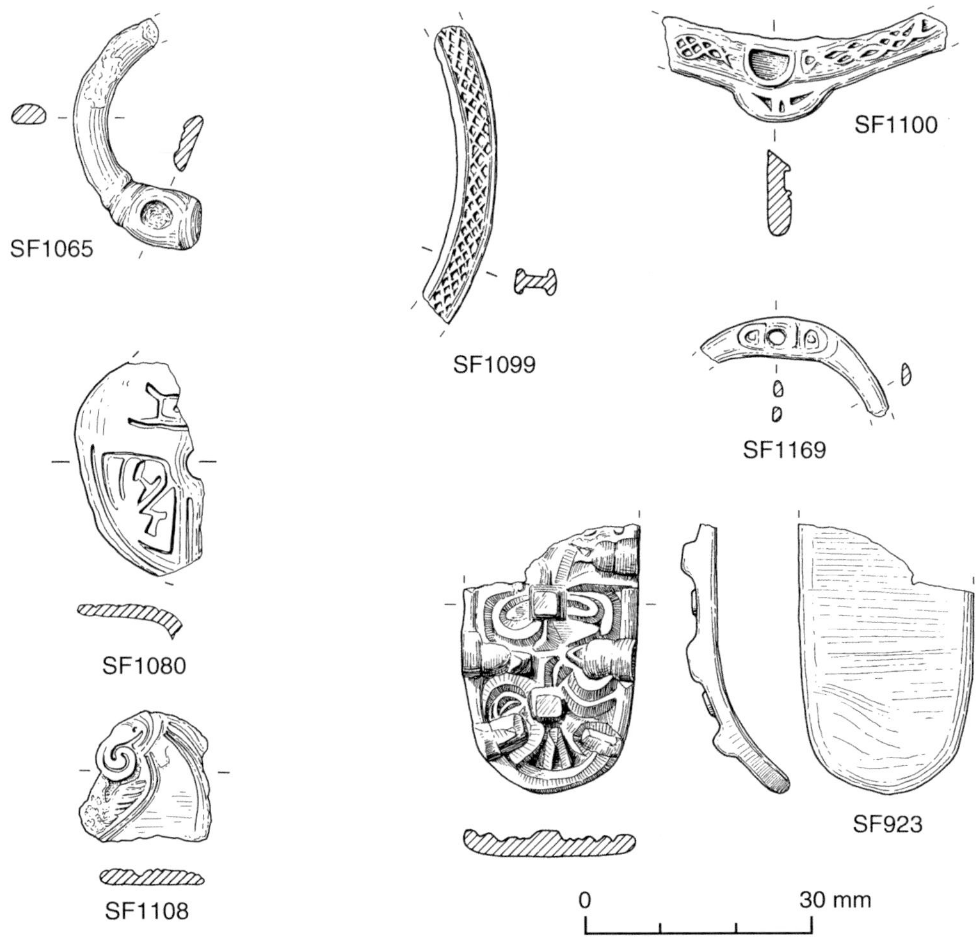

Figure 16 Annular or penannular brooch fragments (sfs1065, 1099, 1100 and 1169), possible disc brooches (sfs1080 and 1108) and possible trefoil brooch fragment (sf923). © York Archaeological Trust

examples include a slide with Borre-style decoration with matching strap-end found at Wharram Percy.

Penannular brooch terminal **(Fig. 16)**

Sf1065 is the terminal of a silvered copper-alloy penannular brooch, which may be most closely identified with Graham-Campbell's Type G3 (Dickinson 1982, 44–5). Other brooches which fall into this grouping include the silver brooch of the mid-9th-century Trewhiddle hoard (Webster and Backhouse 1991, 272, no. 246h), with other examples predominantly recovered from Northern Ireland and western Scotland, and dating from the 7th–9th centuries (Dickinson 1982, 43).

Annular or penannular brooch fragments **(Fig. 16)**

Fragments of the hoops of either annular or penannular copper-alloy brooches with gilding, and decorated with chip-carved interlace, include sfs1099 and 1100: the latter has a sub-circular lip on the hoop exterior, and an empty sub-circular setting slightly off-centre of the lip and set into the hoop. Too little of either brooch survives for their forms to be identified but, in their decoration, they resemble examples of both forms, as seen on an annular ring brooch from Co. Louth, Ireland, and a penannular brooch from Westray, Orkney, which was made in an Irish tradition (Youngs 1989, 199–200, nos 194–5). Both are likely to date to the 8th century. Sf1169, made of copper alloy, also appears to be a brooch hoop fragment and has a perforation with depressions to either side, possibly for settings now lost; it seems likely that the hole is a secondary feature, the fragment perhaps being reworked.

Possible disc brooches **(Fig. 16)**

Sf1080 may be an unfinished disc brooch or mount fragment, with unclear decoration in one quadrant, and broken across a central perforation. The defining of a decorated quadrant on this piece is similar to that on an unfinished disc-shaped piece found at Bawsey, Norfolk, which portrayed a sketched-out Trewhiddle-style beast (Webster and Backhouse 1991, 231–2, no. 188a). The Bawsey fragment has been linked stylistically to the early 9th-century disc brooches in the nearby Pentney (Norfolk) hoard (*ibid.*, 232). Sf1108 is possibly part of an openwork disc brooch, apparently comprising the end of a splayed arm of a cross, and featuring the paw and part of the leg of a Trewhiddle-style beast. This may be compared to a silver brooch found at Elmsett in Suffolk (West 1998, 25, fig. 24.6).

Possible trefoil brooch fragment **(Fig. 16)**

Sf923 is a tongue-shaped fragment which has been broken across its upper end, but may represent one of three arms of a copper-alloy trefoil brooch. It has been decorated with two central square bosses, and also possibly animal head bosses along the edges which may imitate the Borre-style

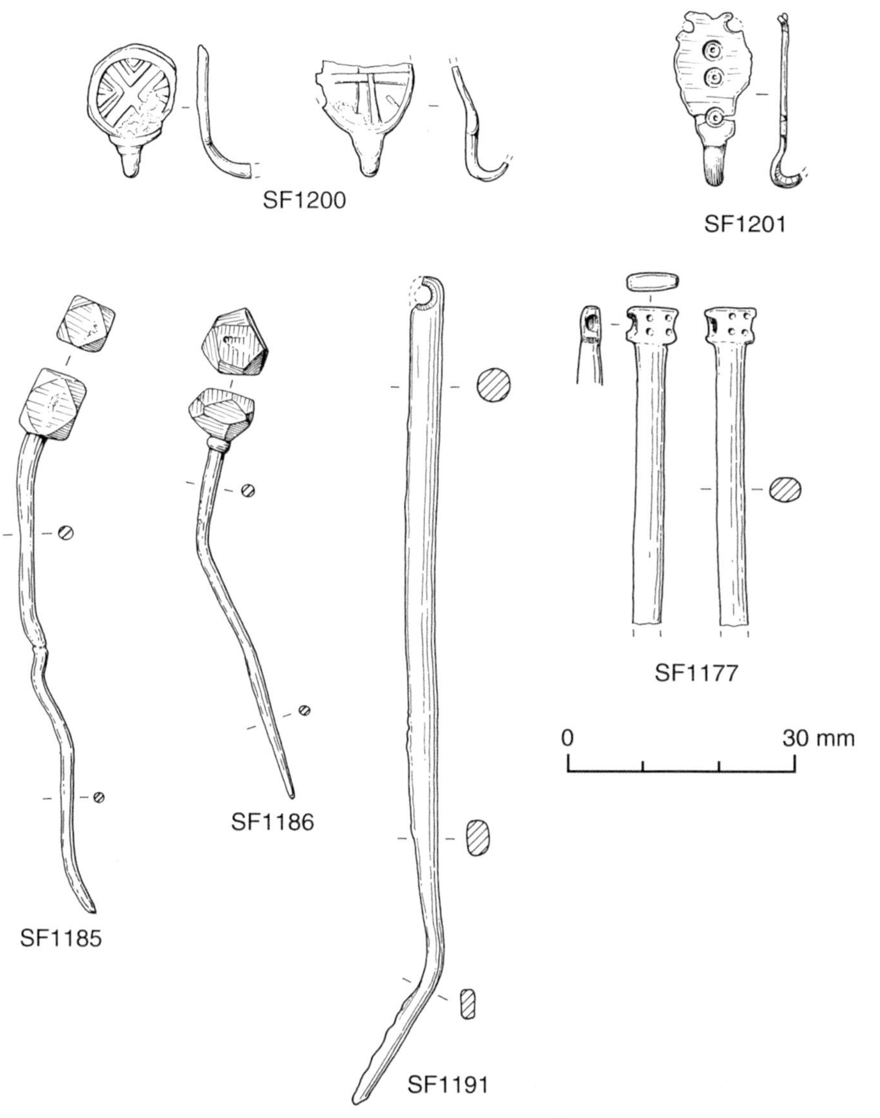

Figure 17 Hooked tags (sfs1200 and 1201) and dress pins (sfs1177, 1185, 1186 and 1191). © York Archaeological Trust

decoration seen on other trefoil brooches, such as that from Stallingborough, Lincolnshire (Leahy 2007b, 168, fig. 67/3). Deeply carved plant ornament fills the areas between the bosses.

Trefoil brooches were widely used in Scandinavia as a third brooch worn by a woman between the pair worn high on the chest (Roesdahl *et al.* 1981, 77, nos E28–9) and typically date to the late 9th to the second half of the 10th century (Graham-Campbell 1980, 37). A fragment of a clay mould for casting trefoil brooches was found at Blake Street in York (Roesdahl *et al.* 1981, 118, no. YMW14).

Hooked tags **(Fig. 17)**

Four copper-alloy hooked tags were identified, of which one was triangular (sf1199), two circular (sf1200), and one oval (sf1201). The circular tags both carry cross motifs, the larger but less complete tag also having been silver plated, while oval tag sf1201 has three ring-and-dot motifs. Two main forms of hooked tags, namely triangular and circular, were in use during the Anglo-Saxon period, the triangular form being the earlier, first appearing during the late 7th and 8th centuries (Geake 1997, 66). The circular form and its sub-circular variants may have been a late 8th-century development (Thomas 2009, 17; Riddler, with Evison and Rogers, 2014). Both forms seem to have remained in use until the 11th century (Hinton 1990, 549), but the circular form may have been the more popular in the latter part of the period (Thomas 2009, 17).

The perforations in the upper corners of these insubstantial fasteners suggest that they were sewn on to light fabric of some kind, and were not intended to take much strain (Hinton 1990, 548); possible functions include garter fastenings (Webster and Backhouse 1991, no. 200), fastening the hems of garments (Dickinson 1973, 116–17) or securing money-bags or purses (Graham-Campbell and Okasha 1991, 225), this latter use being favoured most recently by specialists in Anglo-Saxon costume and clothing (Walton Rogers 2007a, 134; Owen-Crocker 2004, 154–5).

Dress pins **(Fig. 17)**

Perhaps surprisingly, apart from the early Anglo-Saxon pin noted above (sf1110), only ten copper-alloy dress pins feature in the assemblage, of which two are ringed pins (see below). The other eight pins may be divided by head shape into three forms. Five (sfs1179 [two pins], 1180, 1185 and 1186) have polyhedral (i.e. cuboidal or other polygonal) heads, three of

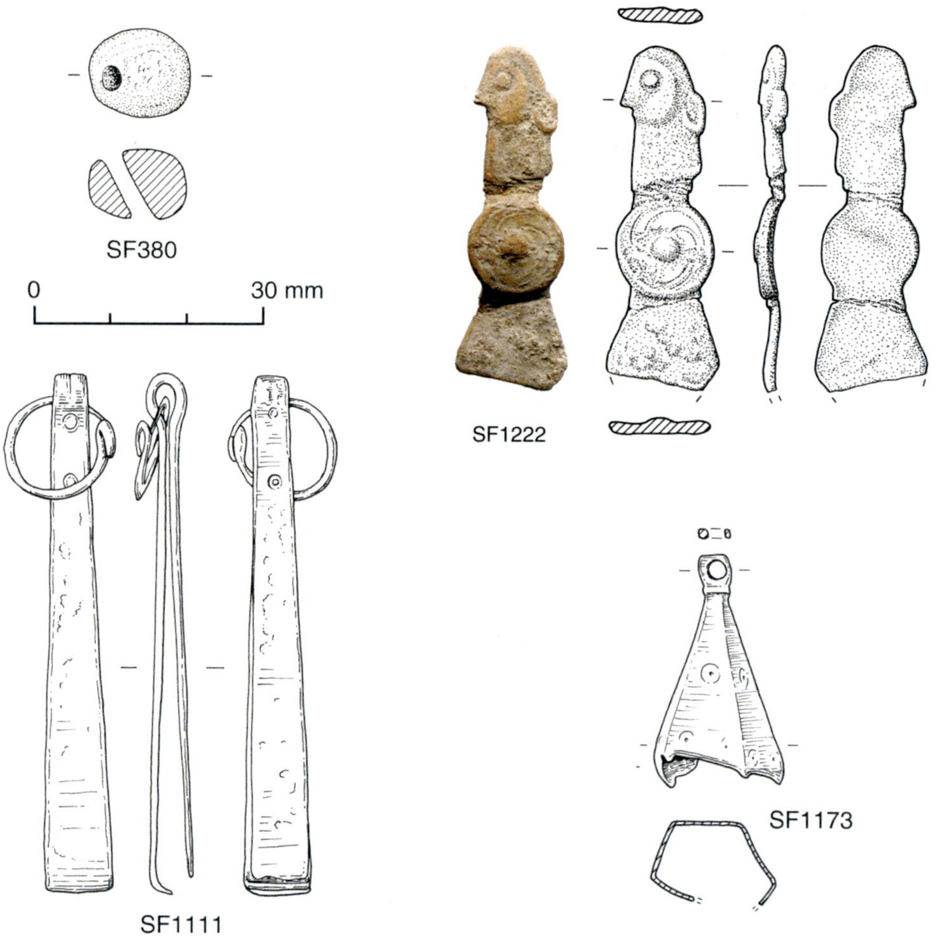

Figure 18 Globular amber bead (sf380), Valkyrie figure or amulet (sf1222), copper-alloy tweezers (sf1111) and copper-alloy bell (sf1173).

which (sfs1179 and 1180) are decorated with ring-and-dot motifs. Sfs1183 and 1184 have biconical heads, and sf1188 has a globular head – these are undecorated. These pin forms represent three of the four most common forms identified at sites of the 8th–9th centuries such as Brandon, Suffolk (Riddler, with Evison and Rogers, 2014), Flixborough, Lincolnshire (Rogers 2009, 33, fig. 1.13), Coppergate, York (Mainman and Rogers 2000, 2577), Hamwic (Hinton 1996, 35) and the Royal Opera House, London (Blackmore 2003, 266–8).

The two ringed pins from the site are both lacking a ring, and feature different head forms. Sf1191 is a loop-headed pin, a simple form often found with a plain ring; a pin of this type was also recovered from the hoard (sf141). This is a type known from pre-Viking and Viking contexts in Ireland, and is the dominant type in most Viking areas outside Ireland, dating to the 8th–10th centuries (Fanning 1994, 16–17). In York, three pins of this form were recovered at Coppergate (Mainman and Rogers 2000, 2580), and another was found at All Saints, Pavement (Tweddle 1986, 229, no. 1233).

Sf1177 is a crutch-headed ringed pin, which would originally have had a stirrup ring. Fanning notes that most known examples of this pin form have been found in Dublin, with some further examples from elsewhere in Ireland, all falling into a date range of the 11th–12th centuries (Fanning 1994, 44–5). Fanning noted only four crutch-headed ringed pins from England, of which one came from a grave at Wharram Percy, Yorkshire (Goodall 1987, 173).

Twisted wire ring

Sf286 comprises three adjoining fragments of a copper-alloy twisted wire ring. Such rings were simply formed by twisting one end of the hoop around the other, and were used commonly in the Anglo-Saxon and Anglo-Scandinavian periods as suspension loops for objects such as tweezers, toilet sets and hones as well as in jewellery (West 1998, 14, fig. 13.1; Mainman and Rogers 2000, 2583).

Beads **(Fig. 18)**

A globular amber bead (sf380) was found during the excavations in a pit fill which also produced a copper-alloy styca of *c.* 854–55 (sf381). Amber beads occur in 6th-century graves, but rarely in those of the 7th century (Leahy 2007a, 166–7); they are also found in Anglo-Scandinavian deposits (Mainman and Rogers 2000, 2597–8), and it seems most likely that sf380 is contemporary with the mid-9th-century coin with which it was found.

A fragmentary blue glass bead, possibly of conical shape originally (sf756), was found during the excavation; sf1220, a fragment of a polychrome glass bead, bright green with a red dot, was recovered by a detectorist. Both are likely to be parts of beads of the early–mid-Anglo-Saxon period (Rogers 1993, 1385).

Valkyrie figure/amulet **(Fig. 18)**

Sf1222 is an object made of lead-alloy sheet, comprising a standing Valkyrie-like figure with an oval head facing left in profile, with a single eye and protruding nose, with hair apparently tied up or knotted and hanging down her back. Below this is a disc decorated with a spiral emanating from the centre, with a sub-trapezoidal projection below. The clothing is unclear, but appears to represent a long dress; no feet are visible. However, this object is crudely made, and lacks the detail found in a number of other examples of comparable figures produced as brooches or pendants in silver (or occasionally copper alloy), including a fine example from Wickham Market in Suffolk, as well as others from Scandinavia (Williams 2014a, 79). Comparison with other examples clearly indicates that the disc is intended to represent a shield, although the figure lacks the accompanying sword or spear found on other figures, while such figures typically have full-length dresses with more elaborate drapery. Such objects typically represent either a single left-facing standing figure, or a similar figure facing a horseman, and should be regarded as distinct from representations of other female figures without shields, although these often have similar hair and dresses. There is no particular reason to identify the female figures without other attributes as Valkyries, and they may equally well represent other female supernatural figures, or even *völur* (human sorceresses) (*ibid.*, 79; Price 2014a, 116; 2014b, 166).

Variations of this figure carry horns or beakers rather than shields and have been portrayed on metalwork such as toilet implements (Graham-Campbell 1980, 50, 176), and amuletic pendants (*ibid.*, 154–5, nos 517–18), as well as on picture-stones (*ibid.*, 141, 480). These have been sometimes been interpreted as Valkyries welcoming warriors to Valhalla. One of the pendants was found in a hoard dated to the late 9th to the second half of the 10th century (*ibid.*, no. 518). The shield-bearing female figures are often also interpreted as Valkyries, as this would be consistent with their role in Norse mythologies as 'shield-maidens', in addition to their eponymous role as 'choosers of the slain'. The assumption that they necessarily represent Valkyries rather than simply female warriors has been questioned by Neil Price (2014a, 116), although other evidence for female warriors is extremely limited in this period.

Sf1222 appears to have been bent up in antiquity, and subsequently straightened out.

Tweezers **(Fig. 18)**

The virtually complete set of copper-alloy tweezers (sf1111) retains its penannular suspension ring, and has ring-and-dot decoration at the upper ends of the parallel-sided arms. The lack of splay in the arms, the non-expanded tips and the ring-and-dot motifs are all features indicating an Anglo-Scandinavian, rather than a middle Saxon, date (Mainman and Rogers 2000, 2600–1).

Copper-alloy bells **(Fig. 18)**

Two bells, both with hexagonal bodies (sfs1173 and 1175), are of a form which has been increasingly recognised in recent years amongst both metal-detected finds and excavated assemblages (Griffiths 2007, 69–70). Following recoveries from Freswick, Caithness, Scotland, and from pagan graves in Iceland, it was suggested that these had a Norse origin (Batey 1988, 215). More recent discoveries include several from the Irish Sea region, from sites such as Meols, Cheshire (Griffiths 2007, 69–70), and a 10th-century grave at Peel Castle, Isle of Man (Graham-Campbell 2002, 94–5), and others from the area of the Danelaw, including York (Mainman and Rogers 2000, 2599, no. 10528) and Cottam, Yorkshire (Richards 2003a, 162). Functionally, these bells were probably worn as personal ornament (Batey 1988, 215), and possibly had a funerary connection (Griffiths 2007, 70).

Mounts and other decorative metalwork

Possible Irish metalwork **(Figs 19–21)**

Sf1102 may be part of a gilded openwork mount; it has a slightly convex outer edge, and an interlace border, and may originally have been discoidal (**Fig. 19**). A triangular mount dating to the 8th century and thought to have been found on the site of a Viking cemetery in Phoenix Park, Dublin, also has an openwork centre, and the design of the interlace is similar to that on sf1102 (Youngs 1989, 150, no. 145).

Sf1140 is a decorative mount: at the top, a square is divided into four square cells, with a pelta shape below, also divided into cells (**Fig. 19**). One blue glass setting survives within the area of the pelta, but clearly others have been lost. There is a perforated lug on the reverse at the top, possibly for attachment to a horse harness (Graham-Campbell 1986, 282); the pelta shape is also seen on several mounts in the collection of 8th- to 9th-century harness mounts from Athlumney, near Navan, Co. Meath, Ireland (Youngs 1989, 117–18, no. 113; Harrison and Ó Floinn 2014, 191–3, 595–7, 117). Originally with settings, and three perforated lugs on the reverse, sf1086 may also be a harness mount of similar date.

Part of a decorative hinged mount, and possibly cut down, sf1174 bears vertical fields of symmetrically identical interlace, with the possible remains of a lug on the reverse (**Fig. 19**). This mount may have been attached to a casket or a house-shaped shrine; a pair of similarly hinged mounts is present on the sides of a house-shaped reliquary of Irish or Pictish origin found in Norway, and is thought to have been for attachment of a carrying-strap (Graham-Campbell 1980, 90–1, no. 314). Another possible fragment from Ireland is sf1101, which has chip-carved interlace, and appears gilded.

Other decorative metalwork

Possibly one of the earliest fragments of decorated metalwork, sf1081 is sub-triangular, and decorated on both faces, indicating that it was a fitting on which both faces were to be seen (**Fig. 19**). Clearly visible on one face is the head of a beast with ears flowing backwards, open jaw and sub-triangular paw with three toes just under the jaw. The motifs on the other face are less clear, but a similar paw is present. The style of the quadruped represented on sf1081 appears most similar to those found in Salin's Style II, in particular the elongated, parallel-sided jaws, and sub-triangular feet with two or three toes (Tweddle 1993, 1310); this style appears to have been used in England from the late 6th into the 8th century, and it seems likely that sf1081 belongs to the latter part of the date range, as indicated by the long prominent ears (*ibid.*, 1311). X-ray fluorescence analysis shows the presence of copper, tin, lead and silver which indicates a leaded bronze with possible silvering,

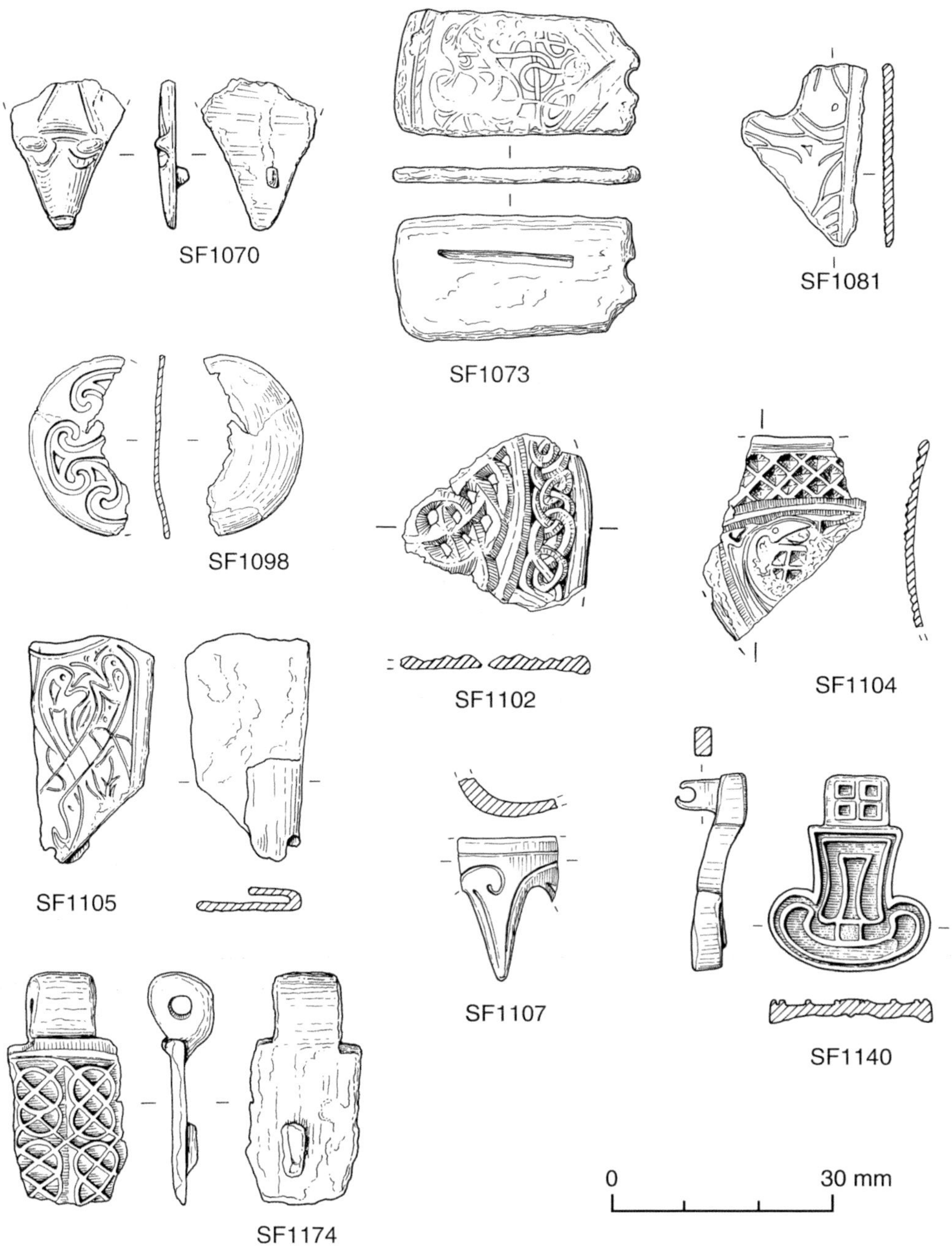

Figure 19 Mounts and decorative metalwork (sfs1070, 1073, 1081, 1098, 1102, 1104, 1105, 1107, 1140 and 1174). © York Archaeological Trust

although this does not show on the surface. The silver may also be part of the alloy as an impurity, if the metal was re-used. There is no indication of the presence of gold. When a swab of acetone was run over the surface of one corner, a gold-coloured substance, possibly paint, was removed.

Sf1069 is a mount fragment, with one arcaded edge with beaded borders, and Trewhiddle-style decoration comprising one almost complete quadruped with open jaw and upright ear, and elements of a further one or two (**Fig. 20**). The edge below the beasts is damaged but appears to have at least two rivet holes within it. This bears a strong similarity to the curved silver mounts found within the Trewhiddle hoard itself, and thought to have been possible bridle or spur attachments (Webster and Backhouse 1991, 272, no. 246e).

The fragmentary sf1070 comprises a terminal formed by a sub-triangular animal mask in relief, the rest of the object – possibly a mount – broken off (**Fig. 19**). Fragments of a possible knot-pattern above the terminal suggest this could be a Borre-style strap mount fragment (Graham-Campbell 1980, 144–5, no. 489). Also incomplete, sf1105 has been made of folded sheet, and may perhaps have been a binding (**Fig. 19**). The upper face is decorated with interlaced confronted serpent-like creatures, whose bodies have been rather crudely delineated. Confronted symmetrical pairs of animals in interlace is a well-known motif of 7th- to 9th-century metalwork and manuscripts (Tweddle 1992, 1158) but the serpent-like beasts on sf1105 may best be compared to those seen in the pages of the late 8th-century Leningrad Gospels (Alexander 1978, 64, no. 39).

Possible mount fragment sf1104 has a chip-carved-type border, and inside this are the remains of a zoomorphic design featuring a long-necked bird with open beak holding a round object (**Fig. 19**). Similar interlaced birds appear in

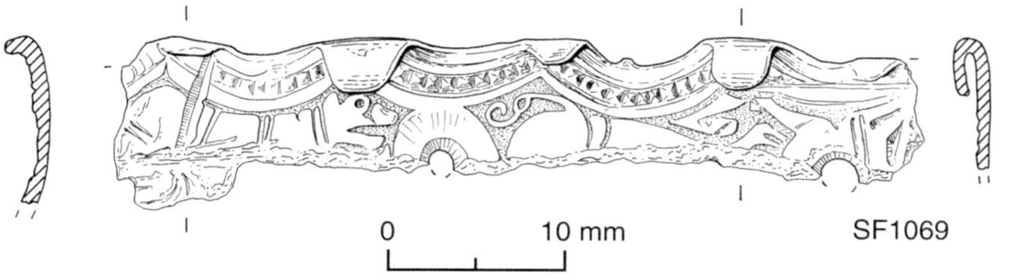

Figure 20 Mount fragment with Trewhiddle-style decoration (sf1069). © York Archaeological Trust

the portrait of an unidentified Evangelist in an early 8th-century Gospel Book now held at Maeseyck, in Limburg, Belgium, but thought by some scholars to have been made in York (Alexander 1978, 50, no. 22).

Sf1073 has been cut down, and appears originally to have been a discoidal mount or perhaps a roundel, probably with a central stud or setting (**Fig. 19**). There is a circumferential border with the main panel filled with possibly chip-carved interlace, and traces of a second border around the incomplete perforation, and the whole has been gilded. Another possible discoidal mount fragment, decorated with a splayed arm cross motif, is sf1098, which has also been gilded (**Fig. 19**). There appears to be the remains of a central rivet hole in the broken edge. Probably contemporary with this metalwork is fragment sf1103 which has also been decorated with interlace, and possible mount fragment sf1107 which was originally circular at its base with a diameter of *c.* 20mm, but is now broken at both sides and has a decorated triangular projection (**Fig. 19**).

Of uncertain date and provenance, sf1223 appears to be a zoomorphic fitting (**Fig. 21**). It comprises a dog-like animal head on a long neck, with a substantial snout, pointed back ears, and sharp teeth, and is tri-coloured, being green on the upper part, black on the lower and with cream/white between. A series of rivet holes appears to go from between the eyes to the jaw, from behind the ears to behind the jaw, and at the far end of the neck. The object is solid and made of a heavily leaded metal, although this has not been analysed.

Iron bell (Fig. 22)

Sf336 is a largely complete bell, excavated from a pit interpreted as of early medieval date. It is made from a sheet of iron which has been folded over, and has non-ferrous brazing and rivets reinforcing the side seams; the rim at the lower edge of the bell also has a brazed reinforcing strip attached (brazing visible on x-ray). A ring which served as both handle and attachment of the clapper projects at the top, the rest of it visible within the bell cavity.

Iron bells with non-ferrous coatings have a long history, and have been found in a range of sizes, the smaller forms thought to be for use on grazing animals (Ottaway 1992, 558); larger bells, such as sf336 have been interpreted differently, however. One possibility is use as ecclesiastical hand-bells (Bourke 1980, 52–66); examples have also been recovered in tool hoards, such as that from Flixborough (Ottaway 2009, 256–67, nos 2450–1), and in the grave of a smith at Tattershall Thorpe, Lincolnshire (Hinton 2000), leading to the suggestion that travelling craftsmen could have used such instruments to announce their arrival (Leahy 2007b, 197). Large iron clappers found at Coppergate, York (Ottaway 1992, 558, nos 2751, 2754–5), and Brandon, Suffolk (Rogers 2014), may also originally have been part of similarly sized bells.

Figure 21 Zoomorphic fitting (sf1223). © York Archaeological Trust

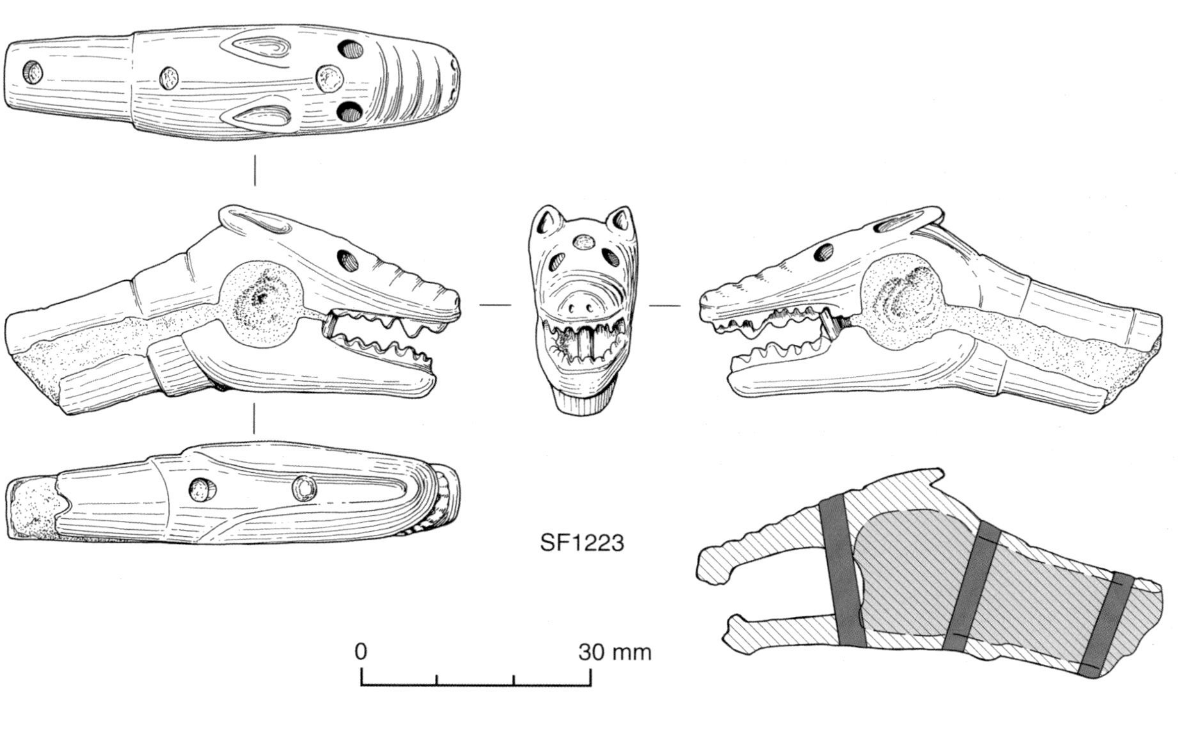

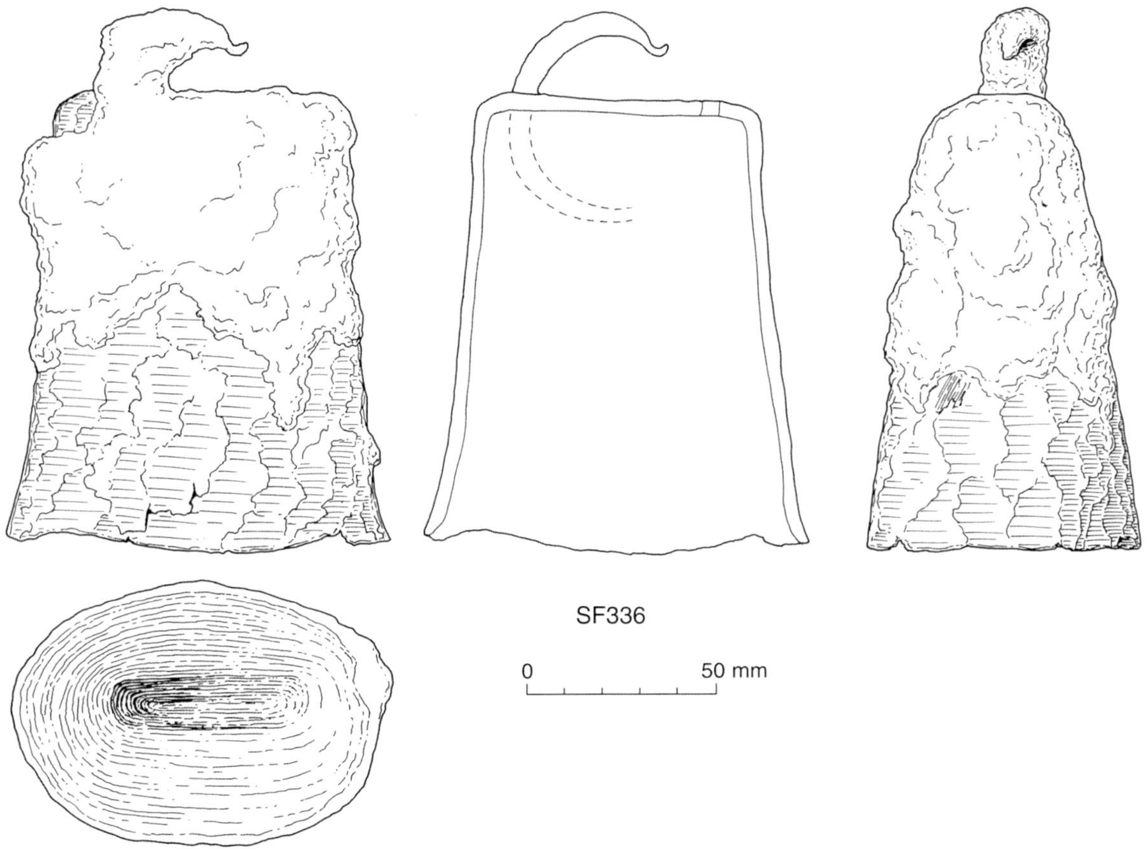

Figure 22 Iron bell (sf336). © York Archaeological Trust

Weaponry

In addition to the swords found in the hoard (sfs132–3; **Figs 4–5**), seven iron hilt fittings and part of a sword blade were recovered.

Hilt fittings

Hilt fittings from three different forms of sword were identified. Sf913 comprises an upper guard, which would be attached to the pommel (**Fig. 23**). It is lentoid, with a central sub-rectangular slot to go over the sword tang, and a circular perforation flanking the slot on each side; these perforations were for the attachment of the pommel via rivets. The base is decorated on all sides with vertical inlaid lines, and plating is also present on the bottom of the guard around the socket. Analyses of the decorative plating reveal that two different non-ferrous inlays were used. On the sides the non-ferrous inlay is made up of an alloy of copper, zinc and tin. Analysis of the area around the socket on the bottom of the guard indicated that the silver-coloured plating is probably an alloy of tin and lead. Another upper guard of this form, although undecorated, is represented by sfs1051 (**Fig. 23**) and 1052.

The classification of Viking-period swords from Norway created by J Petersen in 1919 still forms the basis for the current typologies of swords and their hilts from north-western Europe (Petersen 1919). Sf913 is part of a pommel of a form which fits into Petersen's Type H (*ibid.*, 89–100); elements of such hilts typically have decorative inlaid wires of non-ferrous metals (*ibid.*, 91). For Petersen, Type H held an exceptional position within his typology: this was due to the broad time period it extended across, and also because it was the most numerous of all the sword types from the Viking Age (*ibid.*, 89). These swords had been found across northern Europe, although none from England was known to Petersen. Since his time, however, a Type H sword has been recovered in a Viking grave at Sonning, Berkshire, dated by all the grave goods to the late 9th–10th century (Evison 1969, 330, 333), and another pommel fragment, very similar to sf913, has been identified at Brandon, Suffolk (Rogers 2014). Possible hilt guards from swords of this form have also been found at Coppergate, York (Ottaway 1992, 716–17, no. 3941), and Wharram, North Yorkshire (Webster 2000, 139, no. 257). Petersen dated these swords from *c.* 800–*c.* 950 (Petersen 1919, 98–9), but it has been suggested recently that they may have originated as early as *c.* 775 (Peirce 2002, 18–19).

Four pommels (sfs242–3, 914, 1053 (**Fig. 23**)) all appear to derive from Petersen Type L swords. The pommels are characteristically trilobate with a convex lower face, the socket for the tang tapering slightly from the lower face through the central lobe to the top. Elements of this form of sword have been found particularly in eastern England; several examples come from York, from Coppergate (Ottaway 1992, 716, no. 3943), Fishergate (Rogers 1993, 1431–2, nos 5262–3), and Acomb (Youngs *et al.* 1984, 249; Tweddle *et al.* 1999, 287–8, no. 180, fig. 108), with others from North Yorkshire, from Gilling West (Watkin 1986) and Wensley, as well as Norwich, and Fiskerton, Lincolnshire (Wilson 1965, 33–5, 41–2, pls II–III, VII). Although included in Petersen's classification, Type L swords are thought to have an English origin, as they have frequently been found with Trewhiddle-style decoration (Peirce 2002, 20), and date from the mid-9th–late 10th century (*ibid.*, 18–19). The sword elements found in the hoard (sfs132–3) are also from Type L swords (**Figs 4–5**).

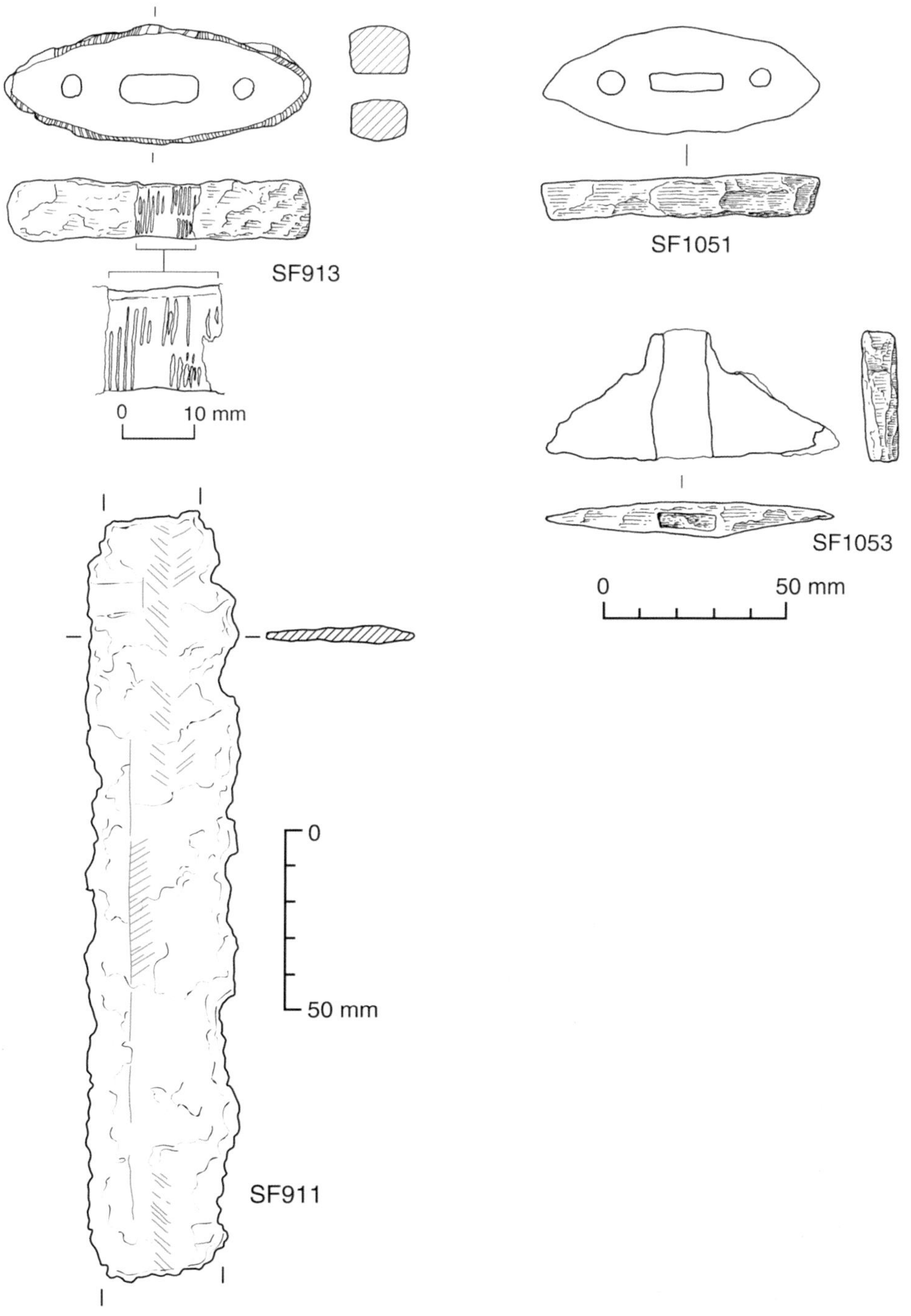

Figure 23 Sword pommels (sfs913, 1051 and 1053) and sword blade (sf911). © York Archaeological Trust

One pommel may be from a Petersen Type X sword: sf241 is unfortunately incomplete, and its original form unclear, but it appears to be one-piece, with a semi-circular upper face, and a slightly tapering central socket. Waterman published two Type X swords from York (Waterman 1959, 71–2, fig. 5, nos 1–2), and pommels found at Fishergate (Rogers 1993, 1433, no. 5261) and Coppergate (Ottaway 1992, 716, nos 3937, 3940) also appear to be from Type X swords. Type X swords may first have appeared by the mid-9th century, and continued in use to the mid-11th century (Peirce 2002, 20).

Sword blade **(Fig. 23)**

Sf911 is a sword blade fragment, broken at both ends, and currently just over 200mm long. The structure of the blade is evident from the x-ray, which reveals one steeled edge, the other probably having been lost, and a clear chevron/herringbone pattern in the pattern welding. Originally, the blade would also probably have had a fuller, a shallow central channel, running much of its length on one or both sides, although this is not visible on sf911.

Such structural features are not particular only to Viking swords, but are found on most sword blades of the period, which have been classified and dated mainly on the basis of their relative dimensions (Peirce 2002, 21–4); as sf911 is incomplete, it is not possible to type it, but it seems most likely that it belongs to a sword of one of the forms represented by the pommels also found on the site. The use of pattern welding certainly indicates a date before *c.* AD 1000, by which time the making of such blades is thought to have ceased (Oakeshott 1960, 148).

Plate 5 Front and back of sf1224, a terminal from a harness mount. Private collection (photo: British Museum)

Horse equipment

Harness mount **(Pl. 5)**
James Graham-Campbell

This unusually shaped mount, sf1224, is a terminal (length 70mm) from a set of interlocking mounts which would have formed part of an elaborate bridle of Irish manufacture, dating stylistically to the 8th/9th centuries AD. The standard of workmanship is high, and the state of preservation is for the most part excellent. Such harness mounts are known not only from Ireland, but also from Viking-Age contexts in Scotland, Norway and England (e.g. Youngs 1989, 117–20, nos 113–17). The mount is in the form of a stylised spread-eagled animal, with downward-facing head, seen from above (**Pl. 5**); it is elaborately decorated with zoomorphic ornament on the front, with the front 'legs' of the spread-eagled animal both in the form of birds seen in profile, while the feet of the hind 'legs' are depicted as animal heads in profile. The expanded 'body' of the spread-eagled animal is divided into variously shaped panels by three interlacing snakes which have heads in profile at both ends of their ribbon-shaped bodies (the main pair being more prominent than the third). The fourth element forming this interlaced framework consists of a ribbon extending from, and linking together, the ears of the main animal head, which also has a neck-like extension connecting it to the central rectangular field of ornament. The reverse is plain, with three perforated lugs, one behind the head and the other two behind the hind-legs (**Pl. 5**).

None of the known Irish harness mounts of 8th/9th-century date takes the form of a spread-eagled animal, making the ARSNY example unique but, in general terms, the mount finds parallels in a number of female graves in Norway as well as in the set of harness mounts from Athlumney, near Navan, Co. Meath (Harrison and Ó Floinn 2014, 191–3, 595–7, 117). These parallels, and the design and function of the piece are discussed in more detail elsewhere (Graham-Campbell 2015). However, one may note that while the object was manufactured as a mount rather than a brooch, most of the 40 or so Scandinavian finds of comparable material were re-used as brooches for female dress (Wamers 1998, 38). The particular interest of the ARSNY example, in addition to its unique design, is therefore that it is in the intermediate state of having been separated from its set of harness mounts, but not yet fitted with a pin for use as a woman's brooch. While it is listed here under horse equipment because of its original function, it is probably better considered among the mounts and other decorative metalwork (see above, pp. 59–61), as there is no evidence that it was ever used as a harness mount on this site. However, this possibility cannot be completely discounted.

Prick spurs **(Fig. 24)**
Nicola Rogers

Two largely complete iron prick spurs (sfs161, 225), and two fragmentary examples (sfs1124–5) were found. The most complete, sf225, lacks only the tip of its goad; it retains both arms with terminals which have been formed by flattening

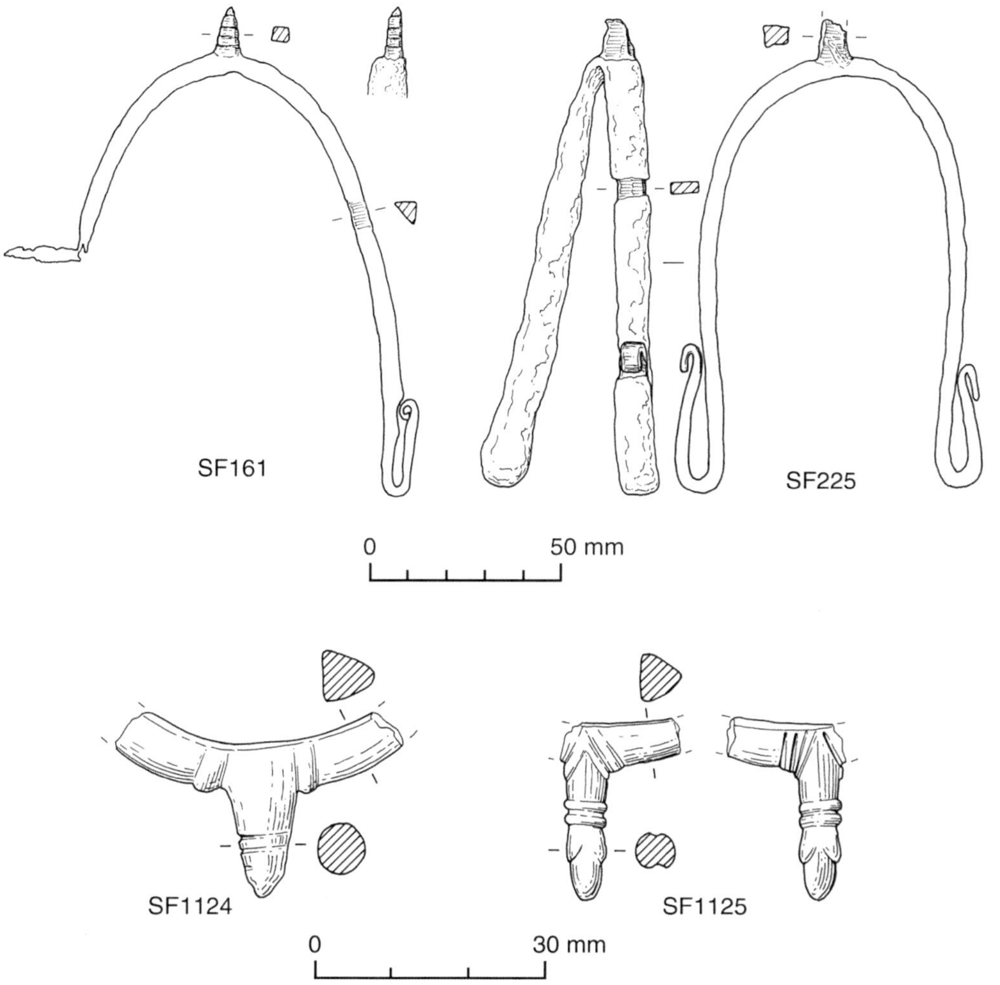

Figure 24 Two largely complete iron prick spurs (sfs161 and 225) and two fragmentary examples (sfs1124 and 1125). © York Archaeological Trust

out the ends and then looping them back to form eyes. Sf161 has lost part of one arm, but the other survives, and has the same terminal form as sf225; this spur has traces of plating in grooves on the arm above the terminal, and on the goad, which is triangular. The form of the goad and terminals on both these spurs indicates Viking origins, as they closely resemble an example from a burial thought to be of a pagan Viking at Middle Harling, Norfolk (Margeson 1995b, 79–80); another example was found at Coppergate, York, where it was dated as probably 9th century (Ottaway 1992, 699–701, no. 3836). Although sfs1124–5 are fragmentary, the goad survives on both, the forms suggesting that these spur fragments are likely to be roughly contemporary with the more complete survivals.

Miscellanea (Fig. 25)

Unusually shaped and smoothed fired-clay fragments (sfs349, 378 and 391) are of uncertain function. Although apparently deliberately shaped, they are not considered to be furnace lining (C. Mortimer, pers. comm.) or unfinished loom weights (P. Walton Rogers, pers. comm.). All the fragments come from excavated deposits of early medieval date containing charcoal and/or other evidence of *in situ* burning. A further 22 samples of not highly fired clay are also unlikely to have been involved in metalworking.

Archaeological excavations

Richard Hall

A variety of agricultural uses in the recent past have disturbed and truncated *in situ* archaeological deposits. Extant animal burrows demonstrate significant intrusions into and disturbance of archaeological deposits; this may also have led to the introduction of intrusive material via ancient, unrecognised burrowing.

Trench locations were metal detected to retrieve items from the plough soil before they were machine stripped down to undisturbed deposits, and all spoil heaps were spread so that they could be thoroughly metal detected. Features were either sampled in section or were fully excavated. The well-drained sandy deposits resulted in extremely poor organic preservation, and the poor condition of surviving human and animal bone.

Here, only those trenches which provided evidence for early medieval activity are discussed; prehistoric and Romano-British activity will be published elsewhere.

Investigating the hoard site (Figs 26–7)

Between 15 and 26 March 2004 D.T. Evans of YAT excavated two trenches in order to determine whether there was any evidence for a Viking (ship) burial, and also to elicit further information about the nature of archaeological deposits and their preservation in this part of the site.

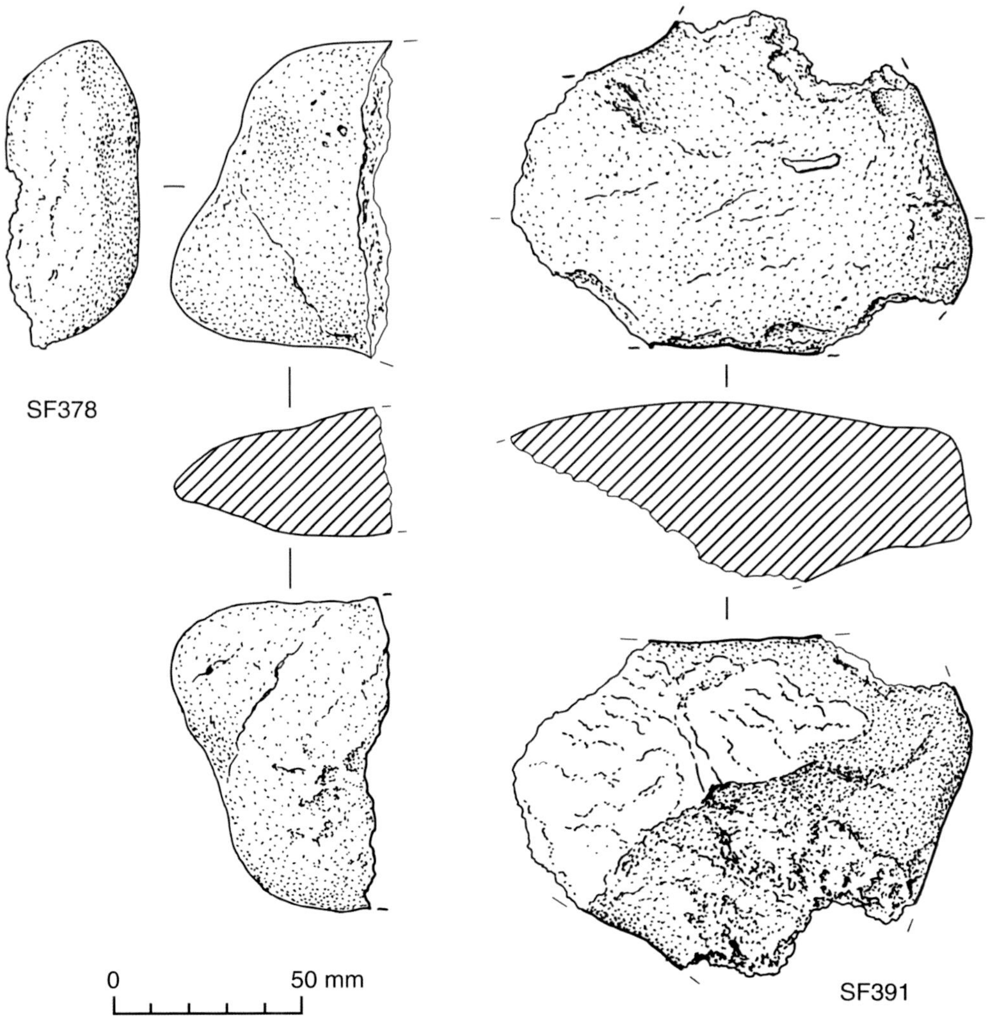

Figure 25 Shaped and smoothed fired clay fragments (sfs378 and 391) of uncertain function. © York Archaeological Trust

Trench 1, 10m x 1.5m, was laid out where the detectorists reported a concentration of nails. Natural sand deposits were encountered throughout; the southern half of the trench had been severely eroded by a natural drainage channel. Some features were created by animals; others may have been pit bases or post-holes, but all are thought to be of later medieval date or even later. No evidence for a boat burial was recovered.

Trench 2 was intended to investigate the area where the hoard had been found (**Fig. 27**). Initially 3m x 3m, it eventually had maximum dimensions of *c.* 5m x 4.5m, impinging on the western limit of Trench 1. Much of the northern 2m was occupied by silt deposits, penetrated by a variety of features. One of these features (with upper fill 2012) may have been a large pit; only the uppermost part was excavated. At the western limit of the trench was a feature of uncertain function (2024), perhaps a post-hole. Towards the centre of the trench was a partly truncated slot (2010) measuring *c.* 1.5m x 0.35m x 0.55m deep. This may have been a robbed-out beam slot, possibly associated with the post-hole mentioned above. The southern part of Trench 2 had been almost completely destroyed by a large, irregular modern cut (2002) which was *c.* 3.6m east to west, 2.4m north to south, *c.* 0.8m deep and penetrated *c.* 0.4m into the natural sand. This was identified as the hole dug by the detectorists when retrieving the hoard.

The slot and a possible post-hole could conceivably have been contemporary with the deposition of the hoard; they could represent one or more structures, such as a building in/beside which the hoard was buried, or features defining or associated with a grave. This, however, is mere speculation which cannot be investigated further, for erosion hereabouts, identified as a problem before 2004, continued to reduce any surviving deposits in the area of the drainage channels and, together with evidence for recent contamination in this vicinity, mitigated against further investigations in this part of the site.

Evaluation excavations

A YAT team directed by Rhona Finlayson excavated 21 trial trenches during 4–19 July and 22 October–29 November 2005. Heavy rain during both campaigns, and baking sun or freezing cold, affected ground conditions. Altogether *c.* 1544m², approximately 0.5% of the total area of the site, was excavated. Trenches excavated within or overlapping the enclosure totalled *c.* 1103m², which represents *c.* 1.1% of its area.

The large enclosure

The large sub-rectangular enclosure revealed by geophysical survey was investigated at its putative north-east corner, where its line had not been determined (Trench 5), along its

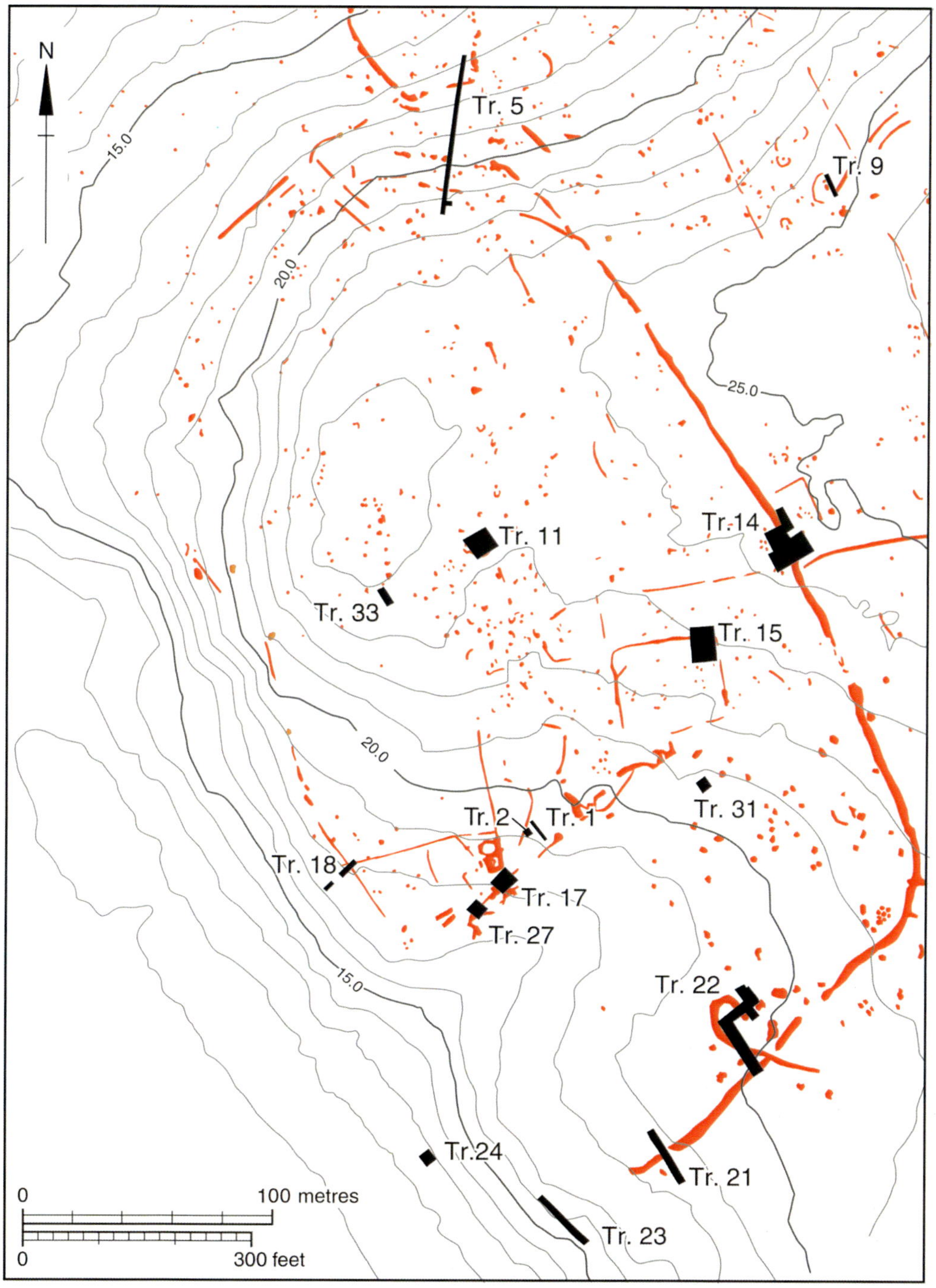

Figure 26 Location of excavation trenches in relation to features revealed by geophysical survey. © York Archaeological Trust

southern arm (Trenches 21 and 22), and at the putative entrance towards the centre of its eastern side (Trench 14) (**Fig. 26**).

In Trench 5 (**Fig. 28**) a ditch (5007) 3.6m wide and at least 1m deep appears to be the northern return of the large enclosure ditch. Time constraints prohibited full excavation of its fills, which included substantial sandy deposits (5006 and 5003). The upper fill included many large fragments of animal bone in very poor condition, as well as an iron rivet.

Within the enclosure was a post-hole or pit (5002) with almost vertical sides, *c.* 1.40m in diameter and *c.* 0.76m deep. At its base was a charcoal-rich silty sand (5005) incorporating small fragments of burnt bone and a copper-alloy strip (sf753). Two samples of charcoal from the layer above (5001) gave calibrated (95% confidence) radiocarbon dates *cal AD 690–950* and *660–890*, with posterior density (95% probability) estimates of, respectively, *cal AD 680–860* and *cal AD 680–830* (p. 76, **Table 10**). An Anglo-Scandinavian lead weight (sf780) was recovered from the plough soil here.

At the opposite corner of the enclosure, in Trench 21 (**Fig. 29**), the earliest features were part of a steep-sided sub-circular cut (21028) *c.* 0.80m in diameter and, to the south, two other sub-circular pits, centred *c.* 4.5m apart, which were *c.* 1.20m in diameter and 0.15m deep. No dating evidence was recovered from them, and they had been truncated by two parallel linear ditches, so it is not known from what level they were cut.

The two parallel linear ditches (21026 and 21036) were aligned north-east/south-west and were *c.* 1.5m apart; their fills were fully defined only in section. The northern ditch

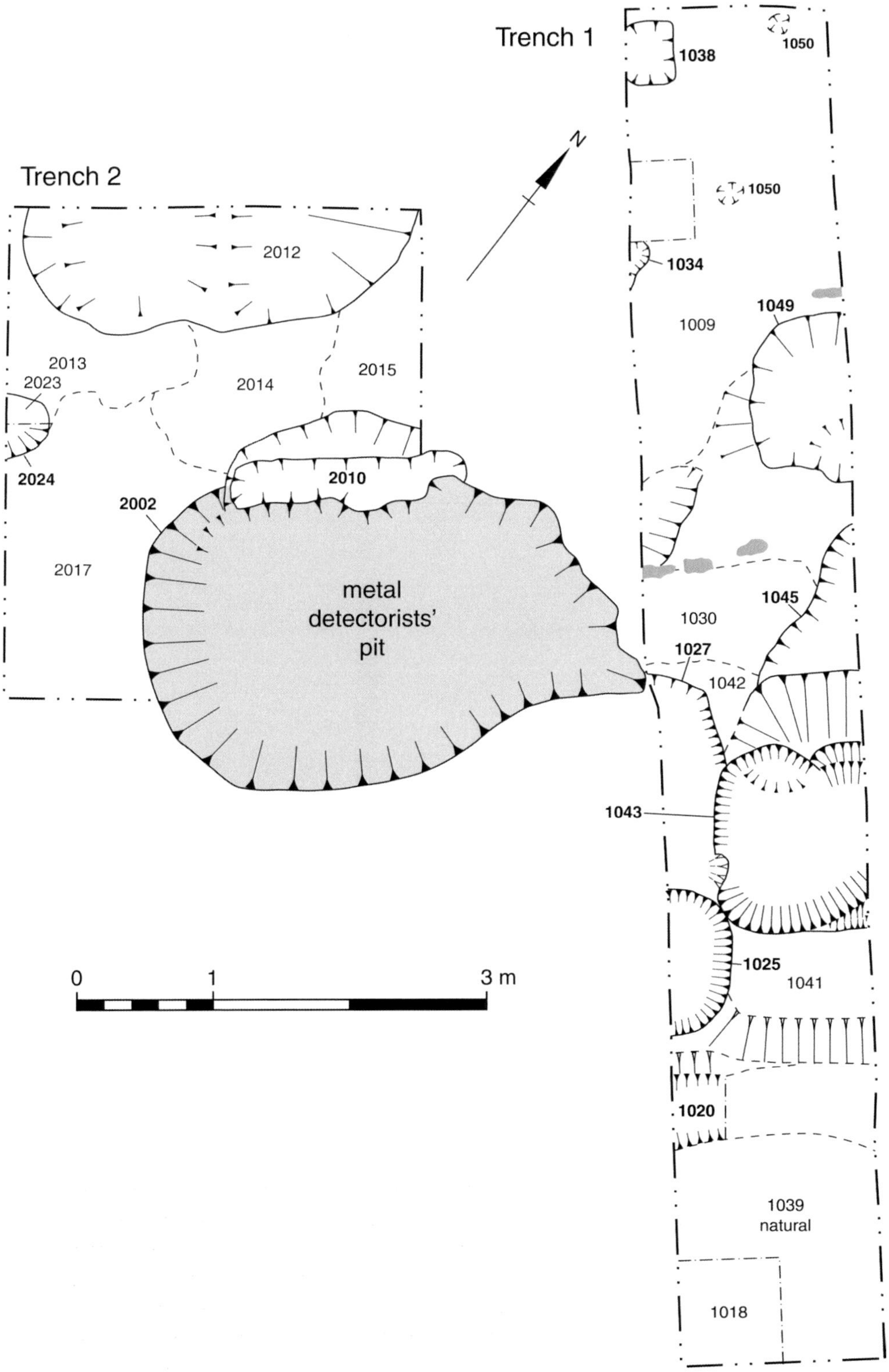

Figure 27 Plan of Trench 1 and Trench 2, the latter showing the pit dug by metal detectorists when retrieving the hoard.
© York Archaeological Trust

(21026) was *c.* 0.65m deep and *c.* 2.50m wide, with a U-shaped profile; a single folded piece of lead sheet (sf839) was in a lower fill and a single abraded Romano-British gritty sherd was also recovered from this ditch. The southern ditch (21036) was *c.* 0.85m deep and *c.* 2m wide, with a U-shaped profile widening towards the top. A single sherd of 4th-century pottery came from the uppermost fill. Worked flint was found in both ditches. These ditches may be contemporary features in a double ditch system used to define a significant area.

Cut from the same height as both ditches but stratigraphically independent of them was a sub-circular post-hole or pit cut (21032) which was partly beyond the east-facing section. It was *c.* 0.45m deep and *c.* 0.65m in diameter, and contained a single piece of Romano-British pottery.

Stratigraphically later than the backfill of the southern ditch were two post-holes (21008 and 21005), 0.50m and 0.87m in diameter and *c.* 0.55m and 0.27m deep respectively. They were located on the south side of the ditch, cutting its backfill (21040), and may indicate that the enclosure

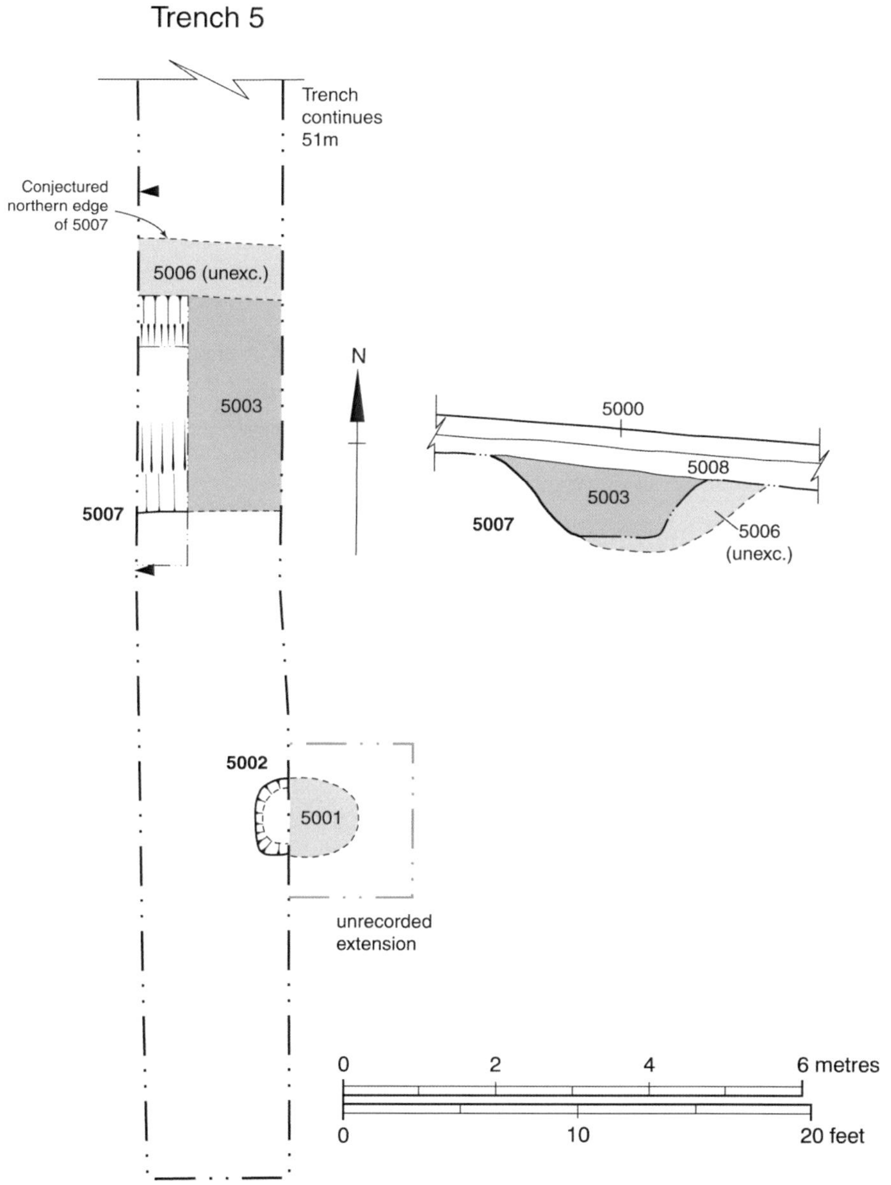

Figure 28 Plan of Trench 5 and section through ditch 5007. © York Archaeological Trust

continued to be defined by a series of posts after the ditch had fallen out of use. Stone pot-boilers were found within 21004, and a fragment of worked stone with one smooth face (sf904) was recovered from 21007.

Trench 22, irregularly shaped, investigated a circular feature recorded by the geophysical survey (see **Fig. 26**), and cut another section through the main enclosure ditch (**Fig. 30**). The archaeological sequence here was found to be relatively complex; all features were sampled, but a full examination of the depositional sequence and understanding of the activities represented here was not possible.

At the north-eastern edge of excavation was a natural gully or stream-bed which had subsequently silted up. Stratigraphically later was a 14m length of curving ditch (22045) aligned north-west/south-east, *c.* 1.30m wide and *c.* 0.40m deep. Lead-alloy spillage (sf752) and a ferrous nail fragment (sf764) from the upper silty fill suggest an early medieval date for this feature. Several cut features located to the east of the ditch are undated and uninterpretable.

Above the silted-up ditch or stream-bed were layers (22037, 22027/41) including small lenses of burnt sand, occasional charcoal and burnt cobbles. Between them, extending over and beyond an area *c.* 14m^2, was a scatter of burnt and heat-shattered cobbles (22038), perhaps introduced to consolidate the area. Eighteen fragments of burnt clay from these deposits are thought to be oven rather than furnace lining. Metalworking debris was also found within these contexts, including a deposit of casting sand (sf348), ferrous slag (sfs387, 388, 864 and 865), a possible iron punch (sf389), an iron weight (sf815), and clench bolts and roves (sfs383, 384, 386 and 760). These bolts could be Roman or early medieval in date, and although they are frequently found in association with ships they were also used on carts, buildings and coffins. Pottery of Iron Age, Roman and early medieval date was recovered from these contexts. A single sample of charcoal from 22037 has a calibrated (95% confidence) radiocarbon date of *380–170 cal BC* indicative, like the Iron Age pottery, of residual material.

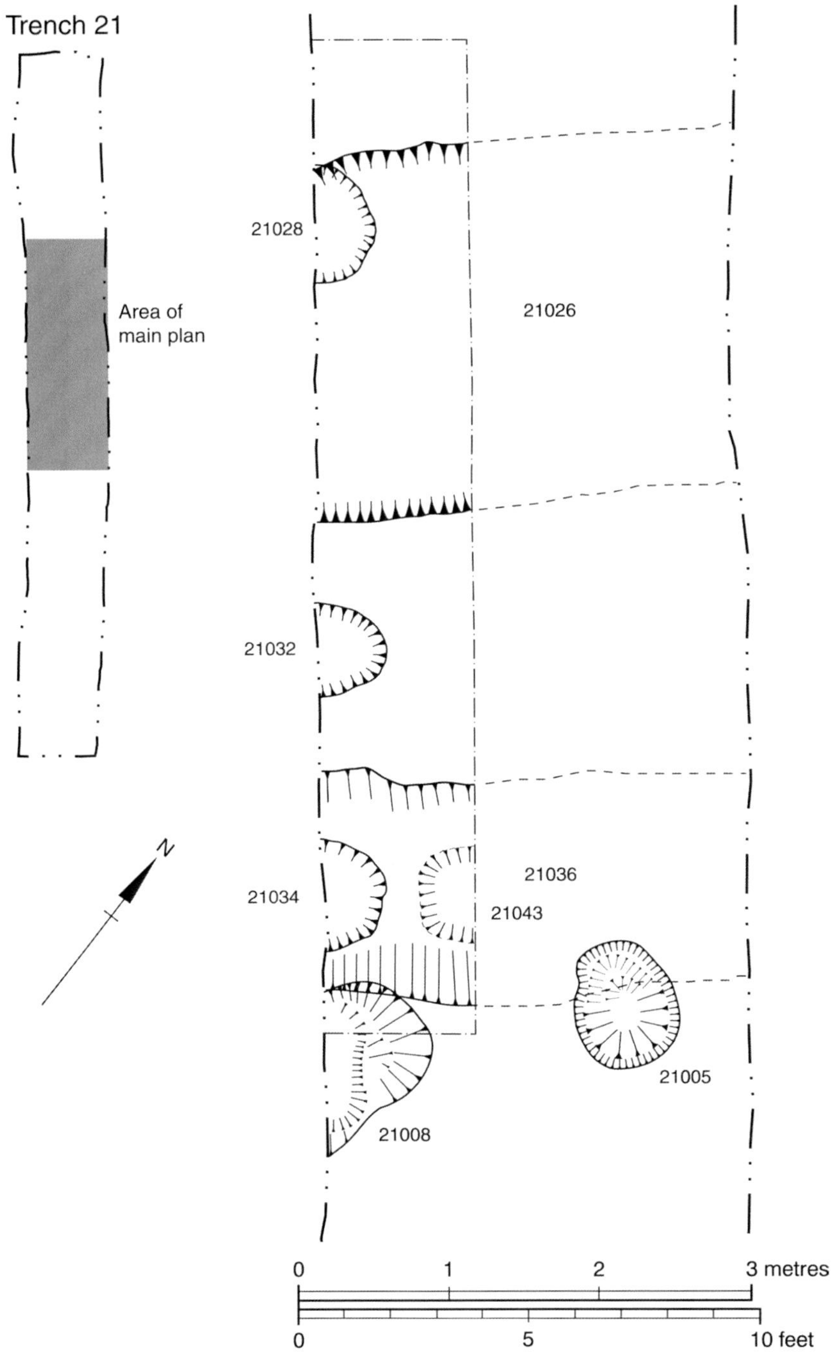

Figure 29 Plan of part of Trench 21 showing parallel linear ditches 21026 and 21036. © York Archaeological Trust

A later circular cut (22039) was *c.* 0.80m in diameter and *c.* 0.40m deep. Its lower fill comprised cobbles, apparently heat-shattered *in situ*, with sand and charcoal in the voids (22036); there was no scorching or burning of surrounding sand. Three fragments of burnt clay, thought to be oven lining, were found here. The cut widened towards the top and here the cobbles (22005), although burnt and shattered, had clearly been redeposited, with no suggestion of *in situ* burning. The upper fill (22004) was a thin layer of fine-grained sand stained by charcoal, with occasional burnt bone and charcoal flecks. Two samples of charcoal from the lower fill (22036) gave calibrated radiocarbon dates (95% confidence) of *cal AD 660–870* and *cal AD 650–780*, both with posterior density estimates (95% probability) of *cal AD 670–780*, and the upper fill (22004) gave a similar date of *cal AD 660–870*, *cal AD 690–830*. This feature may have been a post-hole, with the cobbles as packing, although there was no void representing a removed timber; alternatively, it may have served another, unknown, function.

The main enclosure ditch (22030) here measured *c.* 3m wide. In its lowest fill (22022) was a large, unabraded sherd of Roman pottery (sf330). A piece of ferrous slag (sf329), a clench bolt (sf760) and another Romano-British sherd were recovered from upper ditch fills, which had been extensively infiltrated by animal burrows.

Immediately to the north of this ditch (22030) examination of the section indicates that there may have been a bank (22034) *c.* 3m wide and *c.* 0.50m high associated with the ditch. A large fragment of limestone was seen within this deposit and it was discernibly different from the adjacent material (22001) which was interpreted as a natural build-up of hill-wash and aeolian sands. The material was

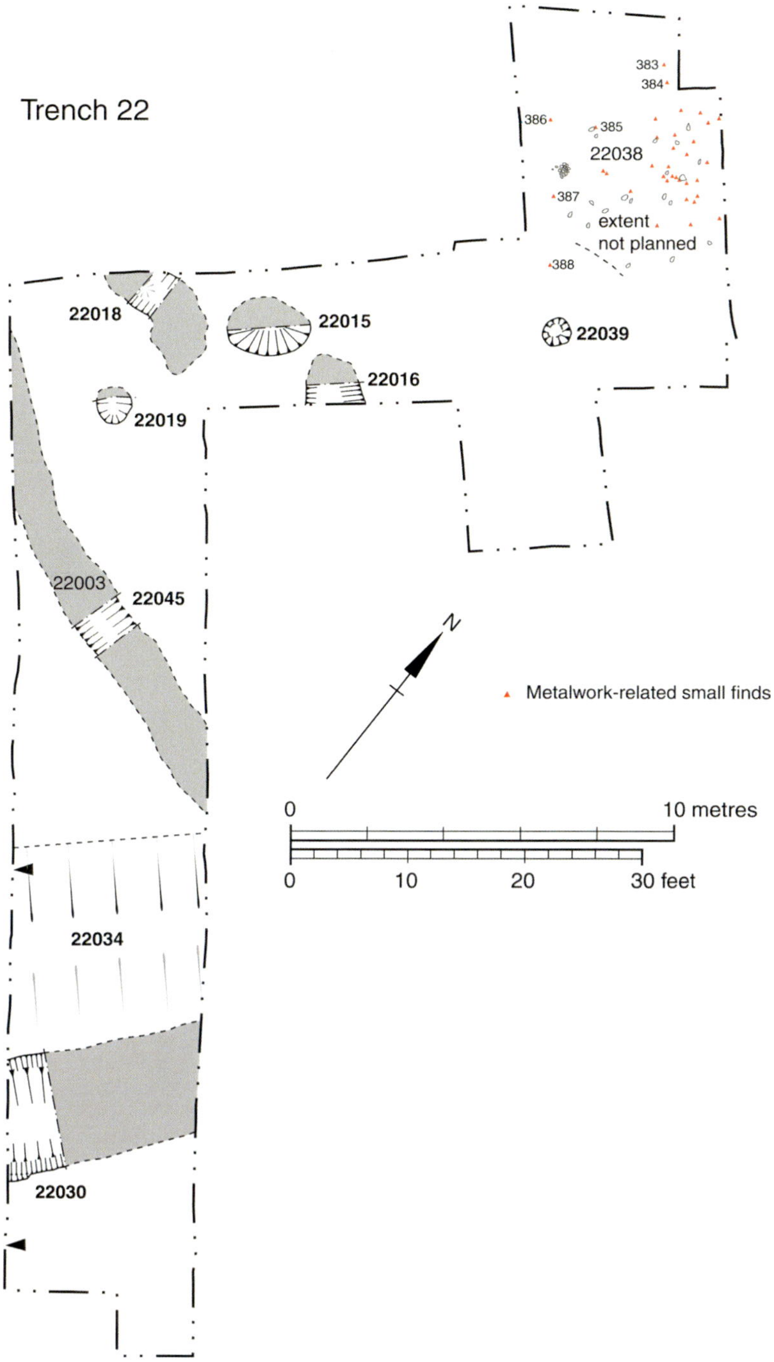

Figure 30 Plan of Trench 22. © York Archaeological Trust

all severely affected by animal burrows, removing clarity, and another interpretation could point to the remnants of ridge and furrow here.

Trench 14 was sited to investigate the putative entrance into the enclosure (**Fig. 31** and see **Fig. 26**). The earliest feature here was a sub-circular pit (14084), *c.* 1.90m in diameter and < 0.50m deep below truncation by the enclosure ditch (14083). A stone pot-boiler and a single droplet of lead run-off (sf325) were recovered from the sandy backfill.

The northern ditch (14083) was *c.* 5m wide and *c.* 0.90m deep, with sandy fills which contained relatively large quantities of metal objects and waste from iron, copper-alloy and lead working, including a fired clay furnace lining (sf901) as well as a lead-alloy weight (sf311). Many fragments of cattle skull and mandibles were also found in these fills, perhaps some form of ritual offering, although the absence of non-head skeletal evidence may reflect poor preservation rather than deliberate selection. Patches of dark grey sand haphazardly located within fill 14075 may represent decayed turves, and may suggest backfilling rather than a slower accumulation of material.

A section through the southern ditch terminal (14028) showed that, below modern truncation, it was *c.* 3.30m wide and *c.* 0.70m deep. In contrast to the northern terminal, its sandy backfill deposits contained no artefacts, although animal bone was recovered from 14017.

In the 5.60m gap between the ditch terminals an approximately linear series of closely spaced truncated features ran for *c.* 13m at a slightly oblique angle to the

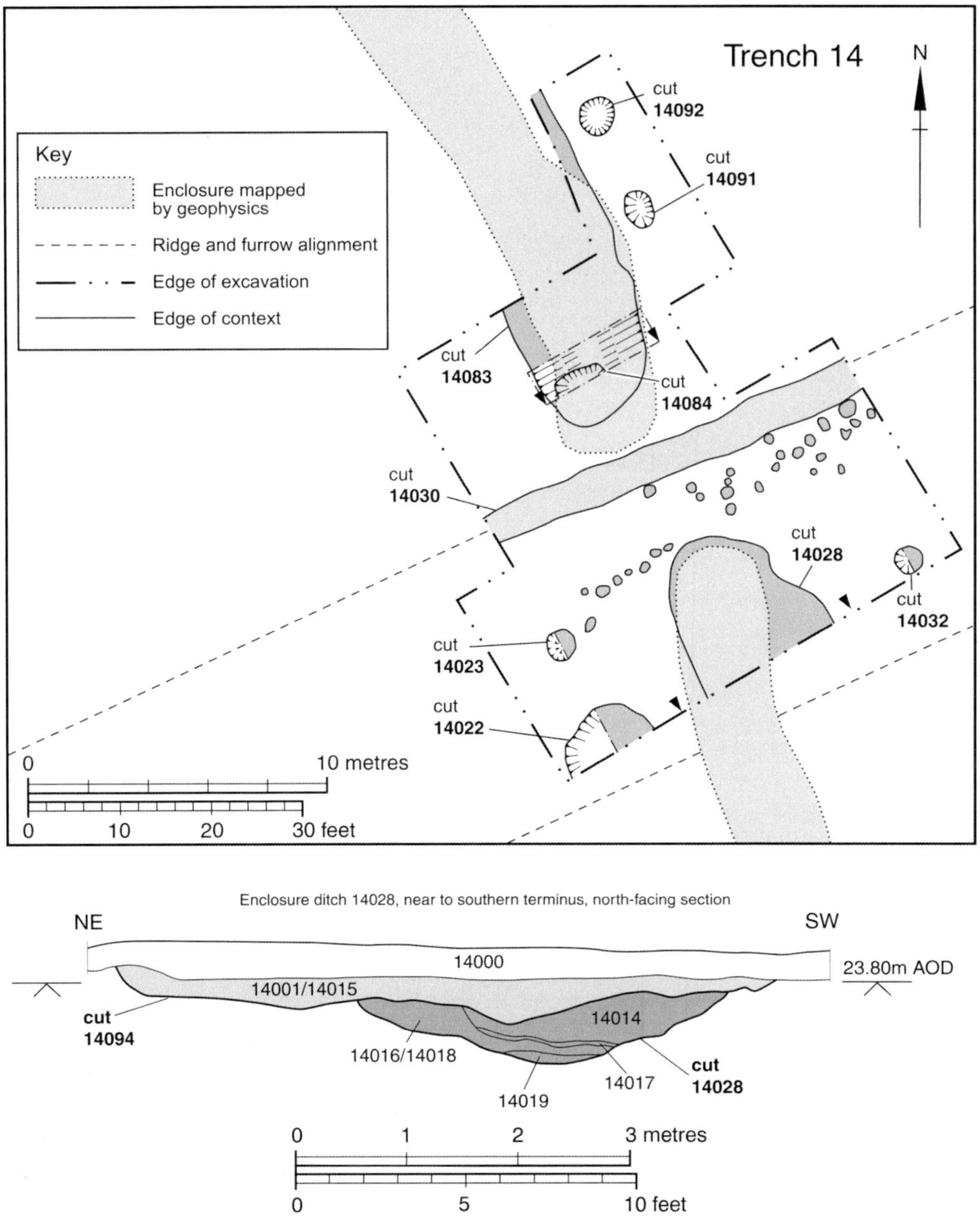

Figure 31 Plan of Trench 14. © York Archaeological Trust

enclosure entrance. The majority were 0.20–0.30m in diameter and 0.07–0.12m deep, but a few were up to 0.55m in diameter. Their sand and pebble fills did not contain any dating evidence, and there is no stratigraphic association between them and the enclosure ditch. Some may be the bases of post-holes; others may represent variations in the natural.

Adjacent to these cuts was a linear feature (14030) aligned north-east/south-west, parallel to the current field boundary, measuring 1.30–1.60m wide and *c.* 0.14m deep. Similar features were found in Trench 15, and, on both spatial and formal grounds, this feature is interpreted as a remnant of ridge and furrow cultivation of the field dating from the medieval to post-medieval period.

Two larger post-holes were located close to the enclosure entrance, one (14023) inside and the other (14032) outside. 14032 was *c.* 0.92m in diameter and *c.* 0.25m deep; 14023 was *c.* 0.95m in diameter and 0.43m deep with evidence of a post socket in the base. No dating evidence was recovered from these features.

Approximately 0.60m outside the northern terminal, and centred 3.5m apart, were two sub-circular pits or post-holes (14091 and 14092), each *c.* 1.40m in diameter and *c.* 0.35m deep. Two pieces of lead-alloy spillage (sfs346 and 347) were recovered from 14091.

Approximately 2m inside the southern ditch terminal was a large stone-lined pit (14022), *c.* 3.50m in diameter and *c.* 1.05m deep, its sides breaking sharply from the surface and sloping steeply, almost vertically, to a flat base. A charcoal-rich deposit (14020) in the base, *c.* 0.40m thick, resulted from burning which could have taken place *in situ* in the base of the pit. The pit was lined with closely packed small pebbles 0.03–0.13m in diameter, forming a *c.* 0.10m thick lining for almost the full depth of the pit. This feature may have functioned as a large storage pit. It was subsequently backfilled with a homogeneous coarse-grained sandy deposit (14002) with few inclusions but disturbed by root and animal burrow activity. Two samples of charcoal from this backfill produced calibrated (95% confidence) radiocarbon

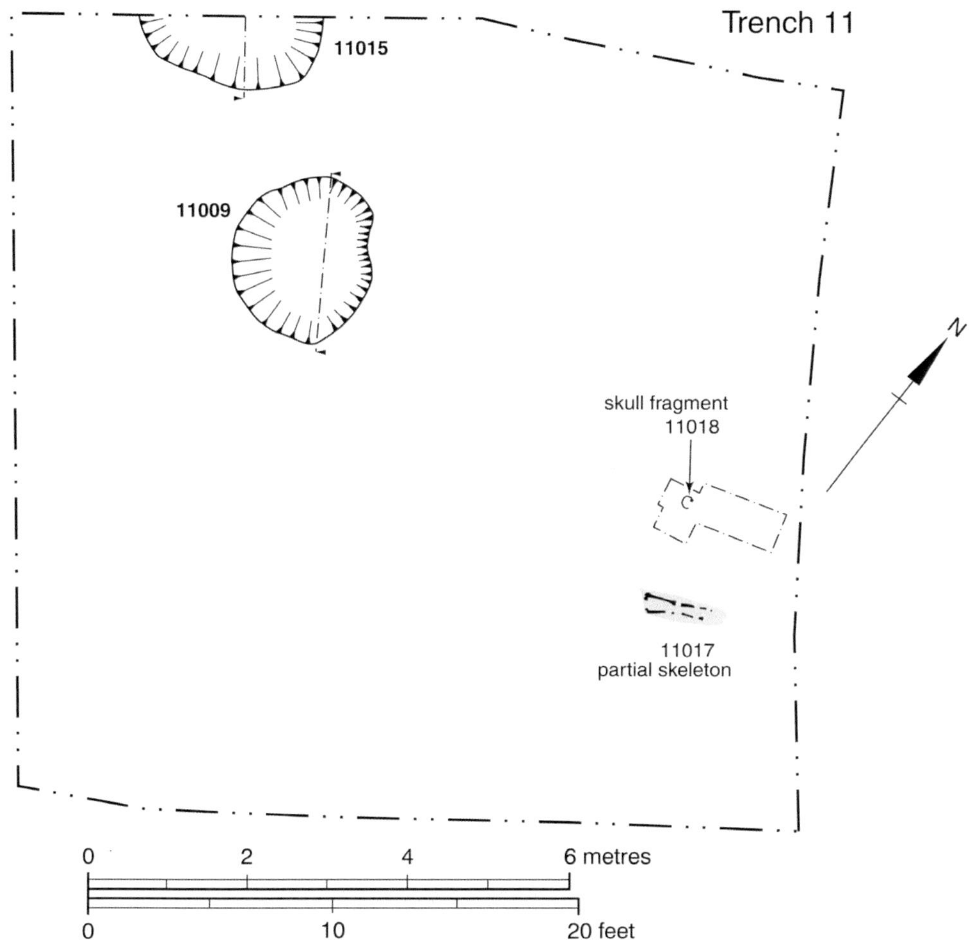

Figure 32 Plan of Trench 11. © York Archaeological Trust

dates of *cal AD 680–940* and *cal AD 660–880*; their posterior density estimates (95% probability) are, respectively, *cal AD 680–850* and *cal AD 670–820.*

Within the large enclosure

Trench 11

Trench 11 (10.5m x 10m) was located on the eastern slope of a plateau of some of the higher ground within the site. Interleaving variations in the natural strata coincided with curving geophysical anomalies. Wind-blown/hill-washed sand, containing a Roman coin, flints, and ferrous and lead-alloy metalworking waste, was cut by two pits (**Fig. 32**). One (11015) was *c.* 2.30m in diameter and *c.* 0.50m deep; its sandy backfill (11006) contained much large animal bone, a plated iron key (sf260) of Roman or later date, an iron ring (sf257), an iron nail head (sf263), ferrous slag (sf256) and an undated styca (sf272).

The other cut (11009), 2.10m in diameter and 0.65m deep, had a similar backfill (11003) in which was a penny of Burgred of Mercia (sf267) dated AD 852–74, a large quantity of animal bone, apparently butchery waste, an iron looped staple (sf251), a drop handle (sf269) with Anglo-Scandinavian to medieval parallels, possible silver waste (sf266) and copper-alloy waste (sfs262 and 271), and iron slag (sf761). Five handmade sherds are thought to be of 6th- to 9th-century date. A dark gritty sandy deposit (11002) south of this pit, which contained a fragment of quern (sf259) dated pre-1100 and a discoid lead weight (sf258), may represent a dump or build-up of industrial waste.

Parts of two severely truncated human skeletons were encountered in the south-east area of the trench. No grave cuts were visible but, like the pits, these burials were stratigraphically above the hill-wash. 11018 was a fragment of a human skull, of indeterminable age and sex, lying as if for an *in situ* supine burial from which other bones had been ploughed away. Some 1.25m to its south were the lower leg, *os coxa* and feet of an adult's supine skeleton (11017, SK1), orientated east–west; the remainder had been removed by a modern cut. Two radiocarbon samples from this skeleton have a weighted mean calibrated date (95% confidence) of *cal AD 890–1020*, with a posterior density estimate (95% probability) of *cal AD 890–1020.*

Disturbed/overlying layers included a sherd of an Anglo-Saxon pedestal base (see **Fig. 35**).

Trench 33 (Figs 26, 33)

A sub-circular pit (33005) measured *c.* 1.50m in diameter and was *c.* 0.70m deep. Its lower fill, a very compacted sand (33007) contained a copper-alloy Roman bracelet (sf813); from its upper fill, a friable soft sand (33003), came a styca of Bishop Wulfhere (*c.* 854–900) (sf381), an irregularly globular amber bead (sf380), a metalworking punch or awl (sf814) and iron rivets (sfs379 and 817).

Trench 15 (Fig. 34)

Trench 15, 15m x 10m, was positioned to examine a rectilinear enclosure, measuring *c.* 42m east–west and *c.* 36.5m north–south, identified by geophysical survey (see **Fig. 26**). Excavation confirmed the north-west quarter of

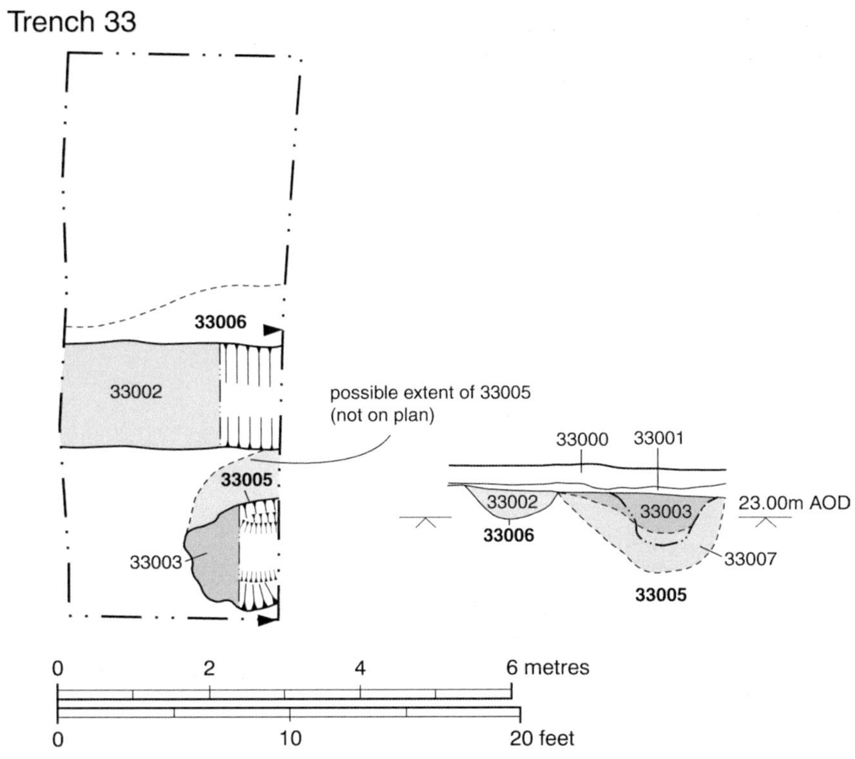

Figure 33 Plan of Trench 33 and section through pit 33005. © York Archaeological Trust

this feature. The defining ditch was *c.* 1.30–1.50m wide and *c.* 0.75m deep, with a U-shaped profile. In the uppermost backfill were a possible anvil stone sf327, pot-boilers and animal bone fragments apparently representing butchery waste.

Two sub-circular pits (15006, 15010), *c.* 1.50m in diameter x 0.36m deep, and *c.* 1.45m in diameter x 0.45m deep respectively, were investigated. Both had sandy fills and both contained quantities of large animal bones, representing butchery waste, and several unusual finds. A large iron bell (sf336) of early medieval form, an iron drop handle (sf278) of either Roman or early medieval date, and a piece of iron slag (sf279) were recovered from 15004, a fill of pit 15006. The finds from 15010 included a possible textile spike (sf338) which could also be of early medieval date, a key (sf280), a copper-alloy twisted wire ring (sf286), a stone hone (sf285), an iron looped staple (sf282), a lead-alloy spindle whorl (sf287), gilt copper-alloy mounts (sfs276, 277 and 290), lead run-off and spillage (sfs281 and 289) and copper-alloy waste (sf288).

Although these pits were located 'within' the rectangular enclosure there was no stratigraphic evidence to define their

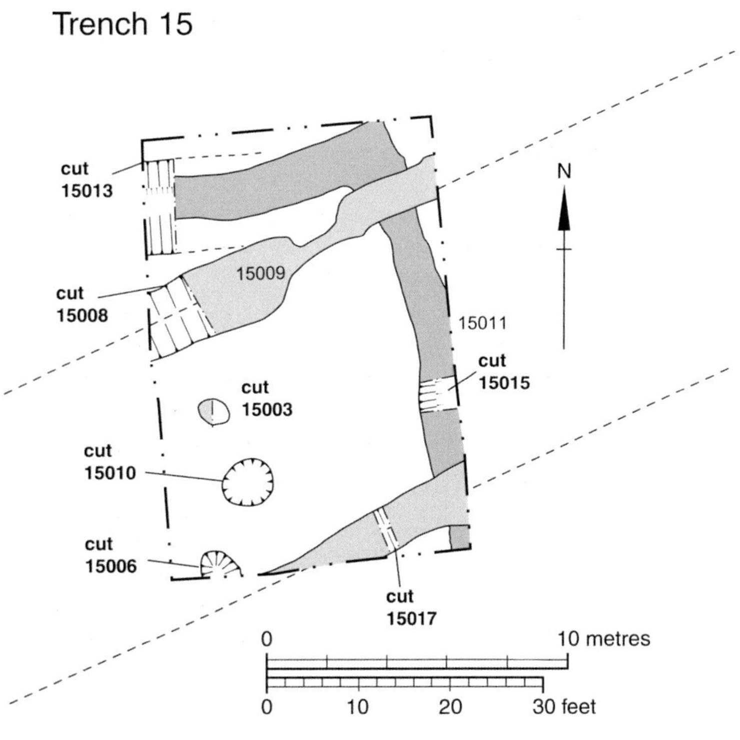

Figure 34 Plan of Trench 15 showing postulated line of ridge and furrow. © York Archaeological Trust

chronological relationship to it. The finds from the pits suggest metalworking, and, possibly, textile production and woodworking in the vicinity.

Pottery
Ailsa Mainman

The assemblage of only 157 sherds was small, and dated from the later 3rd millennium BC to the 20th century AD. Some of the material is difficult to interpret. Most sherds are small and very abraded, characteristic of a collection from well-cultivated fields. This alone often makes identification difficult but, in addition, there are groups of sherds whose date and significance are unclear.

A small quantity of Early Bronze Age and Iron Age material indicates activity over a very long time frame, while equally small quantities of Roman and possible early–middle Anglo-Saxon material extend this into the 1st millennium AD. It is striking that there is no pottery which is clearly Anglo-Scandinavian in date, despite the evidence from the metalwork, although it is possible that a jar of indeterminate date from Trench 22 belonged to this episode. The post-Norman, medieval and post-medieval periods are all represented in the abraded and broken form typical of field assemblages, where their presence might be accounted for by the spreading of farm middens.

The possible Anglo-Saxon material recovered from Trench 11 included a pedestal base in a dark grey burnished fabric (**Fig. 35**). It is almost certainly part of the same vessel as a burnished sherd in the same fabric which has traces of a shallow groove decoration. Fabric, surface treatment and decoration all suggest an Anglo-Saxon date. Pedestal bases are not uncommon amongst vessels of the 5th–7th century (Myres 1977, figs 201–6) and, although they are more common in the south-east and midlands, there are examples from Yorkshire (e.g. *ibid.*, no. 108, fig. 204, from The Mount, York). In this case, however, there is too little surviving to be certain of date or form. Seven further handmade sherds, including a rounded base angle in a micaceous sandy fabric, might all be from a single vessel but the edges are eroded and there are no visible joins. One of the sherds is a similar type to that described below from Trench 22.

Trench 22 produced an assemblage of 27 sherds. Apart from Romano-British, medieval and post-medieval wares, the remainder fall into two groups which were also examined by Terry Manby. One group, comprising five handmade sherds of a reduced, dark brown vesicular fabric which include a flat-topped rim sherd, is certainly Iron Age. The other group comprises ten handmade body sherds in a thick, coarse, hard-fired fabric with roughened surfaces, probably all from one large vessel. No rim or base survives and there is no trace of decoration or surface burnishing. The lack of defining features makes dating uncertain but if, as Manby suggests, they are not Iron Age, they presumably date to the post-Roman era, although they do not resemble other Anglo-Saxon wares. If these sherds do represent only one vessel, then it might be that this was an unusual example. It appears to have been a large jar with wall thickness of 11–12mm, made of a hard gritty fabric with angular quartz temper and a thin carbonised coating. A similar sherd was recovered from context 11003 in Trench 11.

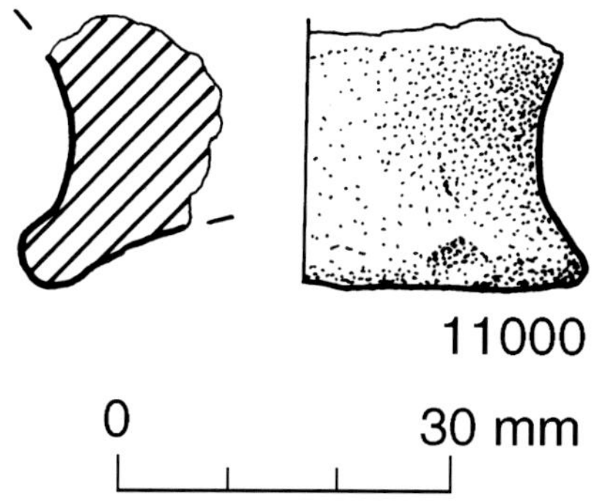

Figure 35 Anglo-Saxon pedestal base in a dark grey burnished fabric recovered from Trench 11. © York Archaeological Trust

There is no clear pattern to the spatial distribution of the material. Most of the pottery came from trenches in the southern half of the area excavated, where the full range of material was found, particularly in Trench 22, which produced the most interesting groups. The pottery, therefore, serves to illustrate the long history of activity on the site without casting much light on the unusually large spread of early medieval metalwork.

Radiocarbon dating
Derek Hamilton, Gordon Cook, Rhona Finlayson, Richard Hall and Peter D. Marshall

Twelve samples were submitted for dating by Accelerator Mass Spectrometry at the Scottish Universities Environmental Research Centre (SUERC), East Kilbride. The samples consisted of ten pieces of short-lived charcoal, and two pieces of human bone from a single burial. The charcoal samples were prepared using methods outlined in Slota *et al.* (1987), and the human bone was prepared following a modified version of Longin (1971). All samples were measured as described by Xu *et al.* (2004). The SUERC laboratory maintains a continual programme of quality assurance procedures, in addition to participation in international inter-comparisons (Scott 2003). These tests indicate no laboratory offsets and demonstrate the validity of the measurement quoted.

Results

The results, given in **Table 10**, are conventional radiocarbon ages (Stuiver and Polach 1977), and are quoted in accordance with the international standard known as the Trondheim convention (Stuiver and Kra 1986). The calibrations of these results, relating the radiocarbon measurements directly to calendar dates, have been calculated using the calibration curve of Reimer *et al.* (2004) and the computer program OxCal (v3.10) (Bronk Ramsey 1995; 1998; 2001; 2009). The calibrated date ranges for these samples are given in **Table 10** and have been calculated using the maximum intercept method (Stuiver and Reimer 1986); they are quoted in the form recommended by Mook (1986), with the end points rounded outwards to 10 years if the error term is greater than or equal to 25 radiocarbon years. The graphical distributions of the calibrated dates, shown in **Figures 36–7**, are derived from the probability method (Stuiver and Reimer 1993).

Lab ID	Sample ID	Contextual information	Material	δ^{15}N (‰)	δ^{13}C (‰)	C/N ratio	Radiocarbon age (BP)	Calibrated date (95% confidence)	*Posterior density estimate (95% probability)*
SUERC-10642	Sample 101; Context 11017, SK1 A	burial (11017)	human bone, acetabulum *os coxa*	11.6	−20.6	3.4	1060±35	–	–
SUERC-10511	Sample 101; Context 11017, SK1 B	burial (11017)	human bone, femur	10.1	−21.4	4.2	1095±35	–	–
weighted mean SK1	T'=0.5, v=1, T'(5%)=3.8		(Ward and Wilson 1978)	–	–	–	1078±25	*cal AD 890–1020*	*cal AD 890–1020*
SUERC-10161	Sample 103; Context 22036 A	pit (22039)	charcoal, Salicaceae	–	−25.0	–	1270±35	*cal AD 660–870*	*cal AD 670–780*
SUERC-10162	Sample 103; Context 22036 B	pit (22039)	charcoal, *Quercus* sp., s/w	–	−27.0	–	1290±35	*cal AD 650–780*	*cal AD 670–780*
SUERC-10163	Sample 104; Context 5001 A	pit/post-hole (5002)	charcoal, *Ulex/Cytisus*	–	−24.5	–	1200±35	*cal AD 690–950*	*cal AD 680–860*
SUERC-10164	Sample 104; Context 5001 B	pit/post-hole (5002)	charcoal, *Corylus avellana*	–	−26.7	–	1250±35	*cal AD 660–890*	*cal AD 680–830*
SUERC-10168	Sample 105; Context 19003 A	ditch (19004)	charcoal, *Quercus* sp., s/w, 5 rings	–	−23.0	–	3715±35	*2210–1980 cal BC*	–
SUERC-10169	Sample 105; Context 19003 B	ditch (19004)	charcoal, *Fraxinus excelsior*, r/w	–	−24.0	–	3330±35	*1740–1510 cal BC*	–
SUERC-10170	Sample 102; Context 14002 A	pit (14022)	charcoal, Pomoideae	–	−29.3	–	1210±35	*cal AD 680–940*	*cal AD 680–850*
SUERC-10171	Sample 102; Context 14002 B	pit (14022)	charcoal, Salicaceae	–	−26.5	–	1260±35	*cal AD 660–880*	*cal AD 670–820*
SUERC-10172	Sample 106; Context 22004	pit (22039)	charcoal, Salicaceae	–	−25.3	–	1270±35	*cal AD 660–870*	*cal AD 690–830*
SUERC-10173	Sample 108; Context 22037	pit (22039)	charcoal, cf. *Corylus avellana*	–	−27.2	–	2185±30	*380–170 cal BC*	–

Table 10 Radiocarbon measurements

Stable isotopes

The stable isotope values (Δ^{13}C and Δ^{15}N; **Table 10**) are consistent with a largely terrestrial diet, with only a very minor marine component that is not likely to affect the radiocarbon dating (Chisholm *et al.* 1982; Mays 2000). DeNiro (1985) suggests that a C/N ratio range of 2.9–3.6 is an indicator of good-quality collagen. Although SUERC-10511 has a C/N ratio of 4.2 (with SUERC-10642 having a C/N ratio of 3.4), the fact that the radiocarbon results on the paired samples from the inhumation (11017) SK1 are statistically consistent gives little reason to reduce our confidence in the radiocarbon determination of this sample.

General approach

The Bayesian approach to the interpretation of archaeological chronologies has been described by Buck *et al.* (1996). It is based on the principle that although the calibrated age ranges of radiocarbon measurements accurately estimate the calendar ages of the samples themselves, it is the dates of archaeological events associated with those samples that are important. Bayesian techniques can provide realistic estimates of the dates of such events by combining absolute dating evidence, such as radiocarbon results, with relative dating evidence, such as stratigraphic relationships between radiocarbon samples. These 'posterior density estimates' (which, by convention, are always expressed *in italics*) are not absolute. They are interpretative estimates, which will change as additional data become available or as the existing data are modelled from different perspectives.

The technique used is a form of Markov Chain Monte Carlo sampling, and has been applied using the program OxCal (v3.10) (http://c14.arch.ox.ac.uk/oxcal3/entire.htm), which uses a mixture of the Metropolis-Hastings algorithm and the more specific Gibbs sampler (Gilks *et al.* 1996; Gelfand and Smith 1990). Details of the algorithms employed by this program are available from the online manual or in Bronk Ramsey (1995; 1998; 2001; 2009). The algorithms used in the models described below can be derived from the structure shown in **Figures 36–7**.

Objectives and sampling

The objectives of the dating programme were, firstly, to provide a date for the inhumation (SK1) and, secondly, to provide a chronology for the occupation of the site.

The first stage in sample selection was to identify short-lived material, which was demonstrably not residual in the context from which it was recovered. Material was selected only where there was evidence that a sample had been put fresh into its context. This included discrete fills in a putative prehistoric circular ditch and three otherwise undated pits. Where possible, duplicate samples from these contexts were submitted, to test the assumption that the material was of the same actual age. The dates for the prehistoric ditch are available in the YAT Archive and will be published at a later date.

Analysis and interpretation

The replicate samples from contexts 14002, 5001 and 22036 were all subjected to a chi-squared test using OxCal (v3.10), following Ward and Wilson (1978). The results are shown in **Table 11**. This analysis shows that the measurements on the charcoal from 14002, 5001 and 22036 are statistically consistent and reliably date their respective contexts. As the measurements on two distinct bones from the burial were statistically consistent, these measurements were combined by taking a weighted mean prior to calibration (Ward and Wilson 1978).

Context	T'	Pass/Fail
14002	1.0	Pass
5001	1.0	Pass
22036	0.2	Pass
19003	60.4	Fail

Table 11 Results of chi-squared test on sample pairs, by context (Ward and Wilson 1978); for all pairs: T'(5%)=3.8, v=1

Nearly all of the other samples produced measurements that calibrate to the Anglo-Saxon period. As such, and considering there was some stratigraphic relationship between some of the contexts, these samples/measurements have all been combined into a Bayesian chronological model (**Fig. 37**). The model consists of two parts: pit features within the D-shaped enclosure and the inhumation. In total, five features were dated, with no stratigraphic relationship between them. However, within one feature, pit 22039, samples were submitted from three contexts that did have stratigraphic relationships. In this pit, sample 108 (22037) is below samples 103 (22036) A and B, with sample 106 (22004) coming out of the upper fill.

The overall index of agreement between the radiocarbon results and their stratigraphic relationships shown in the

Figure 36 Probability distributions of Bronze Age dates. © York Archaeological Trust

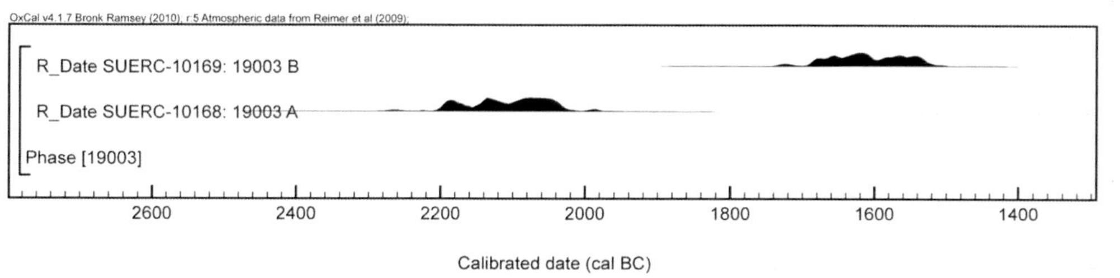

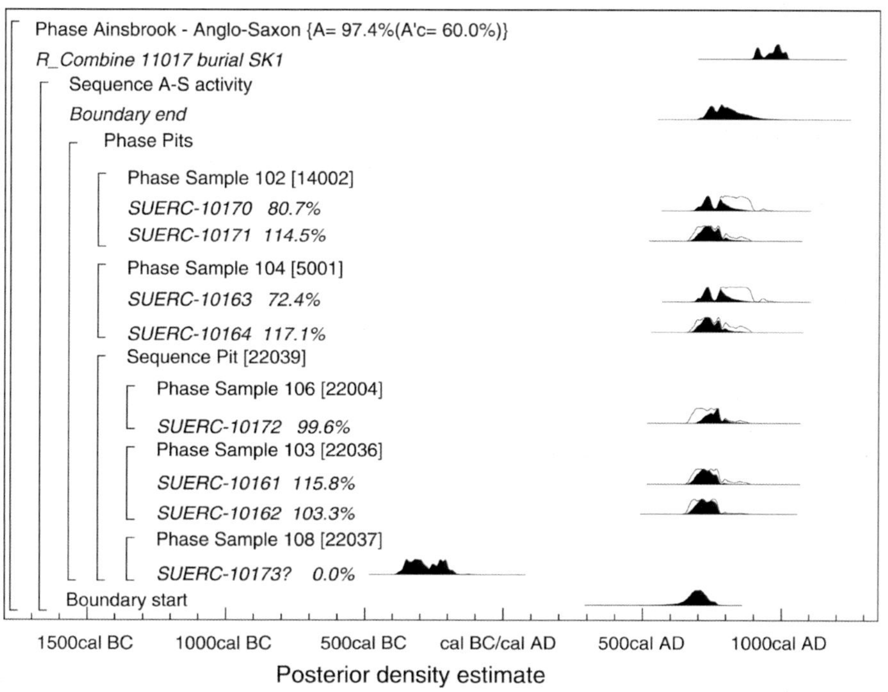

Figure 37 Chronological model of Anglo-Saxon activity. © York Archaeological Trust

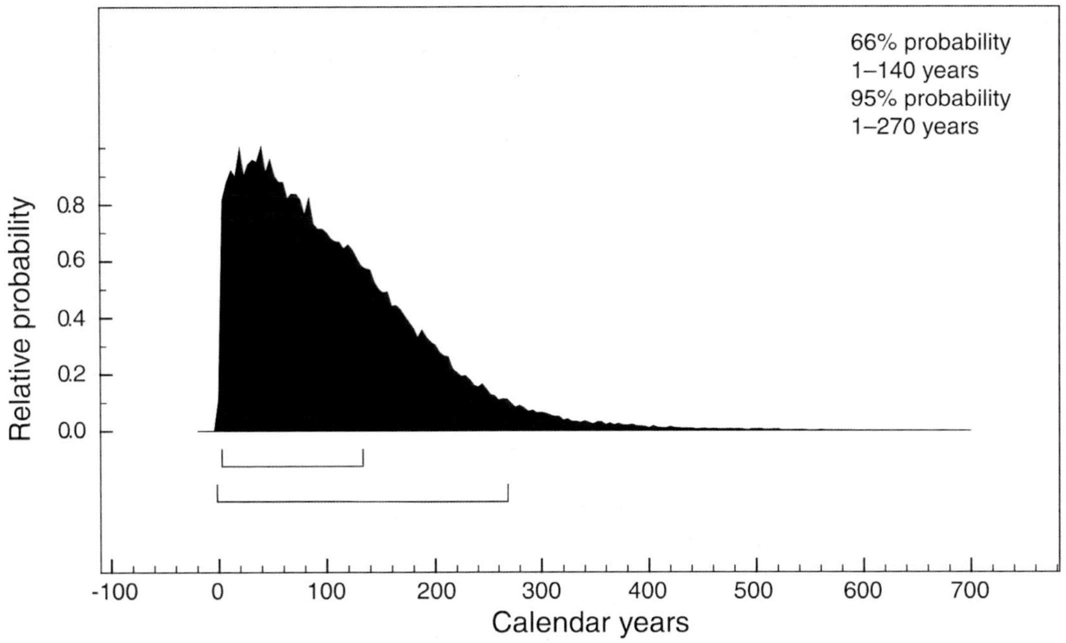

Figure 38 Estimate for the duration of activity resulting in the pit features, as derived from the chronological model in Figure 37. © York Archaeological Trust

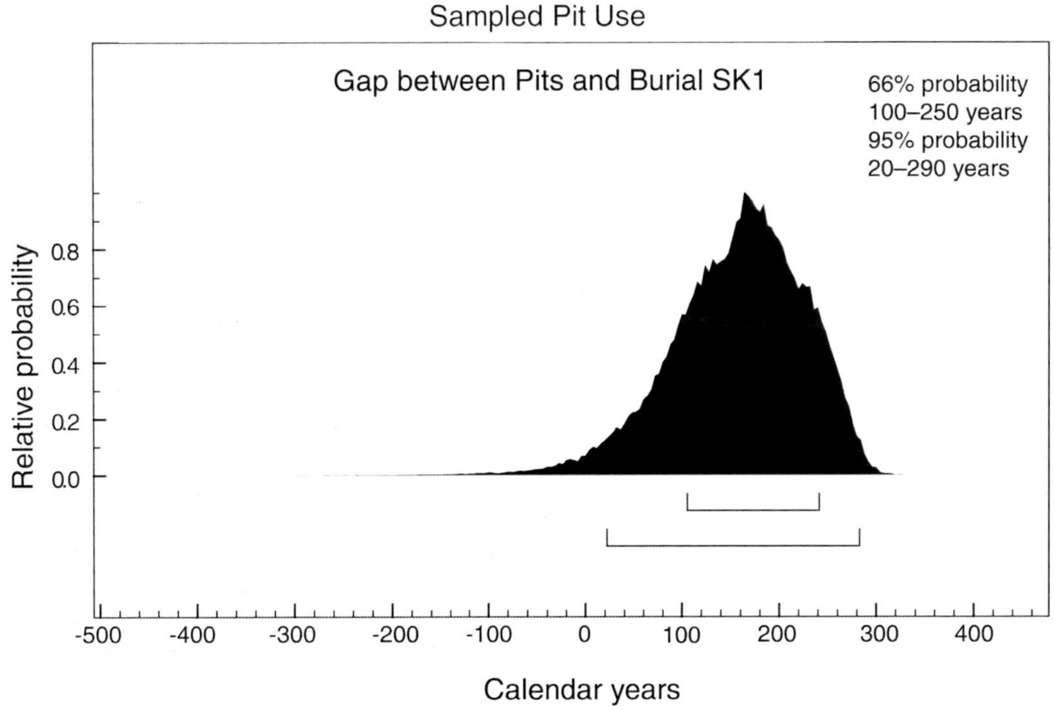

Figure 39 Difference between the probability distributions for burial SK1 and the end of activity as evidenced by the dating of the pits. © York Archaeological Trust

model is good ($A_{overall}$=97.4%, **Fig. 37**). One measurement, SUERC-10173 (Sample 108, 22037), dates to the Iron Age, and suggests that either residual material was incorporated into the lowest fill of pit 22039 when the cobbles were placed at the base, or that it was brought in through identified animal burrowing. This measurement has been left out of the model, as indicated by the '?' next to the laboratory number.

The model estimates that the use of the site, as evidenced by the dating of the pit features, began in *cal AD 610–770* (*95% probability*; **Fig. 37**; *start*) and ended in *cal AD 700–920* (*95% probability*; **Fig. 37**; *end*). The overall span of use for the pits is *1–270 years* (*95% probability*; **Fig. 38**). The small number of dates available is, however, likely to mean that the estimate suggests that activity continues for longer than it really did.

The inhumation, 11017 SK1, has not been included in the estimates for the use of the site during the Anglo-Saxon period, despite clearly being Anglo-Saxon in date. This is because a qualitative evaluation of the radiocarbon dating suggested that the inhumation is of a later period of use. Indeed, this model gives a 98% probability that the posterior density estimate for the burial post-dates the posterior density estimate for the *end* of the use of the pit features.

Furthermore, the model estimates that *20–290 years* (95% probability) or *100–250 years* (66% probability; **Fig. 39**) separates the end of the use of the pits and the burial of SK1.

ARSNY: Overview and conclusions

Overview of the site
Richard Hall

Until the metal-detected discoveries were reported, there was no archaeological evidence to suggest that this locale was of any particular significance in the early medieval period. There is no record of any previous archaeological intervention on the study site itself, and indeed no record of any discovery of early medieval material in the parish. The array of non-invasive techniques deployed by YAT in the investigation of the ARSNY site has revealed a hitherto completely unsuspected multi-period archaeological site at a prominent point within the local landscape.

There is no contemporary documentary evidence that the site had any extraordinary status in the early medieval period. This *lacuna* is not surprising, given the relative paucity of surviving documentation from this period in Northumbria. Yet, had the site been a major permanent focus of activity or occupation, a secular or religious focus of more than merely local significance, it might be hoped, if not expected, that its former function or pedigree would have registered or been reflected in some way within later medieval documentation. No such reference has yet been located, however.

Apart from traces of medieval ridge and furrow (see below, p. 82), two principal earlier landscapes can be detected among the data; additionally, there is a series of features – enclosures, alignments, etc. – which do not obviously relate to either of these two main buried landscapes.

One of these landscapes, which appears to extend over much of the area, looks like a series of Iron Age–Romano-British fields, enclosures and trackways. Some circular features might represent structures, and some other pit-type features might be associated with this phase.

The other is represented by a large ditch that encloses a sub-rectangular area of some 400m x 200m (see **Fig. 1**). One side is now defined by a sharp natural break in slope which was apparently not reinforced artificially; it is not known whether erosion may have removed traces of a man-made boundary here. Elsewhere, most of its course, and an approximately centrally positioned entrance, were indicated by a clear geophysical anomaly. At or towards what might be its northern corner, however, the anomaly becomes intermittent just before it bifurcates and then peters out, leaving unclear the exact position(s) of any westwards return(s).

Four exploratory trenches which straddled the anomaly and its putative continuation were excavated (see **Fig. 26**). Two (Trenches 21 and 22) were in its southern sector, one (Trench 14) lay astride the possible entrance way, and in the fourth (Trench 5) it was hoped to confirm the line or lines of the westwards return(s).

A ditch was located in Trench 5 (see **Fig. 28**). Time constraints precluded its full excavation but it was over 1m deep and is estimated to have been over 3.5m wide. Parallel ditches in Trench 21 (see **Fig. 29**) may have been perpetuated by posts. These ditches may be contemporary features in a double ditch system used to define a significant area.

Only a small number of geophysical anomalies within the enclosure share its main axes; it is not known whether any of the plethora of pit-type features within it are associated with its use. The date and function (as well as some aspects of the form) of this feature remain enigmatic; it could, for example, be an early medieval defended/prestige/high-status site, and thus provide a context within which the remarkable number of early medieval objects – coins, weights, pieces of decorated metalwork, etc. – can be better understood. This metal-detected artefact assemblage, including the hoard recovered from Trench 2 (see **Figs 26–7**), is outstanding among those recorded within the region, and singles out the site as a major focus of economic activity. Yet the precise nature of this activity throughout the period from *c.* 700 until the 10th century remains elusive.

Dating
Gareth Williams

Both excavation and the finds assemblage show intermittent activity on the site over a prolonged period, from prehistory to the post-medieval period, but with a peak of activity in the late 9th century. Both the overall archaeological landscape and individual finds point to Iron Age, Roman and/or Romano-British activity on the site, but this falls outside the remit of the current report.

Pre-Viking activity

The stycas (see p. 36 and **Table 5**) could suggest that there was significant Anglian activity on the site in the mid-9th century in the period prior to the Viking conquest of Northumbria. Stycas are assumed to have been produced until some point (perhaps *c.* 855) in the reign of Osberht, who was killed in 867, although the end of his reign saw him competing with a rival Ælle, for whom no coins are recorded. However, a significant proportion of the later stycas have blundered legends and cannot be dated precisely. The irregular series includes issues derived from several issuers up to and including Osberht (Pirie 2006), and it is coins of this blundered type which represent the latest phase in the styca assemblage on this site. Furthermore, it is uncertain what impact the deaths of Osberht and Ælle had either on the minting or the circulation of these coins. Later sources refer to the installation of an Anglian puppet king, Ecgberht, under the control of the Vikings in 866, and to his replacement in 872 by another puppet king named Ricsige, although the extent and character of their authority remains uncertain (Rollason 2003, 249; McLeod 2014, 177–80). While the anonymous blundered issues certainly began before 866, it is possible that the latest anonymous issues post-date 866. Neither the political nor the economic situation in Northumbria is clear between the conquest of 866–7 and the settlement of 876, and it is entirely possible that there was a degree of continuity in this period. Reassessment of the role of the Mercian king Ceolwulf II (874–*c.* 879) (Keynes 1998; Williams and Naylor 2016), who was also presented as a Viking puppet in later West Saxon sources, casts doubt on the reliability of West Saxon accounts, and the limited post-870 East Anglian coinage in the names of Osberht and Æthelred also raises the possibility of continuity in that kingdom between the death of Eadmund in 870 and the Viking settlement of 875 (Blackburn 2005). The status of Ecgberht, and especially the extent of his authority south of the Tyne, remain obscure, and the same is true of Ricsige, although the fact that the latter is credited in the *Historia Regum* of Symeon of Durham with a reign of three years may indicate that he was displaced at the beginning of the lasting Viking settlement of Northumbria in 876 (McLeod 2014, 177–80).

Against this background, the value of Northumbrian stycas as an indication of 'pre-Viking' activity is limited. Furthermore, as discussed above (see pp. 36, 42–3), it has generally been assumed that there was little place for stycas within the Viking silver economies. However, their apparent availability during the period of Viking conquest and settlement, the direct evidence of re-use of stycas as decoration on Viking weights, and the utility of stycas as raw material for metalworking or even as a form of low-value commodity money, all point to the fact that they are more likely to appear at a Viking site in Northumbria in the late 9th century than has generally been supposed. Thus, while the stycas could point to pre-Viking activity on the site, they do not necessarily have to, and the relative paucity of other Anglo-Saxon finds does not suggest major occupation in the pre-Viking period, although possible fragments of great square-headed brooches (sfs1144 and 1106), cruciform brooches (sfs1075 and 1109) and other early fragments point to early activity on the site. Given the apparent re-use on the site of fragmentary metalwork imported from elsewhere (see below, pp. 59–61, 84), it is possible that the early Anglo-Saxon fragments were also imported rather than indicating early local activity. However, the finds also included a ceramic pedestal base in dark grey burnished fabric, found in Trench 11. While too little remains to be certain of date, the fabric, surface treatment and decoration all suggest an Anglo-Saxon origin, and the use of pedestal bases has parallels in the 5th–7th centuries. In addition, the radiocarbon dating indicates with a 95% probability that use of the pits on the site started in *cal AD 610–770*, and ended in *cal AD 700–920*, with a span of use for the pits of *1–270 years*, although this dating is derived from a sample of only three pits. Nevertheless, the dating of the pits is consistent both with the likely dates of the few early Anglo-Saxon finds and the cessation of non-agricultural activity on the site following the main period of Viking activity in the late 9th century discussed below. On balance, it therefore seems reasonable to accept pre-Viking Anglian activity on the site, perhaps as early as the 7th century, but on a considerably smaller scale than that of the subsequent Viking phase.

Viking and Anglo-Scandinavian

Most of the Viking finds can only be loosely dated to the late 9th or early 10th centuries. The introduction of the cubo-octahedral weights has previously been dated to the 870s–880s on the basis of the finds from Hedeby, but a slightly earlier date of 860s–870s has been suggested on the basis of the Birka and Kaupang finds (see above, p. 20). In either case, the evidence is consistent with the activities of the *micel here* from the mid-860s onwards and certainly with the settlement in the mid-870s. The absence (or rarity) of oblate-spheroid weights, with only one possible example, sf815, may be significant, since these are often found at the same sites in Scandinavia but were apparently introduced slightly later in the 870s–880s. This would support a tighter dating, with the main period of activity on the site being limited to the 870s. However, the absence of this type of weight might also be explained by other factors (see above p. 20).

As discussed, lead weights with coins and fragments of Insular metalwork inset appear to have been produced by the Vikings in Britain and Ireland (and possibly elsewhere). These are again difficult to date with any certainty, since only the inset pieces are diagnostic, and in many cases these may represent the re-use of much earlier material. At least one recorded find, unfortunately unprovenanced, includes a re-used coin of the early 8th century (Williams 1999, 23, no. 5), but the vast majority of those which incorporate coins (now over 30 examples) include either Northumbrian stycas, or Lunettes coins of the type shared by Burgred of Mercia (852–74), Æthelred I of Wessex (865–71) and the first part of the reign of Alfred of Wessex (871–99), prior to his first coinage reform of the mid-870s. It therefore seems reasonable to associate this class of weight with the activities of the *micel here*, although not exclusively, and even though the style may have continued (more rarely) into the early 10th century.

By contrast, the coins in the small hoard suggest a fairly clear *terminus post quem* for the hoard. The hoard terminates in coins of the Lunettes type of both Burgred and Alfred, and particularly with the rare sub-type E ii in the name of Burgred, which probably dates from the very end of his reign, *c.* 873–4. The Lunettes coinage had completely disappeared by the time of the hoards of the 890s and later, such as Ashdon, Stamford and Cuerdale, and is even absent from the Watlington hoard of *c.* 879–80. The ARSNY hoard lacks any evidence of testing by pecking, commonly found in these later hoards. It also lacks any coins of the reformed coinages of Alfred and Ceolwulf II, from *c.* 874–5 and later, any of the anonymous Viking imitations of *c.* 880 and later, and any of the distinctive Anglo-Viking coinages of the 890s. There is thus a firm *terminus post quem* for the hoard of *c.* 874, and, while the small size of the hoard means that one must be cautious about arguing from absence of evidence, it seems very likely that the hoard pre-dates 890, likely that it pre-dates 880, and more likely than not that it dates from the mid-870s.

A dating for the hoard in the mid- to late 870s is also consistent with the main concentration of coins in the 9th-century site assemblage. As discussed above, the stycas probably terminate around the time of the Viking conquest in the 860s, although possibly a few years later, and these are followed by another Lunettes penny of Burgred recovered from Trench 11 during the YAT excavations (sf267), and a solitary example of the Cross-and-Lozenge type of Ceolwulf II (874–*c.* 879) (sf1385), without context. No later silver pennies of the late 9th or early 10th century are recorded from the site, although both Anglo-Saxon and Anglo-Scandinavian coinage of this period is relatively common elsewhere in areas of Viking settlement in England in hoards, and as single finds. There are also no coins dating from the period of the West Saxon conquest of Northumbria, or from the later Viking Age. None of the dirham fragments has been precisely dated, but from what can be seen of them, they are consistent with the dating of the rest of the 9th-century assemblage.

Both coins and weights thus point to the main period of Viking activity on the site commencing in the late 860s to mid-870s, possibly but not necessarily on the site of a former Anglian settlement, and with the more tightly dated pieces focused on the mid-870s. This is entirely consistent with the settlement of Northumbria by a section of the *micel here* under Halfdan in 875 (*Anglo-Saxon Chronicle* A&E, *sub* 876 [875]), and fits well with the similarity of the assemblage to that associated with the Viking winter camp at Torksey in 872–3 (*Anglo-Saxon Chronicle* A&E, *sub* 873–4 [872–3]; Blackburn 2002; 2007c; 2011), while the smaller size of the ARSNY site and assemblage may be explained by the fact that the *micel here* divided before Halfdan led one section to Northumbria in 874, and further divided to share out the land in 875. This is also consistent with the overall size of the site being smaller than Torksey (see below, pp. 84–6). Activity on the site could perhaps be associated with a short-lived occupation by the larger group in 874–5, and/or with continued activity by a smaller group after the settlement of 875, although the site is still very substantial by Viking standards (see p. 92).

Most of the other finds (excluding earlier material which was probably being re-used in the Viking phase, such as the Irish metalwork) can only be broadly dated to the late 9th century, and are thus consistent with the suggested period of core activity in the 870s. However, comparative evidence suggests that some of this material, in particular some of the strap-ends, may date to the very end of the century, or even to the early 10th, which would indicate that there was an element of continued activity on the site over a period of years or even a few decades, although there is nothing to indicate extensive activity on the site after the early 10th century, and the absence of any form of clearly Anglo-Scandinavian pottery also suggests that occupation of the site was comparatively short-lived. This is also consistent with the latest radiocarbon dates for the pits, and for some of the human remains in Trench 11 (see pp. 76–7, **Tables 10–11**). A similar clash between the dating evidence of the strap-ends and that of the coins and weights exists at Torksey. There the evidence is currently interpreted as deriving from a single season of occupation in 872–3 (Hadley and Richards *et al.* 2016, 45), although it is difficult to reconcile such a firm conclusion with the loose dating of many of the finds, and the coins do not in my opinion provide as firm a date as suggested in that publication.

On current evidence, it is impossible to state how long the core period of activity at ARSNY lasted. Given the reassessment of the styca evidence suggested above, together with the parallel evidence from the winter camp at Torksey, there is nothing to indicate that Viking activity pre-dated the documented settlement of Northumbria in 874–5. The hoard, the single coin finds and the relative proportions of oblate-spheroid and cubo-octahedral weights all suggest that the period of activity in trade and exchange on the site did not last beyond the mid- to late 870s, although occupation and perhaps even some production may have lasted rather longer. The core period of activity could thus be very short, perhaps comparable to the documented seasonal over-wintering camps of the period 865–76, such as Torksey and Repton, each of which had a single recorded core period of activity of only a few months. However, since the presence of datable coins or weight types would have required importation of the former from southern England and the latter from Scandinavia, the evidence could also be interpreted as indicating trade and exchange in a purely local context, without the opportunity or need for such imports. If production of metalwork did continue on the site for a longer period, this might suggest that an element of exchange also continued, as the production of strap-ends (and perhaps other metal items) implies an element of demand. Nevertheless, it seems likely that any role in exchange, like that of production, was on a much smaller scale after the core period of at most a few years in the mid- to late 870s.

It is against this background that one must consider the dating of the main earthwork. This appears likely to be early medieval, but cannot be dated very precisely. This allows for the possibilities that it is pre-Viking, contemporary with the Viking settlement, or post-settlement Anglo-Scandinavian. Given the evidence for severe reduction of non-agricultural activity after the initial settlement period, it is hard to see a plausible later Anglo-Scandinavian origin for the earthwork. However, the finds of the core period of activity seem largely to respect the earthwork, with the majority found inside, and a few found in the ditch fill. This leaves the question of whether the earthwork was created to define and perhaps defend the Viking site, or whether the earthwork already existed in the pre-Viking period. There are parallels for D-shaped or sub-rectangular enclosures along rivers at other Viking camps of the 9th century, including Repton and Woodstown (Biddle and Kjølbye-Biddle 1992; 2001; Kelly and Maas 1995, 1999; Kelly and O' Donovan 1998; O'Brien *et al.* 2005; Russell and Hurley, with Eogan, 2014; Kelly 2015; see further discussion below), and combined with the evidence for activity in the 870s, a Viking origin seems the most obvious conclusion. However, Viking winter camps in England, and to some extent in Ireland, appear in many cases to have been based at pre-existing central places, whether towns, monasteries or secular estate centres (Williams 2008b; see below, pp. 94–7), and, as discussed, there is some evidence for pre-Viking Anglian activity on the site, so it is possible that the earthwork may already have been a feature of the site when the Vikings arrived. However, this seems less likely, since the limited number of pre-Viking finds does not suggest a densely occupied site filling the whole of the enclosure before the 870s. Nevertheless, especially given the limited fieldwork undertaken on the site, it is possible that there was some sort of Anglian estate centre, whether secular or monastic, with agricultural land around it also enclosed within the earthwork. Ulmschneider (2000, 68) points to the presence of a *vallum monasterii* as a possible indicator of ecclesiastical character when considering 'productive sites'. Petts (2008) also points to the importance of well-defined boundaries for ecclesiastical precincts, and Hall (2011, 604) has noted that such boundaries may have contributed to the use of the term *burh* (more typically used in the context of secular defences and enclosures) to refer to monastic sites. Without further investigation, however, the existence of a pre-Viking enclosure can only be a hypothesis, and the coincidence of an earthwork with similarities to Viking sites elsewhere, together with a core period of activity at the time of the Viking settlement, suggests that a Viking attribution for the earthwork is a stronger possibility. However, this begs the question of the character of the Viking site, which is discussed further below.

Later medieval and post-medieval

Ridge and furrow agriculture, probably dating from the medieval period, had apparently taken place widely across the site. Evidence for it was found in Trenches 14, 15, 33 (**Fig. 40**) and possibly 22. The two coins of Edward the Confessor, both without context but dating from the mid-1060s, together with the small metal-detected assemblage of late medieval and post-medieval coins and jettons, considerably post-date the main period of activity on the site, although they point to continued activity on a much-reduced scale throughout the Middle Ages and post-medieval period. A single strap-end (sf928) with 11th-century Ringerike- and Urnes-style decoration (**Fig. 12**) reinforces the evidence for limited activity in the 11th century, but the fact that there is only one example of this type and few other finds of the period suggests that this represents a chance loss rather than production or even necessarily occupation. There was otherwise very little residual cultural material from the medieval period, suggesting the absence of structures or any activity other than agriculture on the site after the early 10th century. The same is true of the post-medieval period. The limited evidence of medieval and later pottery suggests the redeposition of abraded fragments, possibly spread across the site as the result of the use of material from middens to manure the fields. This is thus consistent with the evidence for ridge and furrow and the limited finds in indicating purely agricultural use.

Character of the site and comparators elsewhere
*Gareth Williams and Richard Hall**

**This section was compiled by Gareth Williams. It is based in part on notes by Richard Hall, in part on the interpretation of the finds and comparators by Gareth Williams, and in part on recollections of discussion between the two. As far as possible, the interpretation represents the views of both authors. However, the circumstances in which it was completed, combined with the fact that there have been important developments in the interpretation of Torksey, Repton and Woodstown since 2011, mean that Richard never read or approved the final version, and holds no responsibility for any errors which it may contain.*

The hoard and the quantity of other material of early medieval (particularly 8th- to 10th-century) date suggest that the site was a major focus of activity during this period. Such basic questions as to whether it was episodic, continuous, variable over time, and extensive or intensive in terms of the archaeological remains preserved in situ, require an answer in order to understand its full significance in the regional settlement pattern. Not all of these questions can be answered on the basis of the current evidence, but it seems safe to say that in addition to evidence of prehistoric and Roman activity on the site, there was Anglian occupation of some sort, whether continuous or episodic, and this was succeeded by a period of intense activity at the time of the Viking settlement of the kingdom of Northumbria in the 870s. However, it is uncertain whether there was Anglian activity on the site immediately prior to the Viking occupation. The core period of activity on site seems to have lasted no more than a few years at most, and possibly no more than a few weeks or months, but the typology of some of the metalwork suggests continued activity on a smaller scale possibly into the early 10th century. Thereafter, there is no evidence to suggest occupation or non-agricultural activity.

Anglian and Anglo-Scandinavian activity

Pits containing quantities of large animal bone and cultural material dating to the Anglian and Anglo-Scandinavian period were found in Trenches 11, 15 and 33. Animal bone from pit fills in Trench 11 and in Trench 15 appears to represent butchery waste. The bone is consistent with the site being occupied, but does not indicate the exact scale, dates or duration of this occupation.

Charcoal samples from the fills of other singular cut features found in Trenches 5, 14 and 22 (5002, 14022 and 22039 respectively) have all yielded radiocarbon dates in the Anglian and Anglo-Scandinavian periods. These were a deep circular cut (5002), a large deep pebble-lined possible storage pit (14022) close to the southern terminal of the enclosure, and an unusual pit (22039) containing heat-shattered cobbles. These features and deposits indicate activity over a large part of this site; such activity is likely to have been varied in character, ranging from possible structural activity to possible storage, together with a variety of crafts. An oven may have been located in the vicinity of Trench 22 and various types of craftworking in this period are indicated.

Metalworking

Several different types of metalworking took place on or around the site, in locations as yet undiscovered. Iron smithing took place in the vicinity of the pits, with the very large smithing hearth bottom fragment suggesting a relatively large hearth. Copper-alloy casting and silver working seem to have been of lesser importance than lead working, using casting and cold-working techniques. Metalworking, textile and woodworking tools were present among the artefacts, and the finds also include litharge cakes and other waste products, together with stray droplets of silver which are likely, but not certain, to relate to production rather than exchange.

The dating of much of this production activity is not certain. Some metalworking on site can be more firmly dated to the late 9th century (possibly through to the 10th century) on stylistic grounds. This includes unfinished

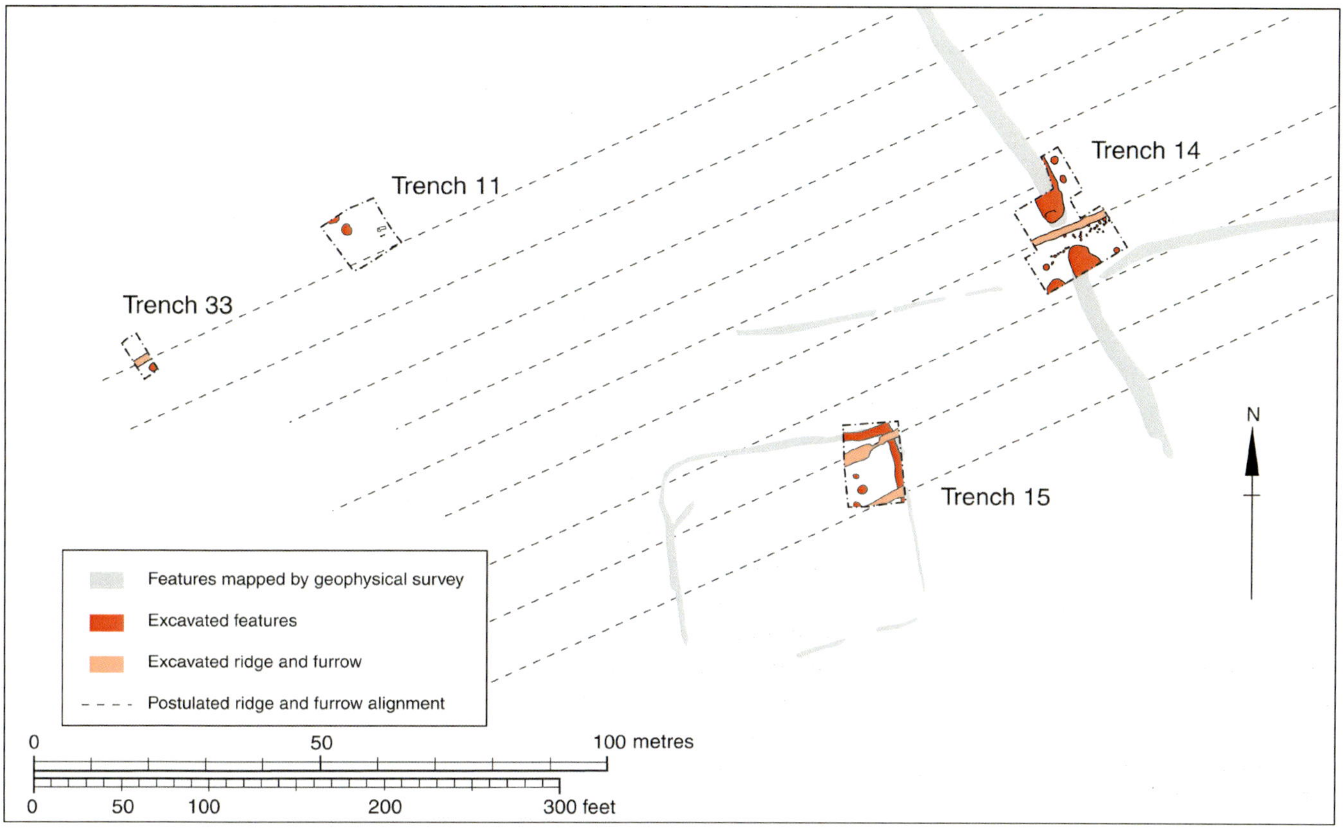

Figure 40 Plan of Trenches 11, 14, 15 and 33 showing excavated ridge and furrow as well as postulated ridge and furrow alignments

strap-ends sfs920 and 1151, discarded due to poor casting (**Fig. 13**), and two part-made or unfinished strap guides with casting flashes still attached. These match Class E strap-ends, also with a central rib, and also possibly made on site (**Fig. 13**). The lead-alloy strap-end sf927 may be a pattern or model for casting in copper alloy (**Fig. 13**). Sf1080 may possibly be an unfinished disc brooch or mount fragment (**Fig. 16**) and mount sf1073 appears to have been cut down for re-use (**Fig. 19**). The complete large Irish harness mount sf1224 (**Pl. 5**) may also have been intended for reworking as a brooch, which is typical for this class of object, but had not yet received any secondary treatment when it was lost. Finally, some of the large number of weights on the site may have been used for measuring alloys for metalworking, rather than or as well as for exchange, while the presence of weights ornamented with stycas and fragments of decorative metalwork (which can be seen as characteristic Insular Viking objects of the late 9th century) (pp. 15–16, 22) could suggest that some of them were produced on site. None of the objects suggest pre-Viking metalworking, and, while the possibility cannot be excluded, there seems no particular reason to suppose that any of the undated evidence of metalworking pre-dates the Viking phase.

Trade and exchange

In addition to the evidence for production in the late 9th century, there is also extensive evidence for exchange in the same period. The site has one of the largest assemblages of weights of this period discovered so far in Britain and Ireland, and larger than anything but a small number of urban sites and other central places in Scandinavia, indicating that this is a site of international significance for the understanding of Viking trade. If anything, the significance of this group is probably understated, given that weights are among the items which the metal detectorists who discovered the site have indicated that they found and sold before they began systematically recording finds from the site. All of the weights that can be dated are consistent with the suggested core period of the mid- to late 870s, but the possibility that some of these may pre-date the Viking settlement or extend into the early 10th century cannot be excluded. Both the hoard and the single finds also include coins terminating in the mid-870s, together with hack-silver which cannot be so precisely dated, while the single finds also include two pieces of hack-gold. Together, the weights, coins and hack-silver point clearly to a system of exchange based on silver bullion valued by weight and, more debatably, perhaps also based on the use of gold, copper alloy and even lead as bullion. Northumbrian stycas may indicate that the site was also a centre for exchange in the pre-Viking period, but the presence of the stycas need not necessarily date from before the Viking occupation. The character of exchange on the site compared with other evidence for exchange in Viking Yorkshire, including hoards, single finds and finds from the Coppergate excavations, is discussed separately by Kershaw (this volume, pp. 123–7) and Williams (Chapter 5).

Weaponry

In addition to items relating to manufacture and trade, ornaments and domestic items, the assemblage includes seven sword hilt fittings and a sword blade, as well as fragments of two swords found together with the hoard.

Other items of ironwork may also derive from weapons, and the finders report the earlier discovery of items which were interpreted as an axe head and a shield-boss respectively (Mark Ainsley, pers. comm.). Given that the dating of the core period of activity on the site coincides with the settlement of Northumbria in the mid-870s by part of the *micel here*, and that the recorded weapons are all of types current in the late 9th century, it is difficult to avoid the conclusion that the weapons relate to this period of military settlement, whether or not the site itself was of military character. The presence of the large earthwork (although its original height cannot be determined) is consistent with at least an element of defence around the site. Clench nails may also indicate the repair of boats or ships on the site, which would be consistent with its location on a navigable river. Especially given the evidence for trade and exchange on the site, it does not necessarily follow that any ships or boats repaired on the site were military in character, but given the dating of the main period of occupation plus the presence of weapons and the earthwork enclosure, it seems likely. In any case, on current evidence it is unclear whether purpose-built trading ships distinct from those which carried large crews of warrior-rowers had already been developed in Scandinavia as early as the 870s (Williams 2014b, 45–8).

Irish finds

A number of finds of Irish origin have been identified from the site. One of these, a crutch-headed ringed pin of the 11th–12th century (sf1177, **Fig. 17**), is one of the small number of stray finds from this period, long after the main period of activity, and indicates continued contact between Ireland and the north of England. However, most of the Irish finds are consistent with the main period of activity in the late 9th century. These include a strap-end (sf931) (**Fig. 13**), and assorted mounts (sfs143, 276–7 and 290, 1174, 1224) (**Figs 2, 10, 19**; **Pl. 5**). All of these appear to be of 8th- or 9th-century date and, if not necessarily recently produced at the time of the Viking settlement in England in the 870s, then at least recent enough to be available through plunder, tribute or trade in Ireland during the decades leading up to the settlement. Some of the decorated lead weights (sfs1568–9, 1571, 1577, 1699–1700, 1703) also contain fragments of ornamental metalwork, some of which appear to be of Irish origin. As discussed above, there are parallels for the use of enamelled, capped and inset lead weights in Woodstown and other Irish finds, and the overall distribution of such weights suggests that they were an Insular Viking creation, which cannot be entirely localised exclusively to either England or Ireland. A political axis between Dublin and York, supported through dynastic ties, seems to be a product of the end of the 9th or early 10th century (Smyth 1975–79; Dumville 2005; Downham 2007), but both the historical and the archaeological record suggest that Viking raiders moved between England, Ireland and the Continent as opportunities arose (McLeod 2014, 109–71), and the Irish material at ARSNY probably relates to members of the *micel here* having previously been active in Ireland rather than to any more structured contact between ARSNY and Ireland in this period.

Burials

Two human burials were located on the site, orientated east–west. Although a single piece of Iron Age pottery was found in material closely associated with one of the burials, two samples of one skeleton give a radiocarbon date of *c.* AD 900–1000. A human tooth in the material above, but separated from the burials, may indicate that the burials had been disturbed in the historic past. One burial (SK1) had been truncated by a small rectangular pit dug in the recent past. The radiocarbon analysis shows that these burials are of a later date than the activity represented by pit digging. The date range for the one dated burial overlaps with the end of the main period of activity on the site, which may extend into the early 10th century, but much of this date range coincides with a period where there is no other evidence for activity on the site, with single finds suggesting small-scale activity from the 11th century onwards. It is therefore unclear whether the burials relate directly to any other phase of activity on the site, or represent a separate phase (or phases) of their own.

The site in context

Gareth Williams

Commonalities with Torksey

As noted throughout the paper, the finds from ARSNY show strong similarities with the recorded detector finds from Torksey in Lincolnshire. The village of Torksey is located close to the border with Nottinghamshire, where the Foss Dyke from Lincoln joins the River Trent, some miles downstream of Newark-on-Trent. Torksey was the third *burh* of Lincolnshire in the late 10th and 11th centuries, after Lincoln and Stamford, a mint, and a significant centre of pottery production. Archaeological investigation indicates that both *burh* and pottery production were based in the modern village, but metal detecting has revealed a substantial site to the north of the village, which appears to represent an entirely separate phase of activity from that of the late Anglo-Saxon *burh* (Blackburn 2011; Hadley and Richards 2013; 2016, 28–9, 46). Like ARSNY, this sits on a rise sloping down to flat ground along the bank of the river. Finds from the site indicate Roman occupation, and perhaps some form of pre-Viking Anglian settlement, although this is historically unrecorded, and its character remains uncertain. Also like ARSNY, the main evidence for Anglian settlement comes from the presence of Northumbrian stycas and stray pieces of Anglo-Saxon metalwork, but as discussed above, these are objects which could have been brought to the site during the period of Viking occupation, and are not in themselves diagnostic of pre-Viking activity. Unlike ARSNY, Torksey was the recorded site of a Viking winter camp in 872–3 (see p. 81), and the finds from the site have plausibly been interpreted as relating to that event, although as at ARSNY there is some doubt as to whether the Torksey finds represent a single season of activity, or a short-lived core of activity which continued on a smaller scale thereafter before apparently ceasing in the early 10th century (Blackburn 2002; 2011; Brown 2006). The selection of the site probably relates in part to its strategic location, but it is also possible that it relates to the existence of other pre-existing sites nearby at Marton and Stow (Lincolnshire), and South Leverton (Nottinghamshire) (Hadley and Richards 2013, 17; 2016, 59–61; see also below, pp. 97–8).

As yet, no enclosure has been discovered at Torksey, but the name Torksey (*Turcesige*) almost certainly includes reference to an island. As noted above, Torksey today sits at the junction of the Trent and the Foss Dyke, with the Trent flowing along the western side of both the modern village and the area to the north where the camp was located, and low-lying land to the east still prone to flooding. A recent collaborative research project on Torksey, carried out by the Universities of York and Sheffield with input from the British Museum and other partners, investigated both the Anglo-Scandinavian *burh*, where previous investigations had revealed 10th-century kilns, and the area which Blackburn (2011) had identified as the site of the Viking camp. Although only very limited excavations were possible in the course of this project, it included a substantial topographical and geomorphological survey of the landscape around Torksey, carried out by Samantha Stein of the University of Sheffield, as part of her PhD thesis (2014). Stein's work, which includes core sampling not just of the Viking camp site but also of the surrounding area, suggests that a palaeochannel curved around the north, east and south of the site of the winter camp, cutting this piece of land off from the site of the later *burh*, which formed a separate island. This channel would have been marshy wetland during the late 9th century, with a water level around 1–2m higher than at present, and the point at which this joined the Trent would have been flooded, providing a complete natural defence without need for defensive structures (Stein 2014; see further below, p. 98).

The Torksey finds show many similarities to those from ARSNY (for summaries of the two main recorded groups of finds from Torksey, see Blackburn 2011). These include weights of Scandinavian oblate-spheroid and cubo-octahedral types, decorated lead weights of Insular Viking type, and plain lead weights. The site also apparently contained a distinct hoard of silver bullion, as well as dispersed finds of both hack-silver and hack-gold, although in both sites the similarity between the putative hoard material and the single finds leaves some doubt as to exactly what should be regarded as associated with the hoard (see above, p. 19; Blackburn 2011, 234–5). Coins from the site include fragmentary Islamic dirhams, base-silver pennies of the Lunettes type, and large numbers of Northumbrian stycas, although Torksey lacks coins of the Cross-and-Lozenge type found at ARSNY. This last point is unsurprising, since the recorded activity at Torksey pre-dates the introduction of this type by perhaps two years, whereas the documented Viking settlement of Northumbria immediately post-dated the introduction of the type. As at ARSNY, the non-numismatic evidence for immediately pre-Viking activity is thin, and since stycas are much more concentrated on the site than elsewhere in Lindsey, Mark Blackburn (2011, 225) has suggested that these represent Viking imports from Northumbria rather than pre-Viking exchange. The Torksey assemblage also contains lead trial-pieces which may indicate the production of Viking coins imitating the Lunettes type and also Carolingian gold solidi (*ibid.*, 225, 228).

In addition to items relating to trade and exchange, Torksey also has some evidence of metalworking, including a set of smith's tools, and trial-pieces for punches and dies (see above, p. 36) (but without the waste products recorded at ARSNY), together with weaponry, domestic items such as spindle whorls, needles, awls, loom and fishing weights, gaming pieces and personal ornaments, indicating a wide range of activities being carried out on the site, and the presence of women as well as men (Blackburn 2011; Hadley and Richards *et al.* 2016, 54–5). In particular, the strap-ends from the two sites show strong similarities, although those from Torksey have not yet been published in any detail.

In addition to the finds previously recorded by Mark Blackburn, others recorded by Rachel Atherton, Kevin Leahy and more through the PAS, and further items reported through the British Museum under the terms of the Treasure Act (1996), the research project also included recording of new metal-detected finds with GPS-linked find co-ordinates. Blackburn's (2011) study of the finds provides detailed discussion only of the coins, bullion and some of the weights, although it lists numbers of recorded objects in other categories. A further discussion of this material, augmented by more recent finds, has been prepared by Andrew Woods (in prep.). There is some discussion of the finds in the recent publication of this project (Hadley and Richards *et al.* 2016, 36–54) and a fuller listing of the finds can be found in the supporting literature. The University of York plans to continue to develop the Torksey project further, and it is to be hoped that there will be opportunities for future more detailed comparisons between the finds from Torksey and ARSNY.

As at ARSNY, the Torksey finds have been recovered from plough soil. Although geophysics indicates the presence of what appears to be a Romano-British farmstead, and other features suggestive of pits or cellared workshops may perhaps be identified as Viking-Age metalworking hearths and workshops, no traces of more substantial Viking-Age structures have yet been discovered, and while carbon-dated remains of two males seem likely to come from graves relating to the late 9th-century occupation of the site, the graves (like any traces of building structures) have probably been destroyed by ploughing and erosion, or covered to a considerable depth by blowing sand (Hadley and Richards 2013, 16–17; Hadley and Richards *et al.* 2016, 37, 56). It is also possible that for a temporary seasonal encampment a significant proportion of the occupation of the site took the form of tents or other temporary structures which would have left only minimal traces regardless of subsequent disturbance.

The total size of the site has previously been published as *c.* 26 hectares (65 acres; Blackburn 2011, 221; Hadley and Richards 2013, 17), but a recent recalculation suggests that the total size of the Viking camp site was even larger, around 55 hectares (Hadley and Richards *et al.* 2016, 26). Given the suggested dates for the two sites, and given that the *Anglo-Saxon Chronicle* records that in 874 the *micel here* divided into two parts, with one part moving south to East Anglia rather than north to Northumbria, it would be surprising if the ARSNY site were not smaller than Torksey, assuming a comparable density of settlement, but both cover very substantial areas compared not only with other Viking camps but also with late Viking towns in Scandinavia (see below, p. 99). The evidence for Roman/Romano-British occupation of the Torksey site, followed by only limited and ambiguous evidence of Anglian occupation prior to the Viking phase, has direct parallels with ARSNY, although ARSNY has not (yet) revealed any Roman/Romano-British structural remains to match those of Torksey.

Commonalities with Woodstown

Woodstown, near Waterford, is a riverine site on the east bank of the River Suir, protected on the landward sides by a bank and ditch structure. This creates more of an elongated B-shaped enclosure than the classic D-shape associated with Viking sites (Hurley 2014, 348), but nevertheless is consistent with a broader pattern of sites (including ARSNY) which combine defences on land with access to a navigable river, although the Woodstown site is considerably smaller than ARSNY. The site shows evidence of military activity, but also of production and trade, and has been tentatively identified as an example of the type of site described in Irish texts as a *longphort* (pl. *longphuirt*), originally 'harbour for warships', and normally interpreted as referring to raiding bases, although the usage became more fluid over time, and recent interpretations suggest a more complex role for the *longphort* than simply a military encampment (Sheehan 2008; Maas 2008; Downham 2010, 97; Harrison 2013; Williams 2015). Whether the site can be identified as a *longphort* has been questioned by some, precisely because it does not conform to the narrow definition of a *longphort* as a purely military site, but this raises the question of whether the term needs to be redefined rather than simply making an overwhelming case for rejecting Woodstown as a *longphort* (Harrison 2013, especially 68–70). That the site had at least a partially military character is suggested by the presence of a weapon burial, and of individual weapons (Harrison 2014b). The enclosure itself probably also originally had a limited military function, since it was protected by an earth bank, possibly topped with a wooden palisade, with a ditch outside, and a second inner ditch, possibly with a revetment. However, while the original height of the bank is uncertain, the relatively small size of the outer ditch, which seems to have begun to be infilled fairly quickly, suggests that the bank and ditch may have been more to define the edge of the site than a serious defence, while pits with evidence of metalworking activity, and multiple layers of infill and silting, show that the ditch in any case lost any defensive function while the site was still occupied (Russell 2014, 28–34).

Unlike ARSNY, the site provided evidence of at least one building, a bow-ended rectangular house *c.* 8.4m x 5.4m, with some stylistic similarities to buildings from Dublin and elsewhere (Hurley 2014, 349–52), although the parallels are not exact. It is uncertain whether the absence of such buildings at ARSNY and Torksey indicates a greater permanence of occupation at Woodstown. The fact that virtually all of the finds at both ARSNY and Torksey have been recovered from disturbed surface layers with no clear underlying strata suggests that comparable structures would probably have disappeared if they ever existed, while the single building recorded at Woodstown does not in itself point to large-scale permanent occupation, nor is there clear evidence for defined plots and/or roads or pathways (*ibid.*, 351–2). There are, however, numerous post-holes and stake-holes across the site, suggesting the presence of several other structures of undetermined form.

Scientific dating of the site places the focus of activity in the period *c.* 850–950, and this is consistent with the objects. These cannot offer such precise dates as some of those for ARSNY and Torksey, but stylistic comparisons suggest that these centre on the second half of the 9th century, possibly spilling over into the opening decades of the 10th century but with a few late outliers (Hurley 2014, 347), and thus broadly comparable with both the ARSNY and Torksey assemblages. As discussed in more detail above, the cubo-octahedral weights from ARSNY have partial parallels at Woodstown (see pp. 20–3, 40–1), while parallels are closer with the decorated lead weights, the hack-silver and the dirham fragments (Wallace 2013; 2014; Sheehan 2014; 2015; Rispling 2014), suggesting that a similar bullion economy existed at Woodstown as at ARSNY and Torksey, although the relative scarcity of the cubo-octahedral weights, introduced in Scandinavia only in the 860s, could suggest that the core period of exchange on the Woodstown site was slightly earlier than ARSNY and Torksey (see p. 20).

Only two coin fragments are known from the site from the Viking Age, both of which are fragmentary Islamic dirhams. The relative scarcity of coins is unsurprising for Ireland, where circulation of even imported coins was unusual before the 10th century, and where most imported coins were probably melted down for recycling prior to the late 10th century. One of the fragments is from an Umayyad dirham minted in Wasit (modern Iraq), *c.* AD 738–43, and consistent with deposition at any point in the 9th century, while the other certainly dates on stylistic grounds from after *c.* 866–7, and can probably be identified as an issue of the Samanid dynasty minted in Samarkand, *c.* 922–3 (Rispling 2014). Allowing time for the passage of the coin via Scandinavia to Ireland, the deposition of this coin can at the earliest be roughly dated to the same period as the apparent concentration of activity at ARSNY in the 870s, while the Samanid interpretation would place it well after the dated coin assemblage of the Viking phases at ARSNY, although Samanid coins are known from other Viking hoards from Yorkshire deposited in the 10th century, indicating continued importation of coins to the British Isles from Scandinavia after the immediate settlement period (Williams, this volume, pp. 108–9; Kershaw, this volume, pp. 117–19).

As at ARSNY and Torksey, weights are among the most important groups of material from the site, and Patrick Wallace records a total of 217 weights from Woodstown, excluding a silver cubo-octahedral object which he rejects as a weight (see pp. 20, 40–1). This is the largest group of weights recorded from Ireland, compared with 180 from excavations in Dublin, and much smaller groups from Kilmainham/Islandbridge on the outskirts of Dublin, and from the River Blackwater in Northern Ireland (Bourke 2010, 71–5; Wallace 2014, 223–4; see also this volume, pp. 19,

40–3). The weights include plain lead weights of different types, but also several decorated examples, many of which include fragments of re-used Insular metalwork, and one of which has what appears to be an enamelled human face. These correspond very closely with the lead weights from ARSNY, Torksey and Llanbedrgoch (see pp. 22–3). Given the other similarities between the objects at Woodstown and those at ARSNY and Torksey, and given that there is both historical and archaeological evidence for movement of Viking forces between Ireland and northern England in the late 9th century (McLeod 2014, 112–32), the scarcity of cubo-octahedral weights is likely to be significant, and probably indicates that the core of the assemblage at Woodstown is slightly earlier than those at ARSNY and Torksey, pre-dating the widespread introduction of this type of weight in the 860s and 870s. However, since there is an observable difference in the character of the bullion economy between the sites, as indicated by the scarcity of coins, the absence of the cubo-octahedral weights may indicate something more than a purely chronological difference between these and the lead weights, with different patterns of use disguised by the large size and disparate character of the forces which occupied Torksey and (probably) ARSNY. It may also be significant that weights of this type are, at the time of writing, largely absent from Ireland (S. Harrison, pers. comm.). Nevertheless, in other respects bullion use at Woodstown appears broadly comparable with that on the two English sites, and that represented in Viking hoards in England in the late 9th and very early 10th centuries. The silver assemblage from the site comprises two complete ingots, 24 hack-silver ingot fragments, six hack-silver fragments of arm-rings, six pieces of casting waste, single hack-silver fragments of a sheet and a rod, a brooch fragment that is possibly hack-silver, and the cubo-octahedral object which may or may not be a weight (Sheehan 2014; 2015). None of these objects would seem out of place at ARSNY, or in Viking hoards from England, and the fact that some of the objects result from metalworking shows the same ambiguity between silver as bullion and silver as a commodity for production as at ARSNY and Torksey (Williams 2015; see also above, pp. 43–5).

Metalworking in various forms appears to be a significant feature of activity on the site. In addition to the silver casting waste, there are also four fragments of cupels, relating to the assaying of silver, while nine out of the 88 crucible fragments recorded from the site were also used for silver or silver-rich alloys, suggesting an important role for silver on the site. The cupels have been interpreted as relating to the testing of silver in its commercial context (Young 2014a, 112; 2014b, 268–9, 272–3). However, while the crucibles could indicate the melting of silver for use in bullion ingots, which feature extensively in some Viking-Age hoards from Ireland (see Sheehan 1998; 2007), they might equally well have been used in the preparation of ornaments or other manufactured items. The other crucible fragments predominantly relate to copper alloys, typically with a high zinc content (Young 2014b, 271–3). This is consistent with the manufacture of brass objects, and although brass is more typical of the mid-10th century onwards in the British Isles, it is also known earlier (Bayley 1992, 809; Young 2014b, 273). However, as noted above, the presence of the Northumbrian stycas (most commonly brass) at both ARSNY and Torksey has been interpreted as possibly indicative of a non-precious-metal bullion economy based on brass (see pp. 44–5). If this interpretation is correct, although no stycas have been discovered at Woodstown, evidence there for the production of brass may also relate to use as bullion as well as or instead of manufacture. Copper-alloy bar ingots at Woodstown have parallels at ARSNY, and York, where moulds for the production of ingots were also found (Bayley 1992, 767–81; Johnson 2014, 116–17; Scully 2014, 126–7). As with the use of silver, if there was bullion use of copper alloy this probably overlapped with the value of the metal as a commodity for use in manufacture. Numerous fragments of copper alloy from the site probably in part reflect recycling and manufacture, relating both to the production of new copper-alloy items and to the manufacture of lead weights with re-used decorative Insular insets (Ó Floinn, with Bourke, 2014; Young 2014b, 271–3). The crucible fragments suggest that the former may have been as important as the latter. However, the size of the weights assemblage relative to the size of the Woodstown site may well indicate that weights were being manufactured there, although lead working is normally extremely rare in pre-Viking Ireland (S. Harrison, pers. comm.).

The site also has extensive evidence for ironworking, including the smelting of iron, probably in a slag-tapping furnace, as well as smithing. The slag-tapping furnace is more typically Scandinavian than Irish, suggesting Viking influence, and chemical analysis indicates that a range of ores were being used on site, some of which must have been imported, probably reflecting Viking trade. The evidence for smithing techniques, however, is more typically Irish, suggesting a native presence in the site, or at least interaction with native culture and production techniques (Young 2014a, 103–12). However, the finds also included a significant number of nails and roves typical of Viking boat building (as well as other non-diagnostic or later nails), and this may indicate that these were being manufactured on site to facilitate the maintenance of Viking ships and boats (Bill 2014). Such repairs are likely also to have been a feature of winter camps in England, taking advantage of the opportunity to carry out such repairs between seasonal campaigns. Finds from the site include 63 rotary whetstones, two possible rotary whetstones, thirteen whetstones, two possible whetstones and eight hones, indicating that sharpening metal objects was an important activity on the site, whether their purpose was to sharpen tools or weapons, or both. It is also unclear whether they were for sharpening existing objects or for finishing newly made objects, but the manufacture and/or maintenance of weapons cannot be ruled out, and there is possible evidence in some of the slag for the manipulation of carbon content in the metal, which is suggestive of attempts to create a higher carbon steel for use in sword-making (Carey 2014; Hurley 2014, 352).

Metalworking was apparently not the only form of manufacture taking place at the Woodstown site, which has produced two complete glass beads, with parallels in both pre-Viking and Viking contexts, but also three glass drops and seven pieces of cullet, or waste from glass-making.

While the composition of the glass has not been analysed, and there are no crucible fragments with traces of glass or the relevant raw materials, the presence of the waste products rather than complete beads alone suggests that glass was being manufactured on the site (Cropper 2014). The site has also produced a number of finds of amber, which occurs naturally in Scandinavia, but not in Ireland, and is typical of Viking sites. An amber pendant has parallels from 10th-century contexts at Fishamble Street, Dublin, and there are also two beads (one of which may not have been complete) and two fragmentary objects which may have been beads or rings. There are again parallels for beads and for beads/rings from Dublin, which had a substantial amber-working industry. Finally there is one fragment of amber with no evidence of secondary treatment and another with minimal evidence of secondary treatment, both with traces of the original cortex covering. They can probably be explained either as raw materials for, or waste from, amber working (Harvey 2014).

Neither the glass nor the amber has recorded equivalents at either ARSNY or Torksey, but the fact that the two together make up only a tiny proportion of the finds corpus from Woodstown, and that almost all the finds from both ARSNY and Woodstown are the product of metal detecting, the current absence of evidence for glass and amber working from both sites is neither surprising nor significant. At the very least, these finds indicate that glass and amber were being traded into Woodstown, and it seems likely that they were being produced there. Given the different circumstances of recovery, it is possible that manufacture of such items may also have taken place at ARSNY, although there is currently nothing to suggest this. It is also important to remember that the Woodstown site appears to have a longer core period of activity than ARSNY so, despite other similarities between the sites, some elements of production and trade at Woodstown may reflect its greater permanency, rather than being typical features of Viking camps in general.

A final point which does show similarities with both ARSNY and Torksey is the presence of nine perforated lead discs of varying proportions, which could be interpreted as either whorls or weights. According to Richard O'Brien (2014), all but one of these could have functioned as spindle whorls. If so, they indicate the presence of spinning, typically interpreted along with other elements of textile manufacture as a characteristically female activity. As noted elsewhere (see p. 91), there is clear textual evidence for a female presence with Viking forces on campaign, confirmed by the skeletal evidence of at least one woman of Scandinavian origin in the mass grave at Repton. As with ARSNY and Torksey, there is therefore no reason to doubt that the population of Woodstown included women as well as men, and this is also consistent with a more detailed argument recently put forward by Shane McLeod (2011) for a high proportion of the original Scandinavian settlers of eastern England in the late 9th century being women (see below, p. 91).

Although the recent publication of Woodstown does not contain a discussion of the overall area of the site, it is considerably smaller than either ARSNY or Torksey. This is not surprising. Other proposed *longphort* sites in Ireland are also much smaller than ARSNY or Torksey (for dimensions of several of the sites, see Sheehan 2008), although the Irish sites are typically larger than the 1.46-hectare enclosure which has been identified as the Viking camp at Repton (Simpson 2005, 21–5). Torksey definitely and ARSNY probably can be identified with the activities of a force described by contemporaries as '*micel*', indicating that it was unusually large. The fact that Repton was also occupied by the *micel here* raises questions about whether 1.46 hectares can realistically represent the whole encampment (see p. 89). In other respects, Woodstown seems very similar to ARSNY, with a combination of an extended waterfront on a navigable river, defended by bank and ditch on the landward side, and with finds suggesting a combination of military activity with production and exchange, as well as the presence of women rather than just the men that might be expected in an 'army' camp. As at ARSNY and Torksey the precise duration of the occupation of the site is uncertain, although it also seems to have begun in the second half of the 9th century. It is uncertain to what extent those differences which are apparent between Woodstown and ARSNY (including evidence for buildings, and for production in a wider range of materials) reflect the apparent longer occupation of the Woodstown site, and to what extent they simply reflect conditions of preservation and the circumstances of recovery.

Other comparators

A number of Viking camps are recorded in Anglo-Saxon, Irish and Frankish sources. These are focused in the period from the mid-9th to the mid-10th century and were of varying degrees of permanence. In England, these include over-wintering places from the 850s, including a sequence of annual over-wintering sites of the *micel here* between its arrival in 865 and the temporary cessation of large-scale raiding for several years in 879 (see pp. 90–9). A further sequence is recorded with the resumption of raiding in the 890s, while others can be related to the Anglo-Scandinavian response to the campaigns of Edward the Elder (899–924) and his sister Æthelflæd (Edgeworth 2008; 2009). Numerous archaeological features have been identified with the historically attested camps by antiquarians and archaeologists, with varying degrees of justification (Graham-Campbell 2004b; Raffield 2013). In a recent survey, Ben Raffield notes that in most cases these features have either disappeared under other developments or can be identified as having been built in other periods, although he notes the possibility that earlier sites may have been re-used in the Viking Age. Although several such sites have been identified morphologically either because they are riverine or coastal D-shaped enclosures, or because they are circular, like the ring-forts of the Trelleborg type, neither of these shapes is uniquely characteristic of the Viking Age. Such evidence as there is suggests a range of site types in England, including islands (e.g. Torksey, Thorney Island), riverine D-shaped enclosures (e.g. Repton, ARSNY, Tempsford) and promontory forts (e.g. Reading). Hoards and other evidence of exchange can be identified in proximity to several sites (Archibald 1998; Brooks and Graham-Campbell 2000; Graham-Campbell 2004b; Sheehan 2008; 2015) but, with the exception of Torksey, none has produced finds on the scale of ARSNY, and few have been investigated in detail.

The notable exception is Repton, documented as a winter camp in 873–4. As noted above (p. 42), there were severe constraints on fieldwork at the site at Repton investigated by Martin Biddle and Birthe Kjølbye-Biddle, while the fact that the site has not been metal detected probably accounts for the tiny number of single finds in comparison with ARSNY or Torksey. The Viking camp clearly involved the re-occupation of the existing Mercian monastery and royal mausoleum, as the church was apparently incorporated into a substantial bank and ditch defence. This can be observed to the west of the church, curving back to what may be interpreted as either the former course of the River Trent or perhaps a branch of the River Trent, and this also extends immediately to the east of the church, although the presence of Repton School beyond this meant that it was impossible to trace this further. This structure was interpreted by the Biddles (Biddle and Kjølbye-Biddle 1992; 2001) as a roughly symmetrical D-shaped enclosure backing on to the river, with the church in the centre, although the eastern end of the proposed structure is necessarily speculative.

Damaged Christian sculptures found in proximity to the church are thought to relate to the destruction of the monastery at the time of the Viking occupation. A few finds of Viking weapons on both sides of the river probably also relate to the winter camp, as do several burials of Scandinavian character both inside and outside the enclosure, including a double-grave containing Viking artefacts inside the enclosure and immediately adjacent to the mausoleum. A mass grave found slightly to the west of the main enclosure has also been linked with the occupation by the *micel here* (Biddle and Kjølbye-Biddle 1992; 2001). This last point has proved more contentious than other elements of the interpretation of the site, although the presence of coins consistent with a deposition date in the mid-870s (see above, p. 37) and the identification through stable isotope analysis of some of the bones in the burial as being of Scandinavian origin point strongly to the mass grave relating at least in part to this phase of occupation (Budd *et al.* 2004). Doubt over the attribution of the mass grave to the Viking Age came from initial interpretation of carbon dating, which appeared to show that while some of the skeletons were plausible for a 9th-century date, others appeared to be far too early, with suggested dates of the 8th or even 7th centuries. However, the skeletal remains have recently been re-examined. With the dates recalibrated to allow for marine reservoir calibration, the dates are now entirely consistent with the historically documented over-wintering of 873–4 (Jarman *et al.* 2018).

It is likely that occupation described as being at Repton may have been over a more extended area. A Viking or Anglo-Scandinavian cemetery at nearby Ingleby (Heath Wood) has also been linked with the Viking winter camp at Repton (Richards 2003b; 2004), while it is unlikely that a naturally defensible site of the strategic importance of Tutbury Castle (the name of which includes the Old English element *burh*) a short distance to the west would have been left unoccupied (Williams 2011c, 88). Even so, the small size of the Repton enclosure stands in stark contrast with both ARSNY and Torksey, with a defended area of only 1.46 hectares (3.65 acres) compared with *c.* 31 hectares (76 acres) at ARSNY and *c.* 55 hectares (137.5 acres) at Torksey. While the relationship with ARSNY is more conjectural, it is hard to believe that a force which occupied a space of *c.* 55 hectares at Torksey in 872–3 could be condensed into 1.46 hectares at Repton the following year. It has been suggested that the Repton enclosure as normally interpreted was even smaller, and that the published figure of 1.46 hectares should read 1.46 acres (0.59 hectares) (Stein 2014, 43), giving an even greater contrast with ARSNY and Torksey.

If the D-shaped enclosure at Repton has been correctly reconstructed (and the B-shaped enclosure at Woodstown provides a possible model for how a more complicated multiple enclosure could hypothetically have extended further to the east at Repton), then it seems unlikely that it represents the entire Viking camp. It may represent a distinct defensive citadel either inside or outside the main enclosure, with parallels in the fortifications at Hedeby and Birka, each of which had a separate fortification outside the main urban enclosure (Clarke and Ambrosiani 1991). A rather larger hypothetical enclosure around the church can be reconstructed on the basis of later road positions and other boundaries, although these may relate to the late medieval church rather than the Viking Age, and full investigation of this possibility lies beyond the scope of this paper. At the time of writing further investigations of the site are being undertaken under the direction of Dr Cat Jarman, and these will undoubtedly add to our understanding in the future.

It is also worth considering that the D-shaped enclosure may have formed a fortified bridgehead controlling access across the river. If, rather than representing the sole course of the Trent at the time, the watercourse below the church formed one branch of the Trent which co-existed with the current course of the river or something similar, this would have created an island close in size to that now postulated as the location of the Viking camp at Torksey (see above, pp. 85–6). This would also be consistent with the discovery of Viking weapons on the other side of the river (Bigsby 1854).

Although Woodstown is the only *longphort* site to have received extensive archaeological investigation so far, a number of potential sites have been identified in Ireland, typically with earthwork defences alongside rivers in areas where there is historical evidence for the existence of *longphuirt*. Some of these appear to re-use earlier enclosures, while others have D-shaped or sub-rectangular enclosures similar to those found at ARSNY, Woodstown, Repton and other Viking sites. In some cases, Viking or Viking-Age objects have also been found in or in close proximity to the proposed sites (Kelly 2015). Most recently, geophysical surveys and trial excavations near Annagassan, Co. Louth, have revealed what has been convincingly identified as the historically attested *longphort* of Linn Duachaill, with a substantial earthwork cutting off the only land access to a promontory otherwise surrounded by a loop in the river (*ibid.*). The Annagassan site was identified some years ago as the likely location of the Linn Duachaill *longphort* (McKeown 2005), and this identification now seems to be supported by the recent investigations. Because of the limited scale of the investigations to date, Annagassan has not yet yielded a comparable body of finds to the sites discussed so far, but what evidence there is does suggest a comparable mixture of military and non-military functions: in addition to the earthwork defences, it has produced two pieces of hack-silver (Kelly 2015; Williams 2015, 115–16). Three separate hoards (one of gold and two of silver) have also been found in close proximity to the potential *longphort* site at Ballaghkeeran Little, Co. Westmeath (Sheehan 2008, 291), and a wider association between the economic use of silver and *longphuirt* seems likely (Sheehan 2015).

Apart from Woodstown, Annagassan and Dublin, sites which have been provisionally identified by Eamonn Kelly and others as *longphuirt* include Dunrally, Co. Laois; Fairyhill near Athlunkard, Co. Clare; Ballaghkeeran Little, Co. Westmeath; Rathmore near Castlemaine, Co. Kerry; Knoxspark, Co. Sligo; Athlumney, Co. Meath; Kellysgrove, Co. Galway; and Dún Dubchomair, Co. Meath (Clinton 2000; Fanning 1983; Gibbons 2004; 2005; Kelly 1982–83; 1993; 2009; Kelly and Maas 1995; 1999; Kelly and O'Donovan 1998). Of these, the place-name Athlunkard appears to contain the element *longphort*, and while not quite representing a single site type in terms of shape, the sites share the key characteristic of being defended by earthworks and sited on or close to navigable rivers, while several have finds of Viking character found in close proximity (Kelly and Maas 1999; Kelly 2015). While until recently evidence of the Viking settlement of Dublin was largely if not completely limited to the 10th century or later, recent excavations have also now identified what appear to be elements of the *longphort* phase of the late 9th century (Simpson 2005; 2010). Opinion remains divided as to whether the Viking burials discovered in the 19th century in the Dublin suburbs of Kilmainham and Islandbridge also relate to the Dublin *longphort* or whether they represent a further late 9th-century settlement further upstream, or whether there was a more extended linear pattern of settlement along the Liffey than typical models of the *longphort* would allow. Whichever of these interpretations one prefers, the grave finds include weapons, weighing equipment and tools relating to textile working, again suggesting that there was no clear differentiation between raiding and more peaceful functions in Viking camps of the late 9th century (O'Brien 1998; Clarke 1998, 350–1; Ó Floinn 1998, 131–43; Johnson 2004; Simpson 2010; Harrison and Ó Floinn 2014).

It is to be hoped that investigations at Annagassan will continue and will reveal additional evidence of the character of the site. In any case, the discoveries at Woodstown and Annagassan, together with the 9th-century phases at Dublin (Simpson 2005; 2010), have stimulated a new interest in the *longphort* phenomenon, amongst both archaeologists and historians, and it seems clear that study of the Irish sites can inform understanding of the character of Torksey, Repton and ARSNY, and vice versa (Williams 2015).

While not directly linked with an identified *longphort*, a body of over 400 single finds has been recovered as a result of the dredging of the River Blackwater in Northern Ireland, along a stretch between Blackwatertown and Lough Neagh. The finds have been in part recorded by metal detectorists and partly through controlled excavation, but the bulk of the material has been removed from its original context, although it includes a group which has in some publications been attributed specifically to Shanmullagh. The assemblage contains a wide variety of material, including weapons, weights, ornaments, both precious and non-precious ingots, and production waste from metalworking (Bourke 2010, 24–34). Despite the lack of a clear context, Cormac Bourke (2010, 32–4) has noted the similarities to the assemblages from Woodstown and Torksey, and has suggested that the Blackwater finds derive from a single site, possibly a *longphort* (noting a number of possible *longphort* sites along the appropriate stretch of the river), and that at least part of the assemblage may possibly represent the stock in trade of a Viking metalworker.

Excavations at Llanbedrgoch on Anglesey have also revealed coins, weights and hack-silver within a defensive earthwork enclosure, while burials at the site indicate violent interaction between the occupants and others, although the exact interpretation of the site in the context of Welsh–Viking relations is unclear. Together with hoards and stray finds of weights, Llanbedrgoch provides clear evidence that the bullion economy observed in Viking contexts in England and Ireland in the late 9th and 10th centuries also existed in North Wales (Redknap 2004; 2009). The site is much smaller than others discussed here, and Llanbedrgoch was certainly not a camp on the scale of Torksey or Woodstown, but it provides a useful reminder that the sorts of activity that took place at such sites might also occur on a variety of scales, and were not necessarily confined to major sites.

Single finds of related material are becoming increasingly common, including pieces of hack-silver and gold, intact ingots, and weights. Much of this has been recorded through the PAS (www.finds.org.uk). The distribution of such finds in rural areas, which is not restricted to known productive sites, suggests that bullion economy was not confined to centres of production and exchange but was widespread in areas of England settled by the Vikings, including East Anglia as well as northern England. The distribution and character of bullion economy in Anglo-Scandinavian England on the basis of single finds is the subject of a recent major study by Dr Jane Kershaw, which considers both actual bullion items such as ingots and hack-silver, and objects relating to the measurement of bullion, such as balances and weights. Dr Kershaw's interpretation of the Yorkshire finds forms a separate chapter within this volume (see Chapter 4), but her broader study will be of great importance in providing better contextual information for the study of the bullion-related finds from ARSNY and the other sites discussed here.

ARSNY: a Viking camp?

The assemblage as a whole from ARSNY clearly suggests a site of Viking rather than Anglo-Saxon or even Anglo-Scandinavian character, and the combination on the site of production, trade and weaponry is suggestive of a Viking camp. The presence of some items such as spindle whorls, which are normally associated with female activity, does not detract from that, even if they date from the Viking occupation of the site. Blackburn (2011, 246) notes that both Anglo-Saxon and Frankish sources record the movement of women and children with Viking armies, and suggests that the *micel here* ('great raiding army'), active in England from 865 until the late 870s, would have been accompanied in its travels by a variety of camp-followers and general hangers-on, as well as interacting with the local population. The importance of a female component within the *micel here* has also been stressed by Shane McLeod. His interpretation of the activities of the *micel here* sees the campaigns of the 860s and 870s as being firmly focused on settlement and migration from the outset, and thus involving mobile populations, rather than 'armies' in the traditional sense, and therefore including a very significant female presence (McLeod 2011; 2014, *passim*). McLeod's emphasis on a planned migration from the outset of the campaign in 865 may be overstated, as may his conclusions on the relative proportions of men and women involved with the *micel here*. Nevertheless, he does demonstrate convincingly that there was a female presence with the *micel here* both in the campaigns of the 860s–70s (and in the later similar campaigns of the 890s), and in the early settlements, so the presence of items reflecting 'female' activity in Viking camps is to be expected. The presence of women and children is also indicated in the skeletal assemblage from Repton, some of whom (although not necessarily all) were apparently of Scandinavian origin (Budd *et al.* 2004; Jarman *et al.* 2018). One may, of course, question whether items relating to textiles necessarily indicate a female presence in the context of Viking camps. Camps presumably provided an opportunity to make and mend, and winter camps in particular must have involved repairs and preparations for the following season. There were probably numerous craftsmen attached to the *micel here* as well as warriors, and it is perfectly conceivable that there were male sail-makers among them. Nevertheless, the unambiguous textual references to Viking forces in this period travelling with women and children mean that there is no particular reason to doubt that evidence for textile working at ARSNY, as also at Torksey and Woodstown, reflects a female presence.

Evidence for trade may seem less obvious for camps associated with the *micel here* in England, since this has typically been interpreted purely either as an army, aiming at the conquests which eventually transpired, or as a raiding force, seeking plunder and/or tribute. Although the term *here* has often been translated as 'army', its use in the laws attributed to Ine of Wessex (*EHD*, 364–72, at p.366, ch.13.1; Liebermann 1898, 94–5, ch.13.1) is in the context of a sliding scale of armed robbery. A *here* is defined as any group of 35 men or more engaged in violent robbery. This does not mean, as suggested by Peter Sawyer (1962, 125; 2nd edn 1971, 127–8), that anything above 35 men constituted an army. Rather, the use of the term *here* in the *Anglo-Saxon Chronicle* to describe Viking forces appears to have been intended as pejorative, emphasising the perception of the Vikings as robbers and raiders in contrast with the term *fyrd*, routinely used for 'legitimate' armies (Halsall 2003, 16, 57–9; Abels 2003). The term *micel here* thus indicates armed robbery on a grand scale, and is consistent with the predominant narrative of Viking raids in the British Isles and Continental Europe to be found in contemporary Anglo-Saxon, Irish and Frankish sources.

However, many, although not all, of the recorded winter camps in England involved making some sort of peace with the kingdom in which the camp was established, and trade seems to have been a feature of making peace even temporarily. The long-term treaty established between Alfred and Guthrum at some point between *c.* 879 and *c.* 886 specifically discusses the terms under which trade could take place across the agreed boundary (*AG*, 171–2). This treaty is the only one of its type to survive from the period, and may or may not be typical. The boundary established by this treaty lasted for several years, and one could argue that there was a greater need for a formal treaty for a long-term boundary settlement than for a seasonal camp. That does rely on the assumption that it was clear at the time when the treaty was drawn up that the boundary was intended to be semi-permanent, an assumption which rests in part on hindsight. However, the fact that Alfred's peace treaty with Guthrum following Alfred's victory over him at Edington in 878 (probably not the surviving treaty, which seems more appropriate to a slightly later political geography) was sealed with Alfred's sponsorship of Guthrum's baptism (*ASC* [A], *sub* 878; *AG*, 171–2), together with the fact that Guthrum's substantive coinage in East Anglia was directly based on Alfred's Two-Line type, issued post-*c.* 880 (Blackburn 2005, 21–2, 30–3), does suggest that both sides may have had hopes for a lasting peace rather than a purely short-term accommodation like those associated with over-wintering.

In any case, trade was probably also a feature of shorter truces, including over-wintering, as when Charles the Bald agreed a truce with Vikings on the Loire in 873 after expelling them from Angers, whereby they were permitted to remain at peace on an island in the Loire until the following February, and to hold a market while they remained there (*ASB, sub* 873; Valante 2008, 41–2). The Vikings were obliged to hand over hostages as part of this agreement, which provides an important indication that over-wintering was not always carried out on terms which left the Vikings in complete control. Trade and interaction with the surrounding community was essential for all but the briefest stay, unless a camp had direct control of a large enough hinterland to supply the occupants (Williams 2015, 115–16). The choice of sites for winter camps was suggested in part by logistical need (McLeod 2007; Williams 2008b; see also pp. 94–9), but the acquisition of a permanent hinterland was one of the things required to make the leap between temporary camp and permanent town (Bradley 1988; Williams 2013a, 19). Trade, and production in order to have something worth trading, can thus be seen as likely components of all but the most temporary Viking camps. It was possible for a camp to make the change from camp to town, as in the case of Dublin, where the 9th-century *longphort* eventually developed into the 10th-century town, but many of the historically recorded *longphuirt* did not make the same development. Traditional views of the *longphort* have emphasised the military role of this type of settlement, but more recent discussions of the phenomenon have stressed a more varied role, including production and trade (Valante 2008, 41–5; Sheehan 2008; Harrison 2013; Williams 2015). The same seems to be true of Torksey (Blackburn 2011, 244–7), and should probably be extended to the interpretation of other recorded Viking winter camps. Although not specifically documented, the ARSNY site seems directly comparable, whether it was a seasonal camp or a temporary settlement.

The size of the site at ARSNY (*c.* 31 hectares/76 acres) is not as large as the estimated size of Torksey (*c.* 55 hectares/137.5 acres), but both are considerably larger than the enclosure at Repton (1.46 hectares/3.65 acres) and larger than the Irish *longphuirt* which have been measured so far (Biddle and Kjølbye-Biddle 2001, 57–60; Simpson 2005, 21–5; Blackburn 2011, 221). They are also rather larger than the defended enclosures at Hereford and Tamworth which have been interpreted as early (and probably pre-Viking) Anglo-Saxon towns (Bassett 2007; 2008; Hall 2011, 605; see p. 99). The distinction between Torksey and ARSNY on the one hand and various *longphuirt* on the other is not in itself surprising, since the force which campaigned for more than a decade in England in the 860s and 870s before settling was consistently described by the *Anglo-Saxon Chronicle* as *micel* ('large', 'great'), indicating an unusual size. However, as noted above, the same *micel here* progressed from Torksey to Repton before one part moved on to settle Northumbria, around the time that the coin evidence suggests the peak of activity. In this context, it makes sense that ARSNY (which has a slightly later *terminus post quem* than Torksey on the numismatic evidence) should be considerably smaller than the comparable site at Torksey, but it is difficult to reconcile the small size of the enclosure at Repton with either Torksey or ARSNY, and it seems that some reinterpretation of the Repton site is needed, although there is no reason to doubt that the existing association of the enclosure and both the mass grave and the individual graves with the over-wintering of the *micel here* in 873–4 is partially correct (see p. 89). Both Repton and Torksey are historically documented as sites of Viking winter camps, and both have produced finds which correspond closely with the historical dating, but on current evidence seem very different in size and character. The fact that ARSNY has been investigated by similar techniques to Torksey makes it unsurprising that it correlates much more closely with Torksey than with Repton. The similarities, other than scale, between ARSNY and Torksey on the one hand and Woodstown and (to a lesser extent) other *longphort* sites, plus Llanbedrgoch, suggests that Torksey provides a more representative model for Viking camps than the established interpretation of Repton, despite the fact that the latter has provided the paradigm for what Viking camps should look like for a generation. The fundamental differences both in size and character between ARSNY and Repton should therefore not be seen as barriers to interpreting ARSNY as a Viking camp.

A final important factor in the identification of ARSNY as a possible Viking camp is its character as a riverine site enclosed on the landward side. The full height and breadth, and thus the defensive capacity, of the bank and ditch enclosure is uncertain (see p. 9), but there is no doubt that it was a substantial construction, and while there is no single form characteristic of a Viking camp (see pp. 88–90), a D-shaped or sub-rectangular enclosure along a navigable river or coast has parallels in Viking sites in Britain, Ireland and Scandinavia. Although the exact location of the site remains confidential, it is located on a river navigable by vessels with the shallow draught apparently characteristic of Viking ships prior to the development of the deeper sea-going vessels of the late 10th century. The term *longphort* makes an association between ships and camps quite explicit in the Irish context, and most if not all of the identifiable *longphuirt* are located along navigable rivers. Although there is probably no direct equivalent to the word *longphort* in Old English (for possible similarities with 'Langport' names, see Williams 2015, no. 20), the majority of recorded camps are also on navigable rivers, or more rarely on the coast. The accessibility of potential camp sites by river was key to their strategic role, as discussed in the following section. On balance, it therefore seems reasonable to identify ARSNY as a historically unrecorded Viking camp, similar to the documented 'winter camps' of the *micel here* of the mid-860s to the late 870s, and possibly, although not certainly, associated with the settlement of Northumbria in 874–6. To understand the significance of this identification, it is necessary first to consider the role of such camps in the campaigns of the *micel here* from 865 to 879, and then to consider the importance of such camps in the transition from temporary raiding to permanent settlement.

Viking camps and the *micel here*

Gareth Williams

Between 865 and the late 870s, the *Anglo-Saxon Chronicle* records the activity of a group which it describes as a *micel here* ('great raiding army'). While the composition of the *micel here* may have changed considerably over time (see below), it existed as a recognisable entity which remained continuously in England throughout this period, and which was active at different times in all four of the main Anglo-Saxon kingdoms, before dividing into two forces in 874. One of these, led by Guthrum, Anund and Oscytel, moved south to Cambridge, and at least part of this force continued to raid until the defeat of Guthrum by Alfred of Wessex at Edington in 878, after which they eventually settled permanently in East Anglia after spending another year in south-west Mercia (*ASC, sub* 875 [874]; 878; 880 [879]). The other, under the leadership of Halfdan, moved north to Northumbria, and after over-wintering at an unspecified location 'on the Tyne' in 874–5, divided up the kingdom and settled in 876, 'ploughing and providing for themselves' (*ASC, sub* 876). It is to this period that the site at ARSNY has been attributed (see pp. 80–2). Although described in less detail in the *Anglo-Saxon Chronicle*, part of the force also settled in eastern Mercia, although it is unclear whether this settlement was undertaken by a third group of the *micel here*, or whether different parts of Mercia can be seen as falling within a 'greater East Anglia' and 'greater Northumbria' respectively. The latter certainly seems to have been the case by the early 10th century (*AG*, 171–2; Blackburn 2001, 132–3; 2006, 212–15; Downham 2008, 343; Williams 2008c; 2011d, 148–9, 152–4; 2013a, 26–30; McLeod 2014, 217–18), but it is less certain that this was the case at the time of the initial settlement. It is also unclear whether or not settlement was planned from the outset. Northumbria was effectively conquered in 866–7, and East Anglia in 870, but it was not until the mid-870s that permanent settlement was recorded in Northumbria and 879–80 in East Anglia. Although the most recent major study of the *micel here* interprets its actions as a planned migration from the outset (McLeod 2014), this fails to explain satisfactorily why it took so long to turn to settlement, given that there were opportunities to settle much earlier.

The division of the *micel here* under its different leaders in 874 points to the probability that it was always a composite force, with multiple leaders combining their followings, and different components joining or leaving the force at different times. The *Anglo-Saxon Chronicle* states that in the year 870–1 nine *jarls* (five of whom were named) and one king (Bagsecg) were killed, along with large numbers of men, although the *micel here* remained a major threat, and the West Saxons were obliged to 'make peace'. By 871 Ívarr, one of the original leaders of the *micel here*, who had probably previously campaigned in Ireland, had apparently left the *micel here* together with some or all of his personal following, as he is recorded campaigning in Strathclyde before moving on to Ireland, where he died in 873 (Downham 2007, 22–3; McLeod 2014, 114–15). His brother Halfdan either remained with the *micel here* or returned to it, as he is named as the leader of the group which moved from Repton to Northumbria in 874 (*ASC*, *sub* 875 [874]), and another unnamed brother was in Wessex in 878, attacking the Devon coast (unsuccessfully) with a fleet (*ASC*, *sub* 878). It is uncertain whether this was a completely independent attack, or a case of a fleet under one leader acting in conjunction with a land-based force under another, as seems to be typical of the strategy of the *micel here* (see below). This leader is named by the later chronicler Gaimar as Ubba, who also appears in other sources, but Shane McLeod plausibly suggests that this was a false association by Gaimar, and that Ubba was the leader of a separate element of the *micel here* which had previously been active in Frisia (McLeod 2014, 133–8). Guthrum, Oscytel and Anund, who led part of the force from Repton south to East Anglia in 874, are not previously recorded in association with the *micel here*, and Clare Downham (2008, 342) has suggested that they may have joined only in 871. Of the three, only Guthrum is named in the context of the later conflicts with Alfred and the West Saxons, suggesting that the other two probably parted company with Guthrum before this, either remaining in East Anglia or moving on elsewhere. It would thus be a mistake to think of the *micel here* as a single entity, remaining intact and unchanged across a ten-year period, quite apart from the losses suffered in battle. Recent approaches have emphasised the temporary and fluctuating nature of the *micel here*, interpreting it as a loose association of smaller warbands, each with its own distinct identity, although these identities might shift in accordance with changes in the leadership of the larger force (Price 2014c; 2016; Raffield 2016; Raffield *et al.* 2016).

Battle must have caused considerable attrition within the force, with as many as nine battles recorded in a single year, with 'great slaughter on either side' at Reading, 'many thousands killed' at Ashdown, and 'great slaughter on either side' again at Merton (*ASC*, *sub* 871 [870]). With so many changes of composition and leadership, it may be unwise to form an interpretation of a single coherent campaign strategy across the whole period of the *micel here*'s activity, however easy it may be to construct such a strategy by analysing the activities of the *micel here* in hindsight.

Nevertheless, many of the component units must have campaigned for many years, and it is likely that some of the individuals concerned may have remained with the *micel here* from its arrival in East Anglia in 865 to its dispersal on leaving Repton in Mercia in 874. Long-term campaigning of this type resumed in England in the period 892–6, and there are also parallels in Viking campaigns in Ireland and in Continental Europe, with long-serving fleets basing themselves in coastal areas such as Frisia and along river valleys such as the Loire and the Seine. Shane McLeod (2014, 109–71) argues persuasively that these were not simply parallel campaigns, but that elements of the *micel here* in England had previously campaigned in Ireland and/or Frisia and elsewhere in the Frankish kingdoms, and that their experiences in these places informed the activities of the *micel here* in England.

Whether or not the campaigns of the *micel here* represent a single coherent strategy, they are remarkable in two respects. As discussed, this was not in any sense a national army, although some of the leaders were of royal status, and this meant that the *micel here* almost certainly lacked some of the social and administrative infrastructure that underpinned the warfare and military organisation of enemies such as the Anglo-Saxons and the Franks (for Anglo-Saxon and Frankish military organisation in this period see Reuter 1985; 1990; Gillmor 1997; Abels 1988). Despite this, the *micel here* was able to campaign on a massive scale, over a prolonged period. The exact size of the army remains uncertain, although contemporary sources indicate that at its largest it comprised hundreds of ships. A minimal interpretation of a force of a few hundred at most was argued by Peter Sawyer (1962, 125; 2nd edn 1971, 127–8), partly on logistical grounds and partly on his interpretation of the legal definition of *here*, although this interpretation has been challenged (see below). However, it did appear to receive some support from the small size of the Viking winter camp at Repton, as interpreted by Martin Biddle and Birthe Kjølbye-Biddle (1992; 2001), and Neil Price's work on possible 10th-century Viking fortifications at Péran and Trans in Brittany also pointed to forces of only moderate size. Such forts were generally occupied temporarily, and there would presumably have been a desire to make the maximum use of space. Price has compared these forts with the rather better documented marching camps of the Roman army. According to Roman military engineering manuals, Roman marching camps had a normal ratio of 740 men per hectare. On this basis, Repton (1.4 ha) could accommodate 1,050 men, Péran (3.7 ha) 2,740 men, and Trans (0.7 ha) 520 men. However, Price also pointed out that these numbers should probably be diminished to take account of space for horses, non-combatants and stores, and also that the Vikings were probably rather less disciplined than the Roman army (Price 1991, 11–13), and these notes of caution seem eminently reasonable.

From a historical perspective, Sawyer's view that the size of the fleets in the *Anglo-Saxon Chronicle* was massively exaggerated was convincingly refuted by Nicholas Brooks (1979), who pointed out that textually independent English, Irish and Frankish accounts of Viking forces broadly agree on the increasing scale of Viking forces throughout the 9th century, and that while there may well be an element of rounding of figures, and some individual accounts may exaggerate, the historical sources between them present a consistent picture of fleets of ships in the low hundreds in the late 9th century. Since ships were not of a standard size, it is difficult to translate the size of fleets into exact numbers of men, but forces in the low thousands seem likely, and the size of the sites at Torksey and ARSNY (see pp. 85–6, 92) seem to point in the same direction. Using the same ratio of up to 740 men per hectare as for the camps in Brittany, this gives a theoretical maximum figure for Torksey of 40,700, and for ARSNY of 22,940 men. However, as noted for Brittany, there is no reason to think that Viking camps in general were as densely populated as those of the highly disciplined Roman army, and the absence of any evidence for any form of housing or shelters on either site means that there is no basis for more specific calculations. In addition, the evidence for production at both sites suggests that some of the space was required for workshops rather than occupation, while it is also likely that some space in both sites was occupied by ships, as over-wintering provided an opportunity for maintenance and repair, which would be difficult during the campaigning season. Finally, it has already been noted that there is both historical and archaeological evidence for the presence of women and possibly children accompanying Viking forces in England in this period. While the relative proportions of combatants and non-combatants remain a matter of conjecture (see McLeod 2011) the balance of evidence certainly suggests that women and children formed a significant part of the total numbers, thereby reducing further the space available for Viking warriors. There is no basis for estimating precisely how much less densely populated Viking camps were than Roman fortifications, but even 10% of the theoretical maximum would give a force of 4,070 for Torksey, and 2,294 for ARSNY, and the possibility of somewhat larger forces cannot safely be excluded.

The text known as the *Burghal Hidage*, which probably dates in its surviving form from the reign of Edward the Elder but reflects the extension of a system introduced by Alfred, lists the fortified *burhs* within the West Saxon kingdom, and the calculations for garrisoning them. This gives a total figure of 27,070 men on garrison service in Wessex, based on the service of one man per hide of land, probably in addition to the West Saxon field army. As a formal military obligation, this indicates a much higher burden of military service than any other reference to military service in Anglo-Saxon England (Abels 1988, 68, 76–7; Brooks 1996, 128–9; Williams 2013b, 133). The introduction of the burghal system probably post-dates the activities of the *micel here*, and the garrisoning of the *burhs* forms part of an important step-change in both the scale and the character of military service within Wessex in the course of Alfred's reign (Abels 1988, 58–78; Williams 2013b, 133–4). The exact date and character of the *Burghal Hidage* remains the subject of debate (e.g. Baker and Brookes 2013; Haslam 2011) and it is possible that it represents a notional blueprint for the development of a burghal system rather than an accurate record of the actual resources available either to Alfred or to Edward the Elder (899–924). Nevertheless, the figures found in the *Burghal Hidage* provide at least some indication of the manpower resources which the West Saxon kings could aspire to control in the late 9th century, even after the depredations of the *micel here*. Even allowing for a lesser figure of one man per five hides, which seems to have been more typical for service in the *fyrd*, then given the figures in the *Burghal Hidage*, it is simply not credible that the West Saxon military establishment in the 860s and 870s did not number in the thousands, or that the *micel here*, which was apparently able to meet West Saxon forces on equal terms on several occasions, should be significantly smaller.

The fact that the Vikings were able to muster such large forces is remarkable in itself, and their achievement is reflected in their success against large and powerful kingdoms. This involved extracting substantial tribute payments in return for peace from various Anglo-Saxon and Frankish rulers. While reference to such payments is often referred to euphemistically in Anglo-Saxon sources in the context of 'making peace', Frankish sources typically refer more specifically to payment of 'tribute' (Coupland 1999). In addition to portable tribute, various 9th-century Viking leaders were able to establish themselves as rulers of parts of Frisia under nominal Frankish overlordship, in a way which prefigured the later and more permanent settlement of Normandy (Coupland 1998). In England, the *micel here* was able to conquer the kingdoms of East Anglia, Northumbria and at least part of Mercia, and one element of it came close to conquering the kingdom of the West Saxons in 877–8, while the *micel here* as a whole had previously fought a campaign in that kingdom in 870–1, in which neither side had an obvious advantage.

Even more remarkable than the fact that such forces were large and often militarily successful is that they were able to campaign for years on end, which required over-wintering in hostile territory which was either conquered (if not necessarily fully subdued), or in which over-wintering was permitted by a temporary truce. Such truces were potentially to the benefit of both parties, and seem to have been a common feature of Viking campaigns in this period, although there are different interpretations of the nuances of 'peace' and 'truce' in the historical sources which fall outside the scope of this paper (*AG*, 313; Lund 1987; Abels 1992; Lavelle 2010, 324–8; McLeod 2014, 209–14). For the Vikings, such agreements potentially offered the chance for tribute in place of loot, the chance to negotiate for supplies (see further below) without either the risk or the effort of foraging in hostile territory, and a greatly reduced risk that rulers with access to the resources of whole kingdoms might organise attacks against them in the dead of winter, when flight and resupply would be at their most difficult. For Anglo-Saxon and Frankish rulers, such truces also offered the chance of reduced risk of attack, and reduced the likelihood of lasting damage to crops and livestock from indiscriminate plundering and forage. The possibility that markets and trade may have formed a normal part of such peace agreements has already been raised (see pp. 91–2), and it is possible that negotiated over-wintering may have provided opportunities for some of the wealth acquired by the *micel here* and other Viking forces to be returned to the hands of the native population. It is notable that despite the documentary evidence for large tribute payments from both Francia and England, 9th-century Frankish and Anglo-Saxon coins are extremely rare in Scandinavia, in contrast to the large quantities of Islamic dirhams deposited in Scandinavia, Russia and other areas of eastern Europe in this period (Coupland 1991; 2011). The paucity of 9th-century finds is also in marked contrast to the large quantities of Anglo-Saxon coins found in Scandinavia from the later period of Viking raiding in the late 10th and 11th centuries. There are various factors which may have influenced this, including the movement of coins not to the Viking homelands but to other areas of Viking settlement (Coupland 2011, 120–5); a conscious rejection of the Christian identity promoted in Frankish and Anglo-Saxon coinage (Williams 2011b, 357–9); and the recycling of coins as raw materials for the manufacture of other types of object (see pp. 22–3, 43–5). However, it is also possible that many of the coins received through plunder or tribute in this period never moved beyond the kingdoms from which they were taken, being returned into the local economy through trade.

While over-wintering offered benefits (or at least limited damage and risk), for both sides, it was nevertheless a major departure from the norms of warfare in northern Europe in the Viking Age. Warfare was typically seasonal, and while garrisons might be left in conquered territory, logistical considerations normally required the bulk of an army to return to its own territory to resupply at the end of a campaign season. This applied even to such powerful and successful rulers as Charlemagne, despite the fact that he had strong centralised power and a far more sophisticated administrative infrastructure underpinning his kingship than the leaders of the *micel here* (Reuter 1985). Even within their own kingdoms, rulers struggled to maintain armies in the field for extended periods. Alfred of Wessex (871–99) is notable not just for the fact that he defeated the *micel here*, and its successor of the 890s, but for his military reforms, introducing the network of fortified *burhs* mentioned above as well as organising his field army to keep half his forces in the field at any time, with the remainder in reserve to replace them (*ASC*, *sub* 894 [893]; Abels 1988, 63–6). This meant that it was easier for the different elements of the field army to resupply, and the *burhs* also had a role in controlling the food supply in their surrounding area to frustrate the campaign strategies employed by the *micel here*, as well as protecting the population (Abels 1997, 258–60; Williams 2008b, 198–9; 2013b, 131–2). Despite all this, even Alfred was unable to maintain forces in the field at all times, even within his own kingdom. In 893 a Viking force was besieged on the islet of Thorney in the River Colne by one part of the West Saxon field army, led by Alfred's son Edward, but this force was obliged to break the siege when the supplies ran out, and to return home before the relief army under Alfred himself arrived (*ASC* [A], *sub* 894 [893]; Abels 1988, 65–6).

It is this ability to campaign over extended periods that sets the *micel here* and other Viking forces of the mid–late 9th century apart from their contemporaries. Such long-term raiding required over-wintering. This is recorded in Ireland from 841, at Dublin and Linn Duachaill (see p. 89), in Francia from 843, on 'a certain island', often identified by modern historians (although not necessarily correctly) as Noirmouiter, and in England from 850–1 at Minster-in-Thanet (Ó Floinn 1998, 162; Coupland 2003, 186–7; Graham-Campbell 2004b, 30–1; Maas 2008, 267–70). Rather than simply campaigning continuously throughout the winter season, over-wintering required the establishment of a temporary base to provide the focus for the occupation and domination of the surrounding area. Many, although not all, of the Irish *longphuirt* discussed above fall into this category, as do the recorded winter camps of the *micel here*, including Torksey and Repton, and the similarities between ARSNY and these other sites suggests that it may also fall into this category. However, there appears to be no single morphological type for such sites in England or in Ireland (see pp. 88–90). Many of the camps seem to have incorporated existing centres. These included monasteries (e.g. Repton), nunneries (e.g. Minster-in-Thanet, Sheppey) royal and ecclesiastical centres (e.g. Reading, Chippenham), and Roman walled cities (e.g. London, Exeter, Chester). Other sites included islands, chosen primarily for their natural defensibility, such as Torksey, and Thorney in Essex, although it is possible that Torksey may have formed part of a royal estate (as it did by the time of Domesday Book), while it was also in close proximity to a suggested market site on the Trent at Marton, and a proposed estate centre at Stow (Hadley and Richards 2013, 17).

Settling down for a period of several months, whether for the purpose of over-wintering or for any other reason, represented a departure from another distinctive feature of Viking campaign strategy in the period of the *micel here*. This was an emphasis on strategic mobility, through a combination of ships and horses. Both ships and horses combined speed with carrying capacity. Speed was essential to strategic surprise, and attacking from the sea generally offered that, but on land horses also offered the opportunity to attack quickly before a defence could be mustered, to outrun pursuit, and to range over a much wider area than on foot, at greater speed, both for the purposes of plunder and for forage. Although the strategic importance of horses is never discussed in detail in contemporary sources in relation to the *micel here* (probably because it was taken for granted), the fact that the force was mounted is frequently mentioned in the *Anglo-Saxon Chronicle* and elsewhere. The *micel here* 'were provided with horses' in East Anglia in 865; in 870 it 'rode to Reading in Wessex, and 3 days later two jarls rode up-country'; in 876 Alfred pursued the 'mounted' *micel here* to Exeter; and the following year the *micel here* 'over-rode and occupied the land of Wessex'. A group of Vikings who had gathered at Fulham in 877 (probably a breakaway group from the *micel here*) moved to the Continent the following year, and after victory in battle at Saucourt in 881 'were provided with horses'. Part of this force attacked Rochester in 884, but elements from this force were surprised by Alfred and 'were there deprived of their horses, and immediately the same summer departed across the sea'. A further force came to Kent in 892 'horses and all', and in 893–4 another (probably overlapping) force at Buttington on the Severn 'devoured the greater part of their horses and the rest were perishing with hunger'.

Horses were important not just for speed but for their carrying capacity. Especially given the evidence that the *micel here* and comparable forces were often if not always accompanied by women and children, it was important to maintain supply lines based on more than could be carried on foot, and without the vulnerability of a slow-moving wagon train, which would have meant abandoning any strategic mobility. The *micel here* had to travel with weapons and armour, with food supplies, tools and other equipment, and with the accumulated plunder and tribute of years of campaigning, and pack-horses as well as riding horses would have been essential in allowing them to do so with speed.

If horses added speed first and carrying capacity second, it was the other way round with ships. Calculations taken from various periods show that, prior to the industrial revolution, the transport of bulk goods from the Roman period onwards was consistently more cost effective and efficient by boat than using land transport (Albrethsen 1997, 210–11). While cost may not have been the prime factor, ships provided a means of moving supplies, valuables and non-combatants much more effectively and probably rather more quickly than by land transport, even deep inland. The shallow draught of Viking ships meant that they were not restricted to the coast, and that most rivers of any size and depth were navigable. While ships on rivers were vulnerable to attack to some extent, especially from missiles, pulling away into mid-stream or to the opposite bank prevented direct assault, making them less vulnerable to direct attack than a conventional baggage train.

This use of ships to carry supplies, loot and non-combatants meant that it was possible for a fast-moving mounted force by land to carry no more than they needed for a set period, otherwise relying on what they could forage, before meeting up by prior arrangement with the ships, and the *Anglo-Saxon Chronicle* describes the *micel here* dividing into a *landhere* and a *sciphere* (e.g. *ASC* 877 [876]). Even when, as most of the time, no such division is mentioned, it can be assumed. The choice of winter camps in particular reflects proximity either to the sea (e.g. Wareham, Exeter, Chester) or to navigable rivers such as the Thames (London, Reading, Fulham), Severn (Buttington) or Trent (Nottingham, Torksey, Repton), and the recorded movements of the *micel here* from one winter camp to another can be traced relatively easily along a combination of rivers and Roman roads or ancient trackways. There is a similar combination of *longphuirt* along river routes in Ireland, while much of the Viking activity in Francia and Frisia was also concentrated either in coastal areas or along major rivers. The name 'A Riverine Site Near York' for the ARSNY site was deliberately chosen since while retaining the anonymity of the site itself, it highlights the key factor that this site was also accessible by river.

As noted, supply was a major issue for all armies in this period, not just for the Vikings. Lacking the facility for mass transportation, even the armies of major rulers were heavily constrained by the difficulties of supply. As Timothy Reuter (1985) has noted, even the largest towns in northern Europe numbered only a few thousand inhabitants, and these were established centres, supplied from their surrounding hinterlands, and with the capacity to store reserves. Campaigning armies had no such advantages, and armies of several hundred or even thousands of men represented the equivalent of whole towns moving around, but without the ability to take their hinterlands with them.

For a campaigning army, especially one campaigning in hostile territory, there were four possible approaches to supply. Firstly, the army itself could take its supplies with it. This would limit the duration of the campaign by the amount of supplies that could be carried, and would also limit the speed of the army to the speed of whatever form of transport was being used to convey the supplies. This is typical of much of early medieval warfare, with short raiding campaigns, withdrawing very quickly.

Secondly, the army could resupply itself, using a separate supply train to link back to stores in safe territory. This meant that the army could move more quickly, and allowed for a larger volume of supplies, but added the risk of the army being cut off and running out of food if the supply line was severed. The Carolingian strategy of seasonal campaigns gradually extending the borders of the Carolingian kingdom, each year attacking beyond established borders (and lines of supply), fits this pattern (Reuter 1985).

Thirdly, the army could rely on foraging as they went along. This allowed greater mobility and did away with the requirement for a vulnerable supply train, but it was extremely risky, since it left the army with virtually no reserve if they were unable to secure supplies in the course of their campaigning. Alfred's willingness to adopt a scorched-earth policy, destroying crops and driving away cattle to deny them to the Vikings, as at Chester in 894, was key to his success in driving the Vikings out of his kingdom (*ASC* [A], *sub* 894–5 [893–4]).

The fourth approach was to combine these different elements. Whichever approach was followed, the difficulty of supply was a major factor in the normal pattern of seasonal warfare, which was based around a campaign season, at the end of which an army would return to the safety and supply of its own lands. The fact that the *micel here* and other forces on the Continent campaigned for years on end in hostile territory is due more to their success in combining campaign strategies with effective logistical organisation than to any particular superiority on the battlefield (Williams 2008b, 197–8).

The combination of fast-moving mounted troops on land with a floating supply train meant that the *micel here* had the ideal combination of strategic mobility combined with effective logistical support. Their ships acted as mobile supply dumps, and would be used in support of land forces where possible. The land forces would carry with them what they could, without sacrificing mobility, and probably also relied to some extent on topping up their supplies through forage.

Winter camps were a response to the fact that this sort of strategic mobility was limited in winter. Although Viking ships were highly effective by the standards of the time, they were nevertheless vulnerable to bad weather. The loss of the *sciphere* at Swanage in 877 on its way from the winter camp of

Wareham to Exeter was a major disaster, and obliged the land force to abandon its campaign at Exeter that year, and to over-winter at unspecified locations in Mercia instead, moving at harvest-time to take advantage of the harvest already being gathered in (*ASC* 877 [876]). Alfred's seizure of cattle and destruction of crops at Chester has already been noted, and in 895 he also took an army to ensure that the harvest in the area around a Viking camp on the River Lea north of London was gathered up by his men rather than the Vikings, again forcing them to move on (*ASC* [A], *sub* 896 [895]). In addition to problems of supply, travel over land was also more problematic in the winter, and moving slowly in hostile territory provided an opportunity for local forces to muster in time to provide an effective threat.

Winter camps provided the focus for an alternative strategy for the period of each year in which strategic mobility was limited. Firstly, they provided a defensible base for the domination of the surrounding landscape during the period of occupation. This does not mean that all members of the *micel here* were necessarily based in the camp for the whole winter, and it is likely that the forces were more widely dispersed (see below), with the camp itself serving as an emergency refuge when required. Secondly, in addition to their location in proximity to transport routes by road and river, the camps were probably selected in advance because they were either existing estate centres, or were defensible sites close to such centres. As noted above, many of the recorded winter camps both of the *micel here* and in the late 9th century generally can be identified as monasteries, nunneries or royal estates. This meant that they had existing supply networks, designed to support substantial populations at something rather more than a subsistence level through the provision of *feorm*, or food rent. Parallels can also be found in the location of some of the Irish *longphuirt* at monastic sites (see above). By arriving at the onset of winter and dispossessing the inhabitants, the *micel here* acquired for itself whatever stockpile had already been accumulated for the winter (Graham-Campbell 2004b, 30–1). This would potentially include not only the produce of the immediate estate, but also the *feorm* of other estates owned by the same landowner, and transported in ready for winter. In the case of royal estates, this might include both *feorm* and taxation in kind from across the whole kingdom. When in the winter of 877–8 the *micel here* under Guthrum captured the royal estate at Chippenham, Alfred of Wessex himself only narrowly avoided capture, and much of his reputation derives from his ability to recover from this adversity to defeat Guthrum's forces. The capture of Alfred at this point might well have been decisive in the conquest of Wessex, and it is possible, though far from certain, that this was part of Guthrum's aim in taking Chippenham by surprise at that point. It is also possible that the supplies brought in to Chippenham to feed Alfred's court and household were considered a more important prize. The timing of the attack just after Christmas shows similarities with the capture of another West Saxon royal estate at Reading in December 870, and Reading on that occasion then served successfully as a base for the *micel here* until the following winter.

The establishment of a winter camp also gave control not just of the immediate locality but of the surrounding area, and often a site seems to have been selected not just to exploit the individual estate at which it was based, but a wider group of nearby estates. Thus the camp at Reading probably involved the exploitation not only of the royal estate at Reading itself, but of another royal estate at Wallingford, as well as the estates belonging to the abbey of Abingdon, while a Viking hoard from Croydon which has been associated with the over-wintering of the *micel here* at London in 871–2 may reflect the exploitation of the archbishop of Canterbury's estates in Croydon (Abels 1997, 258–9; Brooks and Graham-Campbell 2000; see also above, pp. 84–5, 95) for a possible cluster of estates around Torksey). In addition to major estates, such as these, the *micel here* must also have exploited the resources of a wider surrounding area. The reinterpretation of the *micel here* as a force of thousands of men, plus women, children and horses, means that a vast quantity of food was required on a daily basis. At the same time, the size of the force must have given it undisputed control over a substantial area except when an Anglo-Saxon army was in the immediate locality to challenge this. Supplies built up throughout the previous year may well have been brought in by ship when a winter camp was first established, to augment the winter supplies of the estates in the immediate area of the camp, but it is likely that further supplies had to be brought in from further afield throughout the period of occupation.

Exactly how this was done remains uncertain. An element of plunder seems likely. Since the *micel here* rarely stayed in the same kingdom from one season to the next, let alone the same region (the exception being the move from Torksey to Repton), they could afford to exhaust the supplies of the surrounding area in a way which a permanent population, with a requirement for seed corn and breeding stock, could not, before moving on to strip another area the following year. Whether the total stripping of the surrounding area was always necessary, however, is debatable, and depends to some extent on how one interprets the relationship between the *micel here* and the surrounding population. While some plunder is likely to have taken place under almost any circumstances, widespread indiscriminate plunder may not have been necessary. Shane McLeod has noted that on several occasions the *micel here* over-wintered in kingdoms which it had previously conquered. If they maintained authority over these areas, even through local 'puppet kings', this presumably gave them some control over existing administrative structures, potentially including rents and taxes in kind due to the king. These could be exploited directly by the *micel here* if they visited that territory, and could potentially be transported even to a completely different area as required, as long as they had sufficient control over the infrastructure (McLeod 2007). McLeod's broader interpretation of the period of conquest and settlement is precisely that the *micel here* did maintain firm control over its conquests even while they continued to campaign elsewhere, and that the speed of assimilation of Scandinavian settlers in England with the existing population points to considerable continuity of existing practice, in which case the infrastructure required for the collection of *feorm* are likely to have survived throughout the disruption of the 860s and 870s (McLeod 2007; 2014 *passim*).

The evidence for this is not unambiguous, but it is a tenable position, and the *micel here* may well have been able to exploit the resources of previously conquered kingdoms to some extent by peaceful means. If that is the case, then ARSNY's location within the previously conquered kingdom of Northumbria may have permitted this sort of peaceful exploitation. Unfortunately the requirement to keep the site anonymous rules out potentially interesting research into the relationship between the site and evidence for royal landholding in the area, although direct evidence for landholding in Northumbria immediately prior to the Viking incursions is scarce.

If it was necessary to support the *micel here* with supplies from a wider area than the immediate environs of the camp, it is not clear that the whole force would necessarily be based in a single place, except when directly under attack. If they lost the surrounding area, it was only a matter of time before they lost the fortification, unless their attackers ran out of food first, as happened at Thorney Island in 893. It is therefore very likely that the *micel here* spread out over the surrounding area, only concentrating their forces if obliged to do so. The *Annals of St Bertin* record that in 861 Weland's army divided into *sodalitates* ('brotherhoods'), which were billeted in a number of different places along the Seine between Paris and the coast (*ASB*, *sub* 861). This is the only description of such a widespread division of a Viking fleet over winter, which may indicate that it was unusual, but it is not unlikely that when armies are described as wintering in a particular place, they might be billeted over the surrounding area. This had the added advantage of limiting friction between different groups within the larger force as well as making it easier to manage supply. A possible example of this may be found in the Viking cemetery at Heath Wood, Ingleby, a few miles from the Repton camp. The cemetery can be dated to the late 9th century, and shows different burial practices from the Viking burials at Repton itself. It may simply be that the Heath Wood cemetery may relate to a slightly later period following the permanent settlement of the area, as none of the artefacts recovered definitively point to a narrow dating in the early 870s, but Julian D. Richards (2003b; 2004) has interpreted it as evidence that the force based on Repton was divided, with different groups following different burial practices, possibly indicating origins in different regions of Scandinavia.

The dispersed billeting of Weland's forces on the Seine was only possible because of a peace treaty but, as noted above (see pp. 94–5), temporary truces in relation to over-wintering were common, especially when Viking forces were over-wintering within kingdoms which they had not conquered, and did not fully control. An additional benefit to both sides in such truces is that they may have provided an alternative to plunder as a means of supply. 'Making peace' seems generally to have involved payment in silver and/or gold, but could also include provisions. In 861 the Frankish ruler Charles the Bald provided a Viking fleet under Weland with livestock and grain to prevent the need for foraging, in addition to the sum of five thousand pounds of silver. Officially this was payment for Weland's fleet to serve as mercenary troops rather than simply a tribute payment, but such distinctions could often be blurred in practice (*ASB*, *sub* 861; Coupland 1999, 61–2). Provision of livestock and grain may not normally be specified in an Anglo-Saxon context, but may have been a common element in the truces established around the winter camps of the *micel here* (McLeod 2007). For Anglo-Saxon rulers, with access to rents and taxation, passing on a proportion of this to the *micel here* may have seemed preferable to the risk of greater damage associated with indiscriminate forage and plunder. A final element in supply may have been the acquisition of food through purchase. As discussed above, exchange appears to be a major activity in the finds record at both ARSNY and Torksey, while the *Annals of St Bertin* make specific reference to allowing a Viking force to hold a market as part of a seasonal truce in Francia, and the treaty between Alfred and Guthrum also includes provision for cross-border trade (see p. 91). Given the emphasis within law codes of the period on royal regulation of trade (and the references in Alfred-Guthrum are as much about regulation of trade as about trade itself), it is likely that any such trade would only have been officially permitted in authorised markets, which would surely have included the Viking camps. The camps would also have provided obvious central points for the delivery and distribution of any supplies provided to the *micel here* by their Anglo-Saxon hosts.

This emphasis on supply is not to deny the other fundamental role of the camps in defence. While island sites such as Thanet, Sheppey, Torksey and Thorney provided natural defences, most of the sites selected for over-wintering either included existing defences such as Roman city walls, or involved the construction of new or reworked earthwork defences, as at Reading and Repton. ARSNY also seems to fit into this category although the precise dating of the ARSNY enclosure is uncertain (see pp. 81–2). The construction of bank and ditch defences for temporary camps seems to have been commonplace for Viking forces, as indicated by the *Annals of Fulda*, which record that the Vikings on the River Dyle in 891 'pitched their camp untroubled ... and after their fashion surrounded it with a fortified ditch' (*AF*, *sub* 891). Both Anglo-Saxon and Viking siege warfare was fairly rudimentary, and direct assaults on fortifications rarely seem to have been successful for either side, unless the attack was made while the fortification was incomplete, as at York in 866, when the Northumbrians broke into the city (although they subsequently lost the battle), and in the case of an unnamed 'half-made' *burh* (possibly at Appledore) in south-west Kent in 892 successfully attacked by a Viking force landing from the Continent (*ASC* [A], *sub* 867 [866]; 893 [892]). Other recorded sieges involving the *micel here* and comparable forces were only successful if the defenders ran out of food, hence the emphasis on the destruction or seizure of livestock and crops from the surrounding area in Alfred's later campaigns (see above, p. 96), and it was just as likely that the besiegers would run out of supplies first, as at Thorney (see above, p. 95). This would be more problematic for the besiegers the larger their army was, and fortifications were key to the *micel here* being able to avoid battle with potentially superior forces and to negotiate the sort of over-winter truces discussed above. For example, the *micel here* were besieged at Nottingham in 867–8 by the combined forces of the

Mercians and the West Saxons, but 'no heavy fight occurred there, and the Mercians made peace' (*ASC*, *sub* 868 [867]).

Camps thus played an important strategic role in the campaigns of the *micel here*. Without a supply reserve, armies could not reliably forage enough to survive, and would be forced to fragment. Without a secure base where ships, women, children, the wounded and plunder could safely be left, the Vikings also lost their mobility during the campaign season, while the presence of fortifications was instrumental in forcing the various Anglo-Saxon kingdoms to make temporary truces permitting the *micel here* to over-winter, and the winter camps then provided a focus for the gathering and distribution of supplies, even though the *micel here* may well have routinely dispersed over a wider area during their over-wintering.

Viking camps and urbanisation
Gareth Williams

Since the excavations in York and Dublin in the 1970s and early 1980s, towns have been very much a central feature in perceptions of Viking settlement, and individual towns are central to the identities of accepted (if misleading) Viking polities in England such as the 'Kingdom of York' and the 'Five Boroughs' (Williams 2013a). However, towns are not generally a major feature of the first phase of Viking settlements, either in England or Ireland, and the bulk of the surviving evidence from Viking towns in both countries comes from the 10th and 11th centuries, and only to a much lesser extent the late 9th century (Simpson 2010; Hall 2011, 621–5). As discussed in more detail below, while there were undoubtedly pre-Viking sites in England, Ireland and southern Scandinavia that showed some proto-urban characteristics, there were few settlements in any of these countries that provided any sort of substantial model of urban life by the time of the Viking settlement of northern and eastern England in the 870s. Furthermore, even the largest permanent 'towns' were relatively small. The handful of pre-Viking Anglo-Saxon towns identified by Richard Hall (see below, p. 100) were typically 50 hectares or more (Hall 2011, 618), comparable with Torksey, but other towns were such smaller. The Mercian towns of Hereford and Tamworth, which are arguably of pre-Viking date (see below, p. 100), are only *c.* 12.2 and 21.3 hectares respectively (Hall 2011, 621). Towns and proto-towns in Scandinavia and around the Baltic were also smaller than towns such as London and Southampton, and indeed than Torksey and ARSNY. The enclosed area at Hedeby was less than half the size of Torksey, at 24 hectares, and Wolin a little smaller at 20 hectares, while Birka and Ribe were only 12 and 10 hectares respectively (Lilja 1996, 18). As recently noted by Shane McLeod (2014, 132–58), parts of the *micel here* by the mid-870s were probably made up of forces which had earlier campaigned in the Frankish kingdoms, and some may even have temporarily settled in Frisia. Both in Frisia and in other Frankish territories, urbanisation was more developed than in the British Isles or Scandinavia, and Continental influence is also apparent both on minting and on the development of the pottery industry in the Scandinavian settlements in England (Smart 1985; Vince 1993; Blackburn 2005; McLeod 2014, 145–56), both of which are activities normally associated with urbanisation. Frankish towns may thus have been a significant influence in the development of Viking camps and/or Viking towns, although the proportion of the settlers of northern and eastern England who had previously campaigned or temporarily settled in Frisia or Francia remains uncertain. Nevertheless, the vast majority of the Scandinavian settlers of both England and Ireland probably came from rural backgrounds, and had limited experience of town life. While place-names suggest that much of the Scandinavian settlement in England was also rural, the emphasis on towns in the historical record suggests that they were already beginning to evolve by the end of the 9th century, although few (with the exception of York and Lincoln) have yet revealed archaeological evidence of extensive occupation this early (Hall 1989; 2001; 2011; Hall *et al.* 2014; Vince 2001; 2003; Ten Harkel 2010).

As very large (if temporary) settlements, which pre-date many of the excavated 'towns' of the later Viking Age, the Viking camps of the late 9th century thus appear to represent an interesting phase in the development towards urbanisation in both England and Ireland. This begs the question of what constitutes an 'urban' settlement in an early medieval context. Martin Biddle (1976, 100) suggested that the minimum definition of an early medieval town was that it should show at least three or four of the following characteristics: defences; a planned street-system; a market(s); a mint; legal autonomy; a role as a central place; a relatively large and dense population; a diversified economic base; plots and houses of 'urban' type; social differentiation; complex religious organisation; and a judicial centre. Biddle's definitions have not been universally accepted, and may be criticised for underplaying social aspects of urban identity, as well as the relationship between a town and its related territory. There are also practical issues in the application of this model to all but a limited number of historically well-documented sites, since some of the characteristics are archaeologically invisible, while others are visible on clearly non-urban sites. The definitions also fail to provide a clear distinction in terms of scale between towns and other smaller settlements with some urban characteristics, and while specialised production can be seen as part of 'a diversified economic base', the urban excavations of the late 1970s and 1980s suggest that it was of greater importance than Biddle's definitions recognised. Nevertheless, the idea of towns in general, and those of late Anglo-Saxon or Anglo-Scandinavian England in particular, sharing key characteristics found in Biddle's list has received at least a qualified acceptance, implicitly or explicitly, in many discussions of towns and urbanisation (e.g. Scull 1997, 271–2; Astill 2009, 262–5; Hall 2011, 616–17; Hadley and Ten Harkel 2013b). A full discussion of this point goes beyond the scope of the present study. Nevertheless, Biddle's definitions still provide a useful if not necessarily an exhaustive model of the key characteristics of the early medieval town.

To Biddle's definitions, one might add an element of (intended) longevity or permanence, since this is one way of determining the difference between a town and a seasonal market, such as some of the beach markets recorded around the Irish Sea (Griffiths 1992; 2003; 2007; 2010) and, following the interpretations given above, the winter camps in

England and some if not all of the *longphuirt* in Ireland. We know with hindsight that some camps developed into Viking towns – York and Dublin being prime examples – but while York is one of the few settlements in England which can be identified as already partly urbanised immediately prior to the Viking conquest, and the over-wintering of the *micel here* presumably made use of the Roman walls, there is neither archaeological nor historical evidence to suggest that permanent settlement was planned in either Dublin or York at the time of the initial Viking occupation of the respective sites. Indeed, although the *micel here* conquered Northumbria in 866 and apparently over-wintered in or around York in both 866–7 and 869–70, it is not until 876 that Scandinavian settlement in Northumbria is first recorded (*ASC, sub* 876). While many modern discussions of the *micel here* take it for granted, with the benefit of hindsight, that settlement was part of the strategy of the *micel here* from the beginning (e.g. McLeod 2014), this is not clear from the historical accounts, and it is difficult to see why, if the intent was to settle, no attempt was made to do so sooner. Similarly, while an Anglo-Scandinavian town did develop at Torksey in Lincolnshire, the recent investigations make it clear that the Viking camp of the 870s and the later town were in different locations, with no obvious continuity between the two (Hadley and Richards 2013, 17–19). Conversely, although the *burhs* of Alfred of Wessex are often identified as towns rather than simply as fortifications, and many did indeed become major late Anglo-Saxon towns, others apparently did not survive beyond the early 10th century, once their military function had passed. As the *burhs* apparently formed a planned network, it is not unlikely that some or all of these were also intended to become towns, but that other factors intervened. This may be the changing strategic needs of the expanded West Saxon kingdom in the early 10th century, or the fact that the *burhs* were so close together meant that some competed with each other in terms of their non-military functions as centres for regional economy and royal administration (Williams 2013b, 135–49). Again, the intention of permanence is not necessarily archaeologically visible, although it might on occasion be inferred from the scale of planning and building works, but where long-term occupation in a single settlement is visible, this is one characteristic which distinguishes towns from the apparently short horizons of occupation of the Viking camps investigated so far. Returning to Biddle's original twelve characteristics, these fall into a number of different groups, relating to the military, economic, social and civil functions of towns, and I would argue that for a site to be recognised as urban, it needs not just three or four of Biddle's characteristics in total, but a spread across the different groups of functions.

In the case of the Viking camps investigated so far, some of these characteristics are visible, others seem very much to be absent, while others remain uncertain. Defences are apparent at ARSNY, Repton, Woodstown and Annagassan, although the extent to which the Woodstown bank and ditch constitute a serious defence has been questioned (see above, p. 86), while it is argued above that the D-shaped defences at Repton should no longer be considered to define the boundaries of the whole site; the evidence for extensive exchange at ARSNY, Woodstown and Torksey points to the existence of markets; the evidence for production at all three suggests both a diversified economic base and a relatively densely settled population, while all three can be considered large in comparison with other places normally accepted as towns, especially Torksey at *c.* 55 hectares. On Biddle's minimum of three to four characteristics, one could argue that ARSNY, Torksey and Woodstown all qualify as urban, and with further investigation Annagassan might well join them. By contrast, it would be difficult to argue the same for Repton on current evidence. However, the lack of any indication of anything (again, based purely on current evidence) that clearly suggests intended permanence, or which informs our understanding of the social and civil character rather than the purely defensive and economic character of the sites, makes it difficult to describe these convincingly as towns although, as noted above, both ARSNY and Torksey are considerably larger than settlements such as Hereford and Tamworth that have been so interpreted. However, the camps can be seen as representing a pre-urban phase on the way to the development of 'proper' towns.

These seem to be largely a product of the very end of the 9th and the 10th century in England, both in Anglo-Saxon and Viking areas. Although, as mentioned, there is some evidence for defences at Hereford and Tamworth, as well as Winchcombe, and this has been used to argue for a network of boroughs in Mercia in the 8th century, the argument is not entirely compelling on current evidence, although it is certainly possible that the three places in question had a range of urban or pre-urban functions before the Viking settlement (Hall 2011, 605). A small number of other 'towns' can probably also be cautiously identified prior to the reign of Alfred: the four *wics* of London (*Lundenwic*), Ipswich (*Gipeswic*), Southampton (*Hamwic*) and York (*Eoforwic*) probably qualify on archaeological evidence; documentary evidence suggests that Canterbury may already have had an urban layout, in addition to its long established role as a mint and a centre of ecclesiastical authority, while a document of *c.* 889–99 from Worcester seems to point to a range of existing rights before the foundation of the Alfredian *burh*, although it was probably not until the 10th century that it developed a fully urban character (*ibid.*, 602–4, 607).

However, while few *wics* seem to have been on the scale of those mentioned above, there were a wide variety of sites showing combinations of Biddle's urban characteristics, which can be regarded as pre-urban. In recent years, scholarship has moved on from the Hodges (1982) hierarchical model of *emporia* serving primarily to support the acquisition of prestige goods by the elite, to acknowledge a more flexible mixture of sites showing evidence of both production and exchange (Pestell 2011), only some of which appear to fit with Hodges' model. John Blair (2005, 246–90) has argued that minsters had a major role as pre-urban centres both in economic terms and as centres of authority and in some cases also as defensive structures; similar arguments have been made for 'monastic towns' in Ireland, although some of these claims need to be treated with caution (Valante 2008, 26–30). However, *wics* and monastic sites, large and small, seem also to have been supplemented by a range of other categories of site, including elite secular residences and rural sites of rather lower status. The phenomenon of the 'productive site' means that there are many sites at which elements of pre-urban activity can be detected, but whose exact nature cannot be determined; even some excavated sites are ambiguous in terms of their interpretation as secular or monastic settlements. However, the greater range of status implied by productive sites, together with a vastly increased distribution of single finds of coins, leads to the inevitable conclusion that there was already a much greater degree of economic activity, more widespread geographically and involving a wider cross-section of society, than could previously be imagined (Ulmschneider 2000; Pestell and Ulmschneider 2003; Pestell 2011; Hall 2011, 601–5). While relatively little of this may be described as urban, it laid the foundations from which urbanisation could develop with the right stimulus.

The model for urbanisation in Scandinavia in the third quarter of the 9th century was probably even more limited. Current evidence suggests that there were only four sites in southern Scandinavia (Hedeby, Birka, Ribe and Kaupang) which can be considered urban (or something close to it) in this period, together with a few other sites at a comparable stage of development on the southern Baltic coast (Wiechmann 1996; Ambrosiani 2004; 2008; Feveile 2006; Tummuscheit 2003; Skre 2007a; 2007b; 2011a; Bogucki 2007; 2010; von Carnap-Bornheim *et al.* 2010; Hilberg 2008; 2011), although preliminary interpretation of the recently discovered site at Heimdalsjordet near Gokstad in Vestfold suggests that this is another site of comparable status (Jan Bill, pers. comm.). The fact that the new site was until recently completely unknown raises the possibility that others may yet be discovered. Even so, the low total numbers and the fact that their distribution is limited to southern Scandinavia, means that they can hardly be regarded as typical of the Viking homelands as a whole and, as discussed above (p. 40), Scandinavia also lacked the long experience with coin use found in England, while even the bullion economy was only beginning to develop on a large scale. However, a combination of excavation and metal detecting has demonstrated that, as in England, production and exchange were not limited to these few sites, and central places such as Tissø, Uppåkra and Sorte Muld suggest a similar diversity to the productive sites in England (Hårdh 2000; 2008; 2011; Jørgensen 2003; Adamsen *et al.* 2009). In the same way, there were probably many other sites with similar characteristics on a smaller scale, and Sindbæk (2010) has argued for economic interaction within a network of sites of different size and character rather than the traditional model of all activity being limited to a few major trade routes between large 'gateway' centres. Given the high level of investment required to outfit and supply Viking expeditions, it is likely that a much higher proportion of the Viking settlers were familiar with the extended network of economically active pre-urban sites than with the towns alone. The fact that ARSNY and other Viking camps show clear contact with the emerging bullion economy of southern Scandinavia leaves little doubt that there was some familiarity with these sites. Even so, Scandinavia provided few models for the development of towns visible in Viking England and Ireland in the late 9th and 10th centuries.

There seems little doubt that the beginnings of a network of *burhs* was established by Alfred in Wessex in the final decades of the 9th century and extended by his successors in the 10th. The precise definition of a *burh* is problematic, as the word is used in Old English to mean many different things, as are the various Latin terms which are also applied in contemporary texts to refer to settlements described in Old English as *burhs* (Draper 2008; Baker 2013; Yorke 2013). By the time that *burhs* are described in any detail, in law codes and charters of the 10th century, they combined a military role with economic, administrative and judicial functions, or in other words the main groupings of Biddle's urban characteristics described above (Williams 2013b). However, many of Alfred's *burhs* seem to have been short-lived fortifications which disappeared once the immediate threat of Viking attack receded, without making the transition to towns. While urban development can be observed archaeologically in a few of the Alfredian *burhs* in the 9th century, in most cases it appears to be a secondary development in the 10th century. Similarly, the development of towns as centres for administration and a range of civic functions is only fully visible in the 10th century, although there are arguments for suggesting that they may have formed part of Alfred's original conception (Hall 2011, 605–10; Williams 2013b). Viking towns in England seem likewise to have been a product of the very end of the 9th century and the 10th century (Hall 2011, 610–14), and again the development of a full range of urban functions rather than production, exchange and defence seems likely to be a secondary development. However, their defensive role seems to have been a major factor from the beginning, and the extension of West Saxon authority across Mercia and East Anglia in the first quarter of the 10th century appears to have focused on the strategic control of fortified *burhs*, whether initially built by the Vikings or the Anglo-Saxons, although the strategic role of the *burh* should probably be seen as somewhat different in this phase of activity than it was in the defence of Wessex in the late 9th century (Williams 2013b). The development of towns in Ireland in most cases seems on current evidence to be even later, at the very end of the 10th century (Clarke 1998, 353–68), although recent excavations in Dublin suggest a smoother transition from the *longphort* phase to the urban phase than was visible when Clarke was writing (Simpson 2005; 2010). The move from the early Viking raids, launched from a predominantly rural society to the permanent urban settlements of the 10th century and later was thus a gradual one, and the Viking camps represent an important step alongside that development route. Despite their temporary status, they prefigured the range of activities found in later towns, and meet many of the characteristics of 'towns'. At the same time, they also played a part in socialising the Vikings to living in something like an urban environment. The size of the camp sites, and the estimated size of the *micel here*, comes much closer to the urban populations of the late Viking Age than any precursor to towns in the Scandinavian homelands, while there was only limited access to models of urban living in the various lands visited by Viking raiders in the mid–late 9th century. The diverse composition of the *micel here* and other Viking forces also probably necessitated other elements of social organisation that became fixed within permanent towns. Temporary solutions for assigning accommodation and organising work space for production and repair prefigured urban planning, while mechanisms must have been in place for the resolution of disputes, reflecting the later role of towns in the exercise of justice. As also noted, the camps did not function in isolation, but required an interaction with the surrounding landscape both in terms of political and military control, and in terms of supply. Again, this prefigures a permanent relationship between town and hinterland (Williams 2013a, 18–19).

This relationship between town and hinterland was important in the permanent development of towns. John Bradley (1988; 2009) has stressed the importance of understanding the Viking towns in Ireland not just as urban centres, but as larger territories combining rural and urban elements, even if they took their identity from the urban settlements. Something similar is visible in the relationship between the *burhs* in the Burghal Hidage and the territories owing service to individual *burhs*. Within the expanding West Saxon kingdom, this was partly organised through shires, whereas the dating of the shiring of areas of Scandinavian settlement remains obscure (Hinton 1996; Hill 2001), but in addition to the association of the *burhware* (men of the *burh*) who were permanently resident within their particular boroughs, there must have been some identification with the *burh* on the part of the surrounding population responsible for its garrisoning and upkeep, and increasingly reliant on the *burh* as a local focus for economy, justice and royal administration (Williams 2013b). In the same way, the emerging Anglo-Scandinavian towns of the late 9th and early 10th centuries seem to have defined the identities of the surrounding areas even without a shire structure as an additional layer. The story of the West Saxon conquest of East Anglia and Mercia is essentially the story of the conquest and submission of a widespread rural population whose identity was defined in relation to the urban centres that provided a local focus both for defence and for a wide range of other social and economic functions (Williams 2013a). This sort of identity does not seem to have a widespread earlier precedent either in Scandinavia or in England, but to be a product of the settlement itself. As the camps, however temporary, were a defining feature of the period immediately preceding that settlement, they seem likely to have shaped the development of more permanent structures of settlement within the landscape.

The Viking camps thus occupy a transitional phase between a largely pre-urban society in both England and Scandinavia in the mid-9th century and the widespread development of towns in both Anglo-Saxon and Anglo-Viking England in the 10th century. The camps lack the range of attributes that are taken to typify the fully developed early medieval town, but these attributes seem in many cases only to have developed gradually even in those settlements which did become towns. The primary phase of burghal development seems to a great extent to have been concerned with the defensive role of *burhs*, although economic activity developed fairly quickly in a number of sites. This combination of roles is also apparent in the camps, and while more detailed consideration is required of the exact relationship than is possible here, the need for the West Saxons to counter the strategic role of the camps in the campaigns of the *micel here* probably provided a stimulus to Alfred's burghal developments, and while individual *burhs* may have been fortified earlier in the reign, Alfred's burghal policy is only mentioned in historical sources following his defeat of Guthrum in 878, suggesting that it was a reactive policy (Williams 2008b; 2013b). The shift in areas under Viking authority from temporary to permanent settlement following the period in which the camps were used probably led to a natural progression in areas of Viking settlement from camps as temporary defended centres of occupied territory, at which a range of economically driven activities took place, to towns which fulfilled the same functions and more on a more permanent basis.

Conclusion

Richard Hall and Gareth Williams

To conclude, ARSNY can be interpreted as one of a growing group of Viking camps of the late 9th century in Britain and Ireland which, with the exception of Repton, had until recently been almost completely unrepresented in the archaeological record. The large numbers of finds at these sites, together with their size, forces a reconsideration of the extent to which the Repton excavations give a complete picture of that (historically documented) camp, and of the extent to which the published interpretations of Repton can be used as a general model for camps of this period. The finds from ARSNY and other camps demonstrate extensive economic activity, suggesting a more complex range of functions than the purely military role emphasised in contemporary historical references, and ARSNY in particular has a collection of weights, coins and hack-silver surpassed only by the other recently published camp of the same period: Torksey. These camps represent a phase at the beginning of the Viking settlement in England, and one which immediately prefigured, and perhaps stimulated, the main phase of urban development in late Anglo-Saxon and Viking England. Despite the enforced anonymity of the site, and the fact that it is only partially recorded, ARSNY thus has a major role in the reassessment of the process of Viking-Age settlement in Britain and Ireland.

Chapter 3
Viking Hoards from Yorkshire, *c.* 866–954: A Survey

G. Williams

The hoard from ARSNY is one of eleven, or possibly twelve, recorded hoards of Viking character found in Yorkshire and dating from between the Viking conquest of Northumbria in 866–7 and the end of independent Anglo-Viking rule of Northumbria and its lasting assimilation into the emerging kingdom of England in 954. A number of hoards of Northumbrian stycas are recorded which probably date from the period immediately before the Viking conquest (Blackburn and Pagan, n.d., nos 40–4). As discussed above (p. 36), the end of the styca coinage no longer appears to have a clear cut-off with the Viking conquest in 866, so it is possible that some of these hoards may post-date the conquest, and may even have been deposited by Vikings. However, since none of them is recorded as having been found in specifically Anglo-Scandinavian contexts, or have any other Viking associations, the assumption must remain that any hoards containing only stycas should be considered as Anglian rather than Viking unless proven otherwise.

At the other end of the survey period, while the exact chronology of the Anglo-Saxon and Anglo-Viking coinages in northern England in the 940s and early 950s remains uncertain, the imposition of lasting English kingship in 954 undoubtedly brought an end to the distinctive local coinage of Viking Northumbria. On the evidence of the hoards, it may also have brought an end, within those areas now under English control, to the characteristic mixed bullion economy, although this continued in areas such as Cumbria which at this time remained outside the English kingdom. However, the hoard evidence suggests that it is possible that the mixed economy in Yorkshire had already ended in the early 930s (see below) in the years following the earlier West Saxon conquest of Northumbria by Athelstan in 927, although the single finds evidence suggests a somewhat different picture (see pp. 126–7). The uncertainty as to whether eleven or twelve hoards are known from this period depends on the interpretation of two finds from 'Near York' in 2012. The two finds were discovered in close proximity, but appear to represent distinct parcels of material of slightly different character, although of very similar date. The question of whether these represent two distinct hoards or two separate parcels of a single hoard is discussed further below.

Of these hoards, ARSNY, Vale of York, Bedale and 'Near York' have all been discovered in the last 15 years, while Goldsborough has also been republished in rather greater detail than previously (Graham-Campbell 2011, 83, 234–6; Williams 2011e; Williams 2013c, 461–6). The discovery of other Viking hoards of comparable date elsewhere in northern England has also provided additional comparative material, enabling a broader reconsideration of hoards and silver economy within Viking Northumbria. This paper will therefore consider how the new hoards from ARSNY and 'Near York' fit into the wider picture of Viking hoards from Yorkshire and beyond, and how the character of the Yorkshire hoards reflects a wider pattern of economic developments during the period between the Viking conquest and the expulsion and death of the last Viking king.

As discussed elsewhere in this volume (see p. 19), the ARSNY hoard was deposited in the mid-870s, around the

Hoard	Date of deposition	Stycas	A-S coins	A-V coins	Frankish coins	Islamic coins	Intact ornaments	Intact ingots	Hack-silver
1. York (Coney Street), 1760	860s–870s	X	X	–	X	–	–	–	–
2. Lower Dunsforth 1860	Probably mid-870s	–	X	–	–	–	–	–	–
3. ARSNY, 2004	Probably mid-870s	–	X	–	–	X	–	X	X
4. York (Walmgate), 1856	c. 915	–	–	X	–	–	–	–	–
5. Goldsborough, 1858	c. 925	–	X	–	–	X	X	X	X
6. Bossall/Flaxton, 1807	c. 927	–	X	X	–	X	X	?	X
7. Vale of York, 2007	c. 927–28	–	X	X	X	X	X	X	X
8. 'Near York' (a and b), 2012	Probably 930s	–	X	X	–	–	–	–	X
9. York (Coppergate), 1980	c. 940	–	X	X	–	–	–	–	–
10. Near Selby, pre-1893	Late 9th–early 10th century	–	–	–	–	–	X	–	–
11. Bedale, 2012	Late 9th–early 10th century	–	–	–	–	–	X	X	X

Table 12 Summary of Yorkshire hoards of Viking character

time of the first permanent Viking settlement of Northumbria, but some years after the initial conquest and the probable cessation of minting of the pre-Viking Northumbrian copper-alloy coinage known as stycas. In common with the wider assemblage from the site, the hoard indicates a mixed bullion economy, containing a dirham fragment, one silver ingot, four ingot droplets (of varying degrees of purity) and six pieces of hack-silver as well as nine base-silver pennies of the Lunettes coinage from Mercia and Wessex, while there were also both lead weights of Insular Viking style and Islamic-style copper cubo-octahedral weights found in association with the hoard. No stycas appear to have been directly associated with the hoard, but the presence of stycas in the site assemblage points to the continued use of stycas alongside the silver bullion, and perhaps to a wider copper-alloy bullion economy, which is reinforced by the presence of a copper-alloy ingot with the hoard. A poorly documented silver hoard from the comparable site at Torksey in Lincolnshire, together with the larger site assemblage of which it forms a part, suggests much the same picture: the assemblage contains a mixture of silver coins and bullion, and copper-alloy stycas, but the possible hoard (on the limited evidence available) contained only silver (Blackburn 2002, 95; 2011, 223–8, 233–5, 250, nos 20–1; see above p. 85). A further, slightly earlier hoard from Croydon, Surrey, deposited *c.* 870, also reflects the same mixed silver economy, as it contains *c.* 250 coins (of which those which have been identified include Lunettes pennies from both Mercia and Wessex, silver pennies of East Anglia, Carolingian deniers of Louis the Pious and Charles the Bald, and Abbasid dirhams), three complete ingots and a cut fragment of a fourth, and four other pieces of hack-silver (Brooks and Graham-Campbell 2000, 70–9). There were no stycas found in association with the Croydon hoard, but one would not particularly expect this, both because stycas are rarely found south of the Humber (except in Lincolnshire), and because at both Torksey and ARSNY copper alloy seems to have been largely excluded from the hoards, even if the 'silver' Lunettes coinage found in the ARSNY hoard and in a possible hoard from Torksey was of dubious quality. The hoard from near Watlington in Oxfordshire found in 2015 suggests the use of gold bullion alongside silver in the 870s (see pp. 12, 33, 36–7) but this is only reflected in the site finds from ARSNY and Torksey, not the hoards.

The combination of silver coins and stycas on site at both ARSNY and Torksey casts an interesting light on a hoard discovered at Coney Street in York in around 1760. A brief account of its discovery was published in Robert Gough's 1789 edition of Camden's *Britannia*:

> … in a cellar in Conyng Street a bag of about 100 silver Saxon coins, fresh and fair, and a lump of brass sticas, rusted together. Among the silver a few inscribed CHRISTIANIA RELIGIO… Lotharius was king of Kent 670, when Roman temples were standing converted to Christian use. They are more probably of Lothair king of France from 954 to 986 (Camden 1789, iii, 63; Metcalf 1957, 200).

Michael Metcalf has traced this account back to a letter from Mr F. Drake to the antiquary Dr William Stukeley, dated 24 December 1760, which survives in Stukeley's papers. This conveys broadly the same information, but with the slight difference that it refers to the discovery of 'a treasure of Saxon coins … wrapped up in a bag … There were above 100 silver coins, all very fresh and fair; and a large lump of the small brass coins called Sticas, so stuck together by erugo that very few could be separated. Both silver and brass were all coins of the Heptarchy, the latter, I think were particular to our Northumbrian kingdom…' (Metcalf 1957, 200). Both the published account and Drake's letter indicate that the silver and brass coins were found together, but whereas the account in *Britannia* implies that only the silver coins were in a bag, and the lump of stycas was distinct, the earlier account by Drake is more ambiguous, suggesting that both could have been contained in the same bag.

Such a combination of silver pennies and copper-alloy stycas in a single hoard remains highly unusual, with the only documented parallel being the hoard from Talnotrie, Kirkcudbrightshire, deposited *c.* 875, which is in any case generally regarded as an unusual and anomalous hoard (Maxwell 1912–13; Webster and Backhouse 1991, 273, no. 248; Graham-Campbell 1995, 4; see also p. 37). Metcalf noted that the description of the CHRISTIANIA RELIGIO coins in the Coney Street hoard in the name of Lotharius appeared to correspond with coins of Lothair II, king of Lotharingia (855–69), but struggled to reconcile the presence of these within the same hoard as Anglo-Saxon silver pennies and Northumbrian stycas, concluding that there were actually two hoards: one of Northumbrian stycas, deposited *c.* 800–60, and a second containing deniers of Lothair II together with Anglo-Saxon or Anglo-Scandinavian pennies, 'possibly tenth-century Viking issues', and deposited *c.* 900–50, despite the absence of any reference in either Gough or Stukeley that would justify such a late date. Furthermore, the Anglo-Viking coinage of early 10th-century Northumbria was so little known or understood at the time that the hoard was discovered, that it would be surprising if examples of this coinage were to be simply attributed to the 'Heptarchy' by someone curious enough to note the unfamiliar coins of Lothair II. None of the coins from the hoard can be traced with any certainty, and although it has been argued that some Carolingian coins formerly in the collection of Winchester Cathedral may have been derived from the hoard (Dolley 1965–66), this interpretation is questionable. Michael Dolley and Karl Morrison (1963, 78) suggested a date of *c.* 870 for the deposition of the hoard on the basis of their interpretation of the possible Carolingian content, although Mark Blackburn and Hugh Pagan (n.d., no. 45) preferred a date of *c.* 865 in their checklist of Anglo-Saxon hoards.

Carolingian coins appear in a number of Viking hoards from northern England dating from the late 9th and early 10th centuries, the latter including Cuerdale and Silverdale in Lancashire, as well as the Vale of York hoard. Carolingian coins are also comparatively rarely found in England except in areas of Viking activity (for apparent exceptions, see Story 2003, 248–50), but the apparent combination of Carolingian and Anglo-Saxon silver coins said to have been found at Coney Street is comparable to the Croydon hoard, while Carolingian coinage was also found in the Torksey assemblage, and in the Talnotrie hoard. No Carolingian coins have yet been recorded from ARSNY, but the dirham fragments there also point to the unrestricted circulation of imported coin as bullion. Deposition of the silver component of the hoard in the 870s would bring it much closer to the reign of Lothair II, while at the same time it would be consistent with both Croydon and Torksey. As recently noted by Shane McLeod (2014, 150), the presence of Carolingian coins in hoards of the 870s may reflect the presence in the *micel here* in England of Vikings who had formerly raided on the Continent, especially in northern Francia and Frisia. This is very plausible, but does not in itself help to narrow down the dating of the hoard further than providing a *terminus post quem* of the first conquest of Northumbria by the *micel here* in 866–7. With so little of the hoard securely dated, a deposition date anywhere up to the end of the century is perfectly plausible on the evidence of the Carolingian coins alone. However, if the stycas were deposited at the same time, comparison with the ARSNY and Torksey assemblages and the Talnotrie hoard suggests that a date in the 870s is most likely. The description of the discovery of the hoard appears to suggest that the silver and the stycas were found in close association, but were deposited as two distinct groups rather than mixed together. Since stycas did not normally circulate together with silver coinage, and because the styca coinage has been thought to have ended *c.* 855, the idea that these groups were entirely distinct and unrelated has seemed a logical explanation, but this is less obvious given the presence of stycas at both ARSNY and Torksey.

Without any further detail, any attempt to attribute the other silver coins of the 'Heptarchy' can only be speculative. Nevertheless, both ARSNY and Torksey point to a situation in which imported coins, Northumbrian stycas and Southumbrian pennies of the Lunettes type would all have been available at the same time. Together with the fact that this situation occurred shortly after the *terminus post quem* provided by the coins of Lothair II, raises the possibility that the unidentified coins in the Coney Street hoard were Lunettes, or even pre-Viking coins of East Anglia. At the same time, Gough's account which implies that the silver coins and the stycas were bagged separately would fit with the apparent absence of stycas from both the ARSNY and Torksey hoards, despite their availability on both sites. A parallel for separate hoarding of copper alloy alongside silver can be seen in the Spillings hoard from Gotland, buried *c.* 870–1, where the vast quantity of *c.* 67kg of silver found in two obviously related parcels has tended to distract attention from the presence of a third parcel containing over 20kg of copper-alloy objects, including intact and fragmentary personal ornaments and mounts, bars and waste metal (Östergren 2011, 323–5). While the possibility that the Coney Street discovery does indeed comprise two unrelated hoards cannot be ruled out, it is also perfectly plausible that it represents two distinct parcels hoarded together and drawn from the bimetallic currency that seems to be represented at ARSNY. If this reinterpretation is correct, a deposition date anywhere between 866 and the late 870s would seem plausible on current evidence.

Further evidence for a relationship between stycas and Viking silver economies may be found in a hoard of stycas from Kirkoswald in Cumbria, found in 1808. This included at least 542 stycas, buried in a pot, together with an Anglo-Saxon silver trefoil ornament, with filigree decoration and a garnet inset. The exact number of coins in the hoard is unknown, but it terminates in coins of Osberht (*c.* 848–67), Archbishop Wulfhere (854–*c.* 900) and irregular issues, suggesting a deposition date in the late 850s or 860s (Wilson 1964, 139–40, no. 28; Pirie *et al.* 1986, 81–2, no. 96; Graham-Campbell 2011, 17). This has been excluded from listings of Viking hoards on the grounds that all of the objects within the hoard are of Anglo-Saxon origin. However, the dating of the irregular issues at the end of the stycas coinage no longer appears to indicate a certain pre-Viking date (see p. 36), and as James Graham-Campbell (1995, 107; 2001a, 53–4; 2011, 17) has noted, the ornament carries an apparent test-nick of a type normally associated with the testing of bullion within Viking silver economies. While a tested but complete object could have returned to Anglo-Saxon hands, and the whole hoard may thus still be an Anglo-Saxon rather than a Viking deposition, the presence of tested silver alongside stycas reinforces the evidence both from ARSNY and from Coney Street that stycas and silver might circulate in the same contexts.

A third small hoard from the settlement period is recorded from Lower Dunsforth, north-west of York. The hoard was found in 1860, while digging a boundary ditch between the modern churchyard of St Mary's church and School House, and was comprised of around 30 coins, with no trace recorded of any container or non-numismatic silver. The recorded coins are of the Lunettes type of Burgred of Mercia and Æthelred I and Alfred of Wessex, a type represented in both the hoard and the site assemblage from ARSNY. The hoard may also have contained individual coins of Æthelberht of Wessex and Ceolwulf II of Mercia, the latter of which was also recorded as a single find from ARSNY (Blackburn and Pagan n.d, no. 74; Blackburn 2004, 347; see also above, pp. 36, 80). Other coins of Alfred not recorded in detail may plausibly either be further examples of the Lunettes type or of the Cross-and-Lozenge type which he issued concurrently with that of Ceolwulf II. The hoard can thus be dated with reasonable certainty to the 870s, with the possible single coin of Ceolwulf II pulling it into the same date horizon of the mid–late 870s as the ARSNY site assemblage. The fact that this hoard did not apparently contain non-numismatic silver contrasts with both the hoard and the site assemblage from ARSNY, but the small size of the hoard and the lack of container suggests a single small purse of coins, which could have functioned either within a coin-based or a bullion economy.

The next phase of currency is that represented by the hoards from Cuerdale and near Silverdale in Lancashire, both dated to the first decade of the 10th century (Williams 2011a, 64–7; 2012a; 2014c, 27–31; Boughton *et al.* 2012). This phase was characterised on the one hand by a continued mixed bullion economy, and on the other by a very substantial coinage minted wholly or partly in York: many of the coins within this series carry a York mint signature, and those which do not are so closely linked by design (and in some cases by use of the same dies) that it is reasonable to assume that they were also minted in York, although the inscription CVNNETTI found on many coins in the name of Cnut continues to defy interpretation, and the possibility that this represents a second mint cannot be completely excluded (Stewart 1987; Williams 2011a, 43–5). That question aside, there is no doubt that the coinage was strongly associated with York, while the number of different dies in the coinage leaves no doubt that minting took place on a very large scale. It is therefore slightly surprising that as yet there are no hoards of this phase recorded from Yorkshire, although a number of single finds are recorded, both from York and from the surrounding area (Blackburn 2004, 348, nos 13–20). This may be just chance, or it may indicate that Yorkshire itself was relatively peaceful and stable at this time, compared with the situation west of the Pennines. The first decade of the 10th century saw the expulsion of the Vikings from Dublin; Viking settlement on the Wirral and the establishment of an Anglo-Saxon *burh* at Chester to counter this; and a defeat for a Viking army at Tettenhall, near Wolverhampton, close to a Roman road leading up to (or down from) Chester and the Wirral. By contrast, the historical record concerning Yorkshire is silent in this period. This may simply be coincidence, especially given that the *Anglo-Saxon Chronicle* is so uninformative on matters not directly relating to the expanding West Saxon kingdom, and it would be dangerous to read too much into this absence. Furthermore, hoards were not always necessarily deposited in response to specific threats, but might simply represent the safe storage of accumulated wealth, while recent interpretation of hoards in other periods increasingly leans to social rather than economic reasons behind hoarding. As discussed further below, while individual hoards may well be linked with specific historical situations, it is difficult to see a consistent trend linking Viking hoards in Yorkshire to political upheaval. Nevertheless, it remains the case that no coin-datable hoards from Yorkshire can be associated with this phase of prolific Anglo-Scandinavian minting.

There may or may not be a background of unrest to the next hoard from Yorkshire, discovered at Walmgate, York (an area of known Anglo-Scandinavian activity in the early 10th century) in 1856 during the digging of a sewer (Chester 1856; Hall 2004, 494). This hoard contained 'two shovelfuls' of coins, or 'about a hundred', predominantly of the Swordless St Peter type, although some were so corroded that they fell apart when they were cleaned. The Swordless St Peter type carries a York mint signature and was apparently minted on a large scale. Although surviving examples are much rarer than those of the Cuerdale phase, this comparison is distorted by the atypical size of the Cuerdale hoard itself, and the large number of dies within the current corpus of Swordless St Peter coins suggests that this was almost certainly a substantial issue. The Reverend Greville J. Chester, in his brief account of the discovery of the hoard, indicates that there was also considerable variation in the dies of those coins which were sufficiently well preserved to be observed (Chester 1856). Chester also notes that the hoard contained at least two halfpennies of the Swordless St Peter type, one of which he illustrates, as well as two pennies and a halfpenny of the St Edmund Memorial type.

The Swordless St Peter type appears to have commenced either immediately or shortly after the end of the phase of Northumbrian coinage represented in the Cuerdale hoard (Stewart and Lyon 1992, 53; Gooch 2014, 460). On the current dating of Cuerdale, this suggests a start date no earlier than *c.* 905, and not much later than *c.* 910, and this is consistent with at least a brief overlap with the St Edmund Memorial type, also represented in the hoard. This probably continued to be minted until at least *c.* 910 and quite possibly as late as *c.* 917–18 (Blackburn 2001, 132). The Swordless St Peter type probably continued to be issued until *c.* 915, and was replaced in turn by coinage in the name of RAIENALT, identified with Regnald, who established himself as king of Northumbria towards the end of the second decade of the 10th century. Written accounts of Regnald's conquest of Northumbria present a conflicting and problematic chronology, but most recent commentaries have agreed on *c.* 919 as a likely date for the beginning of his kingship (and coinage) in Northumbria, even though he may first have been active slightly earlier (Blunt and Stewart 1983; Stewart and Lyon 1992; Blackburn 2004, 333; Rollason 2004, 310; Downham 2007, 91–4; Williams 2014c, 32–3). The Walmgate hoard could thus have been deposited for security around the time of Regnald's conquest, but there is nothing particularly to indicate this, and it could equally well have been deposited some years earlier. The absence of any historical accounts of what was happening in Yorkshire in the period *c.* 910–15 means that a deposition date at this time does not preclude a background of unrest, but a 'shovelful' of silver would have been worth protecting at any time, and the hoard may simply represent the savings of a trader or craftsman, securely stored until needed, but not subsequently recovered.

The fact that the hoard apparently contained no non-numismatic silver does not in itself prove that a bullion economy had been completely replaced by a coin economy within York at this time, and later hoards demonstrate very clearly a continued bullion economy more widely across Yorkshire and beyond. However, a substantial coin hoard does indicate that there was already a significant coin economy within York in the early 10th century, an interpretation reinforced by the large number of dies employed in both the Cuerdale phase and the Swordless St Peter type. This must indicate minting on a very large scale, which in turn implies a significant demand for coins. At the same time, the near-complete absence in the Walmgate hoard of coin types other than the locally minted Sword St Peter type suggests that other coins were effectively excluded from York, and that within the walls there was a controlled circulation of currency, as seems also to have been the case in areas under Anglo-Saxon authority. This would be consistent with the limited excavated evidence for bullion use from York compared with other Viking trading centres of the late 9th and 10th centuries (see pp. 125–6). It is possible that it is chance that (with a single exception) only Swordless St Peter coins were recorded from the hoard, and that the exclusion of other types suggested above is a false interpretation. However, the description of 'a shovelful' of coins suggests a total number in the low hundreds. While a small group of coins fresh from the mint might plausibly generate a single-type hoard even in a context where multiple types were in circulation, comparison with other Viking hoards in Yorkshire and elsewhere suggests that a hoard of tens or even hundreds of coins would only contain a single type if other types were actively excluded. Furthermore, a parcel fresh from the mint seems unlikely if the hoard did indeed contain coins from a large number of different dies.

The exclusion of other coin types from currency circulation does not mean that all bullion (including imported coins) was completely excluded from the city. It is possible that only coins of the St Peter type were permitted to circulate as currency within the city, but that bullion continued to enter the city as a result of long-distance trade, or indeed through interaction with other areas nearby within which exchange was less tightly regulated. In contrast, the bullion element of other hoards from outside York (see below) was not converted into coin perhaps in part to avoid payment of a premium on minted silver of the sort generally associated (although without specific documentation) with the late Anglo-Saxon coinage (Brooke 1929–30; Grierson 1985; Metcalf 1987; Allen 2012, 8–9, 182–3; Williams 2013d, 59–60). There is no doubt that Viking settlements elsewhere in Britain and Ireland continued to use bullion at this time, and, as discussed by Jane Kershaw (see pp. 126–7), the single finds evidence suggests that a bullion economy still existed across Yorkshire at this point, a view reinforced by the mixed hoards discussed below. However, there is a case that both the Vale of York hoard and the 'Near York' hoard could indicate the presence of a regulated coin-based economy within York itself and a continued mixed economy into the 920s or 930s beyond the immediate environs of the city. This possibility is discussed further below (see Chapter 5).

The next group of hoards does seem to correspond with a period of political unrest. Between them, these hoards cover the period of the first Anglo-Saxon conquest of Viking Northumbria, and also demonstrate a gradual shift in the silver economy, reflecting the expansion of West Saxon royal authority over trade and exchange throughout the emerging kingdom of England. Regnald was succeeded *c.* 921 by Sihtric, another member of the Uí Ímair dynasty of Dublin and, according to some accounts, the brother of Regnald (Rollason 2004, 310; Downham 2007, 97–9). Sihtric ruled Northumbria until his death in 927, and numismatic evidence suggests that he may also have ruled part of the midlands, as the coinage in his name seems largely to have been issued south of the Humber, although at least one example carries a York mint signature. A closely related coinage was struck at York, reverting to the name of St Peter, and another related coinage at Lincoln in the name of St Martin (Blackburn 2006, 209–17; Williams 2008c; 2011d, 148–9; 2014c, 33–5; *pace* Ten Harkel 2013). All of these issues are linked by the use of a sword as the main element in the obverse design.

Sihtric's apparent control of the east midlands contrasts with the narrative of the *Anglo-Saxon Chronicle*, which indicates that the whole of England south of the Humber had submitted to Edward the Elder in 920 (although there is no specific reference to the submission of Lincoln, in contrast to other major midland *burhs*), but does not suggest that it reverted to Viking rule at any point between that date and Athelstan's assumption of authority in northern England following Sihtric's death in 927. It is, however, clear that Athelstan's conquest of Northumbria was contested, unsuccessfully, by Sihtric's brother Guthfrith. Sihtric had met with Athelstan at Tamworth in 926, cementing a peaceful alliance, by marrying Athelstan's sister, which apparently lasted until his death. This meeting has generally been regarded by historians as representing a meeting in the heart of Athelstan's territory, at the Mercian 'capital' of Tamworth (e.g. Foot 2011, 18), and is often though not invariably interpreted as a meeting between a superior (Athelstan) and an inferior (Sihtric) (e.g. Sharp 2001, 82). This would be compatible with the evidence for subordinate kings visiting Athelstan's court in the latter part of his reign, and for the adoption by Athelstan of more imperial titles in his coins and charters following the establishment of his supremacy over assorted northern rulers at Eamont Bridge near Penrith in 927 (Blunt 1974, 55; Williams 2011d, 150; Foot 2011, 26–8, 92, 154–5; and see below, p. 110). However, the numismatic evidence strongly suggests that at least parts of the east midlands were under Sihtric's authority for some period during the 920s. Given also the apparent similarities between this meeting and meetings between Edward the Elder and northern rulers on Edward's northern frontier at Bakewell in 920, and between Athelstan and northern rulers on Athelstan's new northern frontier at Eamont Bridge in 927 (and even to some extent Edgar's meeting with assorted kings from around the Irish Sea at Chester in 973), it makes more sense to interpret the Tamworth meeting in 926 as another frontier meeting, establishing a relationship between Athelstan and a neighbouring ruler (Williams 2014c, 35). Athelstan's expanded authority after Eamont Bridge should not be projected back onto the earlier meetings uncritically, and the meetings at Tamworth and, more debatably, Bakewell, can be seen as meetings between equals (Davidson 2001; Foot 2011, 18). Whether the new frontier was indeed in the Tamworth area or further north, and whatever the relative status of the two kings may have been, there seems little doubt that the meeting was intended to resolve conflict between Athelstan and Sihtric. However, there is no doubt at all that Athelstan's seizure of Northumbria in 927 resulted in further conflict, with the Viking leader Guthfrith (probably the brother of Sihtric) attempting unsuccessfully to recover control of Northumbria (and specifically York) from Athelstan, although it is unclear exactly how quickly peace was re-established thereafter (Foot 2011, 19, 162). While Athelstan probably established his authority in the area relatively quickly, that does not mean that it was universally welcomed, or that the inhabitants of Northumbria in general and Yorkshire in particular assumed that Athelstan's conquest would bring a lasting peace. The resumption of hostilities in 937 resulted in a further victory for Athelstan over an alliance of northern kings including Olaf, son of the Guthfrith who had been driven out a decade earlier.

The 920s thus represent a likely period of prolonged instability, possibly extending into the 930s, and against this background it is not surprising that a number of hoards were deposited, both in Yorkshire and elsewhere. The hoards from Goldsborough, Bossall/Flaxton, the Vale of York and 'Near York' all date from this period, together with hoards from Thurcaston (Leicestershire), Warton (Lancashire) and Flusco Pike 2 (Cumbria) (Williams 2013c). Of the Yorkshire hoards in this group, the earliest is probably that from Goldsborough, discovered in the churchyard by workmen in 1858, although early accounts disagree whether this was during repairs to the churchyard wall, or to the church porch: it is possible that both were being repaired at the same time. The hoard was never fully recorded, and such recording as took place seems to have been somewhat careless, to say the least, and again the details in early records of the hoard conflict with each other. As a result, the exact contents of the hoard are uncertain, but it contained as a minimum three Anglo-Saxon coins (one of Alfred, two of Edward the Elder), and 36 whole or fragmentary Islamic dirhams of assorted ages together with a complete penannular ball-brooch of Irish Sea character, a pendant which may be interpreted as either a Thor's hammer or a cross (or both), plus hack-silver and ingots (Wilson 1957; Graham-Campbell 2001b, 217–18; 2011, 234–6; Williams, 2011c; 2013c, 461–6). The combination of Anglo-Saxon and Islamic coins suggests a deposition date of *c.* 925, but the fact that this is based on such a small sample of Anglo-Saxon coins means that the absence of later coins is not necessarily significant, while not all of the Islamic coins have legible dates, and some of the fragments may be later than the latest datable coins. A slightly later deposition date for the hoard cannot be excluded (Williams 2013c, 465–6).

The absence of any Anglo-Viking coins is notable, given that other coins are present, and has been taken, together with the presence of metalwork from the Irish Sea area, as evidence that the hoard may have been assembled in Ireland (Graham-Campbell 2001b, 217–18). This is certainly historically plausible in the light of the links between Dublin and Northumbria under the Uí Ímair dynasty in this period. However, the presence at both Llanbedrgoch (Anglesey) and Torksey (Lincolnshire) of lead trial-pieces for punches typical of the decoration of Hiberno-Scandinavian punch-marked broad-band arm-rings calls into question the assumption that all such metalwork was necessarily produced in Ireland, and a broader Irish Sea origin now seems preferable, both for the metalwork and the hoard (Redknap 2000, 84, fig 130; 2009, 37–8, Blackburn 2011, 242; see also Kershaw, this volume, pp. 116–17). However, with so few non-Islamic coins in the hoard, together with the poor quality of the initial documentation of the hoard, it is unclear whether the absence of Anglo-Viking coins is genuinely significant, as metalwork of Hiberno-Scandinavian type is also a feature of other Viking hoards from Yorkshire, including Vale of York, Selby and Bedale (see below), although either or both of these may have been deposited before the introduction of Anglo-Viking minting in Northumbria. All of these point to links in the circulation of non-numismatic silver across the Pennines between Yorkshire and the Irish Sea zone, but the fact that Hiberno-Scandinavian metalwork is found in Yorkshire in association with a large number of coins (Vale of York), a relatively small number of coins (Goldsborough) and no coins (Selby, Bedale) is an important warning against building too much interpretation on the presence of this material *per se*. At the very least, however, we can be certain that despite the fact that Goldsborough is a relatively short distance from the major mint of York, the hoard indicates that there was not a wholly coin-based economy across the region by this time, and that even amongst such coins as circulated, the coins of Anglo-Scandinavian Northumbria minted in York did not necessarily predominate. This impression is reinforced by the mixture of coins found in both Bossall/Flaxton and Vale of York, both of which date from the late 920s, but is harder to reconcile with the evidence of the 'Near York' hoard, which probably dates from the 930s, There may thus be a chronological difference in the character of the silver economies from the mid-920s to the mid-930s, probably reflecting increasing Anglo-Saxon (or West Saxon) influence following Athelstan's conquest of Northumbria in 927 (see below).

The next hoard, discovered in 1807, is generally known as the Bossall/Flaxton hoard, although as noted by James Graham-Campbell (1993; 2001b, 214), the recorded find-spot is more accurately described as 'between Claxton and Flaxton'. The hoard was found approximately seven miles from York, 'near' to the road to Malton, although it is unclear from contemporary accounts exactly how close to the road this was. The hoard was found in a wooden box, but was not fully recorded before it was dispersed, meaning that the exact contents of the hoard cannot be reconstructed. However, it is recorded that the hoard contained 'about two pounds' (0.907kg) of silver bullion, and probably more than 270 coins. These included a mixture of Anglo-Saxon coins, dating from the reign of Alfred through to the early part of the reign of Athelstan (924–39); Anglo-Scandinavian coins dating from the Cuerdale phase through to the reign of Regnald (*c.* 919–21) and two Samanid dirhams of unknown rulers, but consistent with an early 10th-century date. The fact that the hoard terminates with a very small number of early coins of Athelstan suggests that it was deposited early in his reign, before his coinage had the chance to enter widespread circulation in Yorkshire, and the hoard has plausibly been linked with the unrest associated with Athelstan's conquest of Northumbria in 927, although there is nothing to indicate conclusively whether the hoard was deposited before or after this conquest (Dolley 1955; Blunt and Dolley 1960; Blunt and Stewart 1983; Stewart 1991; Graham-Campbell 2001b, 214). Of the non-numismatic silver, only a single punch-marked arm-ring survives, of a type with similarities to other examples in the hoards from Cuerdale, Silverdale and Storr Rock (Skye), deposited *c.* 935, which between them bracket the Bossall/Flaxton hoard chronologically, while also pointing to an Irish Sea connection. Otherwise there are references in early accounts to a fragment of silver chain, a cruciform pendant and other less clearly identified items interpreted by James Graham-Campbell (2001b, 215) as arm-rings and (probably) ingots, some of which were fragmented as hack-silver.

There are two interesting aspects to the recorded contents of the hoard, in relation to its date and location. The first is that it contains a mixture of coins of different origins, and a date-span of more than a quarter of a century, together with a larger quantity of non-numismatic silver. The second is that, although Anglo-Scandinavian coins minted in York are present in the hoard, the coinage current in York at the time of deposition was apparently absent, with no Sword St Peter or Sihtric types (*c.* 921–7) recorded in the hoard. The mixture indicates very clearly that all of the contents of the hoard, including the coins, should be considered as bullion, and that a bullion economy still existed only a few miles outside York although Anglo-Scandinavian coins had been minted in York for more than 30 years by the time the hoard was deposited. The fact that there appear to have been no current York issues in the hoard also suggests that however dominant the coinage of Viking Northumbria may have been in exchange within York itself, that coinage had only limited impact further afield (for the evidence of single finds, see pp. 125–6). In both respects the Bossall/Flaxton hoard appears to reflect the same or similar patterns as Goldsborough, located a few miles from York in a different direction, although the larger number of coins in Bossall/Flaxton means that the absence of current York issues in that hoard is more significant than in Goldsborough.

A somewhat different pattern is visible in the Vale of York hoard. This was found only a relatively short distance from Goldsborough, although the precise find-spot has been kept anonymous at the request of the landowner. Like Goldsborough and Bossall/Flaxton, Vale of York was a mixed hoard, comprising a silver-gilt cup, six intact arm-rings (one gold and five silver) of different styles, plus hack-silver, ingots and 617 coins. The entire hoard, apart from the largest ingots, was packed into the cup. The larger ingots were attached to the rest of the hoard, and then a piece of sheet lead was folded around them and around the top of the cup. The cup is Frankish, as are four of the coins; the jewellery is a mixture including elements from the Irish Sea area, Scandinavia and Russia; and the remaining coins are predominantly Anglo-Saxon, with some Anglo-Scandinavian and fifteen Samanid dirhams (mostly fragmentary) (Ager 2011; Ager and Williams 2011a; Williams 2011d; Williams and Ager 2015). Like Goldsborough and Bossall/Flaxton the mixed contents could be taken as indicating a bullion economy, but the larger size of the hoard overall and the larger number of coins may suggest a more complex mixture of economies. The intact arm-rings (like the intact brooch in Goldsborough) may simply represent bullion, or may have had a distinct value in social exchange, particularly given the importance of ring-giving in Viking society (Ager 2011, 127–8), while the cup was also a very valuable high-status item in its own right, as well as containing the hoard. The dirhams and Carolingian deniers must be considered as bullion, and may have reached Yorkshire either directly or via the Irish Sea. In the case of the Carolingian coins these may have circulated in the British Isles for some time, but the datable dirhams seem likely to have been relatively recent imports at the time of deposition. The majority of the Anglo-Saxon pennies in the hoard have revealed no test marks, although testing by 'pecking' and bending is typical of coins in Viking hoards in Britain from the late 9th and early 10th centuries (Archibald 2011). This suggests that the presence of so many Anglo-Saxon coins in the hoard may be the result of ongoing monetary interaction with the expanding West Saxon kingdom to the south, where such coins would have continued in circulation without testing. The Anglo-Saxon component begins with 51 coins of Alfred (871–99) from *c.* 880 onwards, and is dominated by 402 coins (including a number of contemporary imitations) of Edward the Elder (899–924), terminating in 105 coins of Athelstan (924–39). Most of these were early issues, but the hoard contains 36 examples of the normally rare Building type of Athelstan, probably minted for a short period in 927 to celebrate his conquest of Northumbria and the north midlands (Williams 2011d, 150). The fact that several of these carry a York mint signature means that there is no doubt that the deposition of the hoard post-dates Athelstan's conquest of Northumbria, but a more precise dating for the hoard is suggested by the presence of a single coin of Athelstan's Circumscription Cross type, giving him the title (in abbreviated form) of *Rex Totius Britanniae* (King of All Britain). This title was probably assumed on Athelstan's coinage following the submission of a number of northern kings to Athelstan at Eamont Bridge near Penrith on 12 July 927, and remained standard on Athelstan's coinage for the remainder of his reign. The presence of a single example of this type within the hoard provides a firm *terminus post quem* for the deposition of the hoard, but also suggests that it is unlikely to have been deposited much later, as coins of the Circumscription Cross type became extremely common (and were also minted in York). One would expect this type to be better represented if the hoard were deposited more than a few months after the type was introduced (Williams 2011d, 150–1). This gives a clear context for the deposition of the hoard in the period of continued unrest in the aftermath of Athelstan's conquest of Northumbria, and indicates that the bullion economy continued in Yorkshire at least for a short period after the conquest.

The fact that the Vale of York hoard is partly if not necessarily completely a bullion hoard means that it fits typologically as well as chronologically with both Goldsborough and Bossall/Flaxton in indicating a continued bullion economy only a few miles from York in the 920s. However, the Anglo-Scandinavian coins in the hoard present a somewhat different picture from the other two hoards. Goldsborough contained no coins from either Northumbria or East Anglia, while Bossall/Flaxton contained both, but none later than the coinage of Regnald (*c.* 919–21). By contrast, the Vale of York hoard contained no Anglo-Scandinavian coins from before the reign of Sihtric (921–7), but 22 examples of what was probably the latest sub-type of the Sword St Peter type minted in York, and current at the time of Athelstan's conquest. It also contained a contemporary Sword type from the otherwise unrecorded mint of 'Rorivacastr', plus two coins in the name of Sihtric and one in the name of St Martin, minted in Lincoln, which also carried the Sword motif. The absence of any earlier Anglo-Scandinavian issues in so large a hoard (and one which contains so many earlier Anglo-Saxon coins) suggests that this component of the hoard was drawn from the currency circulating in York itself, and that this was regulated to a considerable extent, with coinage apart from the locally minted Sword St Peter type and the other related Sword types effectively excluded from circulation during Sihtric's reign (Williams 2011d, 154). A similar level of exclusion slightly earlier is also suggested by the Walmgate hoard, as (with a single exception) this only contained coins of the Swordless St Peter type (see above, pp. 106–7).

If this interpretation is correct, the hoard evidence suggests a regulated coin economy within York itself by the 920s, and perhaps earlier, but an absence of regulation and a broader pattern of continued bullion use beyond York and its immediate hinterland up to, and slightly beyond, Athelstan's conquest of the kingdom of Northumbria in 927. This pattern appears to continue into the 930s, with two parcels of silver found close together in 2012, and known jointly as the 'Near York' hoard (also referred to in numismatic literature as the Ryedale hoard, and the Eboracum hoard). Like the Vale of York hoard, this name is designed to protect the anonymity of the find-spot, but without revealing the parish it is possible to say that the hoard was found in the same general area as the Bossall/Flaxton hoard, but not in exactly the same place. The first group was a roll of 34 coins, which had probably been wrapped in fabric and leather. All of the coins in this group were Anglo-Saxon, with the exception of a blundered imitation of a Two-Line type penny of Edward the Elder which was probably of Viking manufacture. The remaining coins were two official issues of the same type; one early Two-Line issue of Athelstan; thirteen coins of Athelstan's Building type of *c.* 927, including five minted in York; and seventeen examples of Athelstan's Circumscription Cross type, of which the fifteen legible examples were all issued by the moneyer Regnald of York (Williams 2012b).

The second group was found close to the first, and was quite distinct in its character from the first, although with some overlapping material. This group contained six coins of Athelstan's Building type (one fragmentary), including two minted in York; ten coins of Athelstan's Circumscription Cross type (three fragmentary), including one with a double obverse and one with a double reverse, and with at least seven of the ten minted in York. It also contained one each of Sihtric's Sword/Hammer type (fragmentary), the St Martin of Lincoln type (fragmentary), and the related Anonymous Sword type, as well as thirteen examples of the Sword St Peter/Cross type minted in York (five fragmentary, with one in two fragments, initially recorded as two separate items), and four ingots, three of which are cut fragments, and all of which show edge-nicking (a method used to test the silver content of non-numismatic bullion) (Williams 2012c). The first group is thus wholly Anglo-Saxon in character, as the blundered imitation of Edward would probably have circulated unnoticed alongside the official issues, and predominantly dates from after Athelstan's conquest of Northumbria. The second group as a whole looks more 'Viking', including bullion as coins, and a mixture of pre-conquest Anglo-Scandinavian issues and post-conquest issues of Athelstan. The second group was found slightly deeper in the ground than the first, which may indicate that it was deposited earlier, but it was not directly underneath. Nevertheless, the two groups were found close enough together, and have enough overlap, that it seems reasonable to assume that they are related in some way. There has been no archaeological investigation of the find-spot, so the original context of the deposition is uncertain.

Taken together, the two groups can be interpreted in two very different ways. The presence in both groups of a significant proportion of Athelstan's Circumscription Cross type suggests that both date from a little later than the Vale of York hoard, while the absence of any examples of the revived Anglo-Scandinavian coinage which followed Athelstan's death suggests that both groups were buried during his lifetime, giving a date bracket of *c.* 930–39. If the second group is slightly earlier than the first, as seems plausible given the higher proportion of pre-927 material and the more obviously 'Viking' character, the difference between the two groups could be explained by the mixed bullion economy surviving in rural Yorkshire a little later than the Vale of York hoard (as represented by group 2), but with the bullion economy replaced shortly afterwards by a regulated coin economy (as represented by group 1). However, the latest coins in both groups are of comparable date, and there is no firm evidence that there is any difference in the deposition date of the two groups. If they were deposited around the same time, or even on the same occasion, an alternative explanation would be required for the different character of the two groups. Given the suggestion above that there may already have been a regulated coin economy in York before 927, which one would certainly expect to have continued under Anglo-Saxon rule, and given the proximity of the find-spot to York, it is possible that group 1 was a parcel of coins for use in York itself, while group 2 represents the continued survival of the bullion economy in rural areas. As discussed by Kershaw elsewhere in this volume (see pp. 126–7), single find evidence is consistent with continued bullion use in rural Yorkshire into the 930s, so this interpretation of the 'Near York' hoard is perhaps marginally more likely than a chronological development in exchange systems between the deposition of the two groups, but this can only be conjecture.

The final hoard in the group to contain coins came from the excavations at 16–22 Coppergate in York. Two pennies of Athelstan and two of the Raven type currently attributed to Anlaf (Olaf) Guthfrithsson (939–41) were found in a pile in Tenement D, which also produced a damaged obverse die of the Circumscription Cross type of Athelstan, as well as a Swordless St Peter penny and a separate coin of Athelstan (Pirie *et al.* 1986, 20, 56, nos 50–5). The presence of such a small group within a tenement makes it less certain that this group was deliberately deposited than some of the larger hoards, although the possibility cannot be excluded. The neighbouring Tenement C also contained an obverse die for the latest sub-type of the Sword St Peter type and a trial-piece for a reverse die of Athelstan's Circumscription Cross type in the name of the moneyer Regnald of York, as well as single finds of a fragmentary Danish penny of the early 9th century (of a type now attributed to Ribe, rather than Hedeby, as this coin was originally published, and paralleled by two fragments in the Cuerdale hoard: Malmer 2007; Williams 2007, 187; 2011a, 50), a penny of Sihtric II of Northumbria (*c.* 941–42), and a penny of Eadred (946–55) (Pirie *et al.* 1986, 20, 54–6, nos 43, 45, 50, 56–7; Stewart 1986). The combination of finds, along with a later trial-piece of Eadwig found in residual layers, suggests the presence of minting (although possibly just die-cutting rather than actual minting) in these tenements at least across the period from the 920s to the 940s. As such, the Coppergate site is completely atypical for Viking Yorkshire, and one might expect any hoard from the site to reflect a more monetised economy than was typical for the county as a whole. Of the two Athelstan coins, one was an early Two-Line issue of North-Eastern type, which has stylistic links with York, while the other was of the Circumscription Cross type, minted in Chester. Their presence in a pile with two coins of the subsequent Anglo-Scandinavian phase could be taken to argue against the exclusion of non-current coins in York following the re-establishment of the Uí Ímair dynasty after Athelstan's death but, given the evidence for possible minting on the site, it is possible that all four coins were awaiting recycling for re-use as raw materials for a later issue. This is almost certainly the case with the fragmentary 9th-century Danish penny, as this was found in a 10th-century layer. Thus the Coppergate hoard tells us little about conventional hoarding, but forms part of an assemblage consistent with the arguments above for the exclusive use of coins within York from at least the 920s onwards, and possibly earlier, both under Anglo-Scandinavian rule and under the rule of the West Saxon dynasty. However, the evidence is more ambiguous as to whether the authorities within the town successfully excluded non-current issues from circulation.

Two other coinless Viking hoards are recorded from Yorkshire, but the two are of very different character. The first, from near Selby, was a 19th-century discovery but only recently came to archaeological notice. This contained two arm-rings of different styles, with one made up of plaited rods and the other of twisted rods. Both types are consistent with arm-rings from the general period discussed here, and cannot be dated precisely (Graham-Campbell 2008; 2011, 10–11). As discussed above (pp. 43–4), intact ornaments, and especially arm-rings, could represent a social/status economy, but also had a significant bullion value, and the reason for hoarding the rings might equally relate to either function or both. The hoard is notable as the only example of a Viking hoard of intact ornaments from Yorkshire, but such hoards are in any case rare. Two others are known from Orton Scar and Flusco Pike, both in Cumbria, indicating a wider lack of regional differentiation between types of Viking hoard in northern England (Williams 2009, 78–80). In terms of the quantity of silver represented, even a single arm-ring contained as much silver as the smallest hoards of coins or bullion, and effectively represented a hoard in its own right (*ibid.*, 75; see also Kershaw this volume, p. 117). Hoards such as Selby can thus on the one hand be considered as part of the overall distribution of 'hoards', and on the other as an extension of the single finds of bullion discussed by Kershaw elsewhere in this volume.

The remaining coinless hoard from Yorkshire is on a much larger scale. Found near Bedale in 2012, the hoard contained an iron sword pommel mounted or inlaid with gold foil plaques, together with four gold hoops from the hilt of the sword, six small gold rivets probably from the pommel or hilt, one silver collar and three neck-rings (one cut in two pieces), one silver arm-ring, one fragment of a Duesminde-type ring, one silver penannular brooch, and 29 silver ingots, three of which have incised crosses on the ends. A more detailed account of the hoard is currently in preparation by my colleague Barry Ager, with input from James Graham-Campbell, John Sheehan and Sue Brunning. I am grateful to Barry Ager for sharing his initial Treasure report with me, as well as for the opportunity to examine the hoard in person, and to both Barry Ager, James Graham-Campbell and Jane Kershaw for discussion of the hoard. The hoard is clearly at least primarily a bullion hoard, and the only certain example of a coinless bullion hoard from Yorkshire (see above for the ambiguous status of the Selby hoard), although coinless bullion hoards are also known from Huxley and Eccleston in Cheshire (Williams 2009, 79), and two new hoards in Cumbria in 2014, too late to permit further discussion here.

Much of the contents of the Bedale hoard have direct parallels in other Viking hoards from northern England, although the neck 'collar' and one of the neck-rings are of unprecedented design. The other silver ornaments, ingots and hack-silver all have parallels of sorts in hoards from Britain and Ireland, although the bossed penannular brooch is a hitherto unrecorded type within a well-known Hiberno-Scandinavian series. The parallels range from the Cuerdale hoard to the Vale of York hoard, and thus suggest a broad date of the early 10th century, although it might push back into the late 9th century, which would be consistent with the absence of coins. A similar date is consistent with the sword fittings, which suggest a very high-status version of Petersen's Type L, which is typically attributed to the late 9th century, as in the case of both of the pommels associated with the ARSNY hoard (see pp. 16–17). The presence of gold within a basically silver hoard is unusual, but has parallels in the single gold arm-ring found in the Vale of York hoard (see p. 117) and in the piece of hack-gold in the Watlington hoard (see pp. 12, 33, 36–7). In both cases the gold may simply represent bullion, although in that case the iron core of the pommel from Bedale would suggest that the sword fittings were still in the process of being reclaimed at the time that the hoard was being deposited. Alternatively, just as the gold arm-ring in the Vale of York hoard was still intact, it is possible that the gold sword fittings from Bedale may have been deposited as status items rather than simply as bullion. Swords of Petersen's Type L rarely have gold fittings, so this must originally have been a very high-status item, although its condition at the point of deposition is less certain, and awaits more detailed analysis and discussion by Brunning, which will inform the interpretation of the hoard as a whole.

Conclusion

The hoards from Viking Yorkshire vary considerably in both size and character. Examples can be found of pure coin hoards (Lower Dunsforth and the hoards from Coney Street, Walmgate and Coppergate in York); intact ornaments (Selby); coinless bullion (Bedale), and mixed hoards containing both coins and bullion, with or without intact ornaments (ARSNY, Goldsborough, Bossall/Flaxton, Vale of York and 'Near York'). As a mixture of coins and bullion, the ARSNY hoard thus fits into the largest group, and into a multiple silver economy that remains visible in the hoards into the 930s. At the same time, the fact that all three hoards from York itself (probably spanning a period of over 60 years between the earliest and the latest), contained only coins suggests that York itself may have had a more restricted coin-based economy within a very short period of the initial Viking settlement. This view of a distinction between currency in York and currency in rural Yorkshire is also consistent with the interpretation of distinct parcels within the Vale of York and 'Near York' hoards. The hoards may also show a chronological shift towards a more narrowly coin-based economy in rural areas as well, but this is more ambiguous, depending as it does on the interpretation of the two discrete groups within the 'Near York' hoard of the 930s. As a York find, and one from a site directly associated in some form with minting, not to mention by far the smallest of the hoards discussed, the York (Coppergate) hoard does nothing to elucidate this point, and hoard evidence alone cannot currently resolve this point. A clearly datable hoard from anywhere between the late 930s and 954 has the potential to clarify this further. A final point to be derived from the hoard evidence is that the coins in the ARSNY assemblage and hoard are typical of a transitional period around the time of the settlement of Northumbria in the 870s. Lower Dunsforth demonstrates that the Lunettes coinage was used and valued in Yorkshire at this time despite its relatively low silver content, while the York (Coney Street) hoard is consistent with the interpretation of the ARSNY finds (see p. 36) that pre-Viking Northumbrian copper-alloy stycas may have continued to circulate for a time alongside silver, whether as coins or as a form of bullion. The absence of stycas from any later hoards, however, suggests that such a transition was relatively short-lived, although the gap between Coney Street and Walmgate is over 30 years and possibly closer to 40, making it unclear when exactly such a change occurred.

The hoards as a group thus suggest some consistent patterns, but it is impossible to be certain on the evidence of the hoards alone whether the interpretations suggested above are correct. In the following chapter Jane Kershaw considers the evidence provided by Yorkshire single finds associated with exchange across the same period, and in the concluding chapter I will draw together the evidence from ARSNY, the Coppergate excavations, the hoards and the single finds to suggest a single model of exchange systems in Anglo-Scandinavian Yorkshire from the settlement period to the final Anglo-Saxon conquest of Northumbria in 954.

Chapter 4
Metals and Exchange in Viking-Age Yorkshire: The Contribution of Single Finds

Jane F. Kershaw

Bullion and bullion-related material comprises one of the largest groups of objects from the productive site known as ARSNY. Together with comparable finds from Torksey, Lincolnshire, this assemblage provides crucial evidence for the practice of metal-weight exchange during the earliest phase of Viking settlement in England (the 870s). However, site assemblages represent only part of a growing body of material related to bullion use in England. Hoards and single finds elucidate the Scandinavian silver economy from different chronological and geographic perspectives to productive sites, and all three sources must be considered in order to gain a more rounded view of silver-handling traditions.

In this chapter, I discuss single finds of bullion and bullion-related material from England and how they relate to the evidence of site finds and hoards. My geographic focus is modern-day Yorkshire, an area within the northern Danelaw that has yielded a number of early 10th-century hoards, in addition to the collection from ARSNY. The single finds are predominantly discoveries from the last 20 years, retrieved from topsoil during metal-detector surveys and reported to the PAS. Unlike hoards, they are not confined to precious metal, but also include weights and balances. For the purposes of this chapter, it is assumed that single finds represent accidental losses and, as such, will reflect a more or less random sample of bullion in circulation. In principle, therefore, they ought to provide reliable insights into the scale and location of metal-weight exchange.

The single find material falls into four main categories: ingots, ornaments (both in various stages of fragmentation), Arabic dirhams, and weights and weighing equipment. The silver thus takes a number of different forms, including imported coin and deliberately fragmented or 'hack-' silver, but within a bullion system all forms were valued equally by weight and metal purity. In the case of single finds, without an archaeological context, there is always room for ambiguity concerning their function and context of use. In what follows, I consider other possible uses for the material but nonetheless conclude that the items are most likely to have functioned within a metal-weight system. I discuss each artefact group in turn, focusing on its cultural attribution and date, before moving to consider broader themes relating to the material's economic significance, geographic distribution and chronology. I aim to address two questions: (i) what do the single finds demonstrate about the nature, extent and longevity of bullion exchange in the northern Danelaw? and (ii) how do the single finds differ from regional hoards and site finds?

Metal-weight transactions in context

This text is primarily concerned with evidence for metal-weight payments within a Scandinavian bullion system, but it is important to note that there are a number of possible contexts for such exchange, not all of them commercial. Hack-silver was employed as currency at some Scandinavian sites from the 9th century, and related finds from productive sites in Britain and Ireland have likewise been interpreted as having a commercial role, denoting market-place functions (Hårdh 2007b, 115; 2010, 287–8; Redknap 2009, 38–9;

Location	References	Division	Weight	% silver	No. nicks	Hammering	Groove	Chisel cut
Denby Dale	PAS Find-ID SWYOR-C79E28	complete	19.19g	–	11+	√	X	N/A
Boynton	PAS Find-ID NCL-7D6F54	complete	25.4g	–	0	X	X	N/A
Borrowby	PAS Find-ID NCL-A04B68	complete	3.18g	90%	0	√	X	N/A
nr Easingwold	Blackburn and Bonser 1990	complete	11.66g	–	0	X	X	N/A
Yapham	PAS Find-ID YORYM-29D955	cut at one end	10.7g	–	1	X	X	√
Stillington	PAS Find-ID YORYM-F70826	cut at one end	17.14g	91%	5+	X	X	√
Tadcaster	PAS Find-ID SWYOR-C4D0D2	cut at one end	13.34g	96%	2	√	X	√
Barmby Moor	PAS Find-ID LVPL-16F352	cut at one end	23.09g	99%	4	X	√	√
Melsonby	PAS Find-ID DUR-7563B1	cut at both ends	1.8g	–	0	X	X	√
East Harlsey	PAS Find-ID DUR-147AD6	cut at both ends	7.4g	–	1	X	X	√
Hayton	Hull Museum	cut at both ends	6.8g	–	0	X	X	X
Hayton	Hull Museum	cut at both ends	15.76g	–	2	X	X	√

Table 13 Single finds of silver ingots in Yorkshire

Blackburn 2011, 246–7; Williams, this volume, pp. 40–3). However, silver could be also divided and weighed as part of the division of tribute among troops, or in the payment of compensation, taxes or fines (Archibald 1998, 17; Pedersen 2007, 159–61). Some precious-metal items, such as ingots and rings, may have also had a role in gift-giving or other forms of ceremonial exchange (Samson 1991). The evidence for bullion in Yorkshire is therefore a measure of metal-weight exchange, broadly defined. That said, the single find material from Yorkshire displays a number of characteristics, which suggest a predominantly commercial role, including a high rate of testing and fragmentation and the use of known Scandinavian weight units.

In this context it is worth emphasising that bullion was just one of several potential means of exchange available in 9th- and 10th-century Yorkshire. The exchange of commodities measured in standardised units of account is likely to have been the normal medium of exchange in Viking-Age and later Scandinavian society (Skre 2011b; Gullbekk 2011a and 2011b; Kershaw and Williams 2019). The same was probably true in the Danelaw. At present, however, the dynamics and scale of such exchange, as well as the nature of the commodities involved (cattle, cloth, lead, grain?), remain elusive in both the written and archaeological records.

In Yorkshire, another form of silver currency was coin. The first two decades of Scandinavian settlement coincided with a hiatus in minting at York, but this was resumed, in Scandinavian hands, from the mid-890s. Most coinages issued by local rulers were produced in high volumes, meaning that coinage would have constituted a widely available form of payment, with coins typically circulating by tale, i.e. by being counted out (Gooch 2012, 151). However, coins also appear in a number of mixed bullion/coin hoards, occasionally with bends and 'pecks' that indicate that they have been tested for their silver content. In these instances, they appear to have been treated as just another form of bullion (Williams 2009, 78).

Coin, bullion and probably also commodity economies thus co-existed in late 9th- and 10th-century Yorkshire. The interplay between the different economies is likely to have varied both regionally and chronologically, a theme explored further below. In general, however, a degree of overlap seems likely. Some people probably accommodated a range of different payment methods; others may have altered their chosen exchange medium according to the nature or location of the transaction, or the background of their trading partner. The evidence for bullion-based transactions thus elucidates just one of several potential means of exchange in what was likely a complex and multifaceted economic environment (Kershaw 2017). Nevertheless, this paper will demonstrate that evidence for the bullion economy in the northern Danelaw is substantial. Weighed metal appears to have been a common and widely accepted means of exchange, which remained in use from the onset of Scandinavian settlement in Yorkshire until the mid-10th century.

The single finds

Silver ingots

The first artefact group to be considered here are silver ingots. Within the Scandinavian bullion system, cast bar ingots offered a convenient means of storing, transporting and exchanging silver. Examples with parallel sides, rounded ends and D-shaped, oval or rectangular sections are a common component of Viking-Age hoards from England, including the Yorkshire hoards from Goldsborough (*c.* 925), the Vale of York (*c.* 927/8), Bedale (late 9th–10th century) and 'Near York' (930s) (Graham-Campbell 2011, cat. nos 3:13–14; Ager and Williams 2011a, 138–40, nos 25–57; PAS Find-ID YORYM-CEE620, nos 3–31; PAS Find-ID YORYM-BC3AB2). They are also represented in assemblages from the productive sites of ARSNY and Torksey, as well as other sites linked to Viking activity, such as Llanbedrgoch and Woodstown (Williams, this volume, pp. 40–2; Blackburn 2011, 233, fig. 4; Redknap 2009, 36, fig. 4.5; Russell *et al.* 2007, 24, pl. 3; Sheehan 2014). Twelve silver ingots of typical Viking-Age form have also been found singly in Yorkshire. Four are complete, with the remainder cut at either one or both ends and thus in a form consistent with hack-silver (**Table 13**).

When ingots are found in hoards also containing deliberately fragmented silver and foreign coin, we can be reasonably confident that they passed as bullion. However, the function of ingots found singly, without an archaeological context, is less certain: they may have been used as raw material in metalworking, for instance, or in minting (Hårdh 2011, 282). Fortunately, the form and treatment of all of the single finds from Yorkshire is consistent with that of ingots contained in Viking-Age hoards, and it thus seems likely that they had a bullion role. These features include a high silver content (over 90%); a regular shape and consistent cross-section; hammering on one or more sides and characteristic chisel cuts (**Table 13**). Most ingots have been deliberately cut at either one or both ends, and thus appear to have been in active use as hack-silver (**Pl. 6**). In addition, many ingots carry 'nicks', designed to test their silver content (**Pl. 7**), whereas one has a deep groove, probably intended to direct the cutting process (Graham-Campbell 2011, 78, pls 3–17; Redknap 2009, fig. 4.5; Blackburn 2011, fig. 4).

Since a craftsperson is unlikely to have tested ingots they had recently cast, having satisfied themselves of the quality of silver going into the crucible, it seems unlikely that ingots used in metalworking were regularly nicked. The appearance of such test marks on ingots found singly is thus a solid indicator of their role in exchange. Notably, the rate of nicking is high: of twelve ingots/ingot fragments, seven are nicked, and the number of nicks ranges from 1 to 11+. This pattern suggests that these ingots were frequently exchanged, and implies that the nature of such exchange was commercial. It is nevertheless salutary to note that the ingot with the most nicks is also complete (**Table 13**, **Pl. 6**).

Susan Kruse's analysis of the weights of complete ingots contained in Viking-Age hoards from England and Wales has shown that they were often cast to a weight standard of *c.* 25–6g (Kruse 1988, 294). This is a lighter unit than observed for examples from Scandinavia, Schleswig-Holstein and the Netherlands, and one described by Kruse as 'fuzzy' rather than precise (Kruse 1988, 296–7; Hårdh 2007b, 106–7, table 5.6 and fig. 5.8). The ingots and ingot fragments from Yorkshire range in weight from 1.8g to 25.4g, with no evident clustering at either the lighter or heavier ends of the spectrum. However, one complete ingot, from Boynton, weighs 25.4g, and thus appears to have been

Plate 6 A silver ingot cut at both ends, Melsonby. © Durham County Council

manufactured to a target weight corresponding with those observed in Danelaw hoards.

The remaining complete ingots weigh 19.2g, 11.7g and 3.2g. It is difficult to say whether these were weight-adjusted or not. A weight of 11.7g is close to half of a unit of *c.* 25g, while a weight of 19.2g could represent three-quarters of the same unit, but Kruse found little evidence that half or three-quarter unit weights were aimed for (Graham-Campbell 2011, 76). A weight of 3.2g could possibly represent one-sixth of a *c.* 25g unit, but it could also be unrelated. 3g is roughly the weight of a complete dirham and has been proposed by Hårdh as a target weight for small ingots from Kaupang, Norway (Hårdh 2007b, 107). It is unclear if cut ingots were also intended to conform to weight standards. The weights of cut ingots have been included here, but no attempt was made to correlate them with a particular weight unit.

Plate 7 A complete silver ingot with test marks, Denby Dale (image: West Yorkshire Archaeology Advisory Service)

Plate 8 (above left) Fragment of silver lozenge-sectioned ring, North Yorkshire (length: 49mm). © York Museums Trust

Plate 9 (right) Neck-ring fragment, near Stamford Bridge. © York Museums Trust

What is the likely date of the ingots? None of the single finds derives from archaeologically datable contexts and, since cast bar ingots were current throughout the Viking period, it is impossible to refine the chronology of the Yorkshire finds on typological grounds. They may, then, be contemporary with the productive sites of ARSNY and Torksey, or they may significantly post-date them. The bullion hoards from Yorkshire that can be coin-dated belong to the 920s, and in the case of the 'Near York' hoard probably the 930s (Williams, this volume, pp. 107–11) suggesting an extensive period of bullion use in the northern Danelaw.

Fragmented jewellery

Also found among the single finds from Yorkshire is deliberately fragmented or 'hack'- silver and gold from ornaments. Four pieces of silver are recorded: two from arm-rings, one from a neck-ring and one from a brooch. In addition, a fifth piece belongs to a cut, but complete, arm-ring in gold.

A silver fragment from Barmby Moor has been cut from the side of a Hiberno-Scandinavian broad-band arm-ring (DCMS 2006, 64). It is decorated with transverse rows of bar-stamps, which take the form of a single serrated edge. This particular stamp is uncommon, but it is carried on single broad-band arm-rings from the Cuerdale and Silverdale hoards (deposited *c.* 905–10 and *c.* 900–10 respectively), raising the possibility that all three items were produced in the same workshop (Graham-Campbell 2011, no. 1:517; Ager and Williams 2011b, no. 13).

John Sheehan's in-depth assessment of Hiberno-Scandinavian broad-band arm-rings has shown that they were manufactured in Ireland, primarily in Dublin, during a 50-year period from *c.* 880 to *c.* 930 (2009, 61). However, the recent discovery at Llanbedrgoch, Anglesey, of a stamped lead trial-piece in the form of a broad-band arm-ring, suggests that the type may have been produced over a wider, Irish Sea zone (Redknap 2000, 84, fig. 130; 2009, 37–8). In Britain, most of the 20 find-spots yielding examples of this artefact type are in north-west England and North Wales (Sheehan 2009, 58). Sheehan notes 19 find-spots, to which can be added a hoard find from Bedale, Yorkshire, discovered in 2012 (PAS Find-ID YORYM-CEE620). Just five arm-rings are recorded in Yorkshire and three of these form part of the Goldsborough assemblage, thought to have been composed largely in Ireland or the Irish Sea region (Ager 2011, 130, fig. 15; Graham-Campbell 2011, nos 3:9–11; PAS Find-ID YORYM-CEE620, no. 38). As an item likely to have been lost during a transaction, the Barmby Moor fragment is thus important for showing that Hiberno-Scandinavian arm-rings were actively used as bullion in Yorkshire, outside the primary economic zone in which they were produced.

A second arm-ring fragment comes from a location known only as 'North Yorkshire'. It comprises about one-third of a plain, penannular arm-ring, with faceted sides and a single, tapering terminal (DCMS 2006, 64) (**Pl. 8**). This item was originally identified as a piece of 'ring-money', a term given to a specific type of silver rod arm-ring believed to have circulated as a form of currency in Scotland and the Irish Sea region from *c.* 950 to *c.* 1050 (DCMS 2006, 64; Graham-Campbell 1995, 30, 38–40, 57–9). English-provenanced finds of rings of this type are rare, the only occurrence of fully developed 'ring-money' occurring in the hoard from Castle Esplanade, Chester (*c.* 965), probably assembled in the Isle of Man, although early 'prototype' forms appear in the Cuerdale (*c.* 905–10), Goldsborough (*c.* 925) and Vale of York (*c.* 927/8) hoards (Graham-Campbell 2011, 103). This fact, together with its late date, would thus appear to make the 'North Yorkshire' ring a clear outlier. However, the discovery in 2015 of a comparable penannular silver rod arm-ring from a hoard near Watlington, Oxfordshire, securely dated to 879/80, raises the possibility that the 'North Yorkshire' ring is in fact much earlier. Both rings would seem to belong to an early group of plain, lozenge-sectioned rings with a distribution centred on the Baltic island of Gotland, but which also occur in 9th-century hoards from southern Scandinavia (Wiechmann 1996, 45, 'Armringe vom Typ II 14').

The only Scandinavian neck-ring fragment thus far found singly in England comes from 'near Stamford Bridge' (PAS Find-ID YORYM-30B2B5). The fragment has been cut from the terminal of a silver twelve-rod plaited neck-ring, decorated on its outer surface with three horizontal rows of punched apex-to-apex triangles (**Pl. 9**). The rods have been affected by hammering and are fused by partial melting to a sub-oval-shaped terminal plate. Two short 'nicks' are visible on the opposing edges of the piece, indicating that it has been tested for its silver content.

The identification of a seemingly oval-shaped end-plate identifies this fragment as belonging to Hårdh's neck-ring Type 1, of southern Scandinavian (Danish) origin (Hårdh 1996, 45, fig. 4). Along with eastern Sweden, this is the region that has yielded the highest number of plaited-rod neck-rings, and it thus seems likely that the item from 'near Stamford Bridge' originated there (*ibid.*, 55, table 7). Indeed, the single find has a particularly close parallel in a complete neck-ring from Filborna, southern Sweden, deposited in a hoard in *c.* 955 (Hårdh 1976, 49, no. 66.1, taf. 35,1). This accords with the mid-10th-century date given to neck-rings with oval end-plates more generally, and it thus seems likely that the Yorkshire piece belongs to the same period (Hårdh 1996, 66). Scandinavian plaited neck-rings are rare in England, but fragments belonging to plaited types were found in 2005 in the Flusco Pike (no. 2) hoard, Cumbria (*c.* 925) (DCMS 2008, 101–2). They also form part of an undated assemblage from Bedale, Yorkshire, recovered in 2012 (PAS Find-ID YORYM-CEE620, nos 34–6). This hoard provides a local context for the single find, which is most likely to have arrived in Yorkshire directly from southern Scandinavia.

The final piece of ornament-derived hack-silver to be discussed here is a cut piece from the terminal plate of a silver bossed penannular brooch, found in Snape with Thorp (PAS Find-ID YORYM-CB94B2). The decoration comprises half of a roundel, surrounded by a plain border (**Pl. 10**). The border intersects with a beaded band and divides the panel into two fields, each of which contains engraved ribbon animal-ornament. The fragment can be identified with the largest group of bossed penannular brooches: Johansen's sub-group A (Johansen 1973, 81–4). These brooches are Irish in origin, but may have also been produced in north-west England or elsewhere around the Irish Sea. Their date of production ranges from *c.* 860 to *c.* 930 (*ibid.*, 92–3).

In northern England, such brooches are found in a number of early 10th-century hoards (Graham-Campbell 2011, 113). In Yorkshire, two nicked fragments, including one sub-group A, are contained in the Goldsborough hoard (*c.* 925) while two fragments, both sub-group A, are included in the Vale of York hoard (*c.* 927/8) (Graham-Campbell 2011, nos 3:2 and 3:5; Ager 2011, 128, figs 10–11). A hack-silver piece from a hitherto unknown variant also forms part of the hoard from Bedale (PAS Find-ID YORYM-CEE620, no. 39). When complete, bossed penannular brooches could be worn in elaborate displays of wealth, but the fragmentary and nicked condition of the Yorkshire finds suggests that their role in the northern Danelaw was primarily one of bullion. In this sense, they mark a point of departure from the, usually complete, brooches from Ireland, which appear to have functioned mainly as status objects (Johansen 1973, 118–22).

The final single find to be discussed here, from the York area, differs in that it is gold, rather than silver. Furthermore, although cut and tested, it seems to be complete. It is a massive arm-ring, made of two gold rods twisted together with a single thinner wire that is textured to look like a beaded wire (DCMS 2006, 63–4; for the technique of creating a beaded wire look, see Whitfield

Plate 10 Hack-silver cut from a bossed penannular brooch, Snape with Thorp. © York Museums Trust

1998, 58). The rods taper towards the terminal, where they were originally enclosed within a plain, polyhedral knop, bound on either side by gold wire. Subsequently, the ring was cut near the terminal and partially straightened. A deep nick on the outer edge of one of the rods demonstrates that it was tested for its metal content.

Twisted-rod arm-rings were in widespread use from the second half of the 9th century to the end of the Viking Age, making it difficult to be more specific about the origins and date of this single find (Graham-Campbell 2006, 75–6). However, it does have close parallels in gold arm-rings from Wipholm, Schleswig-Holstein, and Hornelund, Denmark, which may suggest a southern Scandinavian origin (Graham-Campbell 1980, nos 220, 223). Other gold arm-rings, of different construction, are known from Yorkshire, in hoards from Selby and the Vale of York (Graham-Campbell 2008; Ager 2011, 127, fig. 9). These rings are complete, and could thus still be worn, whereas the single find has been cut, flattened and tested, and thus converted into bullion. It is estimated that gold was worth around twelve times the value of silver in the Viking period (Steuer 2004, 116). The 'York area' ring, weighing some 324g, would thus have constituted an enormous sum of wealth, even within the context of Yorkshire's large silver hoards. It demonstrates the very high sums of wealth that could be accommodated within the metal-weight system.

Dirhams

Within a bullion system, coins were valued purely for their metal content. Rather than being accepted at face value, they passed by weight, and were routinely tested for their purity via bending and pecking. In England, this is most clearly demonstrated by finds of Islamic silver coins known as dirhams. Dirhams were imported to Scandinavia via Russia and the Baltic in huge quantities, and provided a crucial source of silver for the Scandinavian bullion economy. When found in England, they provide clear evidence for Scandinavian trading contacts and mercantile activity. The largest contribution of the *c.* 350 dirhams from Britain and Ireland comes from hoards and site finds, but the number of dirhams found singly is increasing. To date, 65 dirhams have been recorded as stray finds from England (Kershaw 2017). Twelve coins, mainly preserved as cut fragments, come from Yorkshire, including one counterfeit coin from York (**Table 14**).

Location	ID	Preservation	Weight	Pecks	Dynasty	Mint date
Hatfield	PAS Find-ID SWYOR-8870E4	–	–	–	Abbasid	770/71
Scampston	EMC 1999.0057	cut fragment	0.91g	4	Abbasid	–
Kingston upon Hull	EMC 1998.2110	cut fragment	1.06g	0	Abbasid	–
nr Saxton	Naismith 2005, table 3, no. 55	whole	–	–	Aghlabid	800–12
Spofforth with Stockeld	PAS Find-ID SWYOR-598651	cut fragment	0.32g	0	Volga Bulgar imitation?	–
Burdale	PAS Find-ID YORYM-CB2703	fragment	0.33g	0	Volga Bulgar imitation?	–
Doncaster	EMC 2001.0927	cut fragment	–	0	Samanid	892–907
nr Tadcaster	EMC 2000.0082	cut fragment	0.58g	0	Samanid	–
Cottam	D. Haldenby, pers. comm.	cut fragment	0.16g	0	Samanid	928/29
nr Acklam	EMC 2012.0081	whole	2.97g	0	Khazar imitation	850–900
Coppergate, York	EMC 1986.0347	whole	3.53g	0	Samanid counterfeit	903–907/08
Studley Roger	PAS Find-ID YORYM-6A1281	–	2.6g	–	–	–

Table 14 Single finds of Arabic dirhams in Yorkshire. PAS: Portable Antiquities Scheme; EMC: Early Medieval Corpus, Fitzwilliam Museum, Cambridge

It is now widely recognised that dirhams imported from the Caliphate into northern Europe fall into one of two groups: an early group composed mainly of Abbasid issues from the central Caliphate, dated to the 8th and 9th centuries, and a later group dominated by Samanid mints, struck further to the east, in Central Asia, from *c.* 890. The first Samanid dirhams probably arrived in Scandinavia from *c.* 900, and soon came to dominate the local coin stock (Blackburn 2007c, 39; Naismith 2005, 199, 201–2). They probably reached England shortly thereafter. In the Yorkshire hoards of the 920s, most dirhams are Samanid issues, although the presence of several late 9th-century Abbasid coins in the Goldsborough hoard (*c.* 925), together with one much older coin, demonstrates that earlier issues could remain in circulation into the early 10th century (Williams 2011e).

The single dirham finds from Yorkshire with identifiable mints are fairly evenly split between the earlier and later groups. As **Table 14** demonstrates, four coins belong to the early group, although only two can be precisely dated. Three are Abbasid issues, one with a mint date of 770–1, while a fourth was minted by the Aghlabid dynasty between 800 and 812. Coins of different dates circulated concurrently in the Caliphate, meaning that these could have been exported along with later coins some time after they were struck. Nevertheless, the two datable coins are very early issues, which are not typical of dirhams found in 10th-century hoards. It therefore seems likely that they circulated in England in the 9th century.

Two further dirhams are contenders for Volga Bulgar imitations. They are in a poor state of preservation and cannot be closely dated. In general, Volga Bulgar imitations date from the late 9th to the first three decades of the 10th century, although most imitate coins struck after 900 (Rispling 1987, 79, 81; 1990). A Khazar imitation found in Acklam is of a type (Rispling's Group B2) which typically appears in very late 9th-century hoards, and may thus be associated with either group. Unusually, it has four piercings at the corners of its central field, suggesting a function other than bullion.

The four remaining dirhams are all Samanid issues or forgeries thereof. Of the three coins that can be more or less precisely dated, one was produced between 892 and 907, while a counterfeit copper-alloy dirham from York copies a Samanid issue struck between 903 and 907/8. The hoard evidence from England and Wales suggests that there was a gap of *c.* 10–15 years between the striking of a Samanid dirham and its deposition in England (Williams 2011a, 66). If a travelling time of *c.* 10 years is conjectured for the single finds, the dirham struck between 892 and 907 can only have reached Yorkshire in the first decade of the 10th century at the earliest. The counterfeit coin from York is perhaps most likely to have been imported along with genuine silver dirhams from the second decade of the 10th century, but it may significantly post-date the coin on which it was modelled.

The latest dirham found singly in Yorkshire, from Cottam on the Yorkshire Wolds, is a Samanid issue from Tashkent, struck in 928/9 (G. Rispling, pers. comm.). This is a late mint date for a dirham from England. Even supposing a quick travelling time of *c.* 5–10 years, the dirham cannot have reached Yorkshire much before the mid-930s, by which time York was ruled by Anglo-Saxon, rather than Scandinavian, kings. Moreover, the dirham is in a highly fragmentary state (it weighs just 0.16g), suggesting that it circulated for an extended period of time. It is therefore reasonable to suggest a date of loss for the coin in the later 930s or even the 940s: perhaps a decade or more later than the latest Scandinavian bullion hoard from Yorkshire.

It is tempting to use this fragment to extend the date range of bullion use in Yorkshire. This is certainly supported by the neck-ring fragment, which comes from a site with a substantial bullion and weight assemblage (see below p. 126). This suggests that a metal-weight economy continued at some level well after the latest hoard was deposited. However, the dirham is an isolated find from a site – Cottam – whose core activity has been dated from the late 9th to early 10th century, and it may be that it was simply lost by a late visitor to the site. Although currently just a single hoard of Scandinavian character post-dates the 920s in Yorkshire (the second parcel of the 'Near York' hoard: see pp. 110–11), dirhams continued to flow into the Irish Sea region into the middle and later 10th century, as attested by their presence in contemporary and later 10th-century hoards from Ireland and Scotland (Naismith 2005, 204–5; Graham-Campbell and Batey 1998, 232–3). The dirham from Cottam may have arrived via this route.

A notable feature of the stray dirhams is their high degree of fragmentation. Of the ten dirhams whose state of preservation is recorded, just three are whole, including the copper-alloy counterfeit from York. The remainder are fragmentary and most show signs of being deliberately cut. The average weight of the six fragmentary dirhams whose weight is recorded is just 0.56g. This is comparable to the average weight of dirhams recorded at Torksey and ARSNY (0.44g and 0.41g respectively), as well as with the high degree of fragmentation observed at Scandinavian market sites, although the single coins from Yorkshire contain a higher percentage of complete coins (Williams, this volume; Blackburn 2007c, 64; Rispling 2004, 35, table 4; Hårdh 2010, 283, fig. 21).

Exactly where such fragmentation took place is an open question. Some dirhams exported after the mid-9th century were already fragmented when leaving the Caliphate, but further fragmentation will have taken place en route to, and in, England. Regional variation in the degree of dirham fragmentation across Scandinavia suggests that dirhams were fragmented locally (Hårdh 2010, 283). Working on the assumption that the degree of fragmentation will reflect the frequency with which dirhams traded hands, the single finds are indicative of a vibrant bullion economy, employing very small amounts of silver. It is nevertheless important to recognise that some dirhams may have been accidentally damaged, or divided for purposes other than exchange, such as to assess their silver content.

Other coin types

Dirhams are an imported coin type that almost certainly reached England as a result of Scandinavian mercantile networks, and are thus an easily recognisable element of the bullion economy. Yet other types of coin could also pass by weight within a bullion system. Carolingian coins are a common component of Viking-Age hoards from Britain (Dolley and Morrison 1963). So too are Anglo-Saxon issues minted in southern England and Viking issues minted in East Anglia and the midlands. Even locally minted coins appear in northern hoards, occasionally with test marks that indicate their treatment as bullion (Williams 2009, 77–8).

Plate 11 Oblate-spheroid weight, near Stamford Bridge. © York Museums Trust

Similar coin types found singly may also be Viking losses from metal-weight transactions (for a list of single coin finds in Yorkshire, as of 2004, see Blackburn 2004, 347–9). However, without an archaeological context, their status as bullion is difficult to prove, particularly in the absence of physical test marks such as bends or pecks. Unlike dirhams, other imported coins types could have reached Yorkshire as a result of trade with the Continent and/or other areas of England, both before and after the Scandinavian settlements. It is now thought that Carolingian coins played a monetary role in the Anglo-Saxon economy, for instance, arriving as a result of direct commercial contact between England and the Continent (Story 2003, 243–55). Carolingian single coin finds may therefore reflect earlier, 9th-century trade, rather than Viking bullion *per se*. Furthermore, since southern Danelaw issues were struck to the same weight standard as coins minted in York, it is possible that they passed by tale alongside local issues. It is thus impossible to know how such coins functioned in Yorkshire. None of the single finds carries test marks, but the possibility remains that they passed as bullion, and were simply weighed, rather than bent or pecked. Such a treatment would be archaeologically invisible, but there is growing evidence to suggest that small, bullion weights were in regular use in the northern Danelaw.

Weights and weighing equipment

One of the benefits in studying single finds is that it allows insights into artefact groups typically excluded from precious-metal hoards. Weights and weighing equipment comprise one such find category. Small bullion weights are found in a range of different materials across Scandinavian-settled regions of England. In Yorkshire, seven standardised copper-alloy/iron weights have so far been recorded, in addition to a larger corpus of lead weights. Also recorded singly are two fragments from folding balances, which may have been used to weigh bullion.

Cubo-octahedral and oblate-spheroid weights

In his discussion of the ARSNY weights (see pp. 20–3), Williams isolated two types of standardised or regulated weight, which are typically associated with the weighing of silver at market sites within Scandinavia: oblate-spheroid weights, with an iron core and copper-alloy shell, and

Plate 12 Cubo-octahedral weight, South Newbald. © North Lincolnshire Museum

copper-alloy cubo-octahedral weights, in the shape of a cube with faceted corners with punched dots on the six square sides (Williams' Type A and B respectively). Both types are represented among single finds from Yorkshire: five oblate-spheroid weights are recorded as well as two cubo-octahedrals.

Included among the five oblate-spheroid weights are two discovered during excavations at 16–22 Coppergate, York (Mainman and Rogers 2000, 2564, fig. 1260), and three single finds (PAS Find-ID YORYM-01C134, **Pl. 11**; SWYOR-E16C55; and North Lincolnshire Museum 0290). All five are poorly preserved, with significant iron corrosion, meaning that the presence of particular weight standards cannot be investigated. Nevertheless, their recorded weights (21.9g; 26.9g; 30.1g; 56.6g and 98.5g) are consistent with a weight range of *c.* 4 to 150g recorded for oblate-spheroid weights more generally (Hårdh 2010, 289, fig. 26). These weights are substantial, and confirm the use of the oblate-spheroids in high-value transactions, involving significant quantities of silver. Of course, the sum of metal that could be weighed could be increased further still when multiple weights were used together. Notably, the two oblate-spheroids from York were found within a metre of each other and may have comprised a pair (Mainman and Rogers 2000, 2564). If used together, they would have had a combined weight of almost 50g.

Just two cubo-octahedral weights have been recorded singly in Yorkshire, both with four punched dots on their square faces (PAS Find-ID NLM687; North Lincolnshire Museum 0289) (**Pl. 12**). Such dots are considered by some to have marked the position of a particular weight within a set, but more recently attempts have been made to link the number of dots to multiples of a weight standard based on either a lighter and heavier unit of *c.* 0.65–0.7g or 0.75–0.8g, depending on the size of the weight (Pedersen 2007, 149–50; Blackburn 2011, 237–8, for a discussion, see Williams this volume, pp. 31–3). This debate is beyond the remit of this paper, although it will be addressed in the present writer's final publication of the single finds from England. Here, it should be noted that while the weight of one of the finds is unfortunately not recorded, the mass of the second weight is 2.61g. This fits extremely well with a light standard of *c.* 0.65g, which is likewise observed among larger weights (with four, three and six dots) from ARSNY and Torksey (Williams, this volume, pp. 31–2; Blackburn 2011, 237–8, table 3, appendix 4). While the use of multiple cubo-octahedral weights in a single transaction would allow for heavier quantities of metal to be weighed, it is clear that these weights were intended primarily for weighing light quantities of silver, such as dirhams. This is supported by concentrations of both cubo-octahedrals and dirhams at Torksey and ARSNY, while the distribution of single finds of both artefact types in England is also broadly correlated.

The presence of both oblate-spheroid and cubo-octahedral weights in Yorkshire points to the existence of both large- and small-scale transactions involving weighed silver. Yet it is clear that oblate-spheroid weights dominate. Significantly, this picture is replicated at a national level: 26 cubo-octahedral weights have been found singly in England, compared with 34 oblate-spheroids (Kershaw 2017). This profile is very different from that of both Torksey and ARSNY, where the reverse trend has been noted: Torksey has yielded at least 57 cubo-octahedral weights and just four oblate-spheroids, ARSNY 28 cubo-octahedrals (including four from the 'hoard') and just one possible oblate-spheroid.

There are a number of possible reasons for such a discrepancy, including a simple bias in recovery. Cubo-octahedral weights are small and lightweight, and while they may be detected during intensive detector campaigns, they may be easily missed during more casual metal detecting. This suggestion is supported by the fact that the finds from the productive sites comprise the full range of cubo-octahedral weights, whereas the smallest/lightest weights (with one dot) are entirely missing from the single find corpus, which is skewed towards the larger, heavier weights (with four or six dots).

Another potentially important factor is chronology. As discussed by Williams above (p. 20), cubo-octahedral weights were introduced to the Baltic and Scandinavia from *c.* 860/70, a whole decade or so earlier than oblate-spheroid weights. This probably explains why oblate-spheroid weights are rare or even absent at Torksey and ARSNY, where the main phases of activity have been dated to the 870s. The implication, in turn, is that many of the single weight finds from England belong to a later settlement phase than represented at these two sites. This is consistent with evidence of the two oblate-spheroid weights from York, excavated from levels dated from the mid–late 9th to the early 10th century (Mainman and Rogers 2000, 2456, table 223, 2564).

Lead weights

Far more common amongst both the site and single finds are lead weights. A significant sub-set of these are capped or inset with ornamental metalwork, principally derived from Anglo-Saxon and Irish sources (Williams, this volume, **Table 2**). They have been identified as an Insular Viking phenomenon, created mainly during the later 9th century, but possibly remaining in production and use into the 10th. The type is usually associated with the weighing of bullion: examples have been found with hand-held balances in Viking-Age graves, and at market and productive sites in presumed commercial contexts (Graham-Campbell 1980, no. 307; Redknap 2009, 38; Blackburn 2011, 240). The

Plate 13 Lead weight decorated with copper-alloy scrap, near Stamford Bridge. © York Museums Trust

Plate 14 Lead weight decorated with a silver anthropomorphic pendant, near Tadcaster. British Museum, 2011,8024.1

function of the added metalwork is unclear, but one possibility is that it served to personalise weights, allowing the owner to recognise their set easily in a trading environment where multiple sets of weights were in use (Williams, this volume, p. 22).

Over 20 decorated lead weights are recorded as single finds from Yorkshire. In most cases, the added metalwork is undiagnostic, simply comprising scraps of copper alloy or, occasionally, glass (for instance, PAS Find-ID YORYM-6AD518 and YORYM-01F154) (**Pl. 13**). In other instances, an Irish origin for the metalwork can be identified, as is the case with a lead weight from Bedale with a near-complete circular plate possibly derived from a late 8th-century bridle mount (PAS Find-ID DUR-181FC7). A remarkable lead weight found near Tadcaster and now in the British Museum carries a gilt silver pendant depicting a man's head with a beard and moustache (PAS Find-ID SWYOR-EF9E81) (**Pl. 14**). The figure may have cult or mythical connections, and finds parallels in early 7th-century Anglo-Saxon and Scandinavian art. A gilded copper-alloy mount found 'near Stamford Bridge' depicts a similar mask, this time with an elongated face, glass cabochon eyes and a horned helmet terminating in fused birds' heads (PAS Find-ID YORYM-024D31). It is not currently attached to lead, but may once have been re-used as decoration for a weight, a suggestion supported by the fact that it comes from the same parish as several other decorated lead weights.

A sub-group of six decorated lead weights from Yorkshire carry coins (for further discussion of this type, see Williams 1999). Four weights carry embedded copper-alloy Northumbrian stycas, one a Lunette of Alfred and one separate, non-matching coin halves from two early 10th-century coins (PAS Find-ID LVPL-5E4310 and YORYM-01F580; Williams 1999, nos 12, 21 and 22; see also Williams, this volume, pp. 20–3). Most, therefore, carry coins issued in the mid–late 9th century, a pattern that suggests that coin-weights were mainly produced during the transition period between Viking conquest and settlement in England, in the 860s and 870s. However, the presence on one weight of two coin halves dated to the early 10th century indicates that the type continued to be produced for an extended period. Certainly, weights with other forms of decorative metalwork appear to have been produced over several decades. A lead weight from Kilnwick is mounted with a fragment from a Scandinavian oval brooch of a type (Petersen's Type 51 E) that dates to the late 9th or early 10th century (Kershaw 2013, 100, 148).

Analysis of several decorated lead weights – from both Britain and Scandinavia – indicates a broad correlation with fractions and multiples of a Scandinavian øre weight between 24g and 26.6g (Blackburn 2011, 240; Redknap 2009, 38; Kilger 2007, 285; Pedersen 2007, 173; Williams 1999, 33–4). Weight standards may have been neither precise nor uniform across the northern Danelaw. However, the weights of 16 well-preserved decorated lead weights appear to correspond well with a unit based on a Scandinavian øre of *c.* 24g (**Fig. 41**). Two weights weigh close to 24g, while there are clusters of weights around the 2-, 3- and 4-øre unit (*c.* 48, 72, 96g). The lighter weights cluster at *c.* 12g and *c.* 16g, suggesting correspondence with a half-øre (*c.* 12g) and multiples of one-third of an øre, a unit called an ertog (*c.* 8g). A heavier weight standard of 26.5g was also applied to the weights but found not to fit as well. These weights would therefore appear to connect to established Scandinavian weight units, while their recorded weights, spanning between *c.* 8g and 140g, reinforces the picture of bullion exchange taking place at a number of different levels. Notably, the weights of the four well-preserved decorated lead weights from ARSNY range from 8.38g to 37.97g, and thus correlate well with the lighter weights found singly (Williams, this volume, pp. 24–9, **Table 2**).

Plain lead weights are difficult to identify among metal-detector assemblages and their precise function remains unclear. Large numbers of variously shaped plain lead weights have been found in workshop areas at Scandinavian sites, but at Kaupang the introduction of plain lead weights in the second quarter of the 9th century (Site Phase II) corresponds with the appearance of hack-silver at the site (Pedersen 2007, 162). The lead weights and silver were spatially related, with both groups clustered in an area in which metal casting was not thought to have taken place, and it therefore seems likely that the weights had a primary role in weighing silver (*ibid.*).

Currently, the only plain lead weights from Yorkshire that can be confidently dated to the Viking Age, apart from those from ARSNY, come from the site of Cottam B on the Yorkshire Wolds, the same site that has yielded a fragmentary dirham. Fifteen well-preserved lead weights

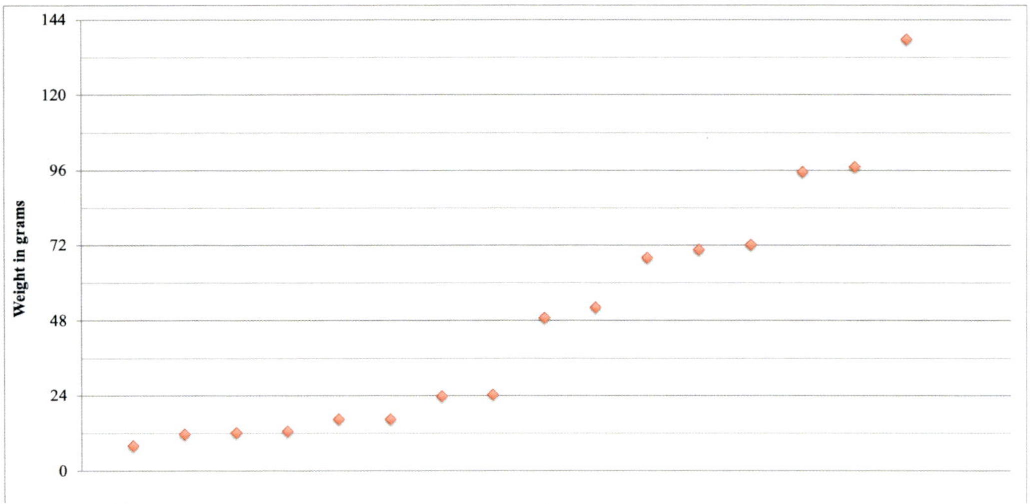

Figure 41 Weight of well-preserved decorated lead weights from Yorkshire

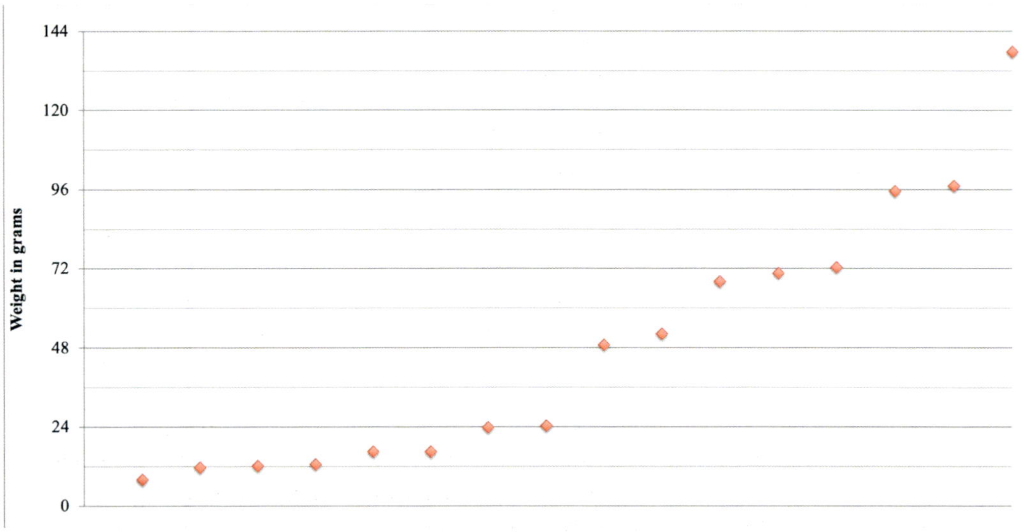

Figure 42 Weight of plain lead weights from Cottam

have been recovered, all from a northern zone independently dated on the basis of its finds signature to the later 9th and 10th centuries (Haldenby and Kershaw 2014). All are regular and well made, with a mid-white patina. They comprise a number of different forms that are paralleled among the Scandinavian lead weight material: seven weights are rectangular or square prisms, six weights are cylindrical, one is a truncated cone and one is ring-shaped. The varied shapes of the weights may have helped to ease their identification. Although plain, a few weights also show signs of decorative or other markings.

The weight distribution of the fifteen lead weights implies the real existence of standards based on a Scandinavian øre of *c.* 24g (**Fig. 42**). Weights range from 8.42g to 94.89g, and thus broadly correlate with the weight range of the decorated lead weights. They are fairly evenly distributed across this range, with pairs of weights clustering at *c.* 8, 12, 20, 24, 32 and 48g. This pairing is an interesting trend, and may suggest the existence of two weight sets. The heavier weights (24g and above) show close correlations with one, two, three and four multiples of an øre of *c.* 24g, while the lighter weights respect the half-øre (*c.* 12g) and ertog (*c.* 8g), and multiples thereof. The deviation from the proposed target weights is very small: under 1g, in most cases. A heavier weight standard of *c.* 26.5g does not correlate as well with the data.

A notable feature of the plain lead weights from Cottam is the absence of light weights, weighing less than 8g. Such weights are well represented at ARSNY, where many plain lead weights weigh just a few grams (Williams, this volume, pp. 24–9, **Table 2**). This discrepancy is unlikely to be due to detector bias, for both sites have been subject to thorough detector surveys over several years, and the wider assemblage from Cottam includes many small artefact types of equivalent size and weight, such as pinheads (D. Haldenby, pers. comm.). Such a pattern may, then, suggest that the average values involved in bullion exchange were smaller at ARSNY than at Cottam, a finding supported by the fact that hack-silver from ARSNY is also very highly fragmented. Nevertheless, the weight assemblage from Cottam is small, and finds of light lead weights may well be made in future.

The apparently widespread use of bullion weights in Yorkshire would have necessitated the use of small, folding balances, capable of a high degree of accuracy. Such balances are relatively common finds in Viking-Age Scandinavian graves, where they often appear in combination with lead or copper-alloy/iron weight sets (Jondell 1974). Two have also been recovered from ARSNY, including one from the 'hoard' also containing weights and silver, alongside other items (Ager, this volume, pp. 13–14; Rogers, this volume, pp. 19–20). Unfortunately, there are few diagnostic features for Viking-period balances, meaning

Plate 15 Copper-alloy arm from a folding balance, Cottam. © Portable Antiquities Scheme

that single finds are difficult to date accurately. Moreover, examples found in association with metalworking debris in urban contexts demonstrate that folding balances were also used in craft production (Kruse 1992, 68–78).

Folding balances

Two copper-alloy balance fragments have been found singly in Yorkshire, both from the same site, Cottam B, that yielded the plain lead weights and late dirham fragment: one comprising a single beam with inlaid silver studs, and a second comprising a central section and beam, ornamented with stamped rings (Haldenby 1994, 55, fig. 3, no. 6; PAS Find-ID FAKL-CC0BE6) (**Pl. 15**). Both types carry distinctive rope-mouldings at the end of the arms, and find parallels among the corpus of Viking-Age balances from Scandinavia (e.g. Jondell 1974, 39, no. 5). Their use in economic transactions, rather than metalworking, cannot be proved. However, Cottam has not yet yielded evidence of metalworking, and given the presence at the site of both bullion weights and bullion (in the form of the dirham fragment), it seems more likely that the scales were used in a commercial context.

Discussion

As this survey demonstrates, evidence for single finds of bullion and related items in Yorkshire is extensive. The finds include both regulated and lead weights, in addition to silver dirhams, ingots and hack-silver: they thus find clear parallels in the bullion assemblage from the 'productive' site of ARSNY, as well as in local hoards. The function of the single finds of silver/gold as currency cannot be proved: precious metal is likely to have been exchanged in different contexts, both social and economic. Nevertheless, the high rate of testing observed on the single finds, coupled with the high rate of fragmentation among the ingots, dirhams and ornaments, strongly suggests a monetary role. This is supported by the fact that regulated weights, associated with the weighing of silver in commercial contexts, are also documented singly, while the lead weights appear to respect an established Scandinavian øre unit. What, then, do the single finds suggest about the practice of a metal-weight economy in the northern Danelaw?

The nature and scale of bullion exchange

At a fundamental level, the single finds indicate that reckoning in weighed silver was commonplace. Silver ingots, cut ornaments and dirhams appear to be common as single losses and are likely to represent only a small proportion of the amount of silver originally in circulation. The number of weights found singly is also considerable, with the high number of decorated lead weights in particular speaking in favour of individual ownership of weight sets. The implication is that many people understood the principles of bullion exchange and could calibrate silver to known units. In addition to weighing, the division and testing of silver seems to have been a regular feature of metal-weight exchange. Overall, nine of the seventeen ingots and ornaments are nicked (53%), while twelve (70%) are deliberately fragmented. The presence of several large bullion hoards from Yorkshire demonstrates that the Vikings had access to very substantial sums of precious metal stored in ingots, rings and imported coin. The single finds show that such silver was not simply stored, but actively cut up, weighed, tested and exchanged as part of a thriving metal-weight economy.

How common was bullion relative to other means of exchange in Yorkshire? At present, evidence for the commodity economy in the Danelaw is elusive, but die estimates have been used to assess the volume of coins produced by the York mint from the mid-890s (Gooch 2012; Blackburn 2009, 56–7). The results show that, notwithstanding variation in output between the different York coinages, the scale of minting was sufficient to sustain a healthy coin-based economy in York and its surrounding region. Indeed, the rate of die use at the York mint under Scandinavian rulers was equivalent to or greater than that in the 11th century, when York was a major mint (Blackburn 2009, 57). This is supported by the fact that local coins are found in significant numbers in select northern hoards, such as Cuerdale and Bossall/Flaxton (Williams 2011a, 43; Graham-Campbell 1993, 79). From the onset of minting in the late 9th century, local coins will, then, have been widely available to the inhabitants of York and the wider region. Since evidence for bullion from both hoards and single finds is likewise extensive, the conclusion must be that, in general, people had a choice in their method of payment (though see below, pp. 124–6; for discussion of a 'dual-currency economy', see Kershaw 2017).

Part of the appeal of bullion may have rested in its flexibility, for the single finds show that the metal-weight system accommodated both silver and gold in high- and low-value transactions. Transactions involving items as valuable

Grams	Number
1–1.9	1
2–3.9	0
4–5.9	2
6–7.9	2
8–9.9	1
10–11.9	2
12–13.9	1
14–15.9	1
16–17.9	1
18–19.9	0
20+	2
Total	**13**

Table 15 Weight distribution of ingot- and ornament-derived hack-silver from Yorkshire

as the gold arm-ring were probably rare, but some plain and decorated lead weights could be used to weigh close to 100g of metal (**Figs 41–2**). One inset lead weight, from Selby, weighs close to 140g. By contrast, the oblate-spheroid weights suggest that transactions involving *c.* 20–50g of silver were routine. This weight range broadly accords with that of most lead weights, and also fits with the weights of the heavier ingots and ingot fragments (**Table 13**; **Figs 41–2**). It is also within the weighing capacity of Viking-Age and later hand-held balances (Steuer 1997, 223; Pedersen 2007, 139).

At the same time, the single finds of silver are skewed towards smaller, lighter fragments. In Yorkshire, the lightest pieces of silver are dirhams, weighing between 0.16g and 3.5g: these may have been exchanged singly, or have been used to top-up larger sums of payment. The weights of the 13 items of ingot- and ornament-derived hack-silver cluster at between 4g and 12g, a weight range roughly equivalent to *c.* 2–8 locally issued coins (**Table 15**). Interestingly, such sums of silver will have been too light to be weighed by most lead weights, but they could be weighed by cubo-octahedral weights. These are currently rare as single finds, but they were probably more common in the northern Danelaw than the current tally suggests. This serves as an important reminder that the smallest items, of both weights and silver, are likely to be under-represented in detector assemblages.

Overall, the degree of fragmentation among the silver finds is consistent with the use of bullion in regular, small- and medium-scale transactions, as well as for occasional high-value payments. However, the rate of fragmentation is not as pronounced as that documented at ARSNY, Torksey, or at other productive sites in Britain and Scandinavia. At ARSNY, for instance, most hack-silver items weigh less than 3g, a pattern that has likewise been noted at both Kaupang and Uppåkra (Ager and Williams, this volume, **Table 4**; Hårdh 2007b, 103, table 5.5; 2010, 287, table 6). The use of very small sums of silver in exchange is also supported by the presence at these sites of large numbers of cubo-octahedral weights, which are comparatively rare as single finds. This pattern no doubt reflects the fact that smaller finds are more likely to be recovered if they are spatially concentrated. However, it is also possible that bullion exchange at ARSNY was more intense than elsewhere in the region, and thus generated smaller sums of silver. Why this might be the case is a question for future research, but it may reflect the presence of a concentrated Scandinavian population, perhaps with close connections to southern Scandinavian central and market places.

Conversely, the weight of the single hack-silver finds does correspond with that of hack-silver found in local hoards. Yorkshire's precious-metal hoards vary in size, composition and function, and not all relate to the use of silver as currency (Williams 2009). However, both the Vale of York and Goldsborough hoards have significant hack-silver elements, in addition to complete objects. **Figure 43** shows that the weight distribution of the hack-silver contained in these two hoards is broadly representative of that found singly, suggesting that the silver from both sources possessed a similar function. Admittedly, the hoards also contain a small number of very heavy hack-silver items (over 40g), which are not reflected in the single finds, but heavy and high-value items are less likely to have been lost from circulation, so we may expect them to be under-represented among stray finds. It would therefore appear that hack-silver from both sources was derived from the same general pool of silver, whereas the hack-silver recovered from ARSNY is of a fundamentally different character. In this way, the single finds help to establish a context for the site finds and hoards, while emphasising the special character of ARSNY in its regional context.

The location of bullion use

Whereas precious-metal hoards could be deposited in locations far removed from the places in which they were assembled, single finds are likely to have been lost when they passed hands during transactions. Their geographic distribution can therefore help to reveal locations of bullion-based exchange. **Figure 44** reveals that, rather than being confined to a limited number of sites, bullion exchange took place across rural Yorkshire, presumably at a range of different sites of variable size and character. The single finds are concentrated along the fringes of the Vale of York. They cluster along the high ground to the east and west, particularly along the western edges of the Yorkshire Wolds and North York Moors. Relatively few items are recorded from South Yorkshire, while just one item, an oblate-spheroid weight, is recorded west of the Pennines, on the western edge of the Yorkshire Dales.

In most instances, the finds represent isolated losses; these probably reflect the small-scale or occasional use of bullion, but are difficult to place in particular site contexts. In other cases, it is possible to identify discrete clusters of finds, which have the potential to reveal hitherto unknown settlements. Small clusters of bullion-related finds point to metal-weight exchange at Barmby Moor and Riplingham, for instance. Neither site has yielded any other archaeological indicators of Scandinavian activity, although the Old Norse origin of the place-name Barmby (meaning 'Bjarni's farm/settlement'

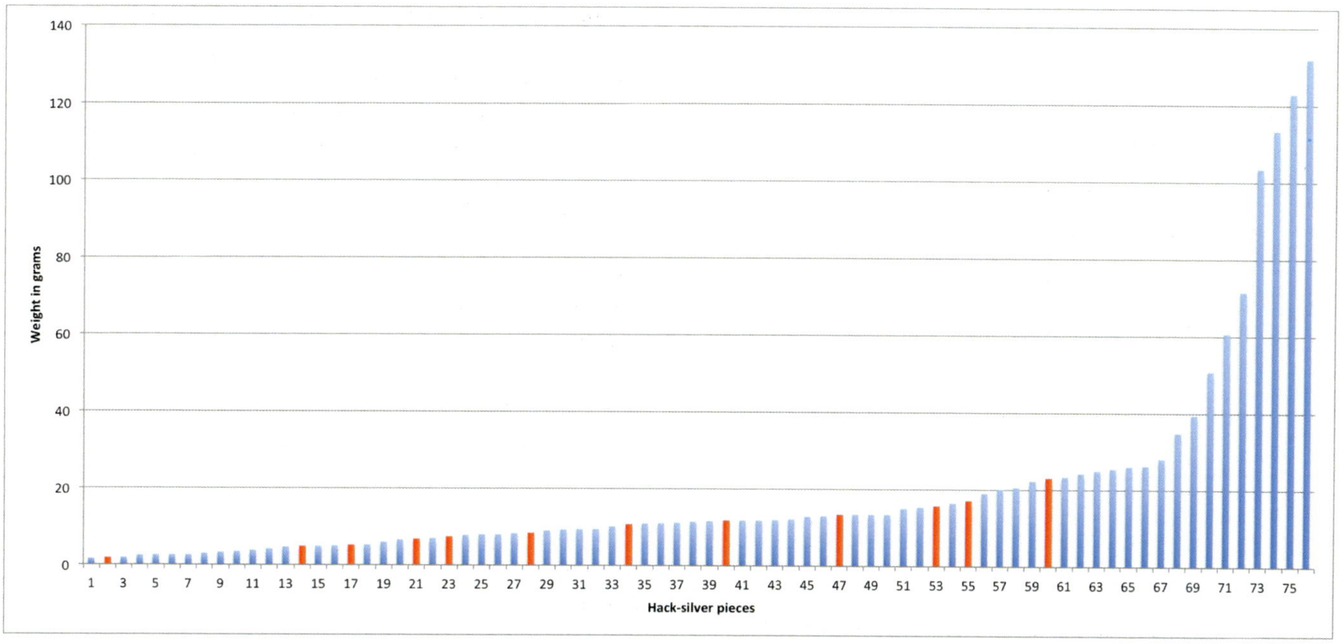

Figure 43 Weight distribution of hack-silver found singly (red) and contained in the Goldsborough and Vale of York hoards (blue)

or 'children's farm/settlement') is suggestive of Scandinavian occupation or influence. The place-name Selby ('willow-tree farm') also derives from Old Norse. It has yielded a hoard containing two complete arm-rings as well as a heavy decorated lead weight, although neither possesses precise find-spots (Graham-Campbell 2008; PAS Find-ID SWYOR-4A40C5).

A significant bullion assemblage, comprising the neck-ring fragment, an oblate-spheroid weight, and at least seven inset lead weights, comes from a parish that can only be described here as 'near Stamford Bridge' (**Pls 9, 11, 13**). The material spans the mid–late 9th to mid-10th century, and seems to reflect concentrated and sustained bullion exchange. This site is of particular interest, since it is close to the location of two silver hoards from Bossall/Flaxton and 'Near York', both of which date to the late 920s/930s and both of which may therefore be linked to Athelstan's takeover of Northumbria in 927 (Graham-Campbell 1993, 83). The precise relationship between the single and hoard material is not yet known, but, to judge from the broad time span of the single finds, the area seems to have attracted Viking activity both before and after the hoards were deposited. Was 'near Stamford Bridge' a longstanding Scandinavian power base and/or a safe haven for those fleeing York after Athelstan's takeover?

Another feature of the single find distribution is the low number of bullion-related artefacts from York itself. Despite extensive excavations, the town has yielded just two oblate-spheroid weights, two inset lead weights and a counterfeit dirham. Moreover, no bullion hoards are known from York, and none of the coins in York coin hoards shows physical signs of testing (Williams 2009, 80). This dearth of material, particularly the low number of weights, provides a sharp contrast with the rich bullion-related assemblages from the productive sites of ARSNY and Torksey and related sites such as Woodstown. It would appear to suggest that, unlike at the productive sites, a Scandinavian metal-weight economy had little or no role within York itself.

York is often regarded as a focus of Scandinavian settlement, trade and culture in England; in this context, it seems odd that it has produced such little evidence for the Scandinavian silver economy. However, from the mid-890s, the Scandinavian kings of York made a concerted effort to establish a large and well-managed coinage (Blackburn 2004, 345). Single coin finds from York suggest that the establishment of a controlled monetary economy was largely successful: new issues regularly replaced old stock and 'foreign' coins were largely excluded (*ibid.*). Within such a system, it is possible that bullion was similarly driven out. Even the few bullion-related artefacts that are known from York may pre-date the onset of minting in the town in the mid-890s. Although the counterfeit dirham belongs to the early 10th century, the weights were probably in use in the mid–late 9th century. They may, then, belong to an early phase of bullion use in York, which began soon after Scandinavian occupation of the town in the late 870s, but which was quickly stamped out following the establishment of a mint in *c.* 895.

Bullion-related finds are not only uncommon in York itself, but also in its immediate hinterland. Just two single finds have been recorded within a ten-mile radius of York: an ingot and dirham fragment, both found along the old Roman road between Tadcaster and York (PAS Find-ID SWYOR-C4D0D2; EMC 2000.0082). One reason for this may be that York's control over a coin-based economy extended beyond the town itself, to cover a larger hinterland in which bullion was similarly excluded. Interestingly, the same area has yielded a handful of locally produced coins, suggesting that the lack of bullion is genuine (Gooch 2012, 201, fig. 4.17).

The extent of this monetary hinterland, if that is indeed what it was, is difficult to gauge. It seems unlikely to have extended beyond the location of bullion hoards, deposited some 15 to 20km from the town, to the south, north-east and north-west (**Fig. 44**). Yet this still leaves a sizeable area within which bullion use appears to have been minimal. Notably, the

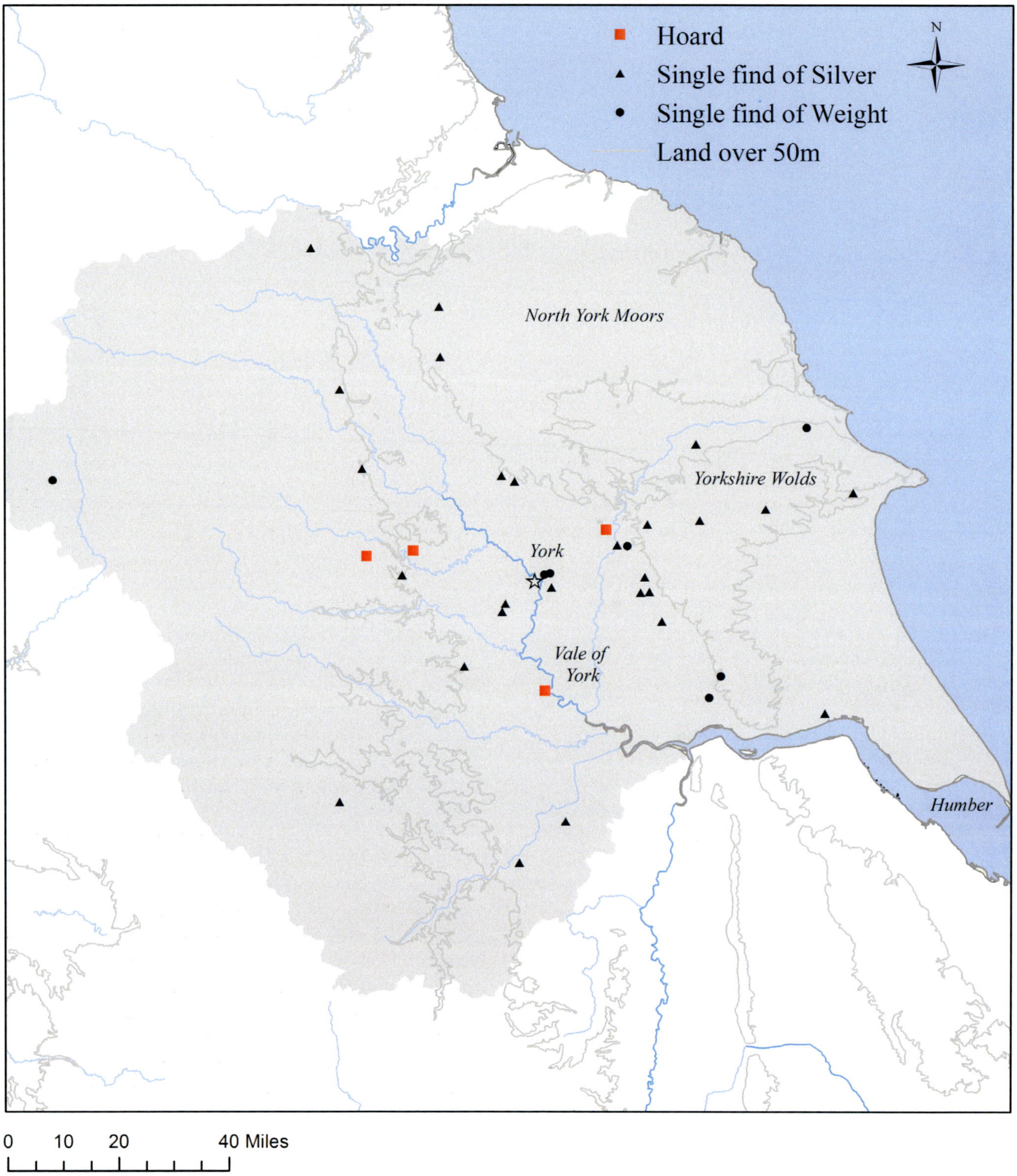

Figure 44 Distribution of bullion and bullion-related material found singly in Yorkshire

distance of the hoards from York corresponds with that of many of the single finds, and it may be that both distributions reflect a geographical shift from a coin to bullion or mixed economy zone, on the outskirts of York's hinterland. The distribution of the single finds, seen alongside that of the hoards, may therefore suggest the existence of two distinct economic zones within Yorkshire: a controlled monetary economy operating in York and its surrounding region, and a dual or mixed silver economy in the rest of rural Yorkshire, in which bullion circulated alongside coin.

Chronology

The final aspect of the bullion economy highlighted by the single finds is its chronology. Combined, the site finds and hoards suggest a long period of bullion use in Yorkshire, stretching from the earliest phases of Scandinavian settlement in the 870s, to the late 920s. Interestingly, the single finds span a similarly broad period, reinforcing the picture of sustained bullion use. The 9th-century material includes the Abbasid/Aghlabid dirhams and most inset lead weights. Cubo-octahedral and oblate-spheroid weights are likely to have circulated in Yorkshire from the 860s and 870s respectively, although they may have remained in use into the 10th century. Whether any of the single finds date to as early a period as the site finds from ARSNY is an open question. Oblate-spheroid weights are documented as single finds, but they are not recorded at ARSNY: they likely predominantly post-date the site, and probably belong to the 880s and 890s. The same may be true of other categories of find, including ingots. These often carry 'nicks', a form of testing which, it was suggested above, does not appear to have been in common usage until the later 870s at the earliest.

Fresh supplies of silver bullion continued to reach Yorkshire into the early decades of the 10th century. This is attested most clearly by the Samanid dirhams, as well as by the various cut ornaments. At least two inset lead weights can also be assigned to this period. A number of single finds have the potential to extend the current end-date of bullion use as suggested by the hoards. The dirham from Cottam was probably lost in the 930s or 940s, and a similar date in the mid-10th century may be supposed for the loss of the neck-ring fragment from 'near Stamford Bridge'. Both post-date the latest hoard on record, the 'Near York' hoard, deposited in *c.* 930.

It is difficult to know whether these finds reflect genuine losses from local bullion-based exchange taking place in the 930s–950s, rather than isolated items that were lost or mislaid by travellers from other bullion-using regions. It would perhaps be surprising if bullion were to have continued as a means of payment much beyond the late 920s. By this date, the York mint was well established, and minting had spread to other towns, a pattern which has been interpreted as marking a transition from a bullion- to coin-based economy (Williams 2009, 81). Moreover, in 927 Athelstan brought the northern Danelaw under Anglo-Saxon control, and at this point probably tried hard to drive out any remaining bullion use (Blackburn 2004, 345).

However, such efforts may not have been entirely successful, and bullion use may have resumed following the reinstatement of Scandinavian rule in York in 938. Certainly, there were advantages in preserving a bullion economy. Viking York maintained strong links with Dublin until its final fall in 954 and Dublin remained a bullion-using society until the second half of the 10th century (Blackburn 2009, 67, fig. 8). The continued use of bullion east of the Pennines would have helped to facilitate economic interchange between the two Viking centres. It is thus entirely possible that metal-weight transactions continued at some level into the middle decades of the 10th century, some years after the latest bullion hoards were deposited.

Conclusions

Recent discoveries of bullion and related items from Yorkshire provide important new evidence for metal-weight exchange in the northern Danelaw. Bullion could change hands in a number of different settings, but the nature of the material suggests that most items had a commercial function, and were used as a form of payment within a Scandinavian economic model. The identity of the bullion users has not been addressed, but the single finds highlight sources of silver and weights in both southern Scandinavia and the Irish Sea region. Settlers and/or visitors from these regions, and their descendants, may have been the principal participants in Yorkshire's bullion economy.

Analysis of the single finds helps to elucidate a number of aspects relating to the scale, location and chronology of the bullion economy. Bullion transactions could accommodate both high- and low-value exchanges, but the majority of transactions seem to have involved small or medium sums of payment. We may therefore envisage bullion being employed to purchase items such as foodstuffs and textiles, perhaps in addition to higher worth items such as livestock. This pattern differs from that at ARSNY, where bullion exchange seems to have involved much lighter sums of silver. This may partially reflect biases in archaeological recovery, but may also highlight genuine differences in the nature of bullion exchange between ARSNY and the wider Yorkshire region.

A second key finding is that bullion transactions were not limited to sites of a particular size or character, but took place at multiple locations across a large geographic area. The notable exception is York and its surrounding area. Here, the use of bullion may have been actively suppressed in favour of coinage, a finding which would suggest that York rulers exercised effective control over monetary circulation, within a limited area. Finally, bullion appears to have continued in use as a form of payment for a longer period than hitherto appreciated. The northern Danelaw continued to receive fresh supplies of silver throughout the early decades of the 10th century, while a small number of objects indicate bullion circulation in the mid-10th century, some 50 years after the establishment of a local mint. The single finds, then, provide new insights into the flexibility, longevity and availability of weighed metal as a form of exchange. Seen alongside the site finds and hoards, they generate a more complete picture of the bullion economy in 9th- and 10th-century Yorkshire.

Chapter 5
Metals and Exchange in Viking-Age Yorkshire: An Overview

G. Williams

This concluding chapter aims to produce a composite picture of the key characteristics of, and developments in, metal-based exchange in Yorkshire from the settlement of the 870s to the expulsion of the last Viking ruler of Northumbria in York. Three different categories of evidence will be considered together and compared: site finds, single finds and hoards. The main site under consideration is naturally the site known as A Riverine Site Near York, or ARSNY for short, together with previously published information concerning York, and particularly the Coppergate excavations. I have summarised the hoard evidence elsewhere in this volume (see Chapter 3), while Jane Kershaw has surveyed the single find evidence relating to bullion and imported coins (see Chapter 4). Single finds of coins of this period from Yorkshire have been previous published by Mark Blackburn (2004, 347–9) as part of a larger study of the 'Coins of Scandinavian York', and although the corpus has increased slightly since then, the pattern of the coin finds has not significantly changed as a result. There is necessarily some overlap between hoards and site finds, and single finds and site finds, while some of the larger and more valuable single finds effectively constitute significant hoards of wealth in themselves, but while the different categories of evidence vary to some degree in both size and character, they present a broadly consistent picture. The main characteristics of this are that there is evidence for multiple types of exchange, that there are chronological developments in the character of exchange which can be divided into several phases, and that for much of the period there appears to be a distinction in practice between York and its immediate hinterland on the one hand and the rest of Yorkshire on the other.

Metal objects can function within a range of different systems of exchange. These include a variety of forms of social exchange; the quasi-monetary use of bullion as a means of exchange and for the storage of wealth; and coin-based exchange with varying degrees of regulation, and based either on imported or locally minted coins. There are no absolute barriers between any of these. Both intact coins and ornaments retained a bullion value based on their metal content, while hack-silver and ingots potentially formed raw materials for recycling either as status items for use in a social economy, or as coins. A further problem of distinction is created by the overlap between metalworking and bullion exchange. In sites such as ARSNY which show evidence of both metalworking and exchange, hack-silver and ingots might plausibly relate to either sphere of activity, but so might waste products from metalworking. Droplets, for example, may suggest metalworking, but the presence of small droplets in hoards such as the massive 40kg hoard from Cuerdale in Lancashire (deposited *c.* 905–10) suggests that they could be used without further treatment within a bullion economy (see p. 44). It is important to recognise that whatever the original function of any of the objects discussed in this or the preceding chapters, that function may have changed before deposition, and thus a simple correspondence between object type and type of economy may be misleading. Nevertheless, one can only interpret the evidence available, and objects should only be considered outside their 'obvious' sphere of exchange if there is good reason to do so.

The most problematic group of objects here are intact ornaments such as brooches, arm-rings and neck-rings. These have a potential social value beyond their bullion content, and if deliberately deposited for safekeeping may equally well have been preserved for their social or their bullion value, and without a clear archaeological context there is no strong argument for preferring either option. However, even where intact ornaments are preserved in the context of mixed bullion hoards, the fact that they have been preserved intact means that they probably retained some social value even if at the time of deposition they may have been considered primarily as bullion. The Selby hoard of two silver arm-rings is the only hoard to contain only intact ornaments from Yorkshire (see p. 111), but Kershaw also notes the existence of a single find of a large gold arm-ring from the 'York area' (DCMS 2006, 63–4, see p. 117). The latter is intact, but shows signs of having been tested, indicating that it has at least been considered as bullion at some point between manufacture and deposition, but the arm-rings from Selby and 'York area' are ambiguous and may have been deposited either as bullion or as status items. All of the other intact precious-metal ornaments have been recovered from mixed hoards, including Goldsborough, Vale of York and Bedale, suggesting that they were at least partly considered as bullion, but their intact state suggests that elements of social exchange continued at least into the mid–late 920s, as they had not been fragmented. The survival of the silver-gilt vessel in the Vale of York hoard points in the same direction.

I have suggested elsewhere that a desire for precious metal as a raw material for status items may have underpinned the initial influx of silver to Scandinavia, effectively as a commodity rather than as a means of exchange, and that this in turn, combined with exposure to coin-using economies both in Western Europe and in the Caliphate and Byzantium stimulated the use of bullion as a means of exchange (Williams 2011b, 345–6, 352–4), but this does not mean that social exchange ceased to be important once the use of bullion became widespread. This raises the wider issue of 'commodity money' (the quasi-monetary use of various types of commodities in set quantities as means of exchange and stores of wealth), which has been an important trend in the discussion of Viking exchange in recent years (Skre 2011b; Gullbekk 2011a; 2011b; Williams 2011b, 352–4; Kershaw and Williams 2019; see also this volume, pp. 31–3, 43–5). However, this is largely invisible archaeologically, so while it may well have had an important role in exchange in Viking-Age Yorkshire, it will not be considered in detail here. Similarly, while it is very likely that the intact ornaments discussed above, or even the act of hoarding, may reflect aspects of social exchange, that is too large a subject to explore here, and the remainder of the paper will focus on coin-based and bullion exchange, what has been labelled as the 'dual economy' of Viking England (Blackburn 2001, 134–5; 2004, 344–6; Graham-Campbell 2001b). However, even with just coins and bullion, the picture appears more complicated than it did a few years ago. Site finds, single finds and now the Bedale hoard (see pp. 111–12) point to the use of gold as well as silver bullion, and while gold coins have not yet been found in Yorkshire from this period, it is apparent that they were circulating in Viking contexts in England (Blackburn 2007a; 2011, 93–5), and it is likely that they circulated in Yorkshire as well as further south. The continued use of pre-Viking Northumbrian copper-alloy stycas now also seems likely, although it is less clear whether they circulated as coins or as a form of copper-alloy bullion, as also possibly represented by a copper-alloy ingot in the hoard from ARSNY, while the possibility of lead bullion cannot safely be excluded (Williams 2011b, 353–4; see also this volume, p. 44). There is thus potential in Viking-Age Yorkshire for both coin-based and bullion economies in at least three different metals (possibly four in the case of bullion), and of these, only gold coinage is currently entirely lacking evidence.

Monetary and bullion exchange appear to fall into five main phases in Yorkshire between 865 and 954 (see **Table 16**). These could probably be further subdivided, since the coinage of Viking Northumbria minted in York certainly has more phases (Williams 2014c, 21–37), but in terms of the changing relationship between coins and bullion, some of these phases within the York coinage can be considered as one for the purposes of this paper.

The first phase relates to the period up to and including the settlement of Northumbria in the mid–late 870s. The most extensive evidence for this comes from ARSNY. Both the 'hoard' and the broader assemblage include intact Anglo-Saxon coins of the base-silver 'Lunettes' type minted in both Mercia and Wessex to *c.* 874–5, and the site assemblage also includes a single silver penny of Ceolwulf II (874–*c.* 879). In both the hoard and the site assemblage these were found together with highly fragmented silver bullion, including fragmentary Islamic dirhams and production waste as well as hack-silver (see pp. 13–14, 33–5, 83). The highly fragmented nature of the bullion matches the pattern of intensive circulation suggested by Birgitta Hårdh (2007b, 100–3) on the basis of site finds in southern Scandinavia, in contrast with typically slightly heavier, less fragmented hack-silver in hoards. This could be seen as evidence of a direct influence from southern Scandinavian market centres such as Kaupang and Uppåkra, where bullion exchange was becoming established in this period, having first been introduced by the middle of the century, slightly earlier than the earliest hack-silver hoards in Scandinavia and elsewhere, which tend to concentrate in the 860s and 870s (*ibid.*, 98–9). It seems likely that at least some members of the *micel here* must have been familiar with these sites (Kershaw, this volume, p. 124), especially as both the hoard and the site assemblage include examples of the cubo-octahedral weights becoming common in southern Scandinavia in the 860s and 870s (see pp. 20–1). However, the site has also produced a much larger number of lead weights, including several with decorative insets, many of which have a specifically Insular character. The distribution of weights of this type, together with the use of Anglo-Saxon coins and other Insular metalwork, suggests that such weights originated in Viking England and Ireland, rather than in Scandinavia. Since the bullion economy seems only to have been widespread in a limited number of trading centres in Scandinavia rather than across the whole of society by the mid-9th century (although from that time it apparently became more

Phase	Dates	Character
1	Mid-870s– *c*. 880	Use of pre-Viking Anglo-Saxon coins, including Northumbrian stycas, base-silver Lunettes and fine silver pennies, as well as imported coins, gold and silver bullion, and arguably base-metal bullion. Introduction of Insular decorated lead weights alongside cubo-octahedral and oblate-spheroid weights of more generically Viking character.
2	*c*. 880–95	Minting of imitative coinage, continued use of bullion in both urban and rural environments.
3.1	*c*. 895–*c*. 910	Regal coinage minted in York and possibly elsewhere, circulating across Yorkshire and more widely across Northumbria, alongside imported coins and bullion. Insufficient evidence to indicate whether restrictions were in place on the circulation of imported coin and bullion in York itself.
3.2	*c*. 910–*c*. 919	Swordless St Peter coinage minted in York and possibly elsewhere, circulating across Yorkshire and more widely across Northumbria, alongside imported coins and bullion. Restrictions on the circulation of imported coin and bullion in York itself, and perhaps the immediate hinterland, but not beyond.
3.3	*c*. 919–27	Coinage in the names of Regnald and Sihtric, and Sword St Peter coinage minted in York and possibly elsewhere, circulating across Yorkshire and more widely across Northumbria, alongside imported coins and bullion. Restrictions on the circulation of imported coin and bullion in York itself, and perhaps the immediate hinterland, but not beyond.
4	927–39	Anglo-Saxon coins of Athelstan minted in York, as well as at mints south of the Humber, and circulation of other coinage and bullion nominally prohibited. These restrictions on the circulation of imported coin and bullion probably enforced in York itself, and perhaps the immediate hinterland, but not beyond.
5	939–54	Coins struck at York in the names of both English and independent Northumbrian rulers, against a background of constantly shifting political authority. Circulation of other coinage and bullion nominally prohibited. These restrictions on the circulation of imported coin and bullion probably enforced in York itself, and perhaps the immediate hinterland, but not beyond.

Table 16 Phases of monetary usage in Yorkshire from the Viking settlement of *c*. 865 to the end of Viking rule in 954

common), it is possible to argue for parallel developments of bullion economies in this period under both eastern and western influence rather than a one-way influence from southern Scandinavia to Viking Britain and Ireland (Williams 2015, 109–12; see also this volume, pp. 40, 43). Examples with coin-insets both from Yorkshire and elsewhere suggest that this style of weight was particularly prevalent in the 860s and 870s, but at least one example seems more likely to date from the late 9th or early 10th century, and while many of the non-numismatic insets re-use earlier metalwork, one from Kilnwick includes a brooch fragment of late 9th- or early 10th-century date (Williams 1999; Kershaw 2013, 100, 148; see also this volume, p. 121), so use of this type of weight was not confined to this phase. The last feature of the ARSNY assemblage is the presence of a significant number of Northumbrian stycas. The most obvious explanation for these, especially given the lack of stratigraphy, is that they are residual finds from pre-Viking occupation. However, the lack of other immediately pre-Viking Anglian finds, and the fact that stycas also appear in large numbers at Torksey in Lincolnshire, which again lacks evidence of immediately pre-Viking Anglian activity, makes it more likely that the stycas were being actively used within the Viking camp. Their function is uncertain, but may relate to a wider use of copper alloy as bullion across the Viking world (Williams 2011b, 353–4; see above, pp. 44–5). The idea of stycas having a continued monetary or bullion function in Viking contexts is also supported by the presence of stycas alongside other objects indicative of Viking bullion economies in the hoards from Kirkoswald, Cumbria and Talnotrie, Kirkcudbrightshire (see pp. 37, 105).

Almost all aspects of the ARSNY assemblage have at least partial parallels elsewhere in Yorkshire. The hoard from Lower Dunsforth also included Southumbrian pennies of the Lunettes type, and possibly also a penny of Ceolwulf II (Blackburn 2004, 347; see also above, p. 106). Unlike ARSNY, these were not found together with bullion, and the fact that the ARSNY pennies (unlike the dirhams) had not been deliberately fragmented (although three had been pierced) may indicate that these had also come to Yorkshire as coin rather than as bullion. Given that the *micel here* returned to Northumbria in 874 after some years in Mercia and Wessex, and given that intact Lunettes pennies are also recorded from Torksey and Repton, it is entirely possible that members of the *micel here* had not only had the opportunity to acquire coins of this type, but to observe the use of such coins within a coin-based economy. There are also three single finds of Lunettes pennies of Burgred from York; from Aldwark, Skeldergate and Tanner Row respectively (Blackburn 2004, 347, nos 1–3). Pennies of the Lunettes type may also have featured in the York (Coney Street) hoard of 1760 among the unspecified silver 'coins of the Heptarchy' but the lack of detail in early accounts means that this can only be supposition (see pp. 104–5).

The Coney Street hoard does appear to provide corroboration for copper-alloy stycas being found in association with silver pennies, but not being hoarded directly with them, suggesting that these were complementary economies rather than a completely mixed bimetallic currency. Again, however, the limited detail available concerning the discovery of this hoard makes this interpretation uncertain. No other hoard from Yorkshire combines the two, and hoards containing only stycas must be considered as probably pre-Viking unless there are other factors such as the balance fragment found in a hoard from Bamburgh in Northumberland (see p. 44), or the nicked silver ornament at Kirkoswald in Cumbria (see p. 105). This is not the case with any of the late styca hoards from Yorkshire, including hoards from Ripon, York (St Leonard's Place), Bolton Percy and Beverley (Blackburn and Pagan n.d., nos 40, 42–4). Stray finds of stycas are similarly uninformative in this respect, since they could equally well have been deposited before or after the Viking conquest and settlement of Northumbria. There were, however, stycas found in the excavations at 16–22 Coppergate in York, spread across phases 3–4b, spanning the period from immediately after the settlement to *c.* 930–5. The later amongst these are almost certainly residual redeposited finds, and this may also be true of the stycas from phase 3 contexts, but Richard Hall noted 'the possibility that the styca coinage retained its local currency deserves recognition' (Pirie *et al.* 1986, 15–17). Whether the stycas continued to function as coinage, or whether they functioned as a form of bullion, it seems very likely on current evidence that they had some function in exchange in the years following the Viking conquest.

The use of bullion also appears to have become fairly widespread in Yorkshire within this period. As discussed by Kershaw (see pp. 114–16), there are single finds from Yorkshire of both ingots (whole and cut) and fragmented jewellery. Without contexts neither group can be dated precisely, although the hack-silver from jewellery can be compared stylistically with other finds from datable contexts. Most of the comparators for the Yorkshire finds come from the 10th century, so while the possibility that some of the finds may have been deposited in this early phase cannot be ruled out, it is likely that most if not all of them are slightly later. The ingots, however, could equally well date from any phase within the period considered here. The fact that the ingots could be as early as the 870s does not mean that they necessarily were that early, and they thus provide only weak corroboration for the bullion phase at ARSNY, although that is supported by other hoards and assemblages from the 870s in other areas (notably Croydon, Torksey and Talnotrie). However, stronger evidence for bullion in Yorkshire in this phase comes from lead weights with decorative insets or caps, with over 20 examples from Yorkshire (see pp. 120–2). As discussed above, this type of weight generally seems to be an Insular Viking development of the 860s–870s, but continuing into the early 10th century. Examples from datable contexts, including ARSNY, concentrate in the 870s, and the sub-set of these weights that includes re-used coins as decoration terminates in the mid-870s with a single exception of probable early 10th-century date. This last example comes from Yorkshire, but there are also four weights with inset stycas, and another with an inset Lunettes penny. On this basis it seems likely (although not certain) that many of the less datable weights were also used in the same period, and this increases the probability that some of the ingot finds may also date from this phase. Finally, Kershaw notes the existence of two single finds of cubo-octahedral weights and two early dirham fragments which are likely to reflect bullion use in this phase.

The next phase covers the period *c.* 880–95. Within this period imitative coins began to be issued in the Viking settlements in England. Most of these are anonymous imitations of Alfred's post-880 issues, and in most cases their production has not yet been convincingly attributed to any particular region, although it is not unlikely that some were produced in Northumbria (Williams 2014c, 25–6). However, a regal type known from a single fragmentary example in Essex has been plausibly linked with Guthfrith, king of Northumbria (Blackburn 1989, 18–20), while two issues in the Cuerdale hoard carry the name ALFDENE or HALFDENE, and have been linked with the Northumbrian king Halfdan (d. 910) (Williams 2011a, 47–8). The dating of the end of this phase is largely based on the recorded burial of Guthfrith in York in 895, who can probably be identified with a 'Guthred' who became king between 880 and 885 (Rollason 2004, 309). If the ALFDENE/HALFDENE coins are correctly identified with the Halfdan who died in 910, this would potentially push the dates of these coins later than this suggested phase, but they fit into this phase stylistically, and not with the Northumbrian coinage of the subsequent phases. Furthermore, although Halfdan died in battle in 910, this is the only record of his kingship, with no indication of his age, so it is perfectly possible that he became king and issued coins before 895, overlapping with Guthfrith, especially since multiple kingship seems to have been a feature of Viking Northumbria in this period (Williams 2011a, 45–8, 65; 2012a).

In addition to the rare regal coins of this phase, there is also evidence for the circulation of anonymous Alfred imitations in Yorkshire in this phase. An imitation London monogram type is recorded from near Doncaster; an imitation Two-Line type from 'Near York'; and an imitation of Alfred's Oxford type from the River Ouse in York (Blackburn 2004, 348, nos 9–11). These numbers are too low to suggest extensive coin use, still less to say anything meaningful about the character of the exchanges in which the coins functioned or the origins of the coins, but they do point to at least limited continued use of coins in Yorkshire in the generation after the initial settlement.

The same phase also saw continued use of bullion. As noted above, both hack-silver and lead weights are hard to date precisely, but it seems likely that some of the recorded examples date from this phase, and although there are no datable hoards containing bullion from Yorkshire in this phase, the fact that they are recorded both before and after this phase means that there is no reason to doubt that there was an active bullion phase as well. It is likely that oblate-spheroid weights were also used in this period, as they were introduced into southern Scandinavia in the 870s and 880s, although they continued to be used later (see p. 120). A total of six weights of this form were found in the excavations at 16–22 Coppergate (Mainman and Rogers 2000, 2561–4, nos 10356–60, 10592): four of brass-coated iron; one of lead-coated iron, and one of lead alloy, coated with copper alloy. The contexts of these vary, and there may be an issue of redeposition in some cases, but two of the weights, possibly a pair, were discovered close together in Period 3 levels, indicating deposition in the late 9th century (*ibid.*, 2563–4). Kershaw (see p. 120) has also recorded three single finds from Yorkshire, indicating that they were used in rural areas as well as in the important trading centre of York.

The next phase is characterised by the minting of a Northumbrian regal coinage between *c.* 895 and *c.* 927, and can be further divided into a number of sub-phases (see **Table 16**). This was minted initially in the names of two kings named *Siefredus* (Sigeferth) and Cnut, as well as another individual named Alwaldus (probably Æthelwold, nephew of Alfred the Great) and another whose name is represented as AIRDECONVT (possibly Harthacnut). These coins were mostly, if not exclusively, minted in York, and the large number of dies found within this series suggests that this coinage was minted in very large numbers, indicating a widespread demand rather than a purely symbolic issue (for more detailed discussion of the coinage within this sub-phase, see Lyon and Stewart 1961; Blunt 1985; Blackburn 2004, 329–32; Williams 2011a, 43–7; 2012a; 2014c, 28–31). This was followed by another coinage minted in York in the name of St Peter (*c.* 910–19), the so-called Swordless St Peter type (Gooch 2014), then by coins in the name of Regnald (*c.* 919–21), then a resumption of minting predominantly in the name of St Peter, but clearly linked with the authority of Sihtric (921–27) (Blunt and Stewart 1983; Blunt *et al.* 1989, 97–107; Stewart 1991; Blackburn 2004, 332–5; 2006, 209–17; Williams 2008c; 2008d; 2011d, 148–9; 2014c, 32–5). Taking this period of *c.* 895–927 as a single phase, this is a period in which three of the coin-dated hoards from Yorkshire were deposited (see **Table 12**, p. 104), and for which there is archaeological evidence for minting at Coppergate, York, in addition to the numismatic evidence of the coins themselves.

There are no datable hoards from Yorkshire from the sub-phase *c.* 895–910, and the coinage is known primarily from the large hoard from Cuerdale, Lancashire (*c.* 905–10), and a smaller hoard from Silverdale, Lancashire (*c.* 900–10). Both hoards combine the coins minted in York with imported coins from outside Northumbria, and with non-numismatic bullion (Graham-Campbell 2011; Boughton *et al.* 2012). This clearly suggests a bullion economy, especially since many of the coins (both locally minted and imported) carry test marks, indicating that they were valued as bullion for their silver content, rather than by tale, according to a nominal value. However, whereas a high proportion of imported coin in the Cuerdale hoard showed evidence of test marks, and in some cases of repeated testing, many of the coins minted in York had no test marks, suggesting that they were accepted as a valid currency without need for testing, although the fact that they were relatively recently minted may also have played a part (Archibald 2011). This does not in itself indicate a fully monetised economy in which the nominal value of the coins exceeded the bullion value of their silver content, but it does indicate that the silver content of this coinage was trusted and familiar, in contrast to the wide variety of imported coin types found in the hoard.

Quite what this means for the circulation of this coinage across Yorkshire as a whole is unclear. Both of the Lancashire hoards contain Irish Sea elements amongst the bullion, and Cuerdale has sometimes been seen as a hoard compiled in Ireland. However, the presence of coins minted in York, many of them fairly freshly minted, clearly indicates a York connection. The question, which cannot be resolved, is whether that component of the hoard was entirely drawn directly from York, or from both York and a wider pool of circulation within Viking Northumbria. The fact that a small proportion of the coins of this series within the Cuerdale hoard do have test marks may indicate that a differentiation already existed between an entirely coin-based economy within York itself and the coins continuing to be seen as bullion elsewhere. However, this tells us nothing about how wide an area around York may have had a purely coin-based economy. A further element of uncertainty is added by the ambiguity of the CVNNETTI inscription on the reverse of coins in the name of Cnut (*c.* 900–05), and whether this represents a separate but unidentified mint within Northumbria (but one with close associations with York) or whether all the coins within this series, including those with CVNNETTI inscriptions, were minted in York itself (see p. 106).

Although there are no hoards of this sub-phase from Yorkshire, there are eight recorded single finds, and these do point to fairly widespread circulation of the locally minted coinage. Two were from York itself, one from 16–22 Coppergate and one from Skeldergate, with the remainder coming from Rufforth and Easingwold in North Yorkshire, and North Ferriby, Pocklington, Stamford Bridge and 'Yorkshire, East Riding' in East Yorkshire. Of these, the example from the 'East Riding' was a coin in the name of Siefredus with a York mint signature, and that from North Ferriby in the name of Alwaldus, probably also minted in York. The remainder were all of the Cnut/CVNNETTI type (Blackburn 2004, 348, nos 13–20). None of the coins is recorded as having test marks, although photographs indicate a possible peck mark on the reverse of the example from Pocklington. The general absence of test marks may indicate that these coins were circulating widely within Yorkshire as coinage rather than as bullion. However, that does not preclude the possibility that a coin economy may have co-existed with a bullion economy, or at least unregulated use of other coin, across the area. The three Alfred imitations of the previous phase may still have been in circulation at this point, as indicated by the presence of similar coins in both Cuerdale and Silverdale, while a halfpenny of the East Anglian St Edmund Memorial issue found around ten miles south of York (*ibid.*, 348, no. 12) probably also dates from this phase, as may some of the single finds of dirhams recorded by Kershaw (see pp. 117–19).

The next sub-phase of the Swordless St Peter coinage is represented by the York (Walmgate) hoard (see pp. 106–7). With the exception of two St Edmund pennies and a St Edmund halfpenny, this hoard contained only locally minted coins of the current type, excluding earlier York coins as well as imported coins and imported bullion. This suggests that by the second decade of the 10th century there was not only a local coinage minted on a substantial scale, but that there was a regulated currency within York itself, and that only coins of the current type were permitted to circulate. The three St Edmund coins point to continued links with East Anglia, and indicate that any exclusion of imported coin was not wholly successful, but they represent only a very small proportion of the hoard, and probably also of the circulating currency within the hoard.

Although the type is known in other hoards from outside Yorkshire, reflecting the wider use of the type in Northumbria west of the Pennines, none of the hoards containing the type was particularly large. As a result, the surviving corpus is much smaller than that of the previous sub-phase, which is dominated by the Cuerdale hoard. Nevertheless, in her recent study of the Swordless St Peter coinage Megan Gooch (2014, 460–5) has argued that the wide variation of dies in relation to the size of the corpus points to this being a much more substantial coinage than current numbers alone would suggest, if not quite as large as that of the series represented in Cuerdale. This view finds some support from the existence of at least six single finds of coins of the type. Four of these are from York itself ('York', 16–22 Coppergate, Skeldergate and St Mary Bishopshill Junior), with the other two from 'Near Doncaster' and Beverley. Further St Peter coins were dredged from the River Ouse in York in *c.* 1740, but it is uncertain whether these were of the Swordless St Peter type or the later Sword St Peter type from the 920s. As with the previous sub-phase, this suggests the use of coins beyond the confines of York and its immediate hinterland. Proportionately, there is a stronger focus on York itself than in the Cuerdale sub-phase, but it would be rash to read too much into such small numbers. Within this sub-phase, there are no single finds that point clearly to a bullion economy either in York itself or elsewhere in Yorkshire, but as in other phases the possibility that hack-silver, weights and ingots which cannot be precisely dated may have been deposited in this period, and as with the previous sub-phase the fact that bullion is known to have been used in Yorkshire both before and after this period, makes it more likely than not that it was used in this period as well.

The final sub-phase from *c.* 919–27 saw the minting in York of coins in the names of Regnald (*c.* 919–21) and Sihtric (921–27), as well as the later varieties in the name of St Peter which feature a sword in the obverse design. There is direct evidence of minting in this phase, in the form of an obverse die of the Sword St Peter type from 16–22 Coppergate (Pirie *et al.* 1986, 34–5; Stewart 1986). There are no hoards from York itself during this sub-phase, but the single find record from Coppergate includes a Danish penny of the 9th century and an imitation dirham, as well a Sword issue of Sihtric, all deposited in Period 4, and thus in the first half of the 10th century (Pirie *et al.* 1986, nos 44–5, 47; Hall *et al.* 2014, 603). The range of coins represented could be taken to indicate a lack of regulation, and that imported coins could circulate as easily in York as locally minted coins. However, the fact that these imported coins come from the Coppergate site, and therefore in close proximity to the site providing evidence of minting, suggests an alternative interpretation that imported coin, as well as bullion, was taken to the mint to be exchanged for current coinage. There are no certain single finds of coins of this sub-phase recorded from Yorkshire, although as noted above St Peter coins dredged from the Ouse *c.* 1740 may relate either to this sub-phase or the previous one. This may indicate a smaller volume of minting, and less extensive circulation than in the two previous sub-phases. However, Mark Blackburn (2006) recorded considerable variation of dies within the Sword St Peter and related coinages. The corpus of this coinage has recently expanded significantly as a result of the discovery of the Vale of York and 'Near York' hoards (see pp. 109–11), as well as another hoard of the 920s from Flusco Pike, near Penrith in Cumbria (Williams 2013c, 471–4). Detailed analysis of these hoards is in progress, but it would currently be premature to comment on what these new finds might tell us about the scale of the coinage as a whole.

The absence of any hoards from York from this sub-phase means that hoards do not throw any light on the character of currency within York itself. However, the hoards from Goldsborough and Bossall/Flaxton clearly suggest that any regulation of currency within York did not extend beyond the immediate hinterland. Both hoards contained a mixture of imported coins and non-numismatic bullion, and while Bossall/Flaxton also contained coins minted in York, these were apparently entirely absent from Goldsborough. The Vale of York hoard bridges this and the following phase, since it was undoubtedly deposited after Athelstan's conquest of Northumbria in 927 and the introduction of minting in Athelstan's name in York (see below). However, it is likely that the hoard was at least in part compiled prior to Athelstan's conquest. The Anglo-Scandinavian coinage within the hoard was almost exclusively limited to the latest sub-type of the Sword St Peter coinage, without test marks but from multiple dies. This suggests a parcel of coins directly from York, but not directly from the mint, which might be expected to be die-identical, or at least from a more limited range of dies. On this basis, the Vale of York hoard also suggests the continued survival into the 920s of a regulated and exclusively locally minted coinage within York itself, but the presence of imported coins and bullion within the hoard supports the evidence of Goldsborough and Bossall/Flaxton for the continued use of bullion beyond York's immediate hinterland.

The apparent distinction within this phase as a whole between York and rural Yorkshire lacks definitive hoard evidence from both the Cuerdale sub-phase and from the sub-phase of the reigns of Regnald and Sihtric. However, it is supported by the almost complete absence of either bullion or weighing equipment from York, while many of the single finds of hack-silver from rural Yorkshire have stylistic parallels within this phase, making it likely that some at least were deposited at this time (see pp. 116–17). As noted by Kershaw, single finds of dirhams also point to the continued use of bullion at this time, with four finds of Samanid dirhams (or contemporary imitations), typical of the hoards of the 920s (see pp. 117–19).

A new phase of monetary activity within York began with the conquest of Northumbria by Athelstan in 927. York already appears as a mint in Athelstan's Building type, a short-lived issue which appears to have begun immediately after Athelstan's assumption of authority over Northumbria and the midlands after the death of Sihtric, but which was quickly replaced by Athelstan's *Rex Totius Britanniae* issue, introduced following a meeting with various rulers from northern Britain and around the Irish Sea at Eamont Bridge near Penrith in July 927 (see p. 110). This coinage was minted at a national network of mints, with a mint signature on all coins of the two types to give Athelstan this title. One of these, the Circumscription Cross type, was minted in York for the remainder of Athelstan's reign. The variety of dies within the York coinage of this period suggests minting on a substantial scale, although only two moneyers are recorded in York under Athelstan, and it appears likely that for most of his reign there was only a single moneyer at any one time (Blunt 1974, 89–90). As part of a national coinage, York coins circulated extensively beyond Yorkshire, while coins from other mints were also permitted to circulate freely in and around York. However, as the only mint recorded in

Northumbria in this period, York coins appear to have dominated the circulating currency in Yorkshire and elsewhere in the former kingdom of Northumbria. The dominance of York in this respect is shown by the prevalence of York issues in both parcels of the 'Near York' hoard (see pp. 110–11).

In addition to the evidence of the coins themselves, a die of this Circumscription Cross type was found at 16–22 Coppergate, at the same tenement as the earlier die of the Sword St Peter type. A trial-piece for a die of the same type, but from the mint of Chester, was also found at 16–22 Coppergate, along with a fragmentary trial-piece for a coin of Athelstan's short-lived Building type, which was probably minted immediately after his conquest of Northumbria (Pirie *et al.* 1986, 34–5; for the Building type, see pp. 119–20). This suggests that Anglo-Saxon minting in the name of Athelstan effectively supplanted Anglo-Scandinavian minting in York following his conquest, and there is no other evidence to suggest the continued minting of anything other than official issues in York in this period. A single blundered imitation of Athelstan's Building type was included in the Vale of York hoard (Williams 2011d, 147, 150), and this must post-date the introduction of that type, and therefore Athelstan's conquest of Northumbria, but there is nothing to indicate where this coin was minted. There is also nothing in the finds evidence from York to suggest that the pattern of the regulated and exclusive use of coinage established there in the previous phase did not continue, although as mentioned this now reflected a wider national coinage across Athelstan's kingdom rather than being limited to locally minted coins. This is consistent with the evidence for the legal exclusion of imported coins found in Athelstan's Grately Code, which is the earliest surviving Anglo-Saxon law code to include sections regulating the minting and circulation of coinage (Blackburn 1996; Screen 2007).

Although both minting and currency circulation may well have been effectively regulated within York under Athelstan, it appears that such regulation continued to be problematic in rural areas, at least initially. The Vale of York hoard, deposited in late 927–8, continues to reflect a mixed bullion economy. The same is true of one of the parcels in the 'Near York' hoard, although the other appears to represent Athelstan's regulated currency. It is unclear whether this discrepancy represents a chronological development between the deposition of the two parcels, with the second parcel representing the extension of effective regulation of currency beyond York and its immediate hinterland between the deposition of the two parcels, or whether one parcel had been compiled specifically for use within the more controlled economy of York while the other reflected the continued use of bullion in the part of rural Yorkshire where the hoard was buried (see pp. 110–11). A few typologically late single finds of bullion may indicate continued bullion exchange in rural Yorkshire in this period (Kershaw, this volume, pp. 126–7), while single finds of coins are too few to provide an argument for extensive penetration of coin use into rural areas.

The final phase of Anglo-Scandinavian currency is one of the richest, but also one of the most confused. Following the death of Athelstan in 939, Northumbrian independence was reasserted under a series of rulers of Scandinavian descent, mostly (although probably not all) members of the Uí Ímair dynasty who continued to rule Dublin. Some of these rulers at least temporarily accepted the overlordship of Athelstan's successors Edmund (939–46) and Eadred (946–55), and there were also brief periods in which all Scandinavian rulers were expelled, but it was not until the death of Eirik Haraldsson (usually identified with the Norwegian Eirik Bloodaxe) in 954 that lasting English rule was firmly re-established, and Anglo-Scandinavian influence brought to an end. With at least seven rulers with enough authority in Northumbria during these fifteen years to have coins minted in their names, the period was one of repeated and rapid political change. Accounts of this period in the different manuscripts of the *Anglo-Saxon Chronicle* are incomplete and contradictory, and there are further clashes with contemporary Irish sources and with sources from both England and Scandinavia which, although certainly complied later in the current form, probably derive in part (but to an unknown extent) from earlier material. As a result there is no scholarly consensus on either an absolute or even a relative chronology for which kings reigned when (Sawyer 1995; Woolf 1998; Downham 2003; Rollason 2004, 310; Williams 2010, 80–103).

Despite (or perhaps because of) the obvious political uncertainty of the period, minting was extensive, with several moneyers issuing coins simultaneously in York, with most of the recorded York moneyers issuing coins in the name of two or more rulers without apparent difficulties as a result of regime change. The coinage itself also shows considerable variety, with York coins of distinctive 'local' style for the five rulers of Scandinavian descent, but also official issues of Edmund and Eadred, and issues of Anglo-Saxon type, but in the names of some of the Scandinavian rulers. It is uncertain to what extent the last group may reflect periods in which the rulers concerned were effectively sub-kings, accepting the overlordship of the West Saxon dynasty, or whether they are simply imitating contemporary Anglo-Saxon designs. Although a received chronology for this coinage can be found in much of the numismatic literature (Dolley 1958; Blunt *et al.* 1989, 211–34; North 1994, 113–16; Blackburn 2004, 336–8), this largely fails to take account of the recent debates on the broader historical chronology, and is in need of revision (Williams 2014c, 36).

This confusion in part results from the lack of substantial hoards of the period, which might demonstrate by association the relative chronology of different coin types (*ibid.*, 36). The only official 'hoard' of the period, containing two coins of Athelstan and two attributed to Anlaf (Olaf) Guthfrithsson, found together at 16–22 Coppergate may represent chance loss as easily as conscious hoarding, and in any case is too small a group to suggest very meaningful conclusions (see p. 111). Given the evidence for continued conflict throughout this period, and given the concentration of hoards during the much shorter period of political uncertainty in the mid-920s, it is perhaps surprising that there are as yet no major hoards from Yorkshire in this period. This absence of large hoards probably means that the overall scale of the coinage is vastly under-represented in the archaeological record compared with earlier phases of coinage which are better represented in the hoards. Northumbrian coins of the period minted in York are known only in small numbers from Viking hoards elsewhere, and as single finds. Nevertheless, the diversity within the current corpus points to minting on a large scale, as does the expansion in the number of moneyers, and die estimates suggest a fairly substantial coinage in total, especially in the Raven type attributed to Anlaf (Olaf) Guthfrithsson and the Triquetra type attributed to Anlaf (Olaf) Sihtricsson (Blunt *et al.* 1989, 229–34; Blackburn 2004, 343–4). At the same time, the fact that minting appears to have continued largely undisturbed through all the political turmoil of the period, and that there were no apparent consequences for the moneyers for the flexibility of their loyalties, may suggest that coin use in York had become so widespread by this time that while new rulers wished to take advantage of coinage as a medium to promote their identities as rulers (reflecting a wider association between minting and a particular model of Romanised Christian kingship: Williams 2007), they saw no advantage in disturbing the status quo of minting. As in earlier phases, there is no evidence to suggest a continued or revived bullion economy in York in this period, and there is therefore no reason to doubt that a coin-based economy remained dominant if not exclusive throughout this period. It is true that most of the Scandinavian rulers in York at this time had links with Dublin, and that the Vikings in Ireland at this point continued to use a bullion economy, albeit one that saw a steady increase in the use of imported coin, especially in Dublin from the 930s onwards (Woods 2014). The mid-10th century also saw the use of standardised weights in Dublin, suggesting the regulated use of bullion (Wallace 1987; 2013). The only authority in Dublin likely to have been capable of such regulation was the king. It could therefore be argued that Hiberno-Scandinavian influence might have resulted in a resurgence of a bullion economy in Northumbria, or at least in the breakdown of the regulated circulation of locally minted coinage. However, the fact that Anlaf Sihtricsson (d. 980) appears to have minted extensively during his brief periods of authority in Northumbria, but not at all during his much longer reign in Dublin, suggests that these rulers were capable of adapting to, and exploiting, the prevailing economy in either region rather than necessarily being in a position to impose a different model.

There are ten single finds of coins of this phase recorded from Yorkshire: three of the 'Raven' type attributed to Anlaf Guthfrithsson (939–41); three of the Triquetra type attributed to Anlaf Sihtricsson (*c.* 941–44/45); one of the Triquetra type in the name of Regnald Guthfrithsson (943–43/45); one of the Triquetra type in the name of Sihtric, who is not mentioned in contemporary sources but who can probably be identified as Sihtric Guthfrithsson on the basis of a later reference by Adam of Bremen (Williams 2014c, 36); one of the Anglo-Saxon king Eadred, who ruled Northumbria intermittently in the late 940s and early 950s as well as after the permanent conquest of 954; and one of the first issue of Eirik Bloodaxe, possibly dating from the late 940s (Blackburn 2004, nos 35–40; EMC 2004.0181; EMC 2007.0258; EMC 2008.0370; EMC 2014.0032). This is not a great number over a total period of around fifteen years, but it does indicate the circulation of coinage throughout the period. None of the coins has any recorded secondary treatment suggesting testing for silver content, so it is reasonable to assume that they circulated as coins rather than bullion. What is also striking about the finds from this phase is how few come from York and the immediate hinterland. The coins of Sihtric and Eadred came from 16–22 Coppergate (Pirie *et al.* 1986, nos 56–7), but these were the only ones deposited in York itself, while one of the coins of Anlaf Guthfrithsson is attributed only to the 'York area'. Another penny of Anlaf Guthfrithsson was found in 'South Yorkshire', and one of the coins of Anlaf Sihtricsson at Campsall, near Doncaster, while the remainder were all found in East Yorkshire. Apart from a penny of Anlaf Guthfrithsson from Dunnington, all of the rest were found in the Beverley area, at different times. Only one of these (Regnald) has a find-spot located in a specific parish, Middleton on the Wolds, with the other three found respectively 'near Beverley', west of Beverley (Anlaf Sihtricsson), and in the 'Yorkshire Wolds, between Malton and Beverley' (Eirik Bloodaxe). Given the lack of more specific find-spots, there is a remote possibility that some of these may be from the same site, indicating either a productive site or a dispersed hoard, but there is no particular evidence to suggest that this was the case. The balance of evidence seems to suggest fairly widespread circulation of coins minted in York elsewhere in Yorkshire, although as in other phases there is currently little evidence for coin use in the north of the county.

The absence of hoards from rural areas in this phase means that there is no coin-dated evidence for or against the continued use of bullion in rural Yorkshire. The evidence of a recent mixed hoard from the Furness area in Cumbria from the late 950s demonstrates that there was a continued use of bullion in areas beyond the direct authority of the expanding English kingdom (Boughton *et al.* 2012). Given the transient authority of the various rulers of Northumbria in the 940s and early 950s, it is hard to imagine that any of them were in a position to expand royal authority over currency circulation in rural areas, so it seems likely, if unproven, that bullion continued to circulate beyond York's immediate hinterland. However, a couple of single finds of hack-silver, namely a piece of 'ring-money' from North Yorkshire and a neck-ring fragment from 'near Stamford Bridge', seem likely to point to continued bullion use into this phase or even slightly beyond, but their deposition cannot be precisely dated (see Kershaw, this volume, pp. 126–7). As noted by Jane Kershaw, apart from the broadly dated Volga Bulgar dirhams already discussed, a single dirham fragment from Cottam, minted in Tashkent in 928–29, also seems unlikely to have reached Yorkshire before the late 930s or 940s, although she is rightly wary of reading too much into a single fragment (pp. 118–19).

What such finds do demonstrate, however, is that whatever the extent of regulation of currency may have been in York, material reflecting the continued use of bullion in the wider Viking world was still entering Yorkshire in the 10th century, whether from the Irish Sea or through trading contacts directly across the North Sea. While this particular fragment is somewhat later than any of the other recorded datable single finds of dirhams (see pp. 117–19) and also later than any of the dated fragments in the hoards attributed to the 920s, it is possible that some of the undated fragments are later than the current attributions of the hoards would suggest. For example, the latest possible date for a dirham in the Goldsborough hoard would push that into this final phase rather than its current date in the mid-920s, although the earlier deposition date remains much more likely (Williams 2011e; 2013c, 465–6). The exact date of the cessation of bullion use in rural Yorkshire thus remains unclear. It seems likely, on the basis of the Cottam dirham fragment and the two late hack-silver fragments, that it extended into this phase, and possibly even slightly beyond, and the circumstantial evidence for weak royal authority in the kingdom of Northumbria throughout this phase would also be difficult to reconcile with the extension of royal regulation of currency into rural areas at this time. However, while the latest single finds could in theory post-date the end of Anglo-Scandinavian rule in 954, there is no compelling evidence to suggest that this was the case.

Conclusion

The combination of site finds, hoards and single finds reveals that there was no single silver economy in Anglo-Scandinavian Yorkshire, nor even the 'dual economy' of some earlier literature, but rather a series of different exchange systems, interacting with each other, and evolving considerably over the period of less than a century that Yorkshire, within the larger kingdom of Northumbria, was under Viking rule. While it has not been possible to explore in any detail the social and political background to those developments, it is fair to say that they took place in the context of political and religious change, and of developments in the nature and extent of royal authority in Northumbria and elsewhere, rather than simply as a response to economic pressure or the assimilation of the Scandinavian settlers into the existing Anglian population, although these are also likely to be factors. Even on the level of material culture alone, the character of the different exchange systems and the precise chronology of developments across the period remain often ambiguous and imperfectly understood. However, such things are clearer than they were, or at least their greater complexity can now be recognised, as a result of a remarkable expansion in the available evidence in recent years. Since this expansion currently shows no sign of slowing down, it seems likely that some of the questions left open here will be resolved wholly or in part over the next few years.

Numismatically, three phases within the overall study period have major issues to be resolved. The typology and attribution of the imitative phase of coinage of the 880s and 890s, and the chronology of the coinage minted in York in the period of 939–54 are questions which have been considered before, but which it has been clear for some time it is important to readdress. However, while the possibility that pre-Viking Northumbrian stycas may have continued in use into the period of Viking settlement has been raised before, the discoveries at ARSNY and other recent sites such as Torksey and Cottam mean that this has become a much more fertile area for future research than previously. If stycas were used (and perhaps even minted) by the Vikings, as the evidence increasingly suggests, this has implications firstly for the process of the Vikings' familiarisation with coinage before the introduction of distinctive regal coinage in Anglo-Scandinavian Northumbria, secondly for the process of assimilation with the existing Anglian population during the early settlement period, and thirdly for the value within exchange and production of copper alloy in addition to the established importance of silver.

Archaeologically, the need to reassess the significance of copper alloy is also important, along with other metals. The potential importance of gold bullion in the late 9th century was highlighted some years ago by Mark Blackburn (2002, 95; 2007a), but the evidence of Torksey and ARSNY, together with a growing body of single finds, now leaves little doubt that gold bullion had an important role in exchange in the early settlement period, and possibly over a longer period (see also Kershaw 2019). Similarly, the idea that copper-alloy ingots in Scandinavia might relate to exchange rather than exclusively to production has also been previously discussed, but the finds at ARSNY and Torksey, combined with the wider recognition in Scandinavia that the mid–late 9th century was an important time in the development of exchange systems in Scandinavia, raise important questions about how copper alloys, and particularly brass, might feature in the developing bullion economies of the period of Viking settlement in England (see pp. 44–5). Within the papers in this volume, this remains more question than answer, but it is an important potential direction for future research.

At the same time, the combination of decorated Insular weights and plain lead weights now found in large quantities at ARSNY, Torksey and Woodstown, as well as in the Blackwater assemblage and increasing numbers of single finds, raises the possibility both that western influence may have been important in the development of bullion economies in the Viking world in addition to the eastern influence that has been a dominant feature of research on the subject in Scandinavia in recent decades, and which is also represented by finds of both cubo-octahedral and oblate-spheroid weights from Yorkshire. In contrast to the eastern-style weights, the lead weights also raise wider issues about the possible role of lead in exchange in addition to the other metals discussed.

All of these points have implications for the development of exchange systems across the Viking world, not just in Yorkshire, and emphasise the significance of ARSNY and comparable sites in that wider context. The study of single finds has added a significant new dimension to artefact studies, providing as it does an important and growing body of evidence for the circulation and loss of different types of objects beyond the limited number of excavated sites. Single finds probably in most cases also represent casual loss, without the element of deliberate selection and compilation potentially involved in the hoards. The fact that most of the single finds come from rural sites is also important in challenging any assumption that monetary or quasi-monetary exchange systems were largely confined to towns and other trading centres. Jane Kershaw's earlier work on ornaments (Kershaw 2013) demonstrates how single finds can offer a contrasting picture to place-names in measuring the extent of Scandinavian settlement in England. In the case of bullion finds in Yorkshire explored in this volume, there is less immediate contrast, but the larger study of single finds of bullion of which Kershaw's analysis here of the Yorkshire finds forms a part, has valuable potential for our understanding of bullion economies across Scandinavian England. Despite this, Kershaw's chapter highlights the limitation of non-numismatic single finds in providing a clear chronological framework for developments in the character of metal-based exchange, since much of the hack-silver can only be dated quite broadly, and the ingots even more so. Site finds and hoards remain vital as reference points for the interpretation of the single finds.

Apart from the range of material relating to different forms of exchange found at ARSNY, the site is of great significance for our understanding of the chronology of exchange in Viking Yorkshire and the rest of the north of England. Prior to the discovery of ARSNY, there was no firmly datable site in Yorkshire providing significant evidence for the character of exchange at the time of the Viking settlement rather than a generation or more afterwards. Cottam also provides important evidence, but is less clear, and the ability to draw comparisons with both ARSNY and Torksey should mean that it will be possible to analyse the monetary/bullion material from Cottam in more detail in the future. The scarcity of hoards from Yorkshire from the beginning of the settlement period means that ARSNY is even more important in this context. The fact that ARSNY is neither an urban nor a wholly rural site also raises important questions about the relationships that developed between different forms of exchange and different types of site in the Viking Age.

The settlement phase now emerges as one of considerable economic complexity, with different media for exchange, and a range of competing influences contributing to the shape of Viking exchange systems in Yorkshire and beyond. By comparing the evidence of ARSNY with finds from York, and with the wider distribution of hoards and single finds, it is possible to trace the evolution of exchange across the whole of the period up to the end of Viking rule in Northumbria. Here the most important element is the evidence that developments took place at different speeds within York itself and more widely in rural Yorkshire and beyond. The focus within the secondary literature on the supposed 'kingdom of York' means that the evidence from York itself has by implication been seen as much more representative than it now appears to be, and it is only towards the very end of the period studied here that use of coins valued by tale rather than by weight seems to have largely supplanted the use of bullion in rural areas, whereas the same change seems to have taken place within a generation or so of the Viking settlement within York itself.

Why such a distinction existed between practice in York and the rest of Yorkshire is still not entirely certain. It could be argued that as the only major town in Northumbria, the urban character of York created different economic pressures from those found in other areas. However, York's role as a major trading centre meant that it had direct contact with other areas in the Viking world which maintained a bullion economy throughout the first half of the 10th century. This remained the case in Ireland, Scotland and most of Scandinavia, while locally issued coinage would not obviously have benefited economic contact with the regulated coin economy of southern England, since Northumbrian coinage would presumably have been excluded from southern England, along with other currency. Anglo-Saxon coins of this period are normally only found in Northumbria in mixed hoards (except during the periods when Northumbria was under the rule of kings of the West Saxon dynasty), suggesting that they only circulated as bullion, and did not circulate as coin.

However, this does not mean that York's urban status was not a factor. The introduction of minting seems to be linked more with the ideology of kingship than with economic factors, at least past the purely imitative phase (see above p. 131; see also Williams 2007 for this point in a wider context), but the fact that both imported coin and bullion seem largely to have been excluded from circulation in York from very early in the 10th century points to active control of the currency rather than symbolism alone. This perhaps suggests that as in other areas where monetary exclusion was practised, there may have been premiums to pay in order to acquire legal currency (see p. 107), which would in turn suggest a considerable degree of royal authority within York itself, and may have been linked with other dues such as tolls on import and/or export, and market tolls. Anglo-Saxon *burhs* in the 10th century seem to have functioned as centres of royal authority, and were also used in the generation of royal revenue through the regulation of trade and through their role in the judicial system (Williams 2013b), and it is possible that York shared more of the administrative and fiscal character of an Anglo-Saxon *burh* before its conquest by Athelstan than can be discerned from the minimal historical record. However, if regulated circulation of coinage within York was a sign of strong royal power, the apparent absence of such control in rural areas is probably also an indication of the limits of royal power, up to and including the period immediately following Athelstan's conquest. The subsequent shift to a broader pattern of rural coin circulation and the disappearance of bullion may well then reflect Anglo-Saxon influence, despite the temporary (and intermittent) re-emergence of Northumbrian independence in the period 939–54.

The conclusions above are speculative, and while more work comparing the material evidence for exchange in Yorkshire pre-954 with the evidence for royal authority and income generation in the late 10th century could be informative, the lack of historical evidence for this area in the period 865–954 means that it is unlikely that there will ever be a sufficiently full chronological framework to permit definitive explanations for monetary developments within that period. Nevertheless, clearer patterns seem to be emerging from the different categories of material evidence, and as the body of evidence continues to grow, these patterns are likely to become clearer still.

To conclude, while the finer points of the chronology discussed above await futher clarification, the combination of site finds, hoards and stray finds establishes some clear trends across the period from the initial Viking conquest of Northumbria by the *micel here* in the 860s, through the subsequent period of settlement a decade later and the later attempts by the sons of Edward the Elder to assimilate Northumbria into the emerging English kingdom. These include the continued use (whether as coins or bullion) of the pre-Viking copper alloy styca coinage, at least into the intial period of settlement, if not necessarily for a long period beyond. This was combined by the establishment of a bullion economy borrowed from the Vikings' Scandinavian homelands, although this now appears to have been a relatively recent development rather than traditional Scandinavian custom. This might explain a degree of experimentation, with use of base metals as bullion, as well as silver (represented by hack-silver, ingots and imported coins) and gold. As with the use of stycas, there is little evidence to suggest that base-metal bullion continued beyond the settlement phase, but single finds suggest that the use of precious-metal bullion in all its various forms had not been completely eradicated from rural areas across Yorkshire by the end of the independent Anglo-Scandinavian kingdom of Northumbria in 954, although it does appear to have become rarer. This was probably in response to another trend, which was the increasingly regulated use of locally minted coinage. While the earliest phases of imitative coinage cannot be attributed with certainty, and did little or nothing to limt the circulation of other forms of currency, York had emerged by the end of the 9th century as the centre of minting within the kingdom, and thereafter the authorities in York seem to have fairly quickly developed sufficient control over exchange within the city to exclude both imported coin and other forms of bullion from circulation within York itself, while locally minted coins increasingly came to dominate the surrounding area. Both the control within York and the wider domination of the York mint seem to have continued with the assimilation of York into the national network of mints established by Athelstan and his successors, even if these 'English' kings were apparently less successful in rural Yorkshire than in some other areas at imposing an exclusive use of officially minted coin at the expense of all other forms of precious-metal currency.

The position of ARSNY at the very beginning of the settlement period means that it plays a dominant role in the interpretation of the continued use of stycas, and of the development of base-metal bullion economies. It also provides important evidence for the establishment of the characteristic 'Viking' precious metal bullion economy which was to last in rural Yorkshire at least until 954, and in those areas of Scandinavian settlement in Britain and Ireland less subject to the control of the expanding English kingdom, for much longer. By contrast, the early date and short duration of the main period of activity at ARSNY means that it predated both the development of the distinctive Anglo-Scandinavian coinage of Northumbria and the re-emergence of York as the centre of both economy and royal authority in the region. York had, of course, been a major centre in Roman times, and while evidence for the character of Anglian York is in many ways more enigmatic than for either the Roman or Anglo-Scandinavian periods, it is likely that it had an important role as a political centre in the pre-Viking period, as well as an ecclesiastical centre and mint. It could therefore be argued that it was only natural that it should develop and expand this role under Viking rule. However, as discussed above (pp. 40, 101; see also Williams 2013a; 2015), there was very limited urbanisation in the Scandinavian homelands, and neither towns nor coinage became universal across all areas of Scandinavian settlement in the Viking Age. With a better understanding of the character of camps such as ARSNY, Torksey and Woodstown, it seems likely that the camp phenomenon played an important part in the development of towns in Anglo-Scandinavian England and in Ireland. ARSNY may only directly demonstrate the earliest phase of the exchange systems discussed in this and the preceding chapters, and there is certainly no evidence that ARSNY or any other Viking camp had the same degree of centralised authority and economic control as emerged in York in the early 10th century. Nevertheless, as the likely focus for the *micel here* in Yorkshire immediately before their settlement of the kingdom of Northumbria, and given the scale of the site and what that implies logistically for interaction with the surrounding area (see pp. 91, 102), ARSNY can also be seen to prefigure York not only as a centre for production and exchange, but as a focus for authority and control over the surrounding hinterland. Thus, while the development of local minting and currency control in and around York has no direct precedent in the ARSNY finds assemblage, it seems reasonable to suggest that ARSNY was an important foundation on which York's later success was built.

Bibliography

Primary

AF: *The Annals of Fulda*, trans. T. Reuter (Manchester and New York: Manchester University Press 1992).

ASB: *The Annals of St Bertin*, trans. J.L. Nelson (Manchester and New York: Manchester University Press 1991).

ASC: *The Anglo-Saxon Chronicle*, ed. and trans. M. Swanton (London: J.M. Dent 1996).

EHD: *English Historical Documents. I. c. 500–1042*, ed. and trans. D. Whitelock (London: Eyre and Spottiswoode 1955).

AG: Alfred the Great. Asser's Life of King Alfred and other contemporary sources, ed. and trans. S.D. Keynes, and M. Lapidge (Harmondsworth: Penguin 1983).

Secondary

Abels, R.P. 1988. *Lordship and Military Obligation in Anglo-Saxon England* (London: British Museum Publications).

Abels, R.P. 1992. 'King Alfred's peace-making strategies with the Vikings', *Haskins Society Journal* 3, 23–34.

Abels, R.P. 1997. 'English logistics and military administration 871–1066: the impact of the Viking wars', in A. Nørgård Jørgensen and B. Clausen (eds), *Military Aspects of Scandinavian Society, AD 1–1300* (Copenhagen: National Museum of Denmark), 257–65.

Abels, R.P. 2003. 'Alfred the Great, the *micel hæden here* and the Viking threat', in T. Reuter (ed.) 2003, 265–79.

Abramson, T. 2011. *Studies in Early Medieval Coinage* II, *New Perspectives* (Woodbridge: Boydell & Brewer).

Adamsen, C., Lund Hansen, U., Nielsen, F.O. and Watt, M. 2009. *Sorte Muld. Wealth, Power and Religion at an Iron Age Central settlement on Bornholm* (Rønne: Bornholms Museum).

Ager, B. 2011. 'A preliminary note on the artefacts from the Vale of York Viking Hoard', in Abramson 2011, 123–36.

Ager, B. and Williams, G. 2011a. 'The Vale of York Viking Hoard: Preliminary Catalogue', in Abramson 2011, 137–47.

Ager, B. and Williams, G. 2011b. Potential find of Treasure: Hoard of Viking silver coins and artefacts from the Morecambe Bay area, Lancashire. Unpublished report for HM Coroner.

Albrethsen, S.E. 1997. 'Logistical problems in Iron Age warfare', in Nørgård Jørgensen and Clausen (eds) 1997, 210–19.

Alexander, J.J.G. 1978. *Insular Manuscripts 6th to the 9th century. A Survey of Manuscripts Illuminated in the British Isles* 1 (London: H. Miller Publishing).

Allen, M.R. 2012. *Mints and Moneyers in Medieval England* (Cambridge: Cambridge University Press).

Ambrosiani, B. (ed.) 2004. *Eastern Connections. Part Two: Numismatics and Metrology*, Birka Studies 6 (Stockholm: Riksantikvarieämbetet).

Ambrosiani, B. (ed.) 2008. 'Birka', in Brink and Price (eds) 2008, 94–100.

Archibald, M.M. 1990. 'Pecking and bending: the evidence of British finds, including Cuerdale', in K. Jonsson and B. Malmer (eds), *Sigtuna Papers, Proceedings of the Sigtuna Symposium on Viking-Age Coinage 1–4 June 1989*, Commentationes de nummis saeculorum IX–XI in Suecia repertis. NS 6 (Stockholm: Kungliga Vitterhetsakademien), 11–24.

Archibald, M.M. 1991. 'Coins', in Webster and Backhouse (eds) 1991, 284–9.

Archibald, M.M. 1998. 'Two ninth-century Viking weights found near Kingston, Dorset', *British Numismatic Journal* 68, 11–20.

Archibald, M.M. 2011. 'Testing', in Graham-Campbell 2011, 51–64.

Armbruster, B.R. 2002. 'Goldschmiede in Haithabu – ein Beitrag zum frühmittelalterlichen Metallhandwerk', in K. Schietzel (ed.),

Berichte über die Ausgrabungen in Haithabu 34, (Neumünster: K. Wachholtz), 85–198.

Astill, G. 2009. 'Medieval towns and urbanization', in R. Gilchrist and A. Reynolds (eds), *Reflections: 50 Years of Medieval Archaeology, 1957–2007*, Society for Medieval Archaeology Monograph 30 (London: Maney), 255–70.

Ayers, B. 2012. 'Richard Andrew Hall (1949–2011)', *Medieval Archaeology* 56, 298–300.

Baastrup, M.P. 2013. 'Irske Lodder', *Skalk* 2013 (4), 12–15.

Baker, J. 2013. 'The language of Anglo-Saxon defence', in Baker, Brookes and Reynolds (eds) 2013, 65–90.

Baker, J. and Brookes, S. 2013. *Beyond the Burghal Hidage: Anglo-Saxon Civil Defence in the Viking Age* (Leiden: Brill).

Baker, J., Brookes, S. and Reynolds, A. (eds) 2013. *Landscapes of Defence in Early Medieval Europe* (Turnhout: Brepols).

Bassett, S. 2007. 'Divide and rule? The military infrastructure of eighth- and ninth-century Mercia', *Early Medieval Europe* 15, 53–85.

Bassett, S. 2008. 'The middle and late Anglo-Saxon defences of western Mercian towns', in S. Crawford and H. Hamerow (eds), *Anglo-Saxon Studies in Archaeology and History* 15 (Oxford: University of Oxford), 180–239.

Batey, C. 1988. 'A Viking-Age bell from Freswick Links, Caithness', *Medieval Archaeology* 32, 213–16.

Bayley, J. 1992. *Non-Ferrous Metalworking from Coppergate*, The Archaeology of York, The Small Finds 17/7 (York: Council for British Archaeology for the York Archaeological Trust).

Bayley, J., Cotton, J., Rehren, T. and Pernicka, E. 2014. 'A Saxon brass bar ingot cache from Kingsway, London', in J. Cotton, J. Hall, J. Keily, R. Sherris and R. Stephenson (eds), *'Hidden Histories and Records of Antiquity': Essays on Saxon and Medieval London for John Clark, Curator Emeritus, Museum of London*, LAMAS Special Paper 17 (London: London and Middlesex Archaeological Society), 121–8.

Besly, E. 2006. 'Few and far between: mints and coins in Wales to the middle of the thirteenth century', in B.J. Cook and G. Williams (eds), *Coinage and History in the North Sea World, c. 500–1250: Essays in Honour of Marion Archibald* (Leiden and Boston: Brill), 701–19.

Bestemann, J. 2004. 'Two Viking hoards from the former island of Wieringen (The Netherlands): Viking relations with Frisia in an archaeological perspective', in J. Hines, A. Lane and M. Redknap (eds), *Land, Sea and Home: Settlement in the Viking Period*, Society for Medieval Archaeology Monograph 20 (Leeds: Maney), 93–108.

Bestemann, J. 2009. 'Westerklief II, a second Viking silver hoard from the former island of Wieringen; with a contribution by Gert Rispling and Simon Coupland', *Jaarboek voor Munt- en Penningkunde* 93–94 (2006–07), 5–80.

Biddle, M. 1976. 'Towns', in D.M. Wilson (ed.), *The Archaeology of Anglo-Saxon England* (Cambridge: Cambridge University Press), 99–150.

Biddle, M. (ed.) 1990. *Object and Economy in Medieval Winchester*, Winchester Studies 7 i and ii (Oxford: Clarendon).

Biddle, M. and Kjølbye-Biddle, B. 1992. 'Repton and the Vikings', *Antiquity* 66, 36–51.

Biddle, M. and Kjølbye-Biddle, B. 2001. 'Repton and the "great heathen army", 873–4', in Graham-Campbell *et al.* (eds) 2001, 45–96.

Biddle, M. and Smith, D. 1990. 'The querns', in Biddle (ed.) 1990, ii, 881–90.

Biddle, M., Blunt, C.E., Kjølbye-Biddle, B., Metcalf, D.M. and Pagan, H.E. 1986a. 'Coins of the Anglo-Saxon period from Repton, Derbyshire: II', *British Numismatic Journal* 56, 16–32.

Biddle, M., Kjølbye-Biddle, B., Northover, J.P. and Pagan, H. 1986b. 'Coins of the Anglo-Saxon period from Repton, Derbyshire', in M. Blackburn (ed.), *Anglo-Saxon Monetary History* (Leicester: Leicester University Press), 111–32.

Bigsby, R. 1854. *Historical and topographical description of Repton* (London).

Bill, J. 2014. 'Nails', in Russell and Hurley with Eogan (eds) 2014, 141–55.

Bill, J. and Løchsen Rødsrud, C. 2017. 'Heimdalsjordet: Trade production and communication', in A.Z. Tsigaridas Glørstad and Kl. Loftsgarden (eds), *Viking-Age Transformations: Trade, Craft and Resources in Western Scandinavia* (London: Routledge), 212–31.

Blackburn, M.A.S. (ed.) 1986. *Anglo-Saxon Monetary History* (Leicester: Leicester University Press).

Blackburn, M.A.S. 1989. 'The Ashdon (Essex) hoard and the currency of the southern Danelaw in the late ninth century', *British Numismatic Journal* 59, 13–38.

Blackburn, M.A.S. 1996. 'Mints, burhs and the Grately code, cap. 14.2', in D. Hill and A.R. Rumble (eds), *The Defence of Wessex, The Burghal Hidage and Anglo-Saxon Fortifications* (Manchester: Manchester University Press), 160–75.

Blackburn, M.A.S. 2001. 'Expansion and control: aspects of Anglo-Scandinavian minting south of the Humber', in Graham-Campbell *et al.* (eds) 2001, 125–55.

Blackburn, M.A.S. 2002. 'Finds from the Anglo-Scandinavian site of Torksey, Lincolnshire', in B. Paszkiewicz (ed.), *Moneta Mediævalis: Studia numizmatycne I historycne ofiaowane Profesorowi Stanisławowi Sochodolskiemu w 65. rocznięe urodzin* (Warsaw: Dig), 89–101.

Blackburn, M.A.S. 2003. 'Alfred's coinage reforms in context', in Reuter (ed.) 2003, 199–218.

Blackburn, M.A.S. 2004. 'The Coinage of Scandinavian York', in Hall *et al.* 2004, 325–49.

Blackburn, M.A.S. 2005. 'Presidential Address 2004. Currency under the Vikings. Part 1: Guthrum and the earliest Danelaw coinages', *British Numismatic Journal* 75, 18–43.

Blackburn, M.A.S. 2006. 'Presidential Address 2005. Currency under the Vikings. Part 2: the two Scandinavian kingdoms of the Danelaw, c. 895–954', *British Numismatic Journal* 76, 204–26.

Blackburn, M.A.S. 2007a. 'Gold in England during the "Age of Silver" (eighth to eleventh centuries)', in Graham-Campbell and Williams (eds) 2007, 55–98.

Blackburn, M.A.S. 2007b. 'Presidential Address 2006. Currency under the Vikings. Part 3: Ireland, Wales, Isle of Man and Scotland during the ninth and tenth centuries', *British Numismatic Journal* 77, 119–49.

Blackburn, M.A.S. 2007c. 'The Coin-finds', in Skre (ed.) 2007b, 29–74.

Blackburn, M.A.S. 2008. 'Presidential Address 2007. Currency under the Vikings. Part 4: the Dublin Coinage, c. 995–1050', *British Numismatic Journal* 78, 111–37.

Blackburn, M.A.S. 2009. 'Presidential Address 2008. Currency under the Vikings. Part 5: The Scandinavian achievement and legacy', *British Numismatic Journal* 79, 43–71.

Blackburn, M.A.S. 2011. 'The Viking winter camp at Torksey, 872–3', in M.A.S. Blackburn, *Viking Coinage and Currency in the British Isles. British Numismatic Society Special Publications* 7 (London: Spink/ British Numismatic Society), 221–64.

Blackburn, M.A.S. and Bonser, M.J. 1990. 'A Viking-age silver ingot from near Easingwold, Yorks', *Medieval Archaeology* 34, 149–50.

Blackburn, M.A.S. and Keynes, S.D. 1998. 'A corpus of the *Cross-and-Lozenge* and related coinages of Alfred, Ceolwulf II and Archbishop Æthelred', in M.A.S. Blackburn and D.N. Dumville (eds), *Kings, Currency and Alliances: History and Coinage of Southern England* (Woodbridge: Boydell), 125–50.

Blackburn, M.A.S. and Pagan, H.E. n.d. 'Checklist of Coin Hoards from the British Isles, c. 450–1180', revised online edition, http://www.fitzmuseum.cam.ac.uk/dept/coins/projects/hoards/index.list.html (accessed 6 June 2014).

Blackmore, L. 2003. 'The non-ferrous metalwork', in G. Malcolm, D. Bowsher, R. Cowie, *Middle Saxon London. Excavations at the Royal Opera House 1989–99*, MoLAS Monograph 15 (London: Museum of London), 264–71.

Blair, J. 2005. *The Church in Anglo-Saxon Society* (Oxford: Oxford University Press).

Blunt, C.E. 1974. 'The coinage of Athelstan, King of England 924–39', *British Numismatic Journal* 42, 35–158.

Blunt, C.E. 1985. 'Northumbrian coins in the name of Alwaldus', *British Numismatic Journal* 55, 192–4.

Blunt, C.E. and Dolley, R.H.M. 1960. 'Coins at Nostell Priory, Yorkshire', *British Numismatic Journal* 30, 360–1.

Blunt, C.E. and Stewart, B.H.I.H. 1983. 'The coinage of Regnald I of York and the Bossall Hoard', *Numismatic Chronicle* 143, 146–63.

Blunt, C.E., Stewart, B.H.I.H. and Lyon, C.S.S. 1989. *Coinage in Tenth Century England: From Edward the Elder to Edgar's Reform* (Oxford: British Academy/Oxford University Press).

Bogucki, M. 2007. 'Coin finds in the Viking age emporium at Janów Pomorski (Truso) and the *Prussian phenomenon*', in S. Sucholdoslki and M. Bogucki (eds), *Monetary Circulation in Antiquity, the Middle Ages and Modern Times. Time, Range, Intensity* (Warsaw: Avalon), 79–106.

Bogucki, M. 2009. 'Two Northumbrian stycas of Eanred and Æthelred II from early medieval Truso in Poland', *British Numismatic Journal* 79, 34–42.

Bogucki, M. 2010. 'Viking Age emporia around the Baltic Sea – a cul-de-sac of the European urbanization?', in A. Buko and M. McCarthy (eds), *Making a Medieval Town: Patterns of Early Medieval Urbanization* (Warsaw: Polish Academy of Sciences/University of Warsaw), 150–65.

Bornholdt Collins, K. 2010. 'The Dunmore Cave [2] hoard and the role of coins in the tenth-century Hiberno-Scandinavian economy', in Sheehan and Ó Corráin (eds) 2010, 19–46.

Boughton, D., Williams, G. and Ager, B. 2012. 'Buried wealth of the Norse of the North West', *Current Archaeology* 264, 26–31.

Bourke, C. 1980. 'Early Irish hand-bells', *Journal of the Royal Society of Antiquaries of Ireland* 110, 52–66.

Bourke, C. 2010. 'Antiquities from the River Blackwater IV, Early Medieval non-ferrous metalwork', *Ulster Journal of Archaeology*, 3rd Series, 69, 24–133.

Bradley, J. 1988. 'The interpretation of Scandinavian settlement in Ireland', in J. Bradley (ed.), *Settlement and Society in Medieval Ireland. Studies Presented to F X Martin OSA* (Kilkenny: Boethius), 49–78.

Bradley, J. 2009. 'Some reflections on the problem of Scandinavian settlement in the hinterland of Dublin in the ninth century', in J. Bradley, A.J. Fletcher and A. Simms (eds), *Dublin in the Medieval World. Studies in Honour of Howard B. Clarke* (Dublin: Four Courts Press), 39–62.

Brink, S. and Price, N. (eds) 2008. *The Viking World* (London and New York: Routledge).

Bronk Ramsey, C. 1995. 'Radiocarbon calibration and analysis of stratigraphy', *Radiocarbon* 36, 425–30.

Bronk Ramsey, C. 1998. 'Probability and dating', *Radiocarbon* 40, 461–74.

Bronk Ramsey, C. 2001. 'Development of the radiocarbon calibration program', *Radiocarbon* 43, 355–63.

Bronk Ramsey, C. 2009. 'Bayesian analysis of radiocarbon dates', *Radiocarbon* 51 (1), 337–60.

Brooke, G.C. 1929–30. 'Quando moneta vertebatur: the change of coin types in the eleventh century; its bearing on mules and overstrikes', *British Numismatic Journal* 20, 105–16.

Brooks, N.P. 1979. 'Ninth-century England: the crucible of defeat', *Transactions of the Royal Historical Society*, 5th Series, 29, 1–20.

Brooks, N.P. 1996. 'The administrative background to the Burghal Hidage', in D. Hill and A.R. Rumble (eds), *The Defence of Wessex: The Burghal Hidage and Anglo-Saxon Fortifications* (Manchester: Manchester University Press), 128–50.

Brooks, N.P. and Graham-Campbell, J. 2000. 'Reflections on the Viking-Age silver hoard from Croydon, Surrey', in N.P. Brooks, *Communities and Warfare 700–1400* (London: Hambledon Continuum), 69–92.

Brown, H. 2006. Torksey, Lincolnshire, in the Anglo-Scandinavian Period. Unpublished MA dissertation, University of York.

Brøgger, A.W. 1921. *Ertog og Øre; den gamle norske vegt* (Kristiania: Dybwad).

Buck, C.E., Cavanagh, W.G. and Litton, C.D. 1996. *Bayesian Approach to Interpreting Archaeological Data* (Chichester).

Budd, P., Millard, A., Chenery, C., Lucy, S. and Roberts, C. 2004. 'Investigating population movement by stable isotope analysis: a report from Britain', *Antiquity* 78, 127–41.

Camden, W. (translated by R. Gough) 1789. *Britannia* (London: T. Payne and Son).

Cardon, T., Moesgaard, J.C., Prot, R. and Schiesser, P. 2008. 'Le premier trésor monétaire de type viking en France', *Revue Numismatique* 164, 21–40.

Carey, A. 2014. 'Stone', in Russell and Hurley with Eogan (eds) 2014, 299–320.

Catt, J.A. 1991. 'The Quaternary history and glacial deposits of East Yorkshire', in J. Ehlers, P.L. Gibbard and J. Rose (eds), *Glacial Deposits of Britain and Ireland* (Rotterdam: Balkema), 185–91.

Chester, Rev G.J. 1856. 'An account of a recent discovery at York', *Archaeological Journal* 13, 283.

Chisholm, B.S., Nelson, D.E. and Schwarcz, H.P. 1982. 'Stable carbon isotope ratios as a measure of marine versus terrestrial protein in ancient diets', *Science* 216, 1131–2.

Clarke, H. and Ambrosiani, B. 1991. *Towns in the Viking Age* (New York: St Martin's Press).

Clarke, H.B. 1998. 'Proto-towns and towns in Ireland and Britain in the ninth and tenth centuries', in Clarke *et al.* (eds) 1998, 331–80.

Clarke, H.B. and Johnson, R. (eds) 2015. *The Vikings in Ireland and Beyond: Before and After the Battle of Clontarf* (Dublin: Four Courts Press).

Clarke, H.B., Ní Mhaonaigh, M. and Ó Floinn, R. (eds) 1998. *Ireland and Scandinavia in the Early Viking Age* (Dublin: Four Courts Press).

Clinton, M. 2000. 'Settlement dynamics in Co. Meath: the kingdom of Loegaire', *Peritia* 14, 372–405.

Coupland, S. 1991. 'Carolingian coinage and Scandinavian silver', *Nordisk Numismatisk Årsskrift* 1985–6, 11–31.

Coupland, S. 1998. 'From poachers to gamekeepers: Scandinavian warlords and Carolingian kings', *Early Medieval Europe* 7 (1), 85–114.

Coupland, S. 1999. 'The Frankish tribute payments to the Vikings and their consequences', *Francia* 26 (1), 57–75.

Coupland, S. 2003. 'The Vikings on the Continent in myth and history', *History* 88 (290), 186–203.

Coupland, S. 2011. 'Raiders, traders, worshippers and settlers: the Continental perspective', in Graham-Campbell *et al.* (eds) 2011, 113–31.

Crawford, B. 1987. *Scandinavian Scotland* (Leicester: Leicester University Press).

Critch, A.J., Harland, J.F. and Barrett, J.H. 2019. 'Tracing the late Viking-Age and medieval butter economy: the view from Quoygrew, Orkney', in Kershaw and Williams (eds) 2019, 278–96.

Cropper, C. 2014. 'Glass', in Russell and Hurley with Eogan (eds) 2014, 282–5.

Davidson, M. 2001. 'The (non)submission of the northern kings in 920', in Higham and Hill (eds) 2001, 200–11.

DCMS 2000. *Treasure Annual Report 1998–1999* (London: Department for Culture, Media and Sport).

DCMS 2003. *Treasure Annual Report 2001* (London: Department for Culture, Media and Sport).

DCMS 2004. *Treasure Annual Report 2002* (London: Department for Culture, Media and Sport).

DCMS 2006. *Treasure Annual Report 2004* (London: Department for Culture, Media and Sport).

DCMS 2008. *Treasure Annual Report 2005/6* (London: Department for Culture, Media and Sport).

DCMS 2009. *Portable Antiquities and Treasure Annual Report 2007* (London: Department for Culture, Media and Sport).

DeNiro, M.J. 1985. 'Post-mortem preservation and alteration of in vivo bone collagen isotope ratios in relation to paleodietary reconstruction', *Nature* 317, 806–9.

Dickinson, T.M. 1973. 'Bronze lace-tags from Site F', in A.C.C. Brodribb, A.R. Hands and D.R. Walker (eds), *Excavations at Shakenoak, IV* (Oxford), 116–17.

Dickinson, T.M. 1982. 'Fowler's Type G penannular brooches reconsidered', *Medieval Archaeology* 26, 41–68.

Dinnin, M.H. 1997. 'The palaeoenvironmental survey of the Rivers Idle, Torne and Old River Don', in R. Van de Noort and S. Ellis (eds), *Wetland Heritage of the Humberhead Levels: An Archaeological Survey* (Hull: Humber Wetlands Project), 81–155.

Dolley, R.H.M. 1955. 'A neglected but vital Yorkshire hoard', *British Numismatic Journal* 28, 11–17.

Dolley, R.H.M. 1958. 'The post-Brunanburh coinage of York: with some remarks on the Viking coinages which preceded the same', *Nordisk Numismatisk Årsskrift*, 1957–8, 13–85.

Dolley, R.H.M. 1965–66. 'New light on the pre-1760 Coney Street (York) find of coins of the Duurstede mint', *Jaarboek voor Munt- en Penningkunde* 52/53 (1), 1–7.

Dolley, R.H.M. and Morrison, K.F. 1963. 'Finds of Carolingian coins from Great Britain and Ireland', *British Numismatic Journal* 32, 75–87.

Downham, C. 2003. 'The chronology of the last Scandinavian kings of York', *Northern History* 40, 25–51.

Downham, C. 2007. *Viking Kings of Britain and Ireland: The Dynasty of Ívarr to AD 1014* (Edinburgh: Dunedin Academic Press).

Downham, C. 2008. 'Vikings in England', in Brink and Price (eds) 2008, 341–9.

Downham, C. 2010. 'Viking camps in ninth-century Ireland: sources, locations and interactions', *Medieval Dublin* 10, 93–125.

Draper, S. 2008. 'The significance of Old English *burh* in Anglo-Saxon England', *Anglo-Saxon Studies in Archaeology and History* 15, 240–53.

Dumville, D.N. 2005. 'Dubliners and New Dubliners in Ireland and Britain: A Viking-Age story', *Medieval Dublin* 6, 78–93.

Edgeworth, M. 2008. 'The Tempsford Project: an interim report', *South Midlands Archaeology* 38, 8–16.

Edgeworth, M. 2009. 'Comparing burhs: a Wallingford-Bedford case-study', in K. Keats-Rohan and D. Roffe (eds), *The Origins of the Borough of Wallingford: Archaeological and Historical Perspectives*, British Archaeological Report (British Series) 494 (Oxford, Archaeopress), 77–85.

Edmonds, F. 2009. 'History and names', in Graham-Campbell and Philpott (eds) 2009, 3–12.

Egan, G. and Pritchard, F. 1991. *Dress Accessories c. 1150–c. 1450* (London: HMSO).

Evans, A.C. 2004. 'Low Santon, North Lincolnshire: Anglo-Saxon silver-gilt disc-headed pin', *Treasure Annual Report 2004* (London: Department for Culture, Media and Sport), 84.

Evans, D.H. and Loveluck, C. (eds) 2009. *Life and Economy at Early Medieval Flixborough c. AD 600–1000. The Artefact Evidence*, Excavations at Flixborough 2 (Oxford: Oxbow).

Evison, V.I. 1967. 'A sword from the Thames at Wallingford Bridge', *Archaeological Journal* 124, 160–89.

Evison, V.I. 1969. 'A Viking grave at Sonning, Berks.', *Antiquaries Journal* 49, 330–45.

Fanning, T. 1983. 'Ballaghkeeran Little, Athlone, Co. Westmeath', *Medieval Archaeology* 27, 221.

Fanning, T. 1990. 'Die bronzenen Ringknopfnadeln aus der Ausgrabung im Hafen von Haithabu', *Berichte über die Ausgrabungen in Haithabu* 27, 127–70.

Fanning, T. 1994. *Viking Age Ringed Pins from Dublin*, National Museum of Ireland, Medieval Dublin Excavations 1962–81, Series B, 4 (Dublin: Royal Irish Academy).

Feveile, C. 2006. *Det ældste Ribe. Udgravninger på nordsiden af Ribe Å 1984–2000* Bind I. Ribe Studier 1.1 (Jyske Arkæologisk Selskabs Skrifter 51), 65–91.

Foot, S. 2011. *Athelstan: The First King of England* (New Haven and London: Yale University Press).

Gaimster, M. 1991. 'Money and media in Viking Age Scandinavia', in R. Samson (ed.), *Social Approaches to Viking Studies* (Glasgow: Cruithne Press), 113–22.

Gaimster, M. 2007. 'Viking economies: evidence from the silver hoards', in Graham-Campbell and Williams (eds) 2007, 123–34.

Gaunt, G.D. 1981. 'Quaternary history of the southern part of the Vale of York', in J. Neale and J. Flenley (eds), *The Quaternary in Britain: Essays, Reviews and Original Work on the Quaternary Published in Honour of Lewis Penny on His Retirement* (Oxford: Pergamon Press), 82–97.

Gaunt, G.D. 1994. *Geology of the Country around Goole, Doncaster and the Isle of Axholme: Memoir for One-Inch Sheets 79 and 88 (England and Wales)* (London: HMSO).

Gaunt, G.D., Fletcher, T.P. and Wood, C.J. 1992. *Geology of the Country Around Kingston Upon Hull and Brigg: Memoir for 1:50 000 Geological Sheets 80 and 89 (England and Wales)* (London: HMSO).

Gaunt, G.D., Jarvis, R.A. and Matthews, B. 1971. 'The late Weichselian sequence in the Vale of York', *Proceedings of the Yorkshire Geological Society* 38, 281–4.

Gazzoli, P. 2012. 'Richard Hall, *Exploring the World of the Vikings* (Thames & Hudson, February 2007)', *Northern Studies* 43, 131–3.

Geake, H. 1997. *The Use of Grave-Goods in Conversion-Period England, c. 600–c. 850*, British Archaeological Report (British Series) 261 (Oxford: Hedges).

Geake, H. 2010. 'Viking-age cubo-octahedral weights recorded on the PAS database: weights and weight-standards', *Medieval Archaeology* 54, 382–400.

Gelfand, A.E. and Smith, A.F.M. 1990. 'Sampling approaches to calculating marginal densities', *Journal of the American Statistical Association* 85, 398–409.

Gibbons, M. 2004. 'The *longphort* phenomenon in Early Christian and Viking Ireland', *History Ireland* 12 (3), 19–23.

Gibbons, M. 2005. 'Athlunkard (Ath-an-longphort): a re-assessment of the proposed Viking fortress in Fairyhill, County Clare', *The Other Clare* 29, 22–5.

Gilks, W.R., Richardson, S. and Spiegelhalther, D.J. 1996. *Markov Chain Monte Carlo in Practice* (London: Chapman and Hall).

Gillmor, C. 1997. 'Charles the Bald and the small free farmers, 862–869', in Nørgård Jørgensen and Clausen (eds) 1997, 28–47.

Gooch, M.L. 2012. Money and Power in the Viking Kingdom of York c. 895–954. Unpublished PhD thesis, Durham University.

Gooch, M. 2014. 'The *Swordless St Peter* Coinage of York', in Naismith *et al.* (eds) 2014, 459–70.

Goodall, A.R. 1987. 'Copper alloy objects', in J.G. Hurst (ed.), *Wharram. A Study of Settlement on the Yorkshire Wolds* III, Society for Medieval Archaeology Monograph 11 (London), 171–3.

Goodall, A.R. and Paterson, C. 2000. 'Non-ferrous metal objects', in P.A. Stamper and R.A. Croft, *The South Manor Area. Wharram A Study of Settlement on the Yorkshire Wolds* 8 (University of York), 126–32.

Goodall, I.H. 1980. Ironwork in Medieval Britain: An Archaeological Study. Unpublished PhD thesis, University of Cardiff.

Graham-Campbell, J. 1980. *Viking Artefacts. A Select Catalogue* (London: British Museum Press).

Graham-Campbell, J. 1986. 'A late Celtic enamelled mount from Galson, Isle of Lewis', *Proceedings of the Society of Antiquaries of Scotland* 116, 281–4.

Graham-Campbell, J.A. 1993. 'A "vital" Yorkshire Viking hoard revisited', in M. Carver (ed.), *In Search of Cult: Archaeological Investigations in Honour of Philip Rahtz* (Woodbridge: Boydell), 79–84.

Graham-Campbell, J.A. 1995. *The Viking-age Gold and Silver of Scotland (AD 850–1100)* (Edinburgh: National Museums of Scotland).

Graham-Campbell, J.A. 2001a. 'The dual economy of the Danelaw. The Howard Linecar Memorial Lecture 2001', *British Numismatic Journal* 71, 49–59.

Graham-Campbell, J.A. 2001b. 'The Northern Hoards; from Cuerdale to Bossall/Flaxton', in N.J. Higham and D.H. Hill (eds), *Edward the Elder, 899–924* (London and New York: Routledge), 212–29.

Graham-Campbell, J. 2002. 'Tenth-century graves: the Viking-Age artefacts and their significance', in D. Freke, *Excavations on St Patrick's Isle, Peel, Isle of Man, 1982–88, Prehistoric, Viking, Medieval and Later,* Centre for Manx Studies Monograph 2 (Liverpool), 83–98.

Graham-Campbell, J. 2004a. 'On the Witham Bowl', *Antiquaries Journal* 84, 358–71.

Graham-Campbell, J.A. 2004b. 'The archaeology of the "Great Army" (865–79)', in E. Roesdahl and J.P. Schjødt (eds), *Beretning fra treogtyvende tværfaglige vikingsymposium* (Højbjerg: Hikuin and Afdeling for Middlealderarkæologi, Aarhus Universitet), 30–46.

Graham-Campbell, J. 2006. 'The rings', in S.H. Fuglesang and D.M. Wilson (eds), *The Hoen Hoard: A Viking Gold Treasure of the Ninth Century.* Acta ad archaeologiam et artium historiam pertinentia (Rome: Bardi Editore), 73–81.

Graham-Campbell, J.A. 2007. 'Reflections on silver economy in the Viking Age', in Graham-Campbell and Williams (eds) 2007, 215–24.

Graham-Campbell, J. 2008. 'Two Viking-age silver arm-rings from near Selby, North Yorkshire', *Medieval Archaeology* 52, 307–10.

Graham-Campbell, J. 2011. *The Cuerdale Hoard and Related Viking-Age Silver and Gold, from Britain and Ireland, in the British Museum,* British Museum Research Publication 185 (London: British Museum Press).

Graham-Campbell, J. 2015. 'An early medieval horse-harness mount, of Irish manufacture, from Yorkshire', in E. Purcell, P. MacCotter, J. Nyhan and J. Sheehan (eds), *Clerics, Kings and Vikings: Studies on Medieval Ireland. Essays in Honour of Donnchadh Ó Corráin* (Dublin: Four Courts Press), 247–50.

Graham-Campbell, J. and Batey, C.E. 1998. *Vikings in Scotland. An Archaeological Survey* (Edinburgh: Edinburgh University Press).

Graham-Campbell, J.A. and Okasha, E. 1991. 'A pair of inscribed Anglo-Saxon hooked-tags from the Rome (Forum) 1883 hoard', *Anglo-Saxon England* 20, 221–9.

Graham-Campbell, J. and Philpott, R. (eds) 2009. *The Huxley Viking Hoard: Scandinavian Settlement in the North West* (National Museums Liverpool).

Graham-Campbell, J. and Williams, G. (eds) 2007. *Silver Economy in the Viking Age* (Walnut Creek, CA: Left Coast Press).

Graham-Campbell, J., Hall, R., Jesch, J. and Parsons, D.N. (eds) 2001. *Vikings and the Danelaw. Select Papers from the Proceedings of the Thirteenth Viking Congress* (Oxford: Oxbow Books).

Graham-Campbell, J., Sindbæk, S. and Williams, G. (eds) 2011. *Silver Economies, Monetisation and Society in Scandinavia AD 800–1100* (Aarhus: Aarhus University Press).

Grierson, P. 1985. 'Domesday Book, the geld *de moneta* and *monetagium*: a forgotten minting reform', *British Numismatic Journal* 55, 84–94.

Grierson, P., Harvey, Y., Metcalf, D.M. and Pagan, H. 1986. 'Other coins of the Anglo-Saxon period from Repton', in Blackburn (ed.) 1986, 124–32.

Griffiths, D. 1992. 'The coastal trading ports of the Irish Sea', in J. Graham-Campbell (ed.), *Viking Treasure from the North West: The Cuerdale Hoard in its Context* (Liverpool: Liverpool Museum), 63–72.

Griffiths, D. 2003. 'Markets and "productive" sites: a view from western Britain', in Pestell and Ulmschneider (eds) 2003, 62–72.

Griffiths, D. 2007. 'Early medieval material: AD 400–450 to 1050–1100', in Griffiths *et al.* 2007, 58–77.

Griffiths, D. 2010. *Vikings of the Irish Sea* (Stroud: The History Press).

Griffiths, D., Philpott, R.A. and Egan, G. 2007. *Meols: The Archaeology of the North Wirral Coast. Discoveries and Observations in the 19th and 20th Centuries, with a Catalogue of Collections,* Oxford University School of Archaeology Monograph 68 (Oxford).

Gullbekk, S.H. 2011a. 'Norway: commodity money, silver and coins', in Graham-Campbell *et al.* (eds) 2011, 93–112.

Gullbekk, S.H. 2011b. 'Money and its use in the saga society: silver, coins and commodity money', in S. Sigmundsson (ed.), *Viking Settlements and Viking Society* (Reykjavík: Hið íslenzka fornleifafélag and University of Iceland), 176–88.

Gurney, D. (ed.) 2001. 'Archaeological finds in Norfolk 2000', *Norfolk Archaeology* 43 (4), 694–729.

Gustin, I. 2004. 'Islamic coins and Eastern contacts', in Ambrosiani (ed.) 2004, 96–120.

Hadley, D.M. and Richards, J.D. 2013. 'Viking Torksey: inside the great army's winter camp', *Current Archaeology* 281, 12–19.

Hadley, D.M. and Richards, J.D. with Brown, H., Craig-Atkins, E., Mahoney-Swales, D., Perry, G., Stein, S. and Woods, A. 2016. 'The winter-camp of the Viking Great Army, AD 872–3, Torksey, Lincolnshire', *The Antiquaries Journal* 96, 23–67.

Hadley, D.M. and Ten Harkel, L. (eds) 2013a. *Everyday Life in Viking Towns: Social Approaches to Viking Age Towns in Ireland and England c. 850–1100* (Oxford: Oxbow Books).

Hadley, D.M. and Ten Harkel, L. 2013b. 'Preface', in Hadley and Ten Harkel (eds) 2013a, vii–xii.

Haldenby, D. 1990. 'An Anglian site on the Yorkshire Wolds', *Yorkshire Archaeological Journal* 62, 51–67.

Haldenby, D. 1992. 'An Anglian site on the Yorkshire Wolds – continued', *Yorkshire Archaeological Journal* 64, 25–39.
Haldenby, D. 1994. 'Further Saxon finds from the Yorkshire Wolds', *Yorkshire Archaeological Journal* 66, 51–6.
Haldenby, D. and Kershaw, J. 2014. 'Viking-Age lead weights from Cottam', *Yorkshire Archaeological Journal* 86, 106–23.
Hall, R.A. 1973. 'A hoard of Viking-Age silver bracelets from Cushalogurt, Co. Mayo', *Journal of the Royal Society of Antiquaries of Ireland* 103, 78–85.
Hall, R.A. 1973–74. 'A check-list of Viking-Age coin finds from Ireland', *Ulster Journal of Archaeology* 36–7, 71–86.
Hall, R.A. 1974a. 'The pre-Conquest *Burh* of Derby', *Derbyshire Archaeological Journal* 94, 16–23.
Hall, R.A. 1974b. 'A Viking grave in the Phoenix Park, Co. Dublin', *Journal of the Royal Society of Antiquaries of Ireland* 104, 39–43.
Hall, R.A. 1978. 'A Viking Grave at Donnybrook, Co. Dublin', *Medieval Archaeology* 22, 64–83.
Hall, R.A. 1984a. *The Viking Dig: The Excavations at York* (London: The Bodley Head).
Hall, R.A. 1984b. 'A late pre-Conquest urban building tradition', in P.V. Addyman and V.E. Black (eds), *Archaeological Papers from York presented to M.W. Barley* (York), 71–7.
Hall, R.A. 1989. 'The Five Boroughs of the Danelaw: a review of present knowledge', *Anglo-Saxon England* 18, 149–208.
Hall, R.A. 1990. *Viking Age Archaeology in Britain and Ireland* (Prince's Risborough: Shire Publications).
Hall, R.A. 1994a. 'Vikings gone West? A summary review', in B. Ambrosiani and H. Clarke (eds), *The Twelfth Viking Congress* (Stockholm 1994), 32–49.
Hall, R.A. 1994b. *Viking Age York* (London).
Hall, R.A. 2000. 'Scandinavian Settlement in England – the archaeological evidence', in S. Stummann Hansen and K. Randsborg (eds), *Vikings in the West. Acta Archaeologica* 71, 147–57.
Hall, R.A. 2001. 'Anglo-Scandinavian urban development in the East Midlands', in Graham-Campbell *et al.* (eds) 2001, 143–56.
Hall, R.A. 2004. 'The Topography of Anglo-Scandinavian York', in Hall *et al.* 2004, 488–502.
Hall, R.A. 2007. *Exploring the World of the Vikings* (London: Thames and Hudson).
Hall, R.A. 2008. 'York', in Brink and Price (eds) 2008, 379–84.
Hall, R.A. 2011. 'Burhs and boroughs: Defended places, trade and towns. Plans defences, civic features', in Hamerow *et al.* (eds) 2011, 600–21.
Hall, R.A. with Coppack, G. 1972. 'Excavations at Full Street, Derby, 1972', *Derbyshire Archaeological Journal* 92, 29–77.
Hall, R.A. with Evans, D.T., Hunter-Mann, K. and Mainman, A.J. 2014. *Anglo-Scandinavian Occupation at 16–22 Coppergate: Defining a Townscape*, The Archaeology of York 8/5 (York: Council for British Archaeology for the York Archaeological Trust).
Hall, R.A., Rollason, D.W., Blackburn, M., Parsons, D.N., Fellows-Jensen, G., Hall, A.R., Kenward, H.K., O'Connor, T.P., Tweddle, D., Mainman, A.J. and Rogers, N.S.H. 2004. *Aspects of Anglo-Scandinavian York*, The Archaeology of York 8/4 (York: Council for British Archaeology for the York Archaeological Trust).
Halsall, G. 2003. *Warfare and Society in the Barbarian West, 450–900* (London: Routledge).
Hamerow, H., Hinton, D.A. and Crawford, S. (eds) 2011. *The Oxford Handbook of Anglo-Saxon Archaeology 2011* (Oxford: Oxford University Press).
Harrison, S.H. 2013. 'Beyond longphuirt? Life and death in early Viking-Age Ireland', in Hadley and Ten Harkel (eds) 2013a, 61–72.
Harrison, S.H. 2014a. 'Historical background', in Russell and Hurley with Eogan (eds) 2014, 11–19.
Harrison, S.H. 2014b. 'Weapons and grave goods', in Russell and Hurley with Eogan (eds) 2014, 155–71.
Harrison, S.H. and Ó Floinn, R. 2014. *Viking Graves and Grave Goods from Ireland* Medieval Dublin Excavations 1962–81, Series B, Volume 11 (Dublin: National Museum of Ireland).
Harvey, P. 2014. 'Amber', in Russell and Hurley with Eogan (eds) 2014, 285–7.
Haslam, J. 2011. 'King Alfred, Mercia and London, 874–86: a reassessment', *Anglo-Saxon Studies in Archaeology and History* 17, 120–46.
Haughton, C. and Powlesland, D. 1999. *West Heslerton, The Anglian Cemetery*, I, *The Excavation and Discussion of the Evidence;* II, *Catalogue of the Anglian Graves and Associated Assemblages* (West Heslerton, N. Yorkshire: The Landscape Research Centre).
Hayeur Smith, M. 2019. 'Vaðmál and cloth currency in Viking and medieval Iceland', in Kershaw and Williams (eds) 2019, 251–77.
Henry, F. 1974. *The Book of Kells. Reproductions from the Manuscript in Trinity College Dublin* (London).
Higham, N.J. and Hill, D.H. (eds) 2001. *Edward the Elder, 899–924* (London and New York: Routledge).
Hilberg, V. 2008. 'Hedeby: an outline of its research history', in Brink and Price (eds) 2008, 101–11.
Hilberg, V. 2011. 'Silver economies of the ninth and tenth centuries AD in Hedeby', in Graham-Campbell *et al.* (eds) 2011, 203–26.
Hill, D. 2001. 'The shiring of Mercia again', in N.J. Higham and D.H. Hill (eds), *Edward the Elder, 899–924* (London and New York: Routledge), 144–59.
Hines, J. 1984. *The Scandinavian Character of Anglian England in the pre-Viking Period*, British Archaeological Report (British Series) 124 (Oxford).
Hines, J. 1997. *A New Corpus of Anglo-Saxon Great Square-Headed Brooches*, Reports of the Research Committee of the Society of Antiquaries of London 51 (London).
Hinton, D.A. 1990. 'Hooked tags', in Biddle (ed.) 1990, 548–52.
Hinton, D.A. 1996. *The Gold, Silver and other Non-Ferrous Alloy Objects from Hamwic*, Southampton Finds, 2 (Stroud: Alan Sutton).
Hinton, D.A. 2000. *A Smith in Lindsey. The Anglo-Saxon Grave at Tattershall Thorpe, Lincolnshire*, Society for Medieval Archaeology Monograph 16 (London: Routledge).
Hodges, R. 1982. *Dark Age Economics: The Origins of Towns and Trade in the West AD 600–1000* (London: Duckworth).
Howard, A.J. 1995. 'Patterned ground in the Lower Trent Valley, near Brough, between Newark and Lincoln', *Mercian Geologist* 13, 183–6.
Howe, M. and Mackreth, D.F. 1996. 'Anglo-Saxon finds', in D.F. Mackreth, *Orton Hall Farm: A Roman and Early Anglo-Saxon Farmstead*, East Anglian Archaeology 76 (Manchester: Nene Valley Archaeological Trust), 102–5.
Hudson-Edwards, K.A., Macklin, M.G. and Taylor, M.P. 1999. '2000 years of sediment-borne heavy metal storage in the Yorkshire Ouse basin, NE England, UK', *Hydrological Processes* 13, 1087–1102.
Hurley, M.F. 2014. 'Discussion and conclusions', in Russell and Hurley with Eogan (eds) 2014, 347–57.
Hårdh, B. 1976. *Wikingerzeitliche Depotfunde aus Südschweden*, Acta Archaeologica Lundensia: Series in 8°, no. 6 (Bonn/Lund: Liber-Läromedel/Gleerup).
Hårdh, B. 1996. *Silver in the Viking Age. A Regional-Economic Study*, Acta Archaeologica Lundensia, Series in 8°, no. 25 (Stockholm: Almkvist & Wiksell International).

Hårdh, B. 2000. 'Uppåkra – a centre in south Sweden in the 1st millennium AD', *Antiquity* 74 (285), 640–8.

Hårdh, B. 2007a. 'Oriental-Scandinavian contacts on the Volga, as manifested by silver rings and weight systems', in Graham-Campbell and Williams (eds) 2007, 135–47.

Hårdh, B. 2007b. 'Hacksilver and ingots', in Skre (ed.) 2007b, 95–118.

Hårdh, B. 2008. 'Viking-Age Uppåkra and Lund', in Brink and Price (eds) 2008, 145–9.

Hårdh, B. 2010. 'Viking Age Uppåkra', in B. Hårdh (ed.), *Från romartida skalpeller till senvikingatida urnesspännen. Nya materialstudier från Uppåkra*, Uppåkrastudier 11 (Lund: Almqvist & Wiksell), 247–316.

Hårdh, B. 2011. 'Viking-Age silver from hoards and cultural layers', in Graham-Campbell *et al.* (eds) 2011, 281–96.

Jarman, C.L., Biddle, M., Higham, T. and Bronk Ramsey, C. 2018. 'The Viking Great Army in England: new dates from the Repton charnel', *Antiquity* 92, 183–99.

Johansen, O.S. 1973. 'Bossed penannular brooches', *Acta Archaeologica* 44, 63–124.

Johnson, C. 2014. 'Ferrous and non-ferrous metal', in Russell and Hurley with Eogan (eds) 2014, 115–25.

Johnson, R. 2004. *Viking Age Dublin* (Dublin: Townhouse).

Jondell, E. 1974. Vikingatidens balansvågar i Norge. C-uppsats i arkeologi, Uppsala University.

Jørgensen, L. 2003. 'Manor and market at Lake Tissø in the sixth to eleventh centuries: the Danish "Productive Sites"', in Pestell and Ulmschneider (eds) 2003, 175–208.

Jørgensen, L. and Vang Petersen, P. 1998. *Guld, Magt og Tro: Danske skattefund fra oldtid of middelalder. Gold, Power and Belief (Danish Gold Treasures from Prehistory and the Middle Ages)* (Copenhagen: National Museum of Denmark).

Kelly, E.P. 1982–83. 'Recent investigations at Navan', *Ríocht na Midhe* 7 (2), 76–85.

Kelly, E.P. 1993. 'Investigation of ancient fords on the River Suck', *Inland Waterways News* 20 (1), 4–5.

Kelly, E.P. 2009. 'Re-evaluation of a supposed inland promontory fort: Knoxspark, Co. Sligo – Iron Age fortress or Viking stronghold', in G. Cooney, K. Becker, M. Coles, M. Ryan and S. Sievers (eds), *Relics of Old Decency: Archaeological Studies in Later Prehistory. Festschrift for Barry Raftery* (Dublin: Wordwell), 485–97.

Kelly, E.P. 2015. 'The *longphort* in Viking-age Ireland: the archaeological evidence', in Clarke and Johnson (eds) 2015, 55–92.

Kelly, E.P. and Maas, J. 1995. 'Vikings on the Barrow: Dunrally fort, a possible Viking longphort in County Laois', *Archaeology Ireland* 9 (3), 30–2.

Kelly, E.P. and Maas, J. 1999. 'The Vikings and the kingdom of Laois', in P.G. Lane and W. Nolan (eds), *Laois: History and Society* (Dublin: Geography Publications), 123–59.

Kelly E.P. and O'Donovan, E. 1998. 'A Viking *longphort* near Athlunkard, Co. Clare', *Archaeology Ireland* 12 (4), 13–16.

Kershaw, J. 2013. *Viking Identities: Scandinavian Jewellery in England* (Oxford: Oxford University Press).

Kershaw, J. 2017. 'An early medieval dual-currency economy: bullion and coin in the Danelaw', *Antiquity* 91, 173–90.

Kershaw, J. 2019. 'Gold as a means of exchange in Scandinavian England (c. 850–1050 AD)', in Kershaw and Williams (eds) 2019, 227–50.

Kershaw, J. and Williams, G. (eds) 2019. *Silver, Butter, Cloth: Monetary and Social Currencies in the Viking Age* (Oxford: Oxford University Press).

Keynes, S. 1998. 'King Alfred and the Mercians', in M.A.S. Blackburn and D.N. Dumville (eds), *Kings, Currency and Alliances: History and Coinage of Southern England in the Ninth Century* (Woodbridge: Boydell), 1–46.

Kilger, C. 2007. 'Wholeness and holiness: counting, weighing and valuing silver in the early Viking period', in Skre (ed.) 2007b, 253–326.

Kirby, J.R. 2001. 'Late-Quaternary marine and perimarine records', in M.D. Bateman, P.C. Buckland, C.D. Frederick and N.J. Whitehouse (eds), *The Quaternary of East Yorkshire and North Lincolnshire: Field Guide* (London: Quaternary Research Association), 25–33.

Kruse, S.E. 1988. 'Ingots and weight units in Viking Age silver hoards', *World Archaeology* 20 (2), 285–301.

Kruse, S.E. 1992. 'Late Saxon balances and weights from England', *Medieval Archaeology* 36, 67–95.

Kruse, S.E. 1993. 'Silver Storage and Circulation in Viking-age Scotland', in C.E. Batey, J. Jesch and C.D. Morris (eds), *Caithness, Orkney and the North Atlantic* (Edinburgh: Edinburgh University Press), 187–203.

Kruse, S.E. 2007. 'Trade and exchange across frontiers', in Graham-Campbell and Williams (eds) 2007, 163–76.

Kruse, S.E. and Tate, J. 1995. 'Appendix II. XRF analysis of Viking-Age silver from Scotland', in Graham-Campbell 1995, 73–9.

Kyhlberg, O. 1980. *Vikt och värde. Arkeologiska studier i värdemätning, betalningsmodel och metrology*. I. *Helgö*. II. *Birka* (Stockholm: Stockholm University).

Lang, J. and Ager, B. 1989. 'Swords of the Anglo-Saxon and Viking periods in the British Museum: a radiographic study', in S.C. Hawkes (ed.), *Weapons and Warfare in Anglo-Saxon England*, Oxford University Committee for Archaeology Monograph 21 (Oxford), 85–122.

Lavelle, R. 2010. *Alfred's Wars. Sources and Interpretation of Anglo-Saxon Warfare in the Viking Age* (Woodbridge: Boydell).

Leahy, K. 2003. *Anglo-Saxon Crafts* (Stroud: Tempus).

Leahy, K. 2007a. *'Interrupting the Pots'. The Excavation of Cleatham Anglo-Saxon Cemetery*, Council for British Archaeology Research Report 155 (York).

Leahy, K. 2007b. *The Anglo-Saxon Kingdom of Lindsey* (Stroud: Tempus).

Liebermann, F. 1898. *Die Gesetze der Angelsachsen I* (Halle: Max Niermayer).

Lilja, S. 1996. 'A "Proto-Urban Stage" – Some tentative reflections on the historical emergence of urbanism', in L. Nilsson and S. Lilja (eds), *The Emergence of Towns. Archaeology and Early Urbanization in Non-Roman North-West Europe. Studies in Urban History* 14 (Stockholm: Stads- och kommunhistoriska institutet, Stockholms Universitet), 15–28.

Long, A.J., Innes, J.B., Kirby, J.R., Lloyd, J.M., Rutherford, M.M., Shennan, I. and Tooley, M.J. 1998. 'Holocene sea-level change and coastal evolution in the Humber estuary, eastern England: An assessment of rapid coastal change', *The Holocene* 8, 229–47.

Longin, R. 1971. 'New method of collagen extraction for radiocarbon dating', *Nature* 230, 241–2.

Lowick, N. 1976. 'The kufic coins from Cuerdale', *British Numismatic Journal* 46, 19–28.

Lund, N. 1987. 'Peace and non-peace in the Viking Age – Ottar in Biarmaland, the Rus in Byzantium, and Danes and Norwegians in England', in J.E. Knirk (ed.), *Proceedings of the 10th Viking Congress: Larkollen, Norway, 1985* (Oslo: Universitets Oldsaksamlings Skrifter), 255–69.

Lyon, C.S.S. and Stewart, B.H.I.H. 1961. 'The Northumbrian Viking coins in the Cuerdale Hoard', in R.H.M. Dolley (ed.), *Anglo-Saxon Coins: Studies Presented to F M Stenton on the Occasion of his 80th birthday* (London: Methuen), 96–121.

Lyons, A.W. and Mackay, W.A. 2008. 'The Lunettes coinage of Alfred the Great', *British Numismatic Journal* 78, 38–110.

Maas, J. 2008. '*Longphort, Dún* and *Dúnad* in the Irish Annals of the Viking Period', *Peritia* 20, 257–75.

Macklin, M.G., Taylor, M.P., Hudson-Edwards, K.A. and Howard, A.J. 2000. 'Holocene environmental change in the Yorkshire Ouse Basin and its influence on river dynamics and sediment fluxes to the coastal zone', in I. Shennan and J.E. Andrews (eds), *Holocene Land-Ocean Interaction and Environmental Change Around the North Sea*, Geological Society of London Special Publication 166, 87–96.

Mainman, A.J. and Rogers, N.S.H. 2000. *Craft, Industry and Everyday Life: Anglo-Scandinavian Finds*, The Archaeology of York, The Small Finds 17/14 (York: Council for British Archaeology for the York Archaeological Trust).

Malcolm, G. and Bowsher, D. 2003. *Middle Saxon London. Excavations at the Royal Opera House 1989–99*, MoLAS Monograph 15 (London: Museum of London).

Malmer, B. 2007. 'South Scandinavian coinage in the ninth century', in Graham-Campbell and Williams (eds) 2007, 13–28.

Manning, W.H. 1985. *Catalogue of the Romano-British Iron Tools, Fittings and Weapons in the British Museum* (London: British Museum).

Margeson, S. 1995a. 'The non-ferrous metal objects', in A. Rogerson, *A Late Neolithic, Saxon and Medieval Site at Middle Harling, Norfolk*, East Anglian Archaeology 74 (Ipswich), 53–68.

Margeson, S. 1995b. 'Objects from burial *451*', in A. Rogerson, *A Late Neolithic, Saxon and Medieval Site at Middle Harling, Norfolk*, East Anglian Archaeology 74 (Ipswich), 79–81.

Matthews, B. 1970. 'Age and origin of aeolian sand in the Vale of York', *Nature* 227, 1234.

Maxwell, H. 1912–13. 'Notes on a hoard of personal ornaments, implements, and Anglo-Saxon and Northumbrian coins from Talnotrie, Kirkcudbrightshire', *Proceedings of the Society of Antiquaries of Scotland* 47, 12–16.

Mays, S. 2000. 'Stable isotope analysis in ancient human skeletal remains', in M. Cox and S. Mays (eds), *Human Osteology in Archaeology and Forensic Science* (London: Greenwich Medical Media).

McKeown, M. 2005. 'Annagassan, a study of a Viking *longphort*', *Journal of the County Louth Archaeological and Historical Society* 26, 67–79.

McLeod, S. 2007. 'Feeding the *micel here* in England, *c.* 865–78', *Journal of the Australian Early Medieval Association* 2, 141–56.

McLeod, S. 2011. 'Warriors and women: the sex ratio of Norse migrants to eastern England up to 900 AD', *Early Medieval Europe* 19 (3), 332–53.

McLeod, S. 2014. *The Beginning of Scandinavian Settlement in England: The Viking 'Great Army' and Early Settlers, c. 865–900* (Turnhout: Brepols).

McNamara, S. 2005. 'Woodstown 6: the finds', in J. O'Sullivan and M. Stanley (eds), *Recent Archaeological Discoveries on National Road Schemes 2004: Proceedings of a Seminar for the Public, Dublin, September 2004* (Dublin: National Roads Authority), 125–30.

Metcalf, D.M. 1957. 'Find-records of medieval coins from Gough's Camden's "Britannia"', *Numismatic Chronicle*, 6th Series, 17, 181–207.

Metcalf, D.M. 1987. 'The taxation of moneyers under Edward the Confessor and in 1086', in J.C. Holt (ed.), *Domesday Studies. Papers Read at the Novocentenary Conference of the Royal Historical Society and the Institute of British Geographers, Winchester, 1986* (Woodbridge: Boydell), 279–93.

Metcalfe, S.E., Ellis, S., Horton, B.P., Innes, J.B., McArthur, J., Mitlehner, A., Parkes, A., Pethick, J.S., Rees, J., Ridgway, J., Rutherford, M.M., Shennan, I. and Tooley, M.J. 2000. 'The Holocene evolution of the Humber Estuary: reconstructing change in a dynamic environment', in I. Shennan and J.E. Andrews (eds), *Holocene Land-Ocean Interaction and Environmental Change Around the North Sea*, Geological Society of London Special Publication 166, 97–118.

Moesgaard, J.C. 2011. 'The Grisebjerggård Hoard and the beginning of pecking in Scandinavia', in Graham-Campbell *et al.* (eds) 2011, 297–308.

Moesgaard, J.C. 2013. 'James Graham-Campbell (red.), The Cuerdale Hoard and related Viking-Age silver and gold from Britain and Ireland in the British Museum (review)', *Nordisk Numismatisk Unions Medlemsblad*, September 2013, 90–2.

Mook, W.G. 1986. 'Business meeting: recommendations/resolutions adopted by the twelfth international radiocarbon conference', *Radiocarbon* 28, 799.

Morris, C.A. 2000. *Craft, Industry and Everyday Life: Wood and Woodworking in Anglo-Scandinavian and Medieval York*, The Archaeology of York, The Small Finds 17/13 (York: Council for British Archaeology for the York Archaeological Trust).

Müller-Wille, M. 1973. 'Eisengeräte aus Haithabu (Ausgrabung 1963–1964)', *Berichte über die Ausgrabungen in Haithabu*, Bericht 6 (Neumünster).

Myres, J.N.L. 1977. *A Corpus of Anglo-Saxon Pottery of the Pagan Period* (Cambridge University Press).

Naismith, R. 2005. 'Islamic coins from early medieval England', *Numismatic Chronicle* 165, 193–222.

Naismith, R., Allen, M. and Screen, E. (eds) 2014. *Early Medieval Monetary History. Studies in Memory of Mark Blackburn* (Farnham: Ashgate).

North, J.J. 1994. *English Hammered Coinage. Volume 1: Early Anglo-Saxon to Henry III, c. 600–1272* (London: Spink).

Nørgård Jørgensen, A. and Clausen, B.L. (eds) 1997. *Military Aspects of Scandinavian Society in a European Perspective, AD 1–1300*, Publications from the National Museum: Studies in Archaeology and History 2 (Copenhagen: National Museum of Denmark).

Oakeshott, E. 1960. *The Archaeology of Weapons* (Woodbridge: Boydell).

O'Brien, E. 1998. 'The location and context of Viking burials at Kilmainham and Islandbridge, Dublin', in Clarke *et al.* (eds) 1998, 203–21.

O'Brien, R. 2014. 'Perforated lead and stone discs', in Russell and Hurley with Eogan (eds) 2014, 255–9.

O'Brien, R., Quinney, P. and Russell, I. 2005. 'Preliminary report on the archaeological excavation and finds retrieval strategy of the Hiberno-Scandinavian site of Woodstown 6, County Waterford', *Decies: Journal of the Waterford Archaeological and Historical Society* 61, 13–122.

Ó Floinn, R. 1998. 'The archaeology of the early Viking Age in Ireland', in Clarke *et al.* (eds) 1998, 131–65.

Ó Floinn, R. with a contribution by Bourke, C. 2014. 'Cast and gilt copper alloy', in Russell and Hurley with Eogan (eds) 2014, 172–93.

Ottaway, P.J. 1992. *Anglo-Scandinavian Ironwork from Coppergate*, The Archaeology of York, The Small Finds 17/6 (York: Council for British Archaeology for the York Archaeological Trust).

Ottaway, P.J. 2009. 'The Flixborough tool hoard', in Evans and Loveluck (eds) 2009, 256–67.

Ottaway, P.J. and Rogers, N.S.H. 2002. *Craft, Industry and Everyday Life: Medieval Finds*, The Archaeology of York, The Small Finds 17/15 (York: Council for British Archaeology for the York Archaeological Trust).

Owen, O. and Dalland, M. 1999. *Scar: A Viking Boat Burial on Sanday, Orkney* (East Linton: Tuckwell Press).

Owen-Crocker, G.R. 2004. *Dress in Anglo-Saxon England* (Woodbridge: Boydell).

Östergren, M. 2011. 'The Spillings Hoard(s)', in Graham-Campbell *et al.* (eds) 2011, 321–36.

Pagan, H.E. 1974. 'Coinage in the age of Burgred', *British Numismatic Journal* 34, 45–65.

Pedersen, U. 2007. 'Weights and balances', in Skre (ed.) 2007b, 119–95.

Peirce, I.G. 2002. *Swords of the Viking Age* (Woodbridge: Boydell).

Penn, K. and Brugmann, B. 2007. *Aspects of Anglo-Saxon Inhumation Burial: Morning Thorpe, Spong Hill, Bergh Apton and Westgarth Gardens*, East Anglian Archaeology 119 (Gressenhall).

Pestell, T. 2011. 'Markets, *emporia*, *wics*, and "productive" sites: pre-Viking trade centres in Anglo-Saxon England', in Hamerow *et al.* (eds) 2011, 556–79.

Pestell, T. and Ulmschneider, K. (eds) 2003. *Markets in Early Medieval Europe: Trading and 'Productive' Sites, 650–850* (Bollington: Windgather Press).

Petersen, J. 1919. *De Norske Vikingesverd. En typologisk-kronologisk studie over vikingetidens vaaben* (Kristiania).

Petts, D. 2008. 'Discussion and conclusions', in J. McComish and D. Petts (principal authors), *Fey Field, Whithorn: Excavations by David Pollock and Amanda Clarke*, section 14. *Archaeology of York Web Series* 10, http://www.iadb.co.uk/yat/publish.htm?PUB=58 (accessed 26 March 2015).

Pirie, E.J.E. 1986. 'The minting evidence', in Pirie *et al.* 1986, 33–41.

Pirie, E.J.E. 2004. 'The Bamburgh hoard of ninth-century Northumbrian coins', *Archaeologia Aeliana*, 5th Series, 33, 65–75.

Pirie, E.J. 2006. 'Contrast and continuity within the coinage of Northumbria, c. 670–867', in B. Cook and G. Williams (eds), *Coinage and History in the North Sea World, c. 500–1250* (Leiden and New York: Brill), 211–39.

Pirie, E.J.E. with Hall, R.A., Archibald, M.M. and Stewart, B.H.I.H. 1986. *Post-Roman Coins from York Excavations 1971–81*, The Archaeology of York: The Coins 18/1 (London: Council for British Archaeology for the York Archaeological Trust).

Pitts, M. 2014. 'News', *British Archaeology*, March–April issue, 6–9.

Price, N.S. 1991. 'Viking armies and fleets in Brittany: a case study for some general problems', in H. Bekker-Bielkson and H.F. Nielsen (eds), *Beretning fra Tiende Tværfaglige Vikingsymposium* (Højbjerg: Hikuin), 7–24.

Price, N.S. 2014a. 'The way of the warrior', in Williams *et al.* (eds) 2014, 116–17.

Price, N.S. 2014b. 'Belief and ritual', in Williams *et al.* (eds) 2014, 162–95.

Price, N.S. 2014c. 'Ship men and slaughter wolves. Pirate polities in the Viking Age', in S. Amirell and L. Müller (eds), *Persistent Piracy: Maritime Violence and State Formation in Global Historical Perspective* (New York: Palgrave Macmillan), 51–68.

Price, N.S. 2016. 'Pirates of the North Sea: the Viking ship as political space', in L. Melheim, H. Glørstad and Z. Tsigaridas Glørstad (eds), *Comparative Perspectives on Past Colonisation, Maritime Interaction and Cultural Integration* (Sheffield: Equinox), 149–76.

Radley, J. and Simms, C. 1967. 'Wind erosion in East Yorkshire', *Nature* 216, 20–2.

Raffield, B. 2013. 'Antiquarians, archaeologists and Viking fortifications', *Journal of the North Atlantic* 20, 1–29.

Raffield, B. 2016. 'Bands of brothers: a re-appraisal of the Viking Great Army and its implications for the Scandinavian colonization of England', *Early Medieval Europe* 24 (3), 308–37.

Raffield, B., Greenlow, C., Price, N. and Collard, M. 2016. 'Ingroup identification, identity fusion, and the formation of Viking warbands', *World Archaeology* 48 (1), 35–50.

Redknap, M. 2000. *Vikings in Wales: An Archaeological Quest* (Cardiff: National Museum and Galleries of Wales).

Redknap, M. 2004. 'Viking-age settlement in Wales and the Evidence from Llanbedrgoch', in J. Hines, A. Lane and M. Redknap (eds), *Land, Sea and Home: Settlement in the Viking Period*, Society for Medieval Archaeology Monograph 20 (Leeds: Maney), 139–76.

Redknap, M. 2009. 'Silver and Commerce in Viking-Age North Wales', in Graham-Campbell and Philpott (eds) 2009, 29–41.

Reimer, P.J., Baillie, M.G.L., Bard, E., Bayliss, A., Beck, J.W., Bertrand, C.J.H., Blackwell, P.G., Buck, C.E., Burr, G.S., Cutler, K.B., Damon, P.E., Edwards, R.L., Fairbanks, R.G., Friedrich, M., Guilderson, T.P., Hogg, A.G., Hughen, K.A., Kromer, B., McCormac, G., Manning, S., Bronk Ramsey, C., Reimer, R.W., Remmele, S., Southon, J.R., Stuiver, M., Talamo, S., Taylor, F.W., van der Plicht, J., and Weyhenmeyer, C.E. 2004. 'IntCal04 Terrestrial Radiocarbon Age Calibration, 0–26 cal kyr BP', *Radiocarbon* 46, 1029–58.

Reuter, T. 1985. 'Plunder and tribute in the Carolingian Empire', *Transactions of the Royal Historical Society* (5) 35, 75–94.

Reuter, T. 1990. 'The end of Carolingian military expansion', in P. Godman and R. Collins (eds), *Charlemagne's Heir: New perspectives on the reign of Louis the Pious (814–40)* (Oxford: Clarendon Press), 391–405.

Reuter, T. (ed.) 2003. *Alfred the Great: Papers from the Eleventh-centenary Conferences* (Aldershot: Ashgate).

Reynolds, A. and Webster, L. (eds) 2013. *Early Medieval Art and Archaeology in the Northern World. Studies in Honour of James Graham-Campbell* (Leiden/Boston: Brill).

Richards, J.D. 2003a. 'The Anglian and Anglo-Scandinavian sites at Cottam, East Yorkshire', in Pestell and Ulmschneider (eds) 2003, 155–66.

Richards, J.D. 2003b. 'Pagans and Christians at a frontier: Viking burial in the Danelaw', in M. Carver (ed.), *The Cross Goes North: Processes of Conversion in Northern Europe, AD 300–1300* (Woodbridge/York: Boydell/York Medieval Press), 383–96.

Richards, J.D. 2004. 'Excavations at the Viking barrow cemetery at Heath Wood, Ingleby, Derbyshire', *The Antiquaries Journal* 84, 23–116.

Richardson, H. 1984. 'Number and symbol in early Christian Irish art', *Journal of the Royal Society of Antiquaries of Ireland* 114, 28–47.

Riddler, I. with Evison, V. and Rogers, N. 2014. 'Dress accessories', in A. Tester, S. Anderson, I. Riddler and R. Carr, *Staunch Meadow, Brandon, Suffolk: A High Status Middle Saxon Settlement on the Fen Edge*, East Anglian Archaeology 151 (Bury St Edmunds: Suffolk County Council), 219–44.

Rispling, G. 1987. 'Coins with crosses and bird heads', *Fornvännen* 82, 75–87.

Rispling, G. 1990. 'The Volga Bulgarian imitative coinage of Al-Amir Yaltawar ('Barman') and Mikail B Jafar', in K. Jonsson and B. Malmer (eds), *Sigtuna Papers, Proceedings of the Sigtuna Symposium on Viking-Age Coinage 1–4 June 1989*, Commentationes de nummis saeculorum IX–XI in Suecia repertis. NS 6 (Stockholm: Kungliga Vitterhetsakademien), 275–82.

Rispling, G. 2004. 'Catalogue and comments on the Islamic coins from the excavations 1990–1995', in Ambrosiani (ed.) 2004, 26–60.

Rispling, G. 2014. 'Numismatic finds: Islamic silver dirham fragments', in Russell and Hurley with Eogan 2014, 259–61.

Roesdahl, E. 1977. *Fyrkat. En jysk vikingeborg* (Copenhagen: Det Kongelige Nordiske Oldskriftselskab).

Roesdahl, E., Graham-Campbell, J., Connor, P. and Pearson, K. (eds) 1981. *The Vikings in England and in their Danish Homeland* (London: Anglo-Danish Viking Project).

Rogers, N.S.H. 1993. *Anglian and Other Finds from Fishergate*, The Archaeology of York, The Small Finds 17/9 (London: Council for British Archaeology for the York Archaeological Trust).

Rogers, N.S.H. 2009. 'The pins', in Evans and Loveluck (eds) 2009, 32–79.

Rogers, N.S.H. 2014. 'Iron bells', in A. Tester, S. Anderson, I. Riddler and R. Carr, *Staunch Meadow, Brandon, Suffolk: A High Status Middle Saxon Settlement on the Fen Edge*, East Anglian Archaeology 151 (Bury St Edmunds: Suffolk County Council), 272.

Rollason, D.W. 2003. *Northumbria, 500–1100: Creation and Destruction of a Kingdom* (Cambridge: Cambridge University Press).

Rollason, D.W. 2004. 'Anglo-Scandinavian York: The evidence of historical sources', in Hall *et al.* 2004, 305–24.

Ross, S. 1991. Dress Pins from Anglo-Saxon England: Their Production and Typo-Chronological Development. Unpublished PhD thesis, University of Oxford.

Russell, I. 2014. 'The excavation', in Russell and Hurley with Eogan 2014, 28–89.

Russell, I. and Hurley, M.F. with Eogan, J. (eds) 2014. *Woodstown: A Viking-Age settlement in Co. Waterford* (Dublin: Four Courts Press).

Russell, I., Harrison, S.H., Nicholls, J., Kinsella, J., McNamara, S. and O'Hare, M. 2007. *Woodstown 6: Supplementary Research Project* (Formerly published online: Archaeological Consultancy Services Ltd), http://www.ahg.gov.ie/ie/Foilseachain/FoilseachainOidhreachta/SeadchomharthaiNaisiunta/47.

Samson, R. 1991. 'Fighting with silver: rethinking trading, raiding and hoarding', in R. Samson (ed.), *Social Approaches to Viking Studies* (Glasgow: Cruithne Press), 123–33 .

Sawyer, P.H. 1962. (Second edition 1971). *The Age of the Vikings* (London: Edward Arnold).

Sawyer, P.H. 1995. 'The last Scandinavian kings of York', *Northern History* 35, 39–44.

Scott, E.M. (ed.) 2003. 'The Third International Radiocarbon Intercomparison (TIRI) and the Fourth International Radiocarbon Intercomparison (FIRI) 1990–2002: results, analysis, and conclusions', *Radiocarbon* 45, 135–408.

Screen, E. 2007. 'Anglo-Saxon law and numismatics: a reassessment in the light of Patrick Wormald's *The making of English law*', *British Numismatic Journal* 77, 150–72.

Scull, C. 1997. 'Urban centres in pre-Viking England', in J. Hines (ed.), *The Anglo-Saxons from the Migration Period to the Eighth Century: An Ethnographic Perspective* (Woodbridge: Boydell), 269–310.

Scully, O. 2014. 'Ferrous and non-ferrous metal', in Russell and Hurley with Eogan 2014, 125–40.

Sharp, S. 2001. 'The West Saxon tradition of dynastic marriage: with special reference to Edward the Elder', in Higham and Hill (eds) 2001, 79–88.

Sheehan, J. 1998. 'Early Viking Age silver hoards from Ireland and their Scandinavian elements', in Clarke *et al.* (eds) 1998, 166–202.

Sheehan, J. 2007. 'The form and structure of Viking-Age silver hoards: The evidence from Ireland', in Graham-Campbell and Williams (eds) 2007, 149–62.

Sheehan, J. 2008. 'The longphort in Viking Age Ireland', *Acta Archaeologica* 79, 282–95.

Sheehan, J. 2009. 'The Huxley Hoard and Hiberno-Scandinavian arm-rings', in Graham-Campbell and Philpott (eds) 2009, 58–69.

Sheehan, J. 2011. '"Bullion-rings" in Viking Age Britain and Ireland', in S. Sigmundsson (ed.), *Viking Settlements and Viking Society* (Reykjavík: Hið Íslenzka Fornleifafélag and University of Iceland Press), 393–46.

Sheehan, J. 2013. 'Viking raiding, gift-exchange and Insular metalwork in Norway', in Reynolds and Webster (eds) 2013, 809–23.

Sheehan, J. 2014. 'Silver', in Russell and Hurley with Eogan (eds) 2014, 194–221.

Sheehan, J. 2015. 'Fighting with silver: The Woodstown assemblage', in Clarke and Johnson (eds) 2015, 161–76.

Sheehan, J. and Ó Corráin, D. (eds) 2010. *Ireland in the Viking* Age (Dublin: Four Courts Press).

Sherlock, S.J. and Welch, M.G. 1992. *An Anglo-Saxon Cemetery at Norton, Cleveland*, Council for British Archaeology Research Report 82 (London).

Simpson, L. 2005. 'Viking warrior burials in Dublin: is this the *longphort?*', *Medieval Dublin* 6, 11–62.

Simpson, L. 2010. 'The first phase of Viking activity in Ireland: archaeological evidence from Dublin', in Sheehan and Ó Corráin (eds) 2010, 418–29.

Sindbæk, S.M. 2003. 'An object of exchange. Brass-bars and the routinization of Viking age long-distance exchange in the Baltic area', *Offa* 58, 49–60.

Sindbæk, S.M. 2010. 'Close ties and long-range relations: the emporia network in early Viking-Age exchange', in Sheehan and Ó Corráin (eds) 2010, 430–40.

Sindbæk, S.M. 2011. 'Silver economies and social ties: long-distance interaction, long-term investments – and why the Viking Age happened', in Graham-Campbell *et al.* (eds) 2011, 41–66.

Skaare, K. 1976. *Coins and Coinage in Viking-Age Norway. The Establishment of a National Coinage in Norway in the XI Century, With a Survey of the Preceding Currency History* (Oslo: Universitetsforlaget).

Skre, D. (ed.) 2007a. *Kaupang in Skiringssal*, Kaupang Excavation Project Publication Series 1, Norske Oldfunn XXII (Oslo/Aarhus: University of Oslo/Aarhus University Press).

Skre, D. (ed.) 2007b. *Means of Exchange: Dealing with Silver in the Viking Age*, Kaupang Excavation Project Publication Series 2, Norske Oldfunn XXIII (Oslo/Aarhus: University of Oslo/Aarhus University Press).

Skre, D. (ed.) 2011a. *Things from the Town*, Kaupang Excavation Project Publication Series 3, Norske Oldfunn XXIV (Oslo/Aarhus: University of Oslo/Aarhus University Press).

Skre, D. 2011b. 'Commodity money, silver and coinage in Scandinavia', in Graham-Campbell *et al.* (eds) 2011, 67–92.

Slota, P.J., Jull, A.J.T., Linick, T.W. and Toolin, L.J. 1987. 'Preparation of small samples for 14C accelerator targets by catalytic reduction of CO', *Radiocarbon* 29, 303–6.

Smart, V. 1985. 'The moneyers of St Edmund', *Hikuin* 11, 83–90.

Smyth, A.P. 1975–79. *Scandinavian York and Dublin*, 2 vols (New Jersey/Dublin: Templekieran Press).

Sperber, E. 1996. *Balances, Weights and Weighing in Ancient and Early Medieval Sweden. Thesis and Papers in Scientific Archaeology* 2 (Stockholm: Stockholm University).

Sperber, E. 2004. 'Metrology of the weights from the Birka excavations 1990–1995', in Ambrosiani (ed.) 2004, 11–25.

Stein, S. 2014. Understanding Torksey, Lincolnshire: A Landscape and Geoarchaeological Approach to a Viking Overwintering Camp. Unpublished PhD thesis, University of Sheffield).

Steinnes, A. 1927. *Ymist um norsk vektfyrre år 900.* Den Norske Vitenskapsakademi avhandlingar II. Hist.-Filos. Klasse 1936, no. 5 (Oslo).

Steuer, H. 1987. 'Gewichtsgeldwirtschaften im frühgeschichtlichen Europa. Feinwaagen und Gewichte als Quellen zur Währungsgeschichte', in K. Düwel, H. Jankuhn, H. Siems and D. Timpe (eds), *Untersuchungen zu Handel und Verkehr der vor- und frühgeschichtlichen Zeit in Mittel- und Nordeuropa, 4: Der Handel der Karolinger- und Wikingerzeit* (Göttingen: Vandenhoeck and Ruprecht), 405–527.

Steuer, H. 1997. *Waagen und Gewichte aus dem mittelalterlichen Schleswig. Funde des 11. Bis 13. Jahrhunderts aus Europa als Quellen zur Handels- und Währungsgeschichte* (Köln: R. Habelt).

Steuer, H. 2004. 'Minting, silver routes and mining in Europe: economic expansion and technical innovation', in J. Heitzman and W. Schenkluhn (eds), *The World in the Year 1000* (Lanham: University Press of America), 105–17.

Steuer, H. 2007a. 'Waagen und Gewichte', in H. Beck, D. Geuenich and H. Steuer (eds), *Reallexikon der Germanische Altertumskunde* 35 (Berlin/New York), 539–86.

Steuer, H. 2007b. 'Wetzstein', in H. Beck, D. Geuenich and H. Steuer (eds), *Reallexikon der Germanischen Altertumskunde* 35 (Berlin/New York), 659–73.

Steuer, H. 2009. 'Principles of trade and exchange: trade goods and merchants', in A. Englert and A. Trakadas (eds), *Wulfstan's Voyage. The Baltic Sea Region in the Early Viking Age as Seen from Shipboard* (Roskilde: Viking Ship Museum), 294–308.

Stewart, B.H.I.H. 1986. 'The date of the St Peter coin die', in Pirie *et al.* 1986, 42–3.

Stewart, B.H.I.H. 1987. 'CVNNETTI reconsidered', in D.M. Metcalf (ed.), *Coinage in Ninth-century Northumbria: The Tenth Oxford Symposium on Coinage and Monetary History,* British Archaeological Report (British Series) 180 (Oxford: Archaeopress), 345–54.

Stewart, B.H.I.H. 1991. 'On the date of the Bossall Hoard', *Numismatic Chronicle* 91, 175–82.

Stewart, B.H.I.H. and Lyon, C.S.S. 1992. 'Chronology of the St Peter Coinage', *Yorkshire Numismatist* 2, 45–73.

Story, J. 2003. *Carolingian Connections. Anglo-Saxon England and Carolingian Francia* (Aldershot: Ashgate).

Stuiver, M. and Kra, R.S. 1986. 'Editorial comment', *Radiocarbon* 28 (2B), ii.

Stuiver, M. and Polach, H.A. 1977. 'Reporting of 14C data', *Radiocarbon* 19, 355–63.

Stuiver, M. and Reimer, P.J. 1986. 'A computer program for radiocarbon age calculation', *Radiocarbon* 28, 1022–30.

Stuiver, M. and Reimer, P.J. 1993. 'Extended 14C data base and revised CALIB 3.0 14C age calibration program', *Radiocarbon* 35, 215–30.

Taylor, M.P., Macklin, M.G. and Hudson-Edwards, K.A. 2000. 'River sedimentation and fluvial response to Holocene environmental change in the Yorkshire Ouse Basin, northern England', *The Holocene* 10, 201–12.

Ten Harkel, L. 2010. Lincoln in the Viking Age: A 'Town' in Context. Unpublished PhD thesis, University of Sheffield.

Ten Harkel, L. 2013. 'The urbanization of Viking Age Lincoln: a numismatic perspective', *The Mediaeval Journal* 13 (1), 1–48.

Thomas, G. 2000. 'Anglo-Scandinavian metalwork from the Danelaw', in D.M. Hadley and J.D. Richards (eds), *Cultures in Contact: Scandinavian Settlement in England in the 9th and 10th Centuries. Studies in the Early Middle Ages* 2, 237–55.

Thomas, G. 2001. 'Strap-ends and the identification of regional patterns in the production and circulation of ornamental metalwork in late Anglo-Saxon and Viking-Age Britain', in M. Redknap, N. Edwards, S. Youngs, A. Lane and J. Knight (eds), *Pattern and Purpose in Insular Art* (Oxford: Oxbow), 39–48.

Thomas, G. 2003. *Late Anglo-Saxon and Viking-Age strap-ends 750–1100: Part 1,* The Finds Research Group AD 700–1700 Datasheet 32.

Thomas, G. 2004. *Late Anglo-Saxon and Viking-Age strap-ends 750–1100: Part 2,* The Finds Research Group AD 700–1700 Datasheet 33.

Thomas, G. 2006. 'Reflections on a "9th-century" Northumbrian metalworking tradition: a silver hoard from Poppleton, North Yorkshire', *Medieval Archaeology* 50, 143–64.

Thomas, G. 2008. 'The symbolic lives of late Anglo-Saxon settlements: a cellared structure and iron hoard from Bishopstone, East Sussex', *Archaeological Journal* 165, 334–98.

Thomas, G. 2009. 'The hooked tags', in Evans and Loveluck (eds) 2009, 17–22.

Thomas, G.W. 1887. 'On excavations in an Anglo-Saxon cemetery at Sleaford, in Lincolnshire', *Archaeologia* 50 (2), 383–406 and pls XXIII–XXV.

Timby, J.R. 1996. *The Anglo-Saxon Cemetery at Empingham II, Rutland,* Oxbow Monograph 70 (Oxford: Oxbow).

Tummuscheit, A. 2003. 'Gross Strömkendorf: a market site of the eighth century on the Baltic Sea coast', in Pestell and Ulmschneider (eds) 2003, 208–20.

Tweddle, D. 1986. *Finds from Parliament Street and Other Sites in the City Centre,* The Archaeology of York, The Small Finds 17/4 (London: Council for British Archaeology for the York Archaeological Trust).

Tweddle, D. 1992. *The Anglian Helmet from Coppergate,* The Archaeology of York, The Small Finds 17/8 (London: Council for British Archaeology for the York Archaeological Trust).

Tweddle, D. 1993. 'Knife handle', in Rogers 1993, 1309–11.

Tweddle, D., Moulden, J. and Logan, E. 1999. *Anglian York: A Survey of the Evidence,* The Archaeology of York, Anglian York 7/2 (York: Council for British Archaeology for the York Archaeological Trust).

Ulmschneider, K. 2000. *Markets, Minsters, and Metal-Detectors: The Archaeology of Middle Saxon Lincolnshire and Hampshire Compared,* British Archaeological Report (British Series) 307 (Oxford: Archaeopress).

Valante, M. 2008. *The Vikings in Ireland. Settlement, Trade and Urbanisation* (Dublin: Four Courts Press).

Vince, A. 1993. 'Forms, functions and manufacturing techniques of late ninth- and tenth-century wheelthrown pottery in England and their origins', in D. Piton (ed.), *Travaux du Groupe de Recherché et D'Etudes sur la Céramique dans le Nord - Pas-de-Calais. Actes du Colloque D'Outreau (10–12 Avril 1992).* Numéro hors-série de Nord-Ouest Archéologie, 151–64.

Vince, A. 2001. 'Lincoln in the Viking Age', in Graham-Campbell *et al.* (eds) 2001, 157–80.

Vince, A. 2003. 'Lincoln in the early medieval era, between the 5th and 9th centuries', in D. Stocker (ed.), *The City by the Pool: Assessing the Archaeology of the City of Lincoln,* Lincoln Archaeological Studies 10 (Oxford: Oxbow), 141–56.

von Carnap-Bornheim, C., Hilberg, V., Kalmring, S. and Schultze, J. 2010. 'Hedeby, the settlement and the harbour: old data and recent research', in Sheehan and Ó Corráin (eds) 2010, 511–24.

Wallace, P.F. 1987. 'The economy and commerce of Viking Age Dublin', in K. Düwel, H. Jankuhn, H. Siems and D. Timpe (eds), *Untersuchungen zu Handel und Verkehr der vor- und frühgeschichtlichen Zeit in Mittel- und Nordeuropa, 4: Der Handel der Karolinger- und Wikingerzeit* (Göttingen), 200–45.

Wallace, P.F. 2013. 'Weights and weight systems in Viking age Ireland', in Reynolds and Webster (eds) 2013, 301–16.

Wallace, P.F. 2014. 'Weights', in Russell and Hurley with Eogan (eds) 2014, 222–55.

Walton Rogers, P. 1997. *Textile Production at 16–22 Coppergate*, The Archaeology of York, The Small Finds 17/11 (York: Council for British Archaeology for the York Archaeological Trust).

Walton Rogers, P. 2007a. *Cloth and Clothing in Early Anglo-Saxon England*, Council for British Archaeology Research Report 145 (York: Council for British Archaeology).

Walton Rogers, P. 2007b. 'The importance and organisation of textile production', in C. Loveluck (ed.), *Rural Settlement, Lifestyles and Social Change in the Later First Millennium AD: Anglo-Saxon Flixborough in its wider context*, Excavations at Flixborough 4 (Oxford: Oxbow Books), 106–11.

Walton Rogers, P. 2009. 'Spinning', in Evans and Loveluck (eds) 2009, 283–5.

Walton Rogers, P. 2014. 'Textile production and treatment', in A. Tester, S. Anderson, I. Riddler and R. Carr, *Staunch Meadow, Brandon, Suffolk: A High Status Middle Saxon Settlement on the Fen Edge, East Anglian Archaeology 151 (Bury St Edmunds: Suffolk County Council), 285–94.*

Wamers, E. 1985. *Insularer Metallschmuck in wikingerzeitlichen Gräbern Nordeuropas. Untersuchungen zur Skandinavischen Westexpansion*, Offa-Bücher 56 (Neumünster: Wachholtz).

Wamers, E. 1998. 'Insular finds in Viking Age Scandinavia and the state formation of Norway', in Clarke *et al.* (eds) 1998, 37–72.

Ward, G.K. and Wilson, S.R. 1978. 'Procedures for comparing and combining radiocarbon age determinations: a critique', *Archaeometry* 20, 19–31.

Warner, R. 1976. 'Scottish silver arm-rings: an analysis of weights', *Proceedings of the Society of Antiquaries in Scotland* 107, 136–43.

Warnke, D. 1992–93. 'Der Horte eines Edlemetllschmeids aus der frühslawischen Siedlung Rostock-Dierkow', *Offa* 49/50, 197–206.

Waterman, D.M. 1959. 'Late Saxon, Viking and early medieval finds from York', *Archaeologia* 97, 59–105.

Watkin, J.R. 1986. 'A late Anglo-Saxon sword from Gilling West, North Yorkshire', *Medieval Archaeology* 30, 93–9.

Webster, G. 1953. 'A Saxon treasure hoard found at Chester, 1950', *Antiquaries Journal* 33, 22–32.

Webster, L.E. 2000. 'Sword fittings', in P.A. Stamper and R.A. Croft, *The South Manor Area. Wharram A Study of Settlement on the Yorkshire Wolds* 8 (York: University of York), 139.

Webster, L.E. and Backhouse, J. (eds) 1991. *The Making of England. Anglo-Saxon Art and Culture AD 600–900* (London: British Museum Press).

West, S. 1998. *A Corpus of Anglo-Saxon Material from Suffolk*, East Anglian Archaeology 84 (Ipswich).

Whitfield, N. 1998. 'The manufacture of ancient beaded wire: experiments and observations', *Jewellery Studies* 8, 57–86.

Wiechmann, R. 1996. *Edelmetalldepots der Wikingerzeit in Schleswig-Holstein: vom "Ringbrecher" zur Münzwirtschaft*, Offa-Bücher 77 (Neumünster: Wachholtz).

Williams, G. 1999. 'Anglo-Saxon and Viking coin weights', *British Numismatic Journal* 69, 19–36.

Williams, G. 2004. 'Land assessment and the silver economy of Norse Scotland', in G. Williams and P. Bibire (eds), *Sagas, Saints and Settlement* (Leiden & New York: Brill), 65–104.

Williams, G. 2007. 'Kingship, Christianity and coinage: monetary and political perspectives on silver economy in the Viking Age', in Graham-Campbell and Williams (eds) 2007, 177–214.

Williams, G. 2008a. 'Burgred "Lunette" type E reconsidered', *British Numismatic Journal* 78, 222–7.

Williams, G. 2008b. 'Raiding and warfare', in Brink and Price (eds) 2008, 193–203.

Williams, G. 2008c. 'RORIVA CASTR: A new Danelaw mint of the 920s', in *Scripta Varia Numismatico Tuukka Talvio Sexagenario Dedicate. Suomen Numismaattisen Yhdistyksen Julkaisuja* 6 (Helsinki: Finnish Numismatic Society), 41–7.

Williams, G. 2008d. 'The coins from the Vale of York Viking Hoard: preliminary report', *British Numismatic Journal* 78, 227–34.

Williams, G. 2009. 'Hoards from the northern Danelaw from Cuerdale to the Vale of York', in Graham-Campbell and Philpott (eds) 2009, 73–83.

Williams, G. 2010. *Eirik Bloodaxe* (Kernavik: Saga Bok).

Williams, G. 2011a. 'The Cuerdale coins', with a contribution by M. Archibald, in Graham-Campbell 2011, 39–71.

Williams, G. 2011b. 'Silver economies, monetisation and society: an overview', in Graham-Campbell *et al.* (eds) 2011, 337–72.

Williams, G. 2011c. 'Chapter 6: History of the castle', in M. Hislop, M. Kincey and G. Williams (eds), *Tutbury: 'A Castle Firmly Built'. Archaeological and Historical Investigations at Tutbury Castle, Staffordshire*, British Archaeological Report (British Series) 546 (Oxford: Archaeopress), 88–117.

Williams, G. 2011d. 'Coinage and monetary circulation in the Northern Danelaw in the 920s in the light of the Vale of York Hoard', in T. Abramson (ed.), *Studies in Early Medieval Coinage*, II (Woodbridge: Boydell), 146–55.

Williams, G. 2011e. 'The coins from Goldsborough', with 'Appendix 5: list of coins in the Goldsborough Hoard', in Graham-Campbell 2011, 236–7, 285–6.

Williams, G. 2012a. 'A new coin type (and a new king?) from Viking Northumbria', *The Yorkshire Numismatist* 4, 261–75.

Williams, G. 2012b Potential find of Treasure. The 'Near York' Hoard, 2012 T341. Unpublished report for HM Coroner.

Williams, G. 2012c 'Addenda' to Potential find of Treasure. The 'Near York' Hoard, 2012 T341. Unpublished report for HM Coroner.

Williams, G. 2013a. 'Towns and identities in Viking England', in Hadley and Ten Harkel (eds) 2013a, 14–34.

Williams, G. 2013b. 'Military and non-military functions of the Anglo-Saxon *burh*, c. 878–978', in J. Baker, S. Brookes and A. Reynolds (eds), *Landscapes of Defence in Early Medieval Europe* (Turnhout: Brepols), 129–64.

Williams, G. 2013c. 'The 'Northern Hoards' revisited: hoards and silver economy in the northern Danelaw in the early tenth century', in Reynolds and Webster (eds) 2013, 459–86.

Williams, G. 2013d. Coins and Kingship in Anglo-Saxon England', in G.R. Owen-Crocker and B.W. Schneider (eds), *Royal Authority in Anglo-Saxon England*, British Archaeological Report (British Series) 584 (Oxford: Archaeopress), 37–61.

Williams, G. 2014a. 'Warfare and military expansion', in Williams *et al.* (eds) 2014, 76–121.

Williams, G. 2014b. *The Viking Ship* (London: British Museum Press).

Williams, G. 2014c. 'Coins and currency in Viking England, AD 865–954', in Naismith *et al.* (eds) 2014, 13–38.

Williams, G. 2015. 'Viking camps and the means of exchange in Britain and Ireland in the ninth century', in H.B. Clarke and R. Johnson (eds), *The Vikings in Ireland and Beyond: Before and After the Battle of Clontarf* (Dublin: Four Courts), 93–116.

Williams, G. and Ager, B. 2015. *The Vale of York Hoard*, revised edition (London: British Museum Press).

Williams, G. and Naylor, J. 2016. *King Alfred's Coins: The Watlington Viking Hoard* (Oxford: Ashmolean Museum).

Williams, G., Pentz, P. and Wemhoff, M. (eds) 2014. *Vikings: Life and Legend* (London: British Museum Press).

Wilson, D.M. 1957. 'An unpublished fragment from the Goldsborough hoard', *Antiquaries Journal* 37, 72–3.

Wilson, D.M. 1964. *Anglo-Saxon Ornamental Metalwork 700–1100*. British Museum Catalogue of the Antiquities of the Later Saxon Period 1 (London).

Wilson, D.M. 1965. 'Some neglected late Anglo-Saxon swords', *Medieval Archaeology* 9, 32–54.

Wilson, D.M. 1984. *Anglo-Saxon Art from the Seventh Century to the Norman Conquest* (London: Thames and Hudson).

Woods, A.R. 2014. 'Monetary activity in Viking-Age Ireland: the evidence of the single finds', in Naismith *et al.* (eds) 2014, 295–330.

Woods, A.R. in preparation. 'Viking Economies and the 'Great Army': Interpreting the precious metal finds from Torksey, Lincolnshire'.

Woolf, A. 1998. 'Erik Bloodaxe revisited', *Northern History* 34, 189–93.

Xu, S., Anderson, R., Bryant, C., Cook, G.T., Dougans, A., Freeman, S., Naysmith, P., Schnabel, C. and Scott, E.M. 2004. 'Capabilities of the new SUERC 5MV AMS facility for 14C dating', *Radiocarbon* 46, 59–64.

Yorke, B. 2013. 'West Saxon fortification in the ninth century: the perspective from the written sources', in Baker, Brookes and Reynolds (eds) 2013, 91–110.

Young, T. 2014a. 'Discussion of metalworking evidence', in Russell and Hurley with Eogan (eds) 2014, 103–13.

Young, T. 2014b. 'Ceramics: crucibles and cupels', in Russell and Hurley with Eogan (eds) 2014, 267–82.

Youngs, S.M. (ed.) 1989. *'The Work of Angels'. Masterpieces of Celtic Metalwork, 6th–9th Centuries AD* (London: British Museum Publications).

Youngs, S.M., Clark, J. and Barry, T.B. 1984. 'Medieval Britain and Ireland in 1983', *Medieval Archaeology* 28, 203–65.

Index

Index note: page numbers in *italic* print refer to illustrations and tables.